Oracle ADF Real World Developer's Guide

Mastering essential tips and tricks for building next generation enterprise applications with Oracle ADF

Jobinesh Purushothaman

[PACKT] enterprise
PUBLISHING   professional expertise distilled

BIRMINGHAM - MUMBAI

Oracle ADF Real World Developer's Guide

First published: October 2012

Production Reference: 1121012

Published by Packt Publishing Ltd.
Livery Place
35 Livery Street
Birmingham B3 2PB, UK.

ISBN 978-1-84968-482-8

www.packtpub.com

Cover Image by Sandeep Babu (sandyjb@gmail.com)

Credits

Author

Jobinesh Purushothaman

Reviewers

Dimitrios Stasinopoulos

Vikram Kohli

Sanjeeb Mahakul

Juan Camilo Ruiz

Acquisition Editor

Rukhsana Khambatta

Lead Technical Editor

Dayan Hyames

Technical Editors

Prasad Dalvi

Jalasha D'costa

Kedar Bhat

Project Coordinator

Arshad Sopariwala

Proofreader

Maria Gould

Indexer

Monica Ajmera Mehta

Graphics

Sheetal Aute

Aditi Gajjar

Production Coordinator

Shantanu Zagade

Cover Work

Shantanu Zagade

About the Author

Jobinesh Purushothaman works with Oracle as a Principal Solutions Architect for the Oracle Application Development Framework. He has over 13 years of experience in the software industry working on Java platforms and various Java-based application frameworks. In his current role with Oracle, he is mainly focused on helping internal and external customers with the adoption of Oracle ADF. He is also involved in the design and architectural decisions of various products using ADF and Java EE technologies, and occasionally he speaks at industry conferences such as JavaOne and Oracle Develop. Links to his blog articles may be found at http://jobinesh.blogspot.com.

Jobinesh holds a Master of Science (M.Sc) degree in Computer Science from Bharathiar University, India, and a Master of Business Administration (MBA) from Indira Gandhi National Open University (IGNOU), India. After completing his M.Sc in Computer Science, he started his career in 1999 with MicroObjects Private Limited, India. His career has taken him to different countries and companies where he worked as developer, technical leader, mentor, and technical architect. Jobinesh joined Oracle India Private Limited in 2008. Prior to joining Oracle, from 2004 to 2008, Jobinesh worked as Senior Software Engineer at the Emirates Group IT, Dubai, where he was part of an IT strategy and architecture team.

Jobinesh currently lives in Bangalore, India, with his wife Remya and son Chinmay.

Acknowledgement

First and foremost, I would like to thank my parents (Mr. Purushothaman M.R and Mrs. Ratnam K.N) for allowing me to realize my own potential. I would like to thank my elder brother Biju for all the support he gave me throughout my life.

Thanks to my lovely wife, Remya, for her love, care, and understanding. Thanks to my son, Chinmay, for being my inspiration in doing this work. I could not have done this work without their support.

I sincerely thank and appreciate the team at Packt Publishing for their unconditional support, professionalism, and commitment.

Thanks to all the technical reviewers for ensuring the quality of the book. They include Dimitrios Stasinopoulos, Juan Camilo Ruiz, Vikram Kohli, and Sanjeeb Mahakul.

Special thanks to Steve Munech (Senior Architect - Oracle ADF) for all the help that he offered throughout my life at Oracle and also for teaching me Oracle ADF.

Many thanks to all members of the Oracle ADF development and product management team for their support and guidance throughout the development of this book. Special thanks to Sathish Kumar, Sung Im, Shailesh Vinayaka, J.R. Smiljanic, and Ken Mizuta for their guidance on specific areas.

I would like to thank my manager at Oracle, Sharad Medhavi, for his support throughout this project. Thanks to all my colleagues at Oracle for their encouragement.

Last, but not least, Special thanks to Rajamani Saravanan, who worked with me at Emirates Group IT (EGIT) Dubai, for teaching me excellence at work.

About the Reviewers

Dimitrios Stasinopoulos is a Certified Application Development Framework Implementation Specialist with more than five years of experience in Oracle Fusion Middleware and more specifically in ADF BC 11*g*. Dimitrios currently works for a big project in the European Commission RTD, which includes technologies such as ADF BC, BPM.

He has worked in the successful migration project of MedNet International as a team leader and was part of the team that designed the migration from Oracle Forms to Oracle ADF BC. In his spare time, Dimitrios is helping the ADF Community by answering technical questions in the Oracle ADF and JDeveloper forum, and maintains a blog about ADF where he writes his findings and his ideas: `dstas.blogspot.com`.

Dimitrios holds a BS in Computer Science from the Technological Educational Institution of Larissa, Greece.

Vikram Kohli is the founder of web startup `PracLabs.com`. He is passionate about learning, teaching, and mentoring. He is an alumnus of XLRI, Jamshedpur, and has completed his masters degree in computers. With more than seven years of experience in the information technology industry, primarily in the Oracle Fusion technology stack, Vikram has worked with the top IT companies in India. Since starting in his college days, Vikram enjoys teaching and mentoring.

In addition to managing day-to-day operations and coding rendered to PracLabs, Vikram teaches and provides consultancy in Oracle ADF to working professionals around the globe.

Sanjeeb Mahakul is Senior Technical Consultant at Speridian technologies, focusing on the Oracle Fusion stack. He has more than five years of experience and more than three years of experience relevant to Oracle ADF and WebCenter. During this tenure, he has worked on three end-to-end product development projects with the Oracle Fusion stack. Prior to this he worked with Mphasis, an HP company and Oracle Financial software services. Now he is an active member of the COE team and is involved in the architectural design of Fusion products.

Sanjeeb is also an active member of OTN and the Oracle EMG group.

You can visit his LinkedIn profile at http://in.linkedin.com/pub/sanjeeb-mahakul/15/429/9b9.

Juan Camilo Ruiz is a computer science information systems professional with more than five years of experience in Java development tools and rich enterprise application development. He is the Principal Product Manager in the Oracle Development Tools organization, currently working for JDeveloper and ADF (Application Development Framework), based in Redwood Shores, California.

Juan has worked with Oracle technologies that co-exist around Oracle ADF for more than seven years, which include Oracle Portal, Oracle SOA Suite, Oracle WebCenter, Oracle E-Business Suite, and Oracle Fusion Applications.

Juan was born in Bogotá, Colombia and has a Bachelor Degree in Software Engineering from the Pontificia Universidad Javeriana.

To my family for their unconditional love and support. Gracias.

www.PacktPub.com

Support files, eBooks, discount offers and more

You might want to visit www.PacktPub.com for support files and downloads related to your book.

Did you know that Packt offers eBook versions of every book published, with PDF and ePub files available? You can upgrade to the eBook version at www.PacktPub.com and as a print book customer, you are entitled to a discount on the eBook copy. Get in touch with us at service@packtpub.com for more details.

At www.PacktPub.com, you can also read a collection of free technical articles, sign up for a range of free newsletters and receive exclusive discounts and offers on Packt books and eBooks.

http://PacktLib.PacktPub.com

Do you need instant solutions to your IT questions? PacktLib is Packt's online digital book library. Here, you can access, read and search across Packt's entire library of books.

Why Subscribe?

- Fully searchable across every book published by Packt
- Copy and paste, print and bookmark content
- On demand and accessible via web browser

Free Access for Packt account holders

If you have an account with Packt at www.PacktPub.com, you can use this to access PacktLib today and view nine entirely free books. Simply use your login credentials for immediate access.

Instant Updates on New Packt Books

Get notified! Find out when new books are published by following @PacktEnterprise on Twitter, or the *Packt Enterprise* Facebook page.

Table of Contents

Preface

Oracle ADF is a powerful Java application framework for building next generation enterprise applications. Oracle ADF in combination with JDeveloper IDE offers visual and declarative approaches to enterprise application development. This book will teach you to build scalable, rich enterprise applications by using the ADF Framework, with the help of many real world examples.

This book discusses the ADF Framework in depth. This book is designed to take programmers beyond visual and declarative programming model and enable them to customize the framework features to meet the real world application development challenges. Many of the framework features are discussed along with real-life use cases and code samples which will definitely help developers to design and develop successful enterprise applications.

This book starts off by introducing the development environment and JDeveloper design-time features. As you read forward, you will learn to build a full stack enterprise application, using ADF. You will learn how to build business services by using ADF, enable validation for the data model, declaratively build user interfaces for a business service, and enable security across the application layers.

What this book covers

Chapter 1, Getting Started with Oracle ADF, introduces Oracle Application Development Framework (Oracle ADF) and its layered architecture. In this chapter, we will develop a simple ADF web application.

Chapter 2, Introduction to ADF Business Components, gives an overview of ADF Business Components, which includes discussion on some topics such as business service layer, building a simple business service, Oracle ADF Model Tester, and so on.

Chapter 3, Introducing Entity Object, explores the Oracle ADF technology stack in depth. This chapter introduces the entity objects, which make up the persistence layer of business components.

Chapter 4, Introducing View Object, discusses about the ADF view object, which is in charge of reading and shaping the data for presenting it to the client. This chapter explains architecture of a view object, its usage, and runtime behavior.

Chapter 5, Advanced Concepts on Entity Objects and View Objects, takes a deeper look into the internals of view objects and entity objects. This chapter focuses on the advanced concepts of these components along with code samples.

Chapter 6, Introducing Application Module,.discusses about the application module component and the service layer for the business components stack. This chapter covers the topics such as core features of an application module, defining an application module, sharing of application module data, and so on.

Chapter 7, Binding Business Services with User Interface, shows how to bind user interface for the data model built from ADF Business Components. This chapter covers the topics such as binding model data with user interfaces, building a simple data bound web page, browsing through page definition file, invoking application module from a Java servlet.

Chapter 8, Building Data Bound Web User Interfaces, covers data bound UI development in detail. This chapter discusses the power of model-driven UI development support offered by Oracle ADF Framework along with JDeveloper IDE.

Chapter 9, Controlling the Page Navigation, discusses about the offerings from the ADF Controller layer to navigate back and forth between views in a Fusion web application. This chapter discusses the basic navigation models provided by the ADF Controller layer.

Chapter 10, Taking a Closer Look at the Bounded Task Flow, covers the topics such as properties of a bounded task flow, building a bounded task flow, working with bounded task flow activities, and so on.

Chapter 11, More on Validations and Error Handling, explains ADF validation cycle for a page and the infrastructure for handling validation exceptions. This chapter covers the topics such as adding validation rules in a Fusion web application, displaying validation exceptions on a page at runtime, and so on.

Chapter 12, Oracle ADF Best Practices, discusses the best practices and coding tips that developers will find useful when building ADF applications. Learning the best practices will help you to avoid common pitfalls that others might have faced.

Chapter 13, Building Business Services with EJB, explains how Oracle ADF helps you to declaratively build user interfaces for Enterprise Java Beans (EJB) based services. You can download this chapter from `http://www.packtpub.com/sites/default/files/downloads/4828EN_Chapter13_Building_Business Services_with_EJB.pdf`.

Chapter 14, Securing Fusion Web Applications, describes how you can visually enable security in different layers of your Fusion web application. You can download this chapter from `http://www.packtpub.com/sites/default/files/downloads/4828EN_Chapter14_Securing_Fusion_Web_Applications.pdf`.

Appendix, More on ADF Business Components and Fusion Page Runtime, discusses various useful features and techniques for ADF Business Components. This chapter covers the topics such as page life cycle for a Fusion page with region, transaction management in Fusion web applications, Building a dynamic model-driven UI with ADF, and so on. You can download this appendix from `http://www.packtpub.com/sites/default/files/downloads/4828EN_Appendix_More_on_ADF_Business_Components_and_Fusion_Page_Runtime.pdf`.

What you need for this book

The examples given in this book utilize the latest release of JDeveloper at the time of writing, namely JDeveloper 11*g* Release 2 (11.1.2.2.0) Studio Edition. The Studio Edition of JDeveloper comes bundled with the necessary ADF libraries and an integrated WebLogic Server installation. Though all the samples are tested primarily against WebLogic Server, they should also work on any ADF-certified application server. In addition, to run examples you may also need an Oracle database with the HR schema (which is a sample database schema). You can use Oracle Database Express Edition (Oracle Database XE) for this which comes with the HR schema.

Who this book is for

If you are an ADF developer looking forward to building healthy and better performing applications by using Oracle ADF, this is the best guide for you. You need to be proficient with Java and need to know a bit of ADF before getting started with this book.

Conventions

In this book, you will find a number of styles of text that distinguish between different kinds of information. Here are some examples of these styles, and an explanation of their meaning.

Code words in text are shown as follows: "The `adf-settings.xml` file keeps the UI project configurations."

A block of code is set as follows:

```
import oracle.jbo.ApplicationModule;
import oracle.jbo.Row;
import oracle.jbo.ViewObject;
import oracle.jbo.client.Configuration;

public class TestClient {

    public static void main(String[] args) {

        String amDef =
        "com.packtpub.adfguide.ch2.model.service.HRServiceAppModule";

        String config = "HRServiceAppModuleLocal";
        ApplicationModule am =
        Configuration.createRootApplicationModule(amDef, config);

        // Work with your appmodule and view object here
        //Find Department View Object Instance
        ViewObject vo = am.findViewObject("Departments");
        //Execute Department query
        vo.executeQuery();
        //Fetch the first record
        Row deptRow = vo.first();
        printRow(vo, deptRow);

        // Clean up resources
        Configuration.releaseRootApplicationModule(am, true);
    }
}
```

When we wish to draw your attention to a particular part of a code block, the relevant lines or items are set in bold:

```
RowIterator rowIter= DeptEOImpl.getEmpEO();
rowIter.reset();
while(rowIter.hasNext()){
  Row row=rowIter.next();
  //Row represent Emp entity instance
}
```

New terms and **important words** are shown in bold. Words that you see on the screen, in menus or dialog boxes for example, appear in the text like this: "The **Rebuild** option allows you to fire an unconditional compilation on the source".

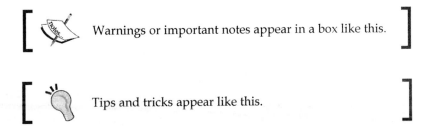

Warnings or important notes appear in a box like this.

Tips and tricks appear like this.

Reader feedback

Feedback from our readers is always welcome. Let us know what you think about this book—what you liked or may have disliked. Reader feedback is important for us to develop titles that you really get the most out of.

To send us general feedback, simply send an e-mail to feedback@packtpub.com, and mention the book title via the subject of your message.

If there is a book that you need and would like to see us publish, please send us a note in the **SUGGEST A TITLE** form on www.packtpub.com or e-mail suggest@packtpub.com.

If there is a topic that you have expertise in and you are interested in either writing or contributing to a book, see our author guide on www.packtpub.com/authors.

Customer support

Now that you are the proud owner of a Packt book, we have a number of things to help you to get the most from your purchase.

Downloading the example code

You can download the example code files for all Packt books you have purchased from your account at http://www.PacktPub.com. If you purchased this book elsewhere, you can visit http://www.PacktPub.com/support and register to have the files e-mailed directly to you.

To locate easily, the example code files for each chapter are grouped under the folders with the respective chapter numbers as names (for example, chapter1). Note that each JDeveloper workspace folder contains a `readme.txt` file which explains the ADF framework features exercised in that sample.

Errata

Although we have taken every care to ensure the accuracy of our content, mistakes do happen. If you find a mistake in one of our books—maybe a mistake in the text or the code—we would be grateful if you would report this to us. By doing so, you can save other readers from frustration and help us improve subsequent versions of this book. If you find any errata, please report them by visiting `http://www.packtpub.com/support`, selecting your book, clicking on the **errata submission form** link, and entering the details of your errata. Once your errata are verified, your submission will be accepted and the errata will be uploaded on our website, or added to any list of existing errata, under the Errata section of that title. Any existing errata can be viewed by selecting your title from `http://www.packtpub.com/support`.

Piracy

Piracy of copyright material on the Internet is an ongoing problem across all media. At Packt, we take the protection of our copyright and licenses very seriously. If you come across any illegal copies of our works, in any form, on the Internet, please provide us with the location address or website name immediately so that we can pursue a remedy.

Please contact us at `copyright@packtpub.com` with a link to the suspected pirated material.

We appreciate your help in protecting our authors, and our ability to bring you valuable content.

Questions

You can contact us at `questions@packtpub.com` if you are having a problem with any aspect of the book, and we will do our best to address it.

1
Getting Started with Oracle ADF

In this chapter we will get an introduction to **Oracle Application Development Framework (Oracle ADF)** and its layered architecture. We will also develop a simple ADF web application towards the end of this chapter.

Here is the brief outline of the topics that we are going to cover in this chapter:

- Introduction to Oracle ADF
- Why Oracle ADF?
- Oracle ADF architecture
- Developing with ADF
- Your first Fusion web application

Introduction to Oracle ADF

Many of today's huge enterprise applications run on the **Java Platform Enterprise Edition (Java EE)** platform. The core Java EE technology has been improved considerably in the recent past. The Enterprise Java application development has become much easier with annotations, dependency injection, **Enterprise Java Beans (EJB) 3.0**, and **Java Persistence API (JPA)**. However, if you take a closer look at the core Java EE technology with a developer's eye, you may notice certain gaps in it:

- The learning curve is steep for a beginner
- Even experienced Java developers find it hard to understand, when he/she goes deeper into the technology stack
- It lacks tooling support that provides a visual and declarative development experience
- Java EE specification does not cover all the generic needs

The way to deal with these problems is to use a framework that abstracts the complexity of the Java EE platform, adhering to standard patterns and practices. The Oracle ADF framework is the most promising one in that category.

The Oracle ADF framework is a complete Java EE framework that simplifies next generation enterprise application development by providing out-of-the-box infrastructure services, and a visual and declarative development experience. In this book, you will explore the core ADF features in detail with real-life code samples.

Why Oracle ADF?

The world moves very fast, and so does technology. It's very important for an enterprise to have dynamic business applications aligned with a growing customer base. In other words, an enterprise application should be smart enough to adapt with the changes in the business eco system and scale with growth of the enterprise. Let us take a look at some of the challenges of enterprise application development with regard to the tools and technology:

- **Choice of the right tool and platform**: The right choice of the tool for development is very critical for the success of any business applications. The tool should be complete, matured, and flexible enough to meet the requirements of different phases of an application lifecycle.

- **The developer's productivity**: The productivity of a developer is the rate at which he/she delivers a quality software product that meets the requirements of the customer. The developer's productivity is thus very important for the success of a product. A tool, which can talk a common language and provides a visual and declarative development experience, has a significant impact on developers' productivity, especially if the application development team is comprised of developers with different skills.

- **One product and many customers**: The unique needs of customers grow more complex every day. In order for a product to do well in the market, besides the generic features, it should also be customizable to meet the unique needs of diverse user groups. A finished software product should always anticipate changes to survive in the market.

- **Businesses grow and so do the business users**: Performance, scalability, and reliability are really important for any enterprise application. An enterprise application should handle increasing demands while maintaining the acceptable performance levels. For example, when a business grows for an enterprise, it may need to consider the large customer base. This may eventually result in an increase in the number of active users for the business applications used in the enterprise. The business application and the underlying technology should be scalable enough to meet tomorrow's needs.

There are many tools and technologies around us that build enterprise applications, but if we need a tool, which is really capable of meeting today's challenges, the list shrinks and we do not have much choice left. Oracle ADF is considered as one among the few best frameworks for building a rich enterprise application.

The following is what makes Oracle ADF one of the best tools for building rich enterprise applications:

- **End-to-end solution**: The Oracle ADF framework provides complete solution for building enterprise applications right from inception to the post-production phase, addressing requirements from each layer of applications.

- **Improved developer productivity**: The declarative nature of ADF improves the developer's productivity, allowing users to focus on the business logic of the application, rather than focusing on technology complexity.

- **Rich Internet Application (RIA) and Web 2.0 enablement**: ADF Rich Client has over 150 rich user interface components, including various graphs and charts, enabled with **Asynchronous JavaScript and XML (AJAX)**. These are model aware components, which can be easily wired to your business data and make your web pages production ready.

- **Technology choice**: Oracle ADF lets the developer choose multiple technologies for each of the layers of the application and does not enforce a specific technology or a specific development style on the developer.

- **Reference architecture**: The enterprise applications built using ADF inherit the layered architecture of the underlying ADF stack, without leaving a chance for you to go wrong on choosing the right architecture.

- **Scalable architecture**: ADF is shipped with a lot of tuning options to meet the increased load of application in production. You are free to override the default tuning parameters based on the usage pattern of the application.

- **Modular architecture**: The Oracle ADF framework supports modular architecture for enterprise scale applications. Multiple modules can be bundled together to build a complete composite ADF application. These modules are also reusable across multiple ADF applications.

Oracle ADF architecture

Oracle ADF has a well-proven, extensible, and layered architecture, which improves the flexibility, maintainability, and scalability of an application.

What does that mean to you?

Some of the core benefits are as follows:

- As an architect, you can pick up the best fitting technology from a wide range of lists while building each of the layers. For example, ADF supports a variety of ways to build business services, which include EJB or (JPA), web services, simple Java objects, and **ADF Business Components (ADF BC)**. On the client tier, applications can choose from Java Swing, core **Java Server Faces (JSF)**, ADF Faces, or ADF, Mobile UI. Oracle ADF along with JDeveloper IDE, offers consistent development experience across different technologies.

- If the use case demands, your ADF application can be easily enhanced later to use other technologies from Oracle Fusion Middleware Stack, such as **Service Oriented Architecture (SOA)**, WebCenter, and so on, with minimal integration effort.

- Oracle ADF follows the **Model-View-Controller (MVC)** design paradigm. The layered architecture of the framework simplifies maintenance, decouples implementations from interfaces, and improves reusability of the components across applications. The layered architecture of the ADF application is really useful when you need to build a **User Interface (UI)** for various channels such as web, mobile, tablet, and desktop, reusing the existing business services.

It is time for us to give a glance at the architectural building blocks of ADF to study how are they put together to build high performing service-oriented applications.

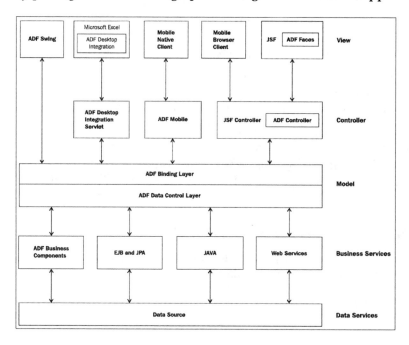

View layer

The View layer contains the UI for the application ADF stack that supports the following view technologies, targeting various presentation channels such as the web browser, desktop, mobile, tablet PC, and Microsoft Excel:

- **ADF Faces**: Rich web UI framework built on top of the **Java Server Faces (JSF)** technology
- **Apache MyFaces Trinidad**: An open source JSF-based web framework (ADF Faces components are based on Trinidad components)
- **JSF**: Core JSF web technology from the Java EE stack
- **ADF Mobile**: ADF Mobile supports both mobile browser client and mobile native clients, which can run on smart phones and tablet PCs
- **Microsoft Excel**: Provides Microsoft Excel frontend for your ADF business services

Controller layer

The Controller layer controls the flow of the application. ADF Controller is used for the ADF Faces application, which provides an improved navigation and state management model on top of JSF. The greatest advantage of ADF Controller over the navigation model offered by core JSF is that it improves the modularity of the system by splitting a single monolithic navigation model to multiple reusable navigation cases known as **task flows**. Task flows are declarative solutions. Developers typically do not need to write any code for defining navigation in applications. Apart from the support for modular application design, ADF task flows also offer a declarative transaction model and state management solutions.

Model layer

The Model layer binds the UI with business services, abstracting the implementation details. The model layer is functionally divided into two components—data control and data binding.

- **Data control**: Data control acts as a proxy cum adaptor for your business services and decouples the view layer from the business service implementation
- **Data binding**: Data binding abstracts the data access from data control and provides a generic interface for invoking common operations

The ADF model layer plays a very vital role in the entire technology stack. It is the model layer along with JDeveloper IDE that provides a visual and declarative UI development experience for the end user, irrespective of the technology used for building business services. The glue code used for binding the UI with the data model is plumbed by the model layer at runtime based on the binding metadata definition
for the page.

Business services layer

The Business services layer provides access to data from various sources and handles the business logic as well. ADF comes with out-of-the-box binding support for the following technologies:

- ADF BC
- EJBs
- Web services
- **Plain Old Java Objects (POJO)**
- **Business Activity Monitoring (BAM)**
- **Business Intelligence (BI)**

You can choose any of these technologies for building the business services.

 The Fusion web application in this book refers to the enterprise web application built using ADF Faces for the view, ADF Model for data binding, ADF Page Flow for the controller, and ADF Business Components for business services.

Comparing the Fusion web application technology stack to the Java EE web application

ADF is built on top of the Java and Java EE stack. If you are familiar with Java EE, this topic is for you. Let us take a quick look at the basic building blocks of these two technologies to see what they have in common:

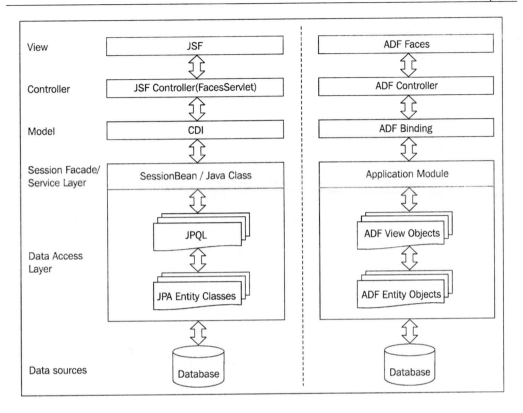

View layer

JSF is a request-driven MVC web framework, which intends to standardize the development of web-based user interface in a Java EE web applications. ADF Faces forms the view layer of a Fusion web application. This is built on top of JSF with lots of extra features, such as graphs and charts, a dialog framework, declarative components, data streaming, embeddable task flows, and rich AJAX-enabled UI components.

Controller layer

In a Java EE web application, it is the JSF controller that intercepts all the page requests and dispatches them to the appropriate view along with the necessary data. The JSF Controller also controls the page navigation. The ADF Controller is extended from the JSF Controller to support modular web application development by decomposing the single monolithic application into multiple reusable web modules, termed as ADF task flows. Each task flow can have its own transaction attributes, resource management, managed bean definitions, and navigation cases.

Data binding layer

The data binding layer of ADF (also known as ADF Model) is quite unique in nature and does not have any real counterparts in the Java EE world. The ADF Model decouples the UI from the business service implementation and provides a generic binding behavior for the collection returned from the business services.

Conceptually, **Context and Dependency Injection (CDI)** does a similar welding job for Java EE web applications, however, feature wise there are many differences, which we will discuss in the coming chapters.

Business service layer

ADF Business Components simplifies the business services implementation by freeing the developer from writing infrastructural code required by enterprise applications. ADF Business Components mainly constitutes of the entity object, view object, and application module.

The ADF entity objects are similar to the **Java Persistence API (JPA)** entities, however functionality wise the former scores. The major advantages of the ADF entity object are out-of-the-box support for caching of data in middle tier, matured transaction management, declarative validation support, and the ability to trigger the SOA process during the transaction post cycle.

The ADF view objects are data shaping components. The ADF view objects are similar to **Java Persistence Query Language (JPQL)** in the Java EE stack. Some of the advantages of ADF view objects over JPQL are the visual and declarative development experience, support for building model-driven UI, and declarative state management.

The ADF application module is the transaction component that wraps your business service — conceptually similar to a session facade built using a session bean in an EJB application. However, we need to keep in mind that these two technologies are in no way related in their underlying implementation, though at the end of the day everything boils down to Java binaries and JDBC calls.

Developing with ADF

The best way to learn technology is to start coding. In the next section, we will build a simple web application and walk through the application source generated by the development tool. In the coming chapters, we will analyze each piece in detail, taking real-life use cases.

Setting up the development environment

Let us set up the environment for building applications with ADF. The development environment setup includes setting up the **Integrated Development Environment (IDE)**, version controlling the source, picking up the right build tool, and setting up team collaboration.

Picking up the tool for development

The success of a development framework is well complimented by a smart development tool, which simplifies the creation of applications by using this framework. Oracle JDeveloper is the IDE that we will be using for building ADF applications. JDeveloper has better tooling support for ADF, covering an end-to-end development lifecycle. You can download and install the studio edition of the latest JDeveloper release from `http://www.oracle.com/technetwork/developer-tools/jdev/downloads/index.html`. The studio version of JDevloper comes packaged with Java EE and ADF libraries.

> If you just want to try out Oracle ADF, installing studio version of JDeveloper alone is enough to keep you going with the technology. In this chapter, you will find some other discussion points such as versions controlling the source, automated build process, and team collaboration. These are required only in real-life enterprise application development with ADF.

Setting up the Software Configuration Management tool

Once you have decided on tools and technologies for development, the next step may be to set up the **Software Configuration Management (SCM)** tool. SCM is the task of tracking and controlling changes in the source code during the application development. There are many source control tools available on the market. JDeveloper is packaged with client support for **Subversion (SVN)** — the most popular version control tool among Java developers. In fact, you are not limited to SVN; JDeveloper can work with most of the popular tools if you have the right extensions installed. The supported version control list includes **Concurrent Version System (CVS)**, Perforce, Serena Dimensions, Rational ClearCase, and so on.

Build tool

JDeveloper has built-in support available for compiling and generating deployable artifacts from the application source. This may be enough when you build less complex applications. However, if you are building more complex enterprise applications and the team size is fairly big, you may need to have automated build support and a **Continuous Integration (CI)** process to improve the quality of the work and fast delivery. In such scenarios, it's required to build the applications outside of JDeveloper. Fortunately, we have multiple options available to address such requirements. Let us take a quick look at the options that are available to build the ADF applications:

- **Built-in Make and Rebuild options on JDeveloper**: When you right-click on a project in JDeveloper and use the **Make** option, the IDE compiles source files that have changed since they were last compiled, or have dependencies that have changed. The **Rebuild** option allows you to fire an unconditional compilation on the source.

- **Ant**: Ant is a Java-based build tool, which automates the build process. JDeveloper has in-built support for using ant as build tool for projects. To learn more about ant, go to `http://ant.apache.org/index.html`.

- **Maven**: Maven is a software management and build automation tool, which bridges ant's shortcomings in many areas. You can learn more about Maven at `http://maven.apache.org`. JDeveloper provides basic infrastructure support through which Maven can be used for building ADF projects. If you plan to use Maven for building an ADF application, you may need to follow some manual tasks such as adding all the dependencies to your project's `pom.xml` and populating the Maven repository with the required ADF libraries.

>
> To learn more about version controlling with JDeveloper and build tools, refer to the *Oracle Fusion Middleware User's Guide for Oracle JDeveloper* documentation. To access the documentation visit `http://www.oracle.com/technetwork/developer-tools/jdev/documentation/index.html` and navigate to **Oracle JDeveloper and ADF Documentation Library | User's Guide for Oracle JDeveloper**. Use the search option to find specific topics..

Team collaboration

When you work on larger projects, you may end up using different tools to perform various tasks at various stages of the application lifecycle. Many of these tools do not run co-operatively and may call for a lot of manual labor to get your job done. What we really need is a platform that will integrate all these tools—making our life easier. JDeveloper supports such a platform, which is shipped as Oracle Team Productivity Center.

Oracle Team Productivity Center is a JDeveloper-based Application Lifecycle Management tool that is useful when we work with a larger team spread across different geographic regions in a connected network. The list of features includes the following items:

- Team navigator, which enables multiple grouping of users and acts as an access point for the team collaborative features

- A build dashboard displaying the nightly built test results on your IDE

- Chat window

- Administration console to manage users and teams

The Oracle Team Productivity Center consists of three components:

- **The Team Productivity Center client software**: This is the JDeveloper client software for the Team Productivity Center. As with any other JDeveloper extensions, this can also be downloaded from the JDeveloper update centre.

- **The Team Productivity Center server software**: The server software manages the connections between the team's Team Productivity Center features in Oracle JDeveloper and data repositories such as a bug database, feature wiki, or directory of product features and specifications.

- **The Team Productivity Center connectors**: As you may have imagined, connectors are used for enabling the connection between the Team Productivity Center client software, running inside JDeveloper and data repositories such as bug-tracking systems, feature databases, and so on. Standard connectors can be installed from the update centre. Even you can build your own connectors, if needed.

In-depth coverage of the Team Productivity Center is beyond the scope of this book. More details on the Oracle Team Productivity Centre including an installation guide and downloads are available at http://www.oracle.com/technetwork/developer-tools/tpc/overview/index.html.

Taking a quick tour of the JDeveloper IDE

Oracle ADF and JDeveloper go hand in hand. JDeveloper is aimed to simplify your job as an application developer by providing visual and declarative aids for development. Let us take a quick tour of the IDE to get familiarized with the commonly used editor windows and tools.

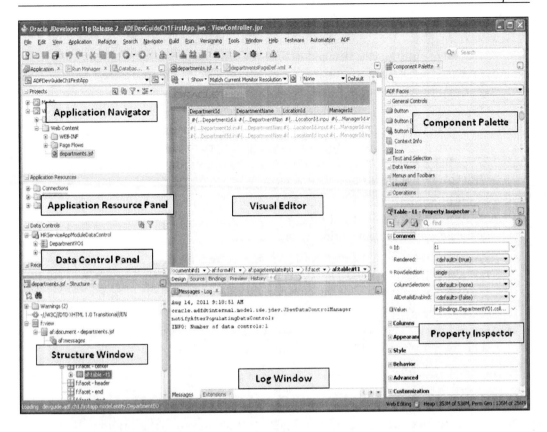

- **Application navigator**: The application navigator window helps us to manage the contents and associated resources of an application. You can create new projects and source files using the options available in this window.

- **Application resource panel**: The application resource panel window displays the application-level resources and configuration files. This includes database connection information, metadata files used to configure ADF Business Components, and so on.

- **Data control panel**: The data control panel displays the data collections, attributes, built-in operations, and business methods from the business services exposed through a data control registry. The exposed items from the data control panel can be dragged-and-dropped on the UI, which will generate a metadata XML file to bind the business data with the UI.

- **Structure window**: The structure window displays a structural view of the data in the document that is currently selected in the active window. Structure window can be used to view or edit the contents. For example, you can drag-and-drop components from any palette to the structure window.

- **Visual editor**: The visual editor window will help you to visually build the UI for ADF applications. It provides a visual WYSIWYG— What You See Is What You Get—editor for HTML, JSP, JSF, Facelets, native mobile UI, and Java Swing. The visual editor allows developers to visually lay out the UI. Note that JDeveloper synchronizes the selection in the structure window with the visual editor and vice versa.

- **Component palette**: The component palette window lists down available components associated with the selected technology that you are using for designing pages or for defining navigation.

- **Property inspector**: A property is a named attribute of a class or component that can affect its appearance or its behavior. The property inspector displays the exposed properties of the component selected in the structure window or in the visual editor.

- **Log window**: The log window displays the logs from various components such as compiler, audit rules, debugger, and profiler.

Your first Fusion web application

It's time for us to break the suspense and get a feel for the smart technology that we are discussing. Are you excited? Good; let us jump start and build a simple Fusion web application. During this course, we will also analyze the generated artifacts by uncovering the magic behind visual and declarative development.

Our use case is very simple, primarily meant for giving you a feel of the development environment and the basic configuration required for an ADF web application to run. In this example, we will build a web application to display the department details from the DEPARTMENTS database table.

Starting JDeveloper IDE for the first time

Once the JDeveloper installation is complete, you are ready to launch it for application development. The first time JDeveloper is run, it will prompt for selecting a role that matches your requirement, as shown in the following screenshot:

JDeveloper IDE enables appropriate features to be used based on the role that you select on startup. The default role selected by the IDE is **Studio Developer**, which includes all the features offered by the IDE. You will use the **Studio Developer** role for building our first example, which we will discuss shortly. You can switch to a specific developer role if you want to restrict IDE from displaying many other features that are not relevant to the application that you are building.

Picking up the right application template

JDeveloper is packaged with a variety of application templates, which may help us to set up the basic skeleton for applications leveraging well proven architectural patterns. Based on the complexity of the application, you are free to extend this basic structure by adding more projects later in the development cycle.

To create an application, perform the following steps:

1. Click on **New Application** within the **Application Navigator** tab in the
    JDeveloper. This will display **New Gallery** with a set of predefined
    templates targeting various technologies.

2. For ADF web applications, select the **Fusion Web Application (ADF)**
    template and click on **OK**.

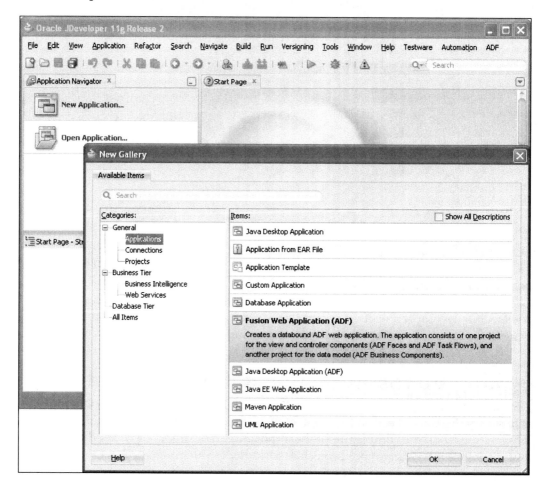

3. Once you select the **Fusion Web Application (ADF)** template, JDeveloper
    will launch the **Create Fusion Web Application** wizard, which may let you
    key in the application name and location to store the source files.

4. The next steps in the wizard will set up the basic skeleton for our application
    by generating the Model and View Controller projects.

As the names suggest, these projects hold your business services and UI-related sources respectively. While navigating through the setup screens for each project, you are free to change the default name of the project and package name of your Java files. As this is our first application, let us leave the default values set by the IDE as they are and finish the wizard.

Analyzing the generated metadata files

When you finish the Fusion web application generation wizard, the following files are generated in your source folder. Let us take a quick look at these metadata XML files to understand the role of each item in our application.

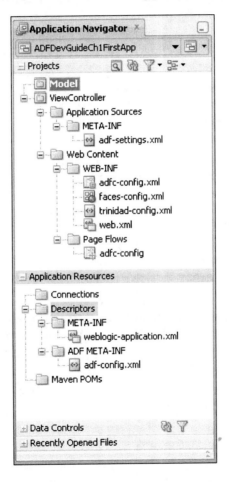

- `adf-settings.xml`: The `adf-settings.xml` file keeps the UI project configurations. This file is present in the `< project-root >/src/META-INF` folder.

- `faces-config.xml`: The `faces-config.xml` file contains the configurations for a web application built using JSF. This file allows us to configure managed beans, data convertors, and validators used in the UI, navigation cases, global resource bundles, view handlers, page lifecycle phase listeners, and custom lifecycle factory implementation for the application.

- `adfc-config.xml`: ADF Faces is built on top of the JSF with a lot of extra features, which are not covered by the core JSF. ADF Faces uses `adfc-config.xml` to keep its configurations. As a Fusion developer, you should use `adfc-config.xml` to configure the navigation cases and managed bean definitions. To run your Fusion web application, you may need both `faces-config.xml` and `adfc-config.xml` files — which is true even if you have not added any custom configuration entries in `faces-config.xml`.

- `trinidad-config.xml`: Apache MyFaces Trinidad forms the base for the ADF Faces component set. In fact, Trinidad components earlier were ADF Faces components, which were donated to Apache Software Foundation later in the journey. By default, the generated `trinidad-config.xml` file contains only the skin family name. However, `trinidad-config.xml` can be used to override the default configurations for accessibility settings, locale settings, state management, and so on.

- `web.xml`: The `web.xml` file acts as deployment descriptor for a Java-based web application. When you generate a Fusion web application by using JDeveloper, a default `web.xml` file with default settings will be created for you. The default entries include context parameters for configuring the runtime state of the system, security filters, data binding filters for web pages, and resource look up filters. The `web.xml` file also includes servlet context listeners for initializing the management and monitoring services for view and model layers.

- `adf-config.xml`: The `adf-config.xml` file contains application-level settings, which manage the runtime infrastructure — such as failover behavior for the application modules, global fetch limit for all the view objects, caching of resource bundles, automated refresh of page bindings, and so on — for your application.

- `weblogic-application.xml`: This file is the WebLogic Server-specific deployment descriptor.

Connecting to the database

The next step is to create a database connection that will be used later in the development phase to generate the data model from database objects.

You can create a database connection by right-clicking on the **Connection** node under the **Application Resource** tab and then choosing the **New Connection** option to connect to the database.

We will be using the HR schema in our samples. The HR schema is included with the Oracle 10g or Oracle 11g database. While you define the database connection, key in the credentials set for your local HR schema.

For building a sample application, you can also use Oracle Express Edition (Oracle Database XE) as the database. Oracle Database XE is an entry-level, small-footprint database. All the examples used in this book use Oracle Database XE as the database. To learn about Oracle Database XE, visit http://www.oracle.com/technetwork/products/express-edition/overview/index.html.

What happens when you create a database connection?

When you create a database connection, JDeveloper generates a set of metadata XML files to keep the connection information. Let us take a quick look at these files.

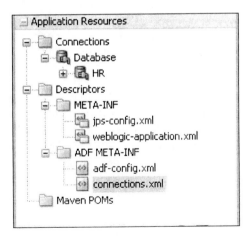

- connections.xml: This file contains the database connection detail that we create for development. If your application consumes web services or map viewer services, the corresponding connection **uniform resource locator (URL)** will also be present in this file.

- jps-config.xml: The jps-config.xml file is used to store the Oracle Platform Security configurations. The location of this file is configured in adf-config.xml. If your application is not configured to use ADF Security, this file, at a minimal level, acts as a pointer to cwallet.sso, which contains the password for the database connection details present in connections.xml.

- cwallet.sso: The cwallet.sso file follows the **Oracle Platform Security Services (OPSS)** specification and it is used as a credential provider in connecting to external systems, such as databases. This file is normally not edited directly.

Generating the data model and business services

The basic infrastructure required for building our first ADF application is in place now. First, we will start the business service implementation by generating the data access layer, followed by the business service layer exposing the services to client.

Our example uses ADF Business Components for building business services where the data access layer is formed by entity objects and view objects. The application module generates the business service layer.

Building entity objects to persist your business data

Entity objects form the data model for your application encapsulating the persistence behavior for items that are used in your application.

An entity definition represents an object in the database such as table, synonym, view, and so on, and an entity instance corresponds to a row from the database object. When you commit a transaction, entity objects are responsible for posting the modified data back to the database.

To generate an entity object, follow these steps:

1. Right-click on your model project in which you want to create entity, and select **New** from the context menu. JDeveloper may respond with the **New Gallery** dialog with a variety of options.

2. In the **New Gallery** dialog, expand the **Business Tier** node, select **ADF Business Components**, and then select **Entity Object**. When you confirm the selection by clicking on **OK**, JDeveloper displays the **Create Entity Object** wizard.

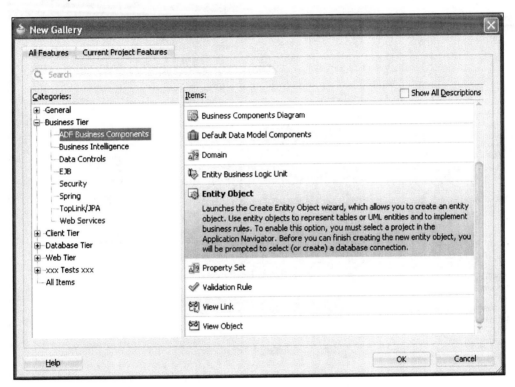

3. In the **Create Entity Object** wizard, you can browse through the schema objects and select the table for which you want to create an entity object, as shown in the following screen shot:

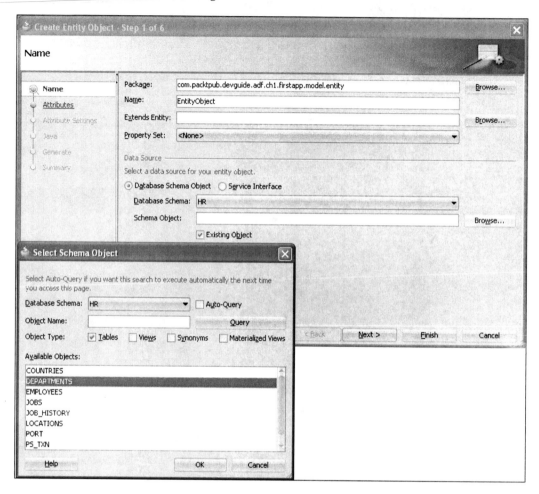

The remaining steps in the wizard's dialog will help you to modify the default properties, such as data types, attribute names, and so on, for entity attributes, and optionally generate Java classes to override the default behavior of entity objects.

In this example, we will generate an entity by selecting the DEPARTMENTS table and modify the default name as DepartmentEO. We will suffix EO with all the entity names in the examples used in this book to improve the readability of the data model. We will skip the remaining steps, accepting the default values generated by the IDE.

Building view objects to shape your business data

Once the entities are generated, the next step is to define a mechanism to populate entities from the database tables. ADF Business Components uses view objects for querying the database.

[In a very simplified form, a view object contains a query to retrieve data from the datasource and data shaping logic to be used by the client.]

To generate a view object, follow these steps:

1. Right-click on your model project in which you want to create a view, and select **New** from the context menu to get the **New Gallery** window.

2. In the **New Gallery** dialog, expand the **Business Tier** node, select **ADF Business Components**, and then select **View Object**. When you confirm the selection by pressing **OK**, JDeveloper will display the **Create View Object** wizard as shown in the following screenshot:

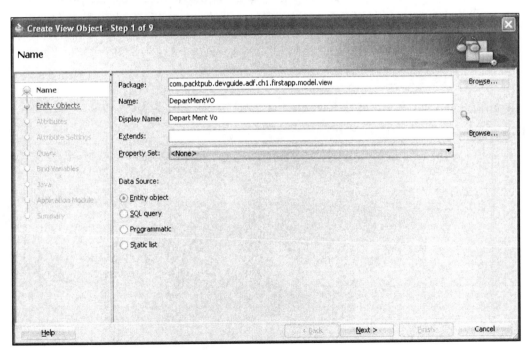

3. In the first step of the **Create View Object** wizard, you can key in the name and select datasource for the view object. In this example, we will build a view object for the `DepartmentEO` entity object that we created in the preceding section. Modify the default name for the view object as `DepartmentVO`. We will suffix `VO` with all the view names in the examples used in this book to improve the readability of the data model. Click on **Next** to continue the wizard.

4. In the **Entity Objects** page of the wizard, select the entity object(s) for which you are building the query. In this example, you will select **DepartmentEO** and click on **Next** to continue.

5. The **Attributes** page displays the attributes from the selected entity objectsfrom the preceding step. You can select the attributes you want to include from each entity usage in the **Available** list and shuttle them to the **Selected** list. For **DepartmentVO**, we will select all the attributes of **DepartmentEO** by shuttling them to the **Selected** list.

6. You can continue with the wizard further if you want to customize the default settings of the view object by altering the default attribute properties that are originally copied from the entity object. The wizard will also let you override the default query in the next step. As the default settings are good enough for **DepartmentVO** used in our example, we will skip these steps by clicking on **Finish**.

Building an application module to facade your business service implementation

We carried out the data access layer implementation in the preceding section step. The next step is to expose the business services to the client through the application module.

 The application module(s) wrap(s) the business service and data model of your application. An application can have multiple application modules depending on the complexity and logical grouping of the services.

To generate an application module, perform the following steps:

1. Right-click on your model project in which you want to create an application module, and select **New** from the context menu.

2. In the **New Gallery** dialog, expand the **Business Tier** node, select **ADF Business Components**, and then select **Application Module**. After clicking on **OK**, JDeveloper will display the **Create Application Module** wizard, as shown in the following screenshot:

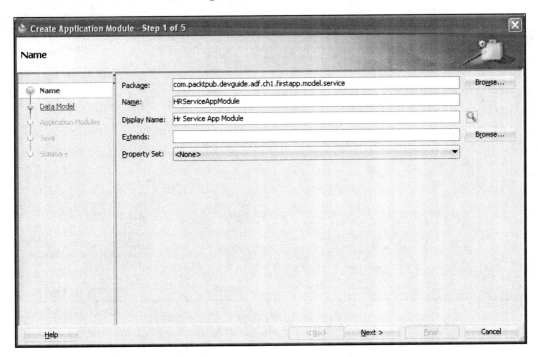

3. On the **Name** page, you can key in the name for the application module and optionally modify the package name. This example names the application module as HRServiceAppModule. Click on **Next** to continue the creation of the application module.

4. The **Data Model** page of the wizard will let you expose the view object instances to the client by shuttling the view object(s) from the **Available** list to **Data Model**. In this example, we will add **DepartmentVO** to the application module as the **DepartmentVO1** instance, which can be consumed from the client later. Either you can finish the wizard at this stage, leaving the default values set by the IDE as they are, or continue the wizard.

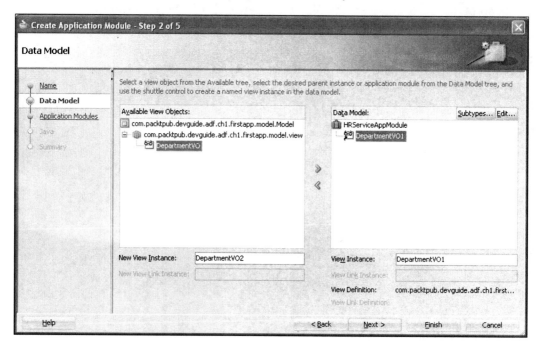

5. If you continue the wizard, the **Application Modules** page may help you to nest another application module (if any) under the current one to build composite services. The **Java** page of the wizard can be used to optionally generate the Java files for the application module, which can be used for adding custom business service methods. These steps can even be performed later during development by editing the existing application module definition.

You can also generate entity objects, view objects, and application modules in a single go by choosing **Business Components** from the **Tables** option displayed in the **New Gallery** window. This feature may save you time, especially when you work on simple applications, proof of concepts, or demos.

What is there in your model project source now?

When you finish generating business components from the database tables by following the steps that we have discussed earlier, JDeveloper will generate metadata XML files and optionally Java classes to hold component definitions for entity objects, view objects, and application modules. Let us take a quick look at the model project source for our example generated by the wizard.

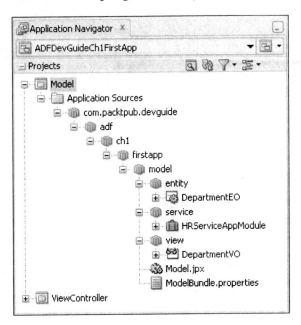

- DepartmentEO.xml: The DepartmentEO.xml file contains the name of the DEPARTMENTS table that we selected for generating the entity and attribute definitions, reflecting the properties of the columns from the DEPARTMENTS table.

- DepartmentVO.xml: The DepartmentVO xml file contains attribute definitions copied from DepartmentEO. this file also contains a query to fetch department records.

- HRServiceAppModule.xml: The HRServiceAppModule.xml file contains information about the view object instances and optional service method definitions. The view object instance used in our example is DepartmentVO1.

- bc4j.xcfg: The bc4j.xcfg file contains metadata information about the application module such as name, database connection, runtime configuration, and so on.

- `Model.jpx`: The `<model-project-name>.jpx` file is used by both ADF design-time tools and runtime components. The `.jpx` file contains the pointers to business component definitions in the `model` project, where each entry describes the package name and type of business components in the package. In more complex applications, it may also contain metadata for the shared application module, which is primarily used at runtime to share the same data between clients. This file is located in the package folder for your `model` project.

When you create an application module, JDeveloper IDE automatically creates a data control that contains all the functionality of the application module. You can click on the refresh icon in the **Data Controls** panel window to view the data control generated for the application module that you added to the `model` project.

The data control exposes the following:

- View object instances as named data collection
- Built-in operations on data collection and custom business methods

You can design a data bound user interface by dragging an item from the **Data Controls** panel and dropping it on a web page as a specific UI component.

Building user interfaces from the model

The next step is to build the user interface for the business services. This is easy if you use ADF data binding, as we will see in this section.

To create a web page, perform the following steps:

1. Right-click on the view controller project and select **New**.
2. In **New Gallery**, expand **Web Tier**, and select **JSF/Facelet**. Select **Page** as item. Confirm the action by clicking on **OK**. Refer to the following screenshot:

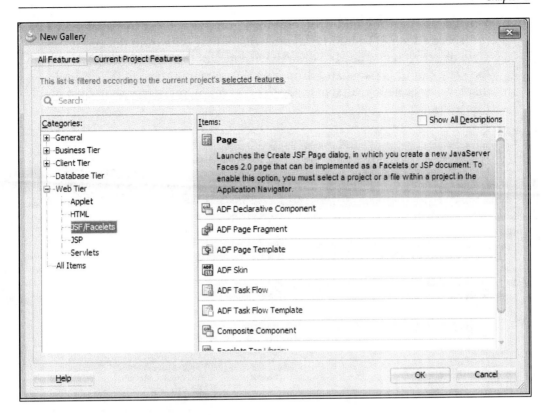

3. In the **Create JSF Page** dialog, you can key in the name for the page and optionally select a template. We will use the **Oracle Three Column Layout** template to build the departments.jsf page for our example.

4. You can use the drag-and-drop offerings from JDeveloper to visually lay out controls on a page. To build a UI table displaying data from the `departments` view object, you just need to drag the instance of the `departments` view from the **Data Controls** panel and drop it on the page by choosing the desired display component available in the list. The following screenshot illustrates this feature:

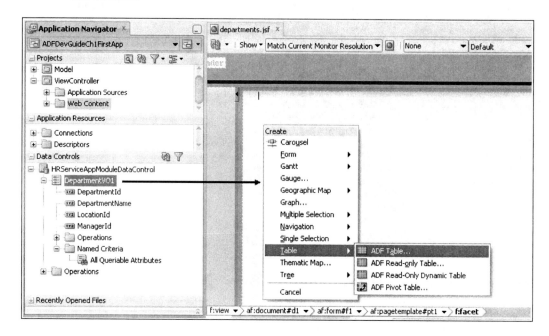

What have you got in your view controller project source now?

It will be interesting to take a look at the `ViewController` project source at this stage. When you drag-and-drop the `departments` view object on the page, the IDE generates two metadata XML files to enable the data binding for the page.

- `departmentsPageDef.xml`: The department page definition XML file is used at runtime to fetch the data when you access the page through the browser. This file will act as binding container for the web pages.

- `DataBindings.cpx`: The `DataBindings.cpx` file defines the binding context for the entire application. This file acts as the registry for page definition files. It also holds metadata for the business services implementations.

- `adfm.xml`: The `adfm.xml` file acts as the registry of registries, holding pointers to each registry metadata file used in the project. In our example, `adfm.xml` contains the path for the `DataBindings.cpx` file.

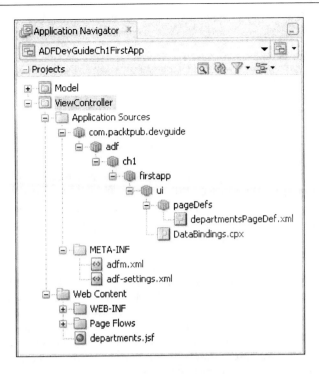

Deploying and running the application

Wow… congratulations! You are done with the implementation even without writing a single line of Java code! We can run this application either by directly a deploying to the application server integrated with JDeveloper, or generating deployable artifact from the application source and then installing to the target server.

 ADF applications are certified against Oracle WebLogic and IBM WebSphere Servers. Oracle ADF essential (free version of ADF) version is also certified against GlassFish 3.1 (or higher).

Running the application using an integrated webLogic server

To run your page by using integrated WebLogic Server, select the .jsf page in the application navigator, right-click on it, and choose **Run**. When running a page by using the integrated application server, JDeveloper creates an exploded EAR at a location that has been pre-configured for the server to look at. Then, the server follows the normal deployment process.

Running the application on a standalone application server

To deploy the application to a standalone server, we may need to prepare the application for deployment. This involves creating deployment profiles for each project and then generating a deployment profile for the whole application, including the required projects. Deployment profiles can be generated by choosing the **New Deployment Profile** option in the **New Gallery** window on your JDeveloper.

The last step is to generate the deployable artifacts, such as an **Enterprise Archive (EAR)** file, for the application by choosing the already created deployment profile. The **Deploy** option is available in your JDeveloper under the **Build** menu of main toolbar.

 To learn more about deploying an ADF application to a standalone sever, refer to the *Oracle Fusion Middleware Administrator's Guide* documentation. To access the documentation visit http://www.oracle.com/technetwork/developer-tools/jdev/documentation/index.html and navigate to **Oracle JDeveloper and ADF Documentation Library | Administrator's Guide**. Use the search option to find specific topics.

Summary

In this chapter, you were introduced to Oracle ADF, its layered architecture, and the advantages of using ADF as an enterprise platform to build next generation applications. We also set up the development environment to use JDeveloper and ADF, and built a simple application to get a feel for the technology stack. This chapter is essential for the easy understanding of what we will learn in the rest of the book. In the coming chapters, we will examine various parts of the Oracle ADF framework in detail.

In the next chapter, we will discuss ADF Business Components, used for building your business services.

2
Introduction to ADF Business Components

The crux of any enterprise application is its business logic implementation. The business service layer of a fusion web application is built using Oracle ADF Business Components. This chapter gives you an overview of ADF Business Components, which includes discussion on the following topics:

- Business service layer
- Overview of ADF Business Components
- Building a simple business service
- Oracle ADF Model Tester
- Java test client for Business Components
- Understanding the runtime behavior of ADF Business Components

The intention of this chapter is to provide you with a brief description of ADF business components. This should hopefully help you to understand the larger picture when we discuss individual business components in the next chapters. If you are already familiar with ADF Business Components, you are free to skip this chapter and move on to the next chapter.

Business service layer

Business logic for an application resides in the area between the UI layer and datasource, fulfilling the requests from the client by interacting with the datasource or other third-party services. A well designed application may have multiple layered structures for business service implementation, where each layer plays a unique role by improving the extensibility of the entire architecture. Let us take a quick look at the various layers found in a multilayered business service implementation:

- **Service layer**: This layer defines the service contracts to be used by a client. The Service layer receives the message sent from the client and delegates it to the appropriate business logic implementation for further processing. The advantage of having a service layer is that it decouples the implementation of services from the service contract, which makes an application more flexible and extensible.

- **Business logic layer**: This layer defines the business logic that is required to perform specific tasks for an enterprise application. The business logic layer is responsible for representing the core business of the system.

- **Data access layer**: This layer is responsible for reading from and writing to a datasource such as a database, file store, or third-party API.

The following diagram illustrates a multilayered business service implementation:

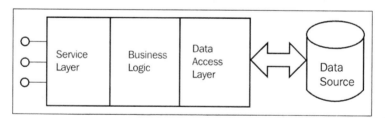

Why ADF Business Components?

This section discusses the advantages of using ADF Business Components for building business services. Business service implementation for any enterprise application generally involves the following three major tasks:

- Building business logic for the application

- Building generic infrastructure services such as connecting to a database, transaction management, business data audit, validation, security, and product customization

- Exposing the services through multiple channels such as EJB, web service, or plain Java to be used by various clients

You, as a developer, may agree that life will be much easier if the underlying technology stack provides the generic infrastructure services required for an enterprise application out of the box. These offerings may free the developers to focus on business logic implementation, eliminating the complexity of the underlying technology.

ADF Business Components and JDeveloper simplify the business service implementation by addressing the aforementioned generic concerns. In the next sections, we will examine how ADF Business Components eases Java EE application development, and what makes this technology an ideal tool to build business services for rich enterprise applications.

Overview of ADF Business Components

ADF Business Components along with JDeveloper provide a visual and declarative development approach for building business logic for an application. By default, business components are configured by using XML metadata files. At runtime, the ADF framework uses the configurations stored in metadata XML definition files for instantiating appropriate business components. If you want to override the default behavior of the business components offered by the framework or want to add custom business logic, then you can generate Java implementation for the desired business components and add your logic there. To customize the default behavior of business components, you must override the appropriate methods from the default base class.

Oracle ADF Business Components' feature list

Oracle ADF Business Components offers many features which are not typically found in other development tools. Let us take a quick look at the ADF Business Components' feature list to understand what makes it a first-class citizen for building business services:

- Oracle ADF Business Components provides a visual and declarative development experience. Business component definitions are kept in XML files and optionally generate Java implementation to write the custom business logic.

- ADF Business Components are built using **Object Relational Mapping (ORM)** concepts by abstracting the underlying data source from the developer.

- Oracle ADF Business Components provides design-time support for exposing business service implementation as web services with very minimal or zero coding.

- Layered architecture of business components improves the reusability and extensibility of each piece used for building the business services.

- Oracle ADF Business Components provides built-in support for managing database connection and middle tier transaction.

- ADF supports building model driven UI components. In this approach, the framework builds UI components on the fly by using UI hints present in the `view` object's XML metadata file. The **list of values (LOV)** and query components are built by leveraging this feature.

- ADF allows you to declaratively synchronize the master and details collection displayed on a page. You can declaratively enable master details co-ordination at the model, which can be leveraged by the binding layer to synchronize the master and detail data display at runtime.

- ADF offers infrastructure services such as paginated queries, validation, security, concurrency management through locking, and business data auditing. The framework also offers declarative tuning support for business components.

Core building blocks

In this section, we will see the core building blocks of business services built by using ADF Business Components. The items in the ADF Business Components stack are shown in the following diagram:

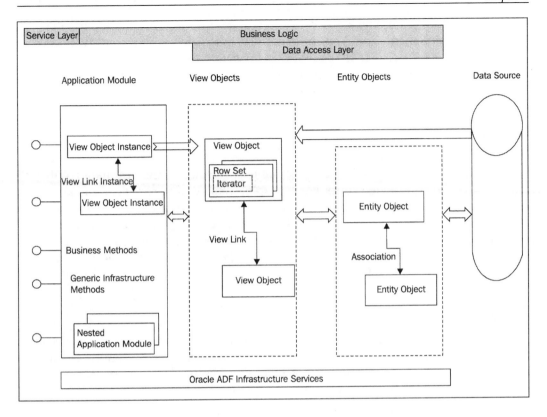

Entity objects

In simple words, an **ADF entity object** represents a database table and an entity object instance represents a single row in that table. The entity object encapsulates application data, validation rules, and persistence logic. An entity implementation has the following artifacts:

- **Entity object definition XML metadata file**: This file stores the entity object definition and declarative settings to control the runtime functionality of the component.

- **Entity definition**: The entity definition describes the structure of an entity object and acts as a template for defining the entity instance at runtime. This is generated at runtime, using the entity object definition XML metadata file.

- **Entity object**: An entity object represents an entity instance, which wraps the business logic for a row in the datasource.

- **Entity collection**: The entity collection caches queried rows for a particular entity implementation. The entity cache is associated with the entity object's `oracle.jbo.server.DBTransaction` object. In other words, entity rows for a particular entity type share the same entity cache only if they are participating in the same transaction.

Associations

Entity object associations define the relation between two entity objects based on the attributes from each side. Associations are useful to access the destination entities from a source entity and vice versa. For example, consider a department and an employee as entity objects. A department can have many employees. This relation can be represented by using association. The number of elements in each side of the association is decided by the cardinality property. When you define association, IDE generates accessor attributes in entities participating in association. These attributes can be used for accessing related entities.

View objects

An **ADF view object** contains logic for reading data from a datasource. It fetches a row set from a datasource and shapes each attribute in a row for presenting them to the client. View objects can be built based on entity objects, a SQL query, or a static list. A view object is composed of the following parts:

- **View object definition XML metadata file**: The view object definition is stored in this file, which contains the query and structure definition of each row in the datasource.
- **View object definition**: The view object definition acts as a Java wrapper for the XML metadata file.
- **View object**: The view object instance manages the query execution life cycle. To intercept the query execution and data population logic, developers can override methods in the default implementation class provided by the framework.
- **View row**: This is a row in the query result.

View links

ADF view links define the relation between view objects. A view link will help you to access the row set present in the destination view object from the source view row and vice versa. View links are defined by mapping attributes of the view object to attributes of a depended view object. If the view object is built using entity objects, the view link can also be defined by choosing the association definition that exists between underlying entity objects. View link is useful for building a master-detail UI.

Row sets

View object uses a special data structure known as **row set** to manage the collection of rows from a query on datasource. The row set contains bind parameter values used in the query, and a default row set iterator implementation to iterate rows from the query. A view object can have multiple row sets. The primary row set used by a view object is termed as default row set. When a view object is executed, by default, it uses the primary row set to hold the rows. The other row sets, which are created explicitly by the client, are secondary row sets.

Query collections

The **query collection** caches the result of executing a view object. A view object instance may contain multiple query collections, depending on the parameter values used by the row sets to execute the parameterized query. All the row sets in a view object are backed up by query collection objects. If two or more row sets use the same parameter values to execute the query, the framework will share the same query collection object to store the rows for those row sets.

Application modules

Application module acts as a service layer for the business services built, using business components. It represents a modular unit of work, and exposes the data model and business method to be used by the client. As the application module is the first layer that a client interacts with, the framework takes special care to reduce the cost associated with the creation and destruction of instances by enabling instance pooling for application modules. Instance pooling reduces the number of application module instances, and thereby the resources needed by service client requests. You can use various configuration parameters to control the pool behavior at runtime.

An application module is composed of the following parts:

- **Application module definition XML metadata file**: The application module definition is stored in this XML file
- **Application module definition**: The application module definition acts as a Java wrapper for the XML metadata file, which will be used at the runtime to create application module instances
- **Application module**: This is an application module instance, which exposes the data model to be used by a client

An application module instance is a work unit container, which aggregates the following component instances and methods:

- **View object instances**: These are the instances exposed to the client to use.

- **View link instances**: View link instances are used to connect view object instances in an application module. Whenever the currently selected row is changed on the master view object instance, the detail view object will be refreshed with new set of rows for the new parent. View link instances are built by using the view links defined between view object definitions.

- **Custom business methods**: These are methods exposed by an application module that implements the business logic that can be used by client.

- **Nested application module**: An application module can act as a composite root application module by nesting existing application modules. This feature is useful for composing services to be used by a client.

Services and service data objects

An application module can be easily extended as web service by using the design-time support provided by JDeveloper. The application module editor allows you to expose application modules as web services that use **Service Data Object (SDO)** components based on the view instance defined in the application module. The service-enabled application module exposes the view object instances, custom business methods, built-in data manipulation operations, and find methods to be used by the client.

To learn more about the SDO standards, visit the Open SOA website at http://www.osoa.org.

Building a simple business service

In this section, we will create a simple ADF model project to get familiarized with the visual aids and tools for building business logic by using ADF Business Components.

Function key *F1* is your friend!
While working with any editor dialog, you can press *F1* to learn more about the features available on the currently active editor window.

To build business services using ADF Business Components, perform the following steps:

1. Right-click on the application navigator in which you want to create the model project, and choose **New Project** to open **New Gallery**.

2. Expand the **General** node, select **Projects**, and then select **ADF Model Project**.

3. In the ADF Model create wizard, enter the name for the project. Optionally, you can enter the package name. The wizard will generate the model project in the application navigator.

4. To generate business components, right-click on the model project and choose **New**.

5. In **New Gallery**, expand **Business Tier**, select **ADF Business Components**, and then choose **Business Components from Tables**.

6. Business component generation needs a database connection to proceed. You can either select an existing connection or create a new connection.

7. The wizard for creating business components from tables will help you to generate the following:

    ○ Entity objects based on database objects
    ○ Updatable view objects from entity objects
    ○ Read-only view objects based on database objects

The following screenshot displays the wizard dialog for creating business components from tables:

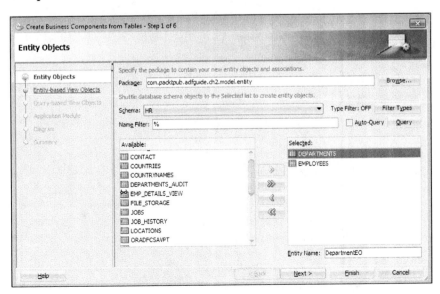

8. Select the desired tables and follow the wizard to generate the appropriate entity objects and view objects.

9. The fourth step in the wizard will optionally generate the application module by exposing the view objects to be used by clients.

10. If you chose to continue the wizard, the next step will allow you to optionally generate a business components diagram for the business components that you generated in preceding steps. It can be used for documenting the business model.

> Each step in the wizard for generating business components from tables will allow the developer to alter the default names generated by the IDE. In real-life application, it is suggested to modify the default business component names and package names, reflecting the naming guidelines and coding standards set for the application.

The following screenshot displays a simple business service implementation generated with ADF Business Components based on the DEPARTMENTS and EMPLOYEES tables from the HR schema. This example logically groups entity objects, entity associations, view objects, view links, and application modules into separate packages by manually altering the default packages generated by the wizard. The default names for the business component definitions and instances have been modified to improve the readability of the components.

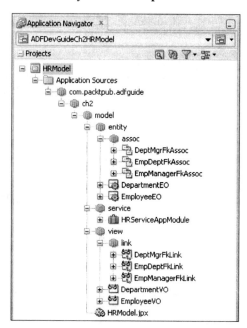

You can set preferences for appending custom suffixes to the default names generated by the business components wizard. The **Preference Settings** dialog box is available under the main menu, **Tools | Preferences | ADF Business Components | Object Naming**.

ADF Business Components configuration files

When you generate business components by using the IDE, the wizard will also generate metadata configuration XML files to manage the runtime behavior of ADF Business Components. Let us take a quick tour of these metadata configuration files. We will be discussing individual configuration entries in the next chapters when we talk about specific components and their usages in depth. These are the configuration files under discussion:

- bc4j.xcfg: The bc4j.xcfg file contains metadata information about the application module and runtime parameters that have been configured to manage the runtime behavior of each application module instance. When you generate an application module, this file will be automatically generated in common subfolders relative to the folder where you create the application module definition. If you edit an application module configuration by using the editor, the modified values are set in the corresponding bc4j.xcfg file.

- adf-config.xml: The adf-config.xml file contains application-level settings for various framework components scattered across different layers of the application. These configuration entries are usually determined at deployment time and will be configured in the adf-config.xml file. However, there are cases where an application administrator may want to modify certain parameters at runtime without bringing down the entire application. You can use the **Oracle Enterprise Manager (OEM)** control to modify the specific settings for business components at runtime without bringing down the application.

To learn more about using Oracle Enterprise Manager to configure ADF web applications, refer to the *Oracle Fusion Middleware Administrator's Guide for Oracle Application Development Framework*. To access the documentation go to http://www.oracle.com/technetwork/developer-tools/jdev/documentation/index.html and navigate to **Oracle JDeveloper and ADF Documentation Library | Administrator's Guide**. Use the search option to find specific topics..

- `<ModelProjectName>.jpx`: The `<ModelProjectName>.jpx` file is used by both design-time editors and runtime framework components. JDeveloper uses the `<ModelProjectName>.jpx` file as a registry to track the contents of the model packages. It also contains metadata for shared application modules present in the project, which is used by both design-time and runtime components.

- `adfm.xml`: The `adfm.xml` file contains path information for other registry files used in the model project. You may not see this file in a model project source during development. IDE generates this file with appropriate entries when you build a model project. The `adfm.xml` records path information for the following files, if they are present in the project:

  ○ `bc4j.xcfg`

  ○ `<ModelProjectName>.jpx`

  ○ `DataControls.dcx`

  ○ `DataBindings.cpx`

Note that this file is used as a registry of registries in the view controller (Web UI) project as well. There, IDE generates this file when you start using ADF binding features. We will discuss this in detail in *Chapter 7, Binding Business Services with User Interface*.

Oracle ADF Model Tester

Smoke testing of the business model implementation is essential for the success of any application development. The JDeveloper comes with a **Graphical User Interface (GUI)** based Model Tester to test your business components.

To test the business components, select the application module in the **Application Navigator** window, right-click on it, and choose **Run** or **Debug**. JDeveloper will display the **Oracle ADF Model Tester** window as shown in the following screenshot:

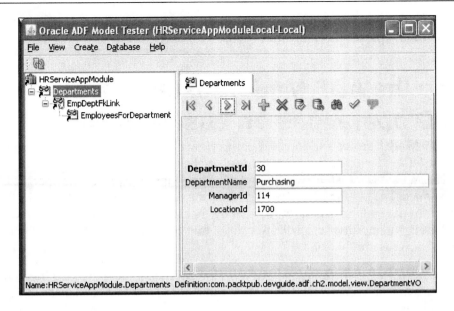

The ADF Model Tester tool will let you test the data model that has been exposed through an application module. This includes executing view object instances to query the datasource, traversing master-child view object instances linked though view links by modifying the attribute values, committing or rolling back a transaction, and invoking business methods.

A quick walkthrough of the commonly used ADF Model Tester toolbar buttons is as follows:

Buttons	Description
	The navigation buttons displayed in the toolbar will help you to navigate between the rows in the collection.
	The green plus toolbar button will create and insert a new row and the red delete button will remove the current row.
	The transaction commit button will save changes to the database. The transaction rollback button will discard the changes since the last save or last query.
	The validate button will run all the validations defined on the entities participating in the current transactions.
	The bind variable edit button will enable you to alter the bind variable value and re-execute the view object.
	The view criteria button will allow you to filter the rows by using query-by-example criteria available on the view object.

In a nutshell, this window can be used to test the basic **Create, Read, Update**, and **Delete (CRUD)** operations on business data.

Using the ADF Model Tester to test the CRUD operations on business data

In the **ADF Model Tester** window, select the view object instance in the data model tree on the left and execute the same by double-clicking on it. Alternatively you can right-click on the view instance and select the **Show** option to execute a specific view object instance. The result will be displayed on the data view page on the right-hand side. You can navigate between rows by using the navigation buttons displayed in the toolbar. If you modify the attribute values, that transaction can be saved by using the transaction commit button.

To test master-detail co-ordination between view objects, double-click on the view link instance displayed between the master and child view object instances in the data model tree.

Testing business methods

There are two instances — application module and view object — through which business methods are exposed in the ADF Business Components architecture.

 To learn about exposing custom methods through the application module or view object, refer to the section *Exposing business service method through data control* in *Chapter 6, Introducing the Application Module*.

To test the methods exposed through an application module instance, double-click on the application module name displayed at the root of the data model in the **Oracle ADF Model Tester** window. This action will display a drop-down list on the data view page with all the exposed methods from the selected application module. You can pick up the desired method and click on **Execute** to test the method. The following screenshot illustrates this feature. This example invokes upd ateDepartmentName(departmentId, departmentName) defined on the application module with user supplied values.

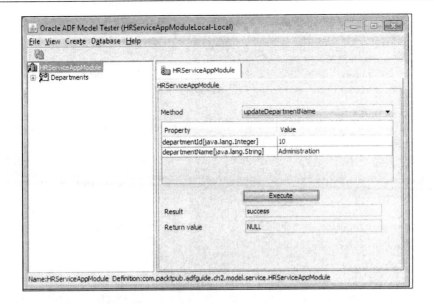

To test the methods exposed through the view object, right-click on the view object instance in the data model tree in the Model Tester window to display the context menu and select the operations menu item. The rest of the steps are the same as testing an application module method that we discussed at the beginning of this section.

This section is intended to briefly introduce you to the Model Tester. To learn more about using the Oracle ADF Model Tester, refer to the chapter *Testing View Instance Queries* in *Fusion Developer's Guide for Oracle Application Development Framework*. To access the documentation visit http://www.oracle.com/technetwork/developer-tools/jdev/documentation/index.html and navigate to **Oracle JDeveloper and ADF Documentation Library | Fusion Developer's Guide**. Use the search option to find specific topics..

Java test client for ADF Business Components

You can generate a Java test client to test the application module and associated data model. The step for generating a Java client is simple and straightforward.

To generate a Java test client class, perform the following steps:

1. Right-click on the project and select **New**.
2. In the **New Gallery** window, select **Java** under the **General** category node and then select **Class** on the right side of the panel. Enter the package and class name.
3. In the generated Java class source, keep the cursor inside the body of the `main (String[] args)` method, type the characters `bc4jclient`, and press *Ctrl + Enter*. This will generate a basic skeleton to invoke the application module.
4. Modify the `amDef` and `config` variables to reflect the names of the application module definition and the configuration that you want to test.

The following code snippet shows a simple test client program to test an application module:

Downloading the example code

You can download the example code files for all Packt books you have purchased from your account at http://www.PacktPub.com. If you purchased this book elsewhere, you can visit http://www.PacktPub.com/support and register to have the files e-mailed directly to you.

```java
import oracle.jbo.ApplicationModule;
import oracle.jbo.Row;
import oracle.jbo.ViewObject;
import oracle.jbo.client.Configuration;

public class TestClient {

  public static void main(String[] args) {
    String amDef =
    "com.packtpub.adfguide.ch2.model.service.HRServiceAppModule";

    String config = "HRServiceAppModuleLocal";
    ApplicationModule am =
    Configuration.createRootApplicationModule(amDef, config);

    // Work with your appmodule and view object here
    //Find Department View Object Instance
    ViewObject vo = am.findViewObject("Departments");
    //Execute Department query
    vo.executeQuery();
    //Fetch the first record
    Row deptRow = vo.first();
    printRow(vo, deptRow);

    // Clean up resources
    Configuration.releaseRootApplicationModule(am, true);
  }
}
```

Understanding the runtime behavior of ADF Business Components

In the previous section, we discussed building a simple ADF model project and learned how to test the business components by using the built-in Model Tester as well as by using the code. You might be wondering now, how do all these things work even without writing down a single line of code? It's time for us to explore the real heroes who do the real jobs behind the scenes.

If you use ADF Business Components for building business logic, you do not really need to worry about the low-level coding, which is otherwise required for querying the database and populating the collection to be used by the client, tracking the modified item, and posting the updates back to the database. In this section, we will learn about the roles and responsibilities of each business component. We will see how they collaborate and work together at runtime to query the datasource and to manage the user transactions.

Roles and responsibilities of the view object, row set, and query collection

Before we dive into the business components' interactions at runtime, let us take a step back and analyze the roles of each business component. The following diagram depicts the core business components, which are responsible for querying the database table and caching the result set to be used by the client:

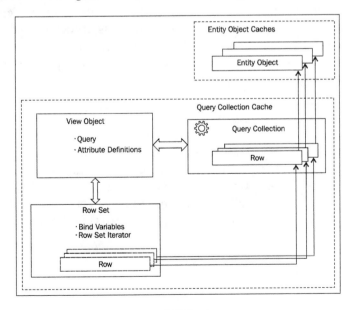

A view object contains a query to read records from the database. It also contains attribute definitions for each column present in the SELECT clause. The framework may use the same view object in multiple places to query the datasource with a different set of **bind variable** (also known as bind parameter) values. For managing the bind variable values used in a query and resulting rows, the framework uses another class known as **row set**. As you might have guessed already, a view object may have many row sets. All row sets that belong to a view object use the same query statement supplied by the view object, but with a different set of bind variable values supplied by the caller. As we discussed a while ago, a view object internally uses a default row set to manage the collection from the query. By default, when a client executes a view object multiple times, the framework populates the default row set each time. A client can explicitly create secondary row sets on a view object, if needed. A row set uses a default row set iterator object to track the current row and iterate over the collection of view rows from the query execution.

The real work horse behind a row set is query collection, which is maintained at view object instance level. The actual query execution and caching of rows is done by a query collection class. Each row in a row set acts as a wrapper over rows from the query collection. If the view object is based on entity objects, the framework generates entity object instances to back up the rows in the query collection. This concept is illustrated in the preceding diagram.

A closer look at query collection

A view object may contain multiple row sets and among these, some row sets might have used the same parameter values for executing the query. While it is necessary to keep the logic for navigation cases and pagination specific to each client, there is no need to replicate the same collection across row sets, if they have queried the database with the same parameter values. So, the framework uses query collection instances to cache the rows from query execution serving multiple row sets with the same bind variable values.

Let us take an example to understand the role of query collection, row sets, and view objects when a client queries the datasource.

In this example, we are taking Product and Supplier view objects. One product can have multiple suppliers in a city and these view objects are linked through a view link. The view link uses the attribute City to connect source and destination view objects. Suppose product 10 and 20 are delivered in New York and product 30 in New Delhi. New York has two supplying agencies Nexus and Shopster, and New Delhi has Simply Shop.

Suppose you want to display Product and Supplier in a tree structure, with Products as parent nodes and Suppliers as child nodes. ADF uses Product and Supplier view objects linked through view links to populate the tree hierarchy. Now, when you query the products view object, the framework populates the default row set in the products view object with products 10, 20, and 30. When the application invokes the view link accessor to get the suppliers from product, each product row will produce a view row set in the Supplier view object. As all collections need to co-exist at this stage, the framework does not touch the default row set, it rather generates a secondary row set in the supplier view object to hold the collection for each caller. Products 10 and 20 show supplying agencies in New York, and product 30 shows the supplying agencies in New Delhi.

As the first two view row sets show the same data, the framework will re-use the same query collection for `city='New York'`, and the third will have its own query collection for `city='New Delhi'` as illustrated in the following diagram:

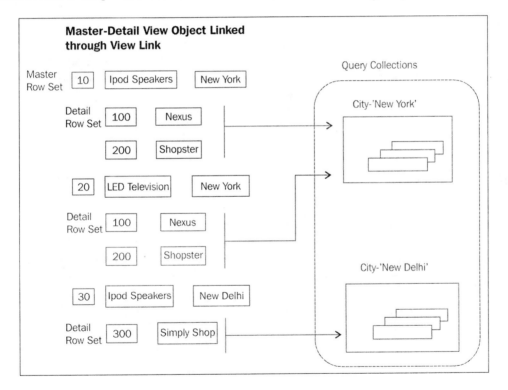

To summarize, when a view object or row set instance is queried for collection, the view object checks an internal query collection hash table to see if a query collection for the row filter key is already in the list, and if found, re-uses it. Otherwise, the query is executed and a new query collection is generated.

What happens when you execute an entity-based view object?

We are prepared for a deep dive now. In this section, we will examine how ADF Business Components work together and complement each other to read data from a datasource. As we discussed at the beginning of this chapter, the business component that is primarily responsible for querying the database table is the view object. However, there are more active items under the hood helping the view object execute the query.

Let us take a simple example to illustrate how a view object queries the datasource and populates the row set. The following code snippet will help you to query the DEPARTMENTS table through the Departments view object. The code snippet contains an implementation to find and execute the view object instance. The last line in the example fetches the first element in the result set:

```
ViewObject vo = applicationModule.findViewObject("Departments");
vo.execute();//execute view object to fetch rows
Row row=vo.first();//Move to the first row in the row set
```

The following sequence diagram highlights how the business components interact with one another to query the database:

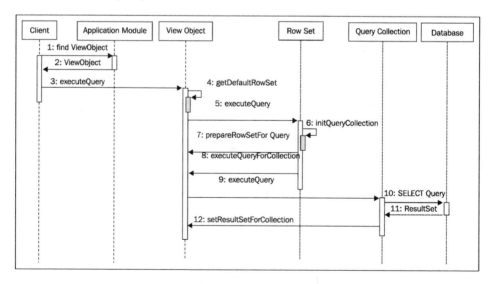

An ADF Business Component client starts the interaction by procuring an application module instance and looking up the view object in the application module. The application module instantiates the view object by using the view object definition and returns the view object instance to the client.

The client then executes executeQuery() on the view object instance to initiate the data fetch operation. The view object instance does not directly query the database, rather it acts as the primary contact point for client. The view object finds the default row set and delegates the call. The row set, as the name suggests, is responsible for managing the row collection for the client. When any view object calls executeQuery() on a row set, it does the following tasks:

- Row set will check the associated view object instance to see if a query collection for the search parameters (row filter) is already available. If yes, use the same query collection object.
- If it does not exist, then a new query collection will be created and this will be added to the view object.

Once the query collection is initialized, the row set will engage the standard query execution lifecycle methods from the view object. The row set instance calls prepareRowSetForQuery() on the view object first. This callback method is the place to hook your custom code (if any) right before the query execution. This is followed by a call to executeQueryForCollection() on the view object. The view object delegates the call to the query collection instance, which is the real hero in the rest of the story. The query collection executes the query by using **Java Database Connectivity (JDBC)** APIs and gets the result set back. This result set will be glued in the query collection instance.

 If you want to intercept the query execution lifecycle for a view object, you may need to generate a view object class and override the standard methods from the oracle.jbo.server.ViewObjectImpl base class.

When the client tries to get the first row in the result set by calling first() on the view object instance, the call will reach the default row set instance in the view object. The row set will now initialize the default row set iterator object, which is responsible for iteration over the view row collection. As the row set is not yet populated with rows, call for the first element by the iterator will put the associated query collection instance into action. The query collection will start serving the call by checking whether the result set from the query has any rows to work on, and if this check returns true, it starts generating a view row for the first item in the result set. While creating the row, if the view object definition is based on an entity object, entity instances will be created and added to corresponding entity cache.

The next step is to populate the newly created entity instances with values from the row in the result set. If there is an entity backup, each row in the query collection will simply act as pointers to corresponding entity instances, and actual data will be present in the entity cache. Once the row is created and storage for the row is set pointing to the entity object, it will be added to the query collection's internal list. If the view object is not built using entity objects, obviously the entity cache would be missing and each row in query collection will be holding the data.

Viewing the object row cache and entity cache

Query result is cached in query collection instance, which is known as **view object row cache**. If the view object is based on an entity object, each view row in the query collection will act as a pointer to the entity usage instance, which is present in the entity cache.

What happens when you commit a transaction?

Let us examine what happens when you modify rows in a view object backed up by entity objects, and later commit the transaction.

This discussion uses the following code snippet to illustrate the transaction post cycle for business components. The code snippet used in this example fetches a row from the DEPARTMENTS table by using the Departments view object, and modifies DepartmentName in the row. The commit() call on the transaction makes changes to the database.

```
ViewObject vo = applicationModule.findViewObject("Departments");
vo.executeQuery();
Row deptRow = vo.first();

//Modify the attribute DepartmentName for first row
deptRow.setAttribute("DepartmentName", "HR Service");

//Commit the transaction
applicationModule.getTransaction().commit();
```

When you modify the attribute value by calling setAttribute() on a row, the call reaches the underlying entity instance on which the row is based. At this stage, the following actions happen:

- The framework pushes the modified attribute value to the entity instance.
- Then, marks it as modified.

Runtime adds the modified entity instance to the transaction listener list and to the validation listener list, maintained by the DBTransaction object attached to the owning application module. Later, when you commit changes by calling commit() on a transaction, the following steps are triggered behind the scenes:

- The DBTransaction object triggers the validate phase. All the modified entities that are available in the validation listener list are validated.

- Transaction manager starts the data post cycle. All the newly created, deleted, and modified entities that were added into the transaction post listener list will be participating in this cycle. During the post changes cycle, the framework performs the following tasks:

  ○ Locks each modified entity
  ○ Generates native SQL for data manipulation based on the type of operation and modified attributes
  ○ Executes JDBC statements, which post modified data to the database

- The last step is committing the transaction. Runtime makes pre- and post-callbacks to enable all the parties participating in the transaction to perform any actions before and after the transaction commits.

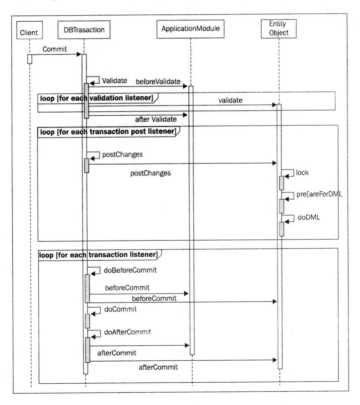

As this is an introductory section, we are keeping things simple. We will cover life cycle methods of business components in depth in the next chapters.

Summary

In this chapter, we discussed the core building blocks of ADF Business Components and how they collaborate and work together at runtime to perform basic CRUD operations on rows from a datasource. In this chapter, you have learned the following:

- Role of business service layer in an enterprise application
- Building blocks of ADF Business Components
- Using JDeveloper to build ADF business components
- How the view object reads data from database
- How the entity object participates in the transaction post cycle

This chapter is intended to give you an overview of business components. We will take a closer look at each business component item in the coming chapters. The next chapter discusses the entity object and its basic features. More advanced features of entity objects are covered in *Chapter 5, Advanced Concepts on Entity Objects and View Objects*.

3

Introducing Entity Object

The previous chapter introduced the fundamentals of ADF Business Components. Now, it is time for us to explore the Oracle ADF technology stack in depth. This chapter builds on the introduction by outlining the entity objects, which make up the persistence layer of business components. The remaining components in the business service layer such as view objects and application modules will be covered in the next chapters. In this chapter, we will discuss the following topics:

- Concepts and architecture
- Core features of ADF entity objects
- Developing entity objects
- Commonly used properties of an entity attribute
- Commonly used properties on an entity object
- Working with entity objects

Introduction

The ADF entity object hides the physical database objects from the developers, and enables them to work with data in the form of Java objects and properties—for example, departments and employees. If you take business logic built by using ADF Business Components, an entity object represents data source definition (for example, a database table) and an entity instance represents a row in the datasource. In this chapter, you will learn using entity objects to build a data model for your business application. This chapter mainly focuses on declarative features offered by the ADF entity object. More advanced features will be explained in *Chapter 5, Advanced Concepts on Entity Objects and View Objects*.

An entity object shields the developer from the complexities of the underlying datasource, using the concept of object relational mapping. The datasource for a typical ADF application could be traditional relational database management systems, such as Oracle, MySQL, MS SQL Server, and DB2, or web services, or even third-party services.

 A full list of supported databases for the Oracle ADF runtime components and JDeveloper IDE is available at the Oracle technology network website (http://www.oracle.com/technetwork/developer-tools/jdev/documentation/index.html) under the **Certification Information** category.

Ingredients of an entity object

In *Chapter 2, Introduction to ADF Business Components* we discussed the constituents of an entity object. In this section, we are revisiting the same topic to analyze the artifacts of an entity object in depth:

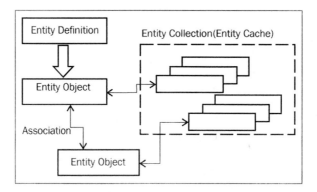

An entity object is composed of the following components:

- **Entity object definition XML metadata file**: This file is an entity descriptor, which holds metadata definition for the entity. This file stores the following configurations for an entity object:
  - ○ This file stores the database object on which the entity is built upon. An entity object can be built from a database table, view, synonyms, or materialized view.

- ○ This file also stores the attribute definition for each column present in the entity object. This includes the datatype, length, precision, validation rules, and updatability of the attribute. Attribute definition also includes UI hints such as label, tool tip, format type, and control type.

- ○ View accessors and entity accessor attributes' definitions are also stored in this file. View accessors and entity accessor attributes' definitions are used for accessing view objects and associated entity objects, respectively.

- ○ Business event definitions that are used for launching business processes in a service oriented environment.

- **Entity definition**: This class acts as a runtime Java class representation for the entity object definition XML metadata file. The default entity definition class used by the ADF Business Components' runtime is `oracle.jbo.server.EntityDefImpl`, which can be extended to provide custom functionalities, if needed.

- **Entity object**: This class represents individual entity instance created from the entity definition at runtime. The default entity object class used by the ADF business components' runtime is `oracle.jbo.server.EntityImpl`, which can be extended to provide custom functionalities, if needed. In simple words, an entity object instance represents a row in the datasource. For example, when you query an `Employee` table in the database by using a view object backed up by the `EmployeeEO` entity object, the framework creates `EmployeeEO` entity object instances for storing employee records returned by the SQL query.

- **Entity collection**: This class represents the cache of the entity object class held in memory for a transaction. The default entity collection (entity cache) class used by the ADF Business Components' runtime is `oracle.jbo.server.EntityCache`, which can be extended to provide custom functionalities, if needed.

Runtime collaboration between business components

At runtime, when an entity instance is created, the framework uses corresponding entity definition class for defining the entity structure. All entity instances inherit the properties from its entity definition class. When the primary key is set for a newly created entity instance, it qualifies for being stored in the entity collection (entity cache). The framework will access the entity instance from the cache thereafter.

Core features of ADF entity objects

Oracle ADF entity objects are not just yet another data access layer built by using an object relational mapping mechanism, rather they are an end-to-end ORM tool with many out-of-the-box features:

- Visual and declarative development
- Associations
- Declarative validation
- Entity inheritance
- Entity caching
- Built-in CRUD operations
- Concurrency handling
- Customizable framework components
- Domain-driven development
- Security-enabled business components

Developing entity objects

In this section, we will learn more about building and configuring entity objects by using JDeveloper IDE.

Creating a database connection

While discussing the ADF Business Component in the previous chapters, you have been introduced to the database connection wizard. We are not repeating the same steps here, rather adding a point on top of what we have learned already:

- The database connection can be defined either at IDE level, which can be copied to multiple ADF model projects to be used, or can be defined individually for each ADF model project in its **Application Resources** section.

- To create a connection at IDE level, navigate to **View | Database | Database Navigator** from the main menu. Right-click on **IDE Connection** and select **New Connection**. The remaining steps remain the same as for defining an application-level database connection.

Initializing the ADF model project

When you opt for generating business components in a model project for the first time, you will see the **Initialize Business Components** dialog box. This dialog box has options to set the SQL platform and datatype map to be used by the model project. The SQL platform decides the native SQL generation by the business components' runtime. The datatype map list decides the Java datatypes to be set for the attributes in the business components. The default datatype map used by JDeveloper for Oracle database is **Java Extended For Oracle**.

> If your application needs to be ported to different databases at a later stage, make sure that you are setting the SQL platform as SQL92 and the datatype map as Java. For more information on this topic, please refer to the white paper *How to Develop with ADF Business Components for Multiple Databases*, which is available online at http://www.oracle.com/technetwork/developer-tools/jdev/multidatabaseapp-085183.html.

Creating entity objects

JDeveloper helps you to build entity objects in two ways:

- **Using Create Business Components from the Tables option**: This option allows you to create multiple entity objects in one go.

  To use this option, right-click on the model project and select **New**. In **New Gallery**, expand **Business Tier**, select **ADF Business Components**, and then select **Business Components** from **Tables**.

- **Using the Create Entity Object wizard**: This option allows you to create a single entity object at a time.

  To use this option, right-click on the model project and select **New**. In **New Gallery**, expand **Business Tier**, select **ADF Business Components**, and then select **Entity Object**.

In this section, we are not going to repeat the same discussion on entity generation that we had in the previous chapters, rather our focus will be on some steps that we skipped by accepting the default settings while using the wizard. You can refer back to the following sections for a quick brush up:

- *Building a simple business service* in *Chapter 2, Introduction to ADF Business Components*

- *Generating the data model and business services* in *Chapter 1, Getting Started with Oracle ADF*

Choosing the database object type

To keep the discussion simple, this section assumes that you are using the **Create Entity Object** wizard for generating an entity object. However, the features that we will discuss here remain the same even if you use **Create Business Components** from the **Tables** option.

The first screen in the **Create Entity Object** wizard will allow you to pick up the schema objects on which the entity objects are based. JDeveloper provides options to build entity objects from the following database object types:

- **Tables**: This option will allow you to define entity object(s) for database tables. This is straight forward and does not need much explanation.

- **Views**: A database view takes the output of a query and makes it appear like a virtual table to the user. If you want to build entity objects by using the database view to insert, update, or delete table rows, the view should be updatable. Database views can be either inherently updatable, or you can create an INSTEAD OF trigger on the view to make it updatable.

  Here is an example for a simple updatable database view defined on the EMPLOYEES and DEPARTMENT tables:

```
CREATE OR REPLACE VIEW  EmployeeDepartmentView AS SELECT Emp.
EMPLOYEE_ID, Emp.FIRST_NAME, Dept.DEPARTMENT_NAMEFROM EMPLOYEES
Emp, DEPARTMENTS Dept WHERE Emp.DEPARTMENT_ID = Dept.DEPARTMENT_
ID;
```

> Note that you can also make a database view-based entity object updatable by overriding the doDML() method of the entity implementation class. This method can contain logic for invoking custom stored procedures for the insert, update, and delete operations as appropriate. We will discuss this topic in the section entitled *Building programmatically managed entity objects* in *Chapter 5, Advanced Concepts on Entity Objects and View Objects*.

- **Synonyms**: A synonym is an alias for any table, view, or materialized view. This option will allow you to define entity object(s) based on synonyms that the schema defines. Here is an example for a synonym defined on the EMPLOYEES table:

```
CREATE OR REPLACE  SYNONYM EMP for EMPLOYEES;
```

- Materialized view: A materialized view is a database object that contains the results of a query. Here is an example for a materialistic view:

```
CREATE  MATERIALIZED VIEW EmployeeMView FOR UPDATE AS SELECT *
FROM EMPLOYEES Employees WHERE Employees.DEPARTMENT_ID = 10;
```

> To learn more about Oracle database objects such as database view, materialized view, and synonym, refer to the *Oracle Database SQL Language Reference* documentation available at http://www.oracle.com/technetwork/database/enterprise-edition/documentation/index.html.
>
> When you generate entities from a view, materialized view, or synonym, the framework may not be able to infer the primary key from the data dictionary. So you as a developer are responsible for specifying the primary key attribute. The primary key is used by the framework to uniquely identify entity rows at runtime. If there is no explicit key set, the framework will set the default primary key to RowID.

Generating Java classes for entity components

ADF provides a visual and declarative way to build your business logic. When you build entity objects by using JDeveloper, the wizard generates entity XML files to store the metadata properties derived from the database object. These configurations will be used by ADF Business Component framework classes to implement the generic CRUD operations on datasource.

The default base classes from the ADF framework may be enough for building most of the generic use cases. However, if you want to go beyond the declarative features to implement custom business logic for your entities, you will need to generate Java classes and override the entity call back methods to add your custom code.

To generate Java classes for entity, double-click on the entity object to display the overview editor. In the overview editor, go to the **Java** tab and click on the **Edit** icon. In the **Select Java Options** dialog, select the types of Java classes that you want to generate:

- **Entity object class**: This class is the more frequently sub-classed class and is used for customizing business logic or runtime behavior for an entity instance. For example, if you want to prevent an update on specific attributes conditionally, you will have to generate an entity object class and override the `setAttributeInternal()` method to add your logic. To learn more about the entity object life cycle methods, refer to the section entitled *Life cycle callback methods of an entity object* in *Chapter 5, Advanced Concepts on Entity Objects and View Objects*.

- **Entity collection class**: This class is for customizing the default entity caching implementation. For example, you may customize the default caching implementation if you want to provide your own caching logic, or to provide custom logic for cleaning up the cached rows.

- **Entity definition class**: This class is used for customizing the default entity definition implementation, and manages entity row creations and defines their structure. For example, if you want to modify the properties of an entity object or attributes of an entity object at runtime, you can override the `resolveDefObject()` method in the `oracle.jbo.server.EntityDefImpl` class, and add custom logic for altering the definition before returning to the caller.

Generally you may not customize an entity collection class and an entity definition class, as the default implementations are good enough to meet most of the use cases.

Commonly used properties of an entity attribute

An entity object attribute has a set of configurable properties, which can be set declaratively to override the default settings.

These properties are configurable either when you create an entity by using the **Create Entity Object** wizard, or later when creating it by using the entity object overview editor. The following screenshot displays the entity object overview editor for the `DepartmentEO` entity object:

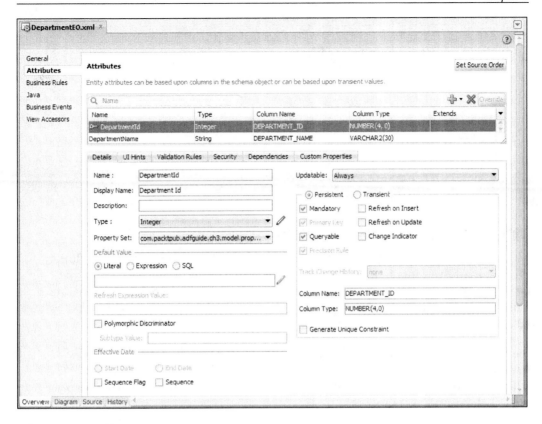

You can open up the overview editor by double-clicking on the appropriate entity object in the model project. Let us take a look at the various properties displayed in this editor.

Attribute names in an entity object

When you generate entities, JDeveloper will use the camel-capped attribute naming convention by default. For example, if you have a column, such as DEPARTMENT_NAME in a table, JDeveloper will pick up the parts separated by the underscore character and will uppercase the first letter in each part. The column DEPARTMENT_NAME turns into DepartmentName in the entity. If you manually edit the names, the attribute name should follow the Java variable naming convention. Also, make sure you use logically meaningful names to improve the readability of the code. If you opt to generate an entity object class with accessors (getter methods for attributes) for your entity object, the framework will generate the accessor methods in the entity object class as follows:

```
/**
 * Gets the attribute value for DepartmentName
```

```
 * @return the value of DepartmentName
 */
public String getDepartmentName() {
   return (String)getAttributeInternal(DEPARTMENTNAME);
}

/**
 * Sets value as the attribute value for DepartmentName.
 * @param value value to set the DepartmentName
 */
public void setDepartmentName(String value) {
  setAttributeInternal(DEPARTMENTNAME, value);
}
```

Attribute types in an entity object

While generating business components from the database objects, the JDeveloper IDE will read the data dictionary for the database object and will try to map the database column with the compatible Java types for the attributes in the generated business components. The datatypes for the attributes in an entity are decided by the datatype map set for the model project.

The default datatype map used by JDeveloper for the Oracle database is Java Extended For Oracle (OracleApps). The following table displays the optimal datatype mapping for business components, when used with the Oracle database and OracleApps-type map:

Database column type	Business components attribute type	Description
VARCHAR2	java.lang.String	VARCHAR2 is mapped to java.lang.String
NUMBER	java.math.BigDecimal	NUMBER type is mapped to java.math.BigDecimal if the scale is not zero or precision is greater than 18
NUMBER	java.lang.Integer	NUMBER type is mapped to java.math.BigDecimal if the scale is zero and precision is between 1 to 9
NUMBER	java.lang.Long	NUMBER type is mapped to java.lang.Long if the scale is zero and precision is between 10 to 18

Database column type	Business components attribute type	Description
DATE	java.sql.Date	DATE type is mapped to java.sql.Date if the table column has no time component and client does not need time zone information
DATE	java.sql.Timestamp	DATE type is mapped to java.sql.Timestamp if the table column has time component and client needs time zone information
TIMESTAMP	java.sql.Timestamp	TIMESTAMP type in database is having nanosecond precision
BLOB	oracle.jbo.domain.BlobDomain	BlobDomain supports streaming and lazy data loading
CLOB	oracle.jbo.domain.ClobDomain	ClobDomain supports streaming and lazy data loading

Using a resource bundle to localize UI hint properties

When you define translatable strings for UI hint properties or validation messages, by default JDeveloper will create a new bundle if there is no resource bundle in the project to hold the translatable text.

Accessing the resource bundle from the entity object class

To access the resource bundle defined for the entity object from the entity object implementation class, refer to the following example:

```
//Access the ResourceBundleDef defined for the entity object
ResourceBundleDef resourceDef = this.getResourceBundleDef();
//Get the user locale
Locale locale = this.getDBTransaction().getSession().getLocale();
//Get the localized value for the key
String retVal = StringManager.getLocalizedStringFromResourceDef(resour
ceDef, key, null, locale, null, false);
```

To access the resource bundle, which is not directly associated with entity object definition, you can use standard `java.util.ResourceBundle` APIs. An example is as follows:

```
//Get the user locale
Locale currentLocale = this.getDBTransaction().getSession().
getLocale();
ResourceBundle myResources = ResourceBundle.getBundle("MyResources",
currentLocale);
```

Property set

There are a number of predefined properties for an attribute in an entity object. Sometimes you may wish to add custom properties for the attributes to store other information and create custom behavior at runtime. ADF offers property set for defining re-usable custom properties. The **property set** is a registry for properties that can be used to logically group the common properties used in business components. These properties are broadly classified into two categories:

- Translatable messages such as attribute labels, short description, and other UI control hints.

  As these values changes with locale setting, they are stored in locale specific properties file, which follows normal resource bundles rules from Java language.

- No translatable key value properties used in the business logic implementation.

Property set allows you to re-use the custom properties across business components.

Creating a property set

To create a property set, do the following:

1. Right-click on the model project and select **New**.
2. In **New Gallery**, expand **Business Tier**, select **ADF Business Components**, and then select **Property Set**.
3. In the **Create** window, enter the property set name and package name. A property set can optionally extend an existing one as well.

Once the property set is created, you can access the translatable and non-translatable properties by using the green plus icon displayed for the **Custom Properties** tab.

Associating the property set with the entity object attributes

To use properties from the property set in an entity object attribute, perform the following steps:

1. Double-click on the desired entity object to open up the overview editor.

2. Click on the **Attribute** tab in the overview editor and select the desired attribute.

3. Under the **Details** tab, select a property set from the drop-down list. This action will associate the property set with the entity attribute, and later you can use the properties in the property set to implement custom behavior for business components.

Using custom properties in business logic

The following example illustrates how you can use custom properties associated with an entity attribute in the business logic. This example uses custom property associated with an attribute to customize the execution at runtime. The setEmail() method reads the custom UPDATE_CHECK_ENFORCED property associated with the attribute and based on this value, it calls isEmailUpdatable() before allowing the data change on the email field. You can use a similar idea in your application to skip unwanted execution.

```
public class EmployeeEOImpl extends EntityImpl {

/**
 * Sets value as the attribute value for Email.
 * @param value value to set the Email
 */
public void setEmail(String value) {
  boolean updateAllowed = true;
  //Read the UPDATE_CHECK_ENFORCED property
  //for the Email field
  String emailUpdateCheckEnforced =
  (String)getDefinitionObject()
  .getAttributeDef(EMAIL).getProperty("UPDATE_CHECK_ENFORCED");
  //If the UPDATE_CHECK_ENFORCED is added to
  //the attribute, then call
  //custom isEmailUpdatable() to check if update is allowed.
  //Call to isEmailUpdatable() may be  expensive and
  //we are doing it selectively using custom property.
  if (("true".equals(emailUpdateCheckEnforced))) {
    updateAllowed = isEmailUpdatable();
  }
  if (updateAllowed)
```

```
        setAttributeInternal(EMAIL, value);
    }
    //Remaining EntityImpl code goes here...
}
```

Persistent and transient attributes

Attributes that are not persisted in the underlying database source, such as the database table, are **transient**. A transient attribute's display values are derived from other attributes either by using Groovy expression or through Java code. In some cases, transient variables can be used as temporary value holders as well as in the business logic implementation.

To define a new transient attribute, open the entity in the overview editor. Go to the **Attributes navigation** tab. Click on the green plus icon and specify the attribute name. To mark this attribute as transient, you can either select the **Transient** radio button in the **Details** tab or set **Persistent** as **false** in the property inspector. The value for the transient attribute can be set either as declarative by using the default value options in the property inspector, or by overriding the appropriate `getter` method for the attribute in the entity implementation class.

 As the transient key forces re-evaluation of the value for each access, you should be careful if marking it as the primary key. The situation becomes much worse if the recalculation is expensive and use case demands frequent access to the attribute value.

Specifying a default value for an entity attribute

As the name suggests, a default value is set to the attribute values:

- The default value defaults the persistent attribute values when you create a new entity instance
- For transient attributes the default value is used when client accesses the attribute as well as during entity instance creation

To specify a default value for an attribute, select the **Attributes** tab in the overview editor of the desired entity object. Choose the appropriate attribute and then open the **Details** tab. Specify the default value by choosing the appropriate options displayed in the **Default Value** section.

There are three ways to specify default values for an attribute:

- **Literal**: It is set to default static value.
- **Expression**: It is set to default values by using the Groovy expression. The following is an expression that is used for defaulting the primary key from a database sequence, namely EMPLOYEES_SEQ:

  ```
  (new oracle.jbo.server.SequenceImpl("EMPLOYEES_SEQ",
  adf.object.getDBTransaction())).getSequenceNumber()
  ```

- **SQL**: The default value is set by using SQL derived expression.

The following screenshot illustrates the declarative support for specifying a default value for an attribute. This example specifies a default value for the EmployeeId attribute, using a database sequence. This will be used at runtime to default the value for the EmployeeId attribute when a new entity instance is created.

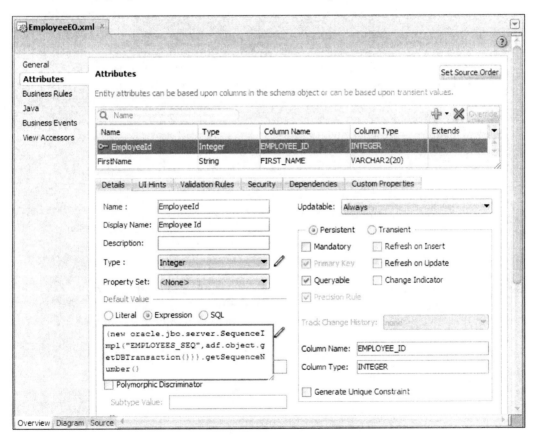

Effective dated entity objects

Effective dated entities are used to provide a view into the dataset pertaining to a specific point in time. For example, consider the job history table for an employee in an organization. This table keeps very sensitive data and is supposed to track all the updates on an employee without overriding the existing data blindly. If the manager wishes, he/she should be able to retrieve all the updates for a specific time frame. To add such functionality, entity components offer effective date feature. To create an effective dated entity, follow these steps:

1. Double-click on the entity on which you want to enable effective dating and then select the **General navigation** tab in the overview editor to display the **Property Inspector** for an entity.

2. In the property inspector window, select **EffectiveDated** for **Effective Date Type**.

3. The next step is to specify attributes from the entity as effective start date and end effective date. Select the **Attributes** tab in the entity overview editor, and then click on the desired attribute and set it as effective start date, either using the **Start Date** drop-down list in the **Property Inspector** window, or using the **Start Date** radio button in the overview editor. Similarly select another attribute in **End Date**. Make sure you are marking the start and end dated attributes as **Keys** (along with the existing keys) in the entity object to prevent multiple records with the same start and end date.

To track multiple changes in a day, you can mark an attribute as **Effective Date Sequence**, which will store the sequence of changes which happened at runtime. And finally to identify the most recent change in the sequence mark an attribute as **Effective Date Sequence Flag**, which will store and indicate the latest modified row.

The runtime behavior of effective date handling is controlled by the effective date mode set for the effective dated entity. The following code snippet sets the effective date mode as EFFDT_UPDATE_CHANGE_INSERT_MODE on an effective dated entity:

```
empEntityImpl.setEffectiveDateMode(Row.EFFDT_UPDATE_CHANGE_INSERT_MODE
);
empEntityImpl.setSalary(10000);
getDBTransaction().commit();
```

In this example, when an effective dated row is updated, the framework splits the modified row into two rows. The modified row is end dated on the effective date -1 and a new row is inserted that fits between the effective date and the start date of the next row in the effective date timeline. Note that the effective date in this example is considered as the current date for a user who is viewing or altering values.

> More effective date modes are available in the `oracle.jbo.Row` interface. To learn more about this, refer to the *ADF Model Java API Reference* documentation available online.`html`. To access the documentation visit `http://www.oracle.com/technetwork/developer-tools/jdev/documentation/index.html`and navigate to **Oracle JDeveloper and ADF Documentation Library | API AND TAG REFERENCES | ADF Model Java API Reference.**

Defining the primary key

The primary key uniquely identifies an entity instance in the collection. When you generate an entity object from the database objects, the design time will try to infer the primary key definition from the data dictionary. If there is no primary key found for the database objects and the underlying database is Oracle, the wizard will pick up the `RowID` pseudo column, which uniquely identifies a row within a table and marks it as the primary key. In all other cases, you as a developer are responsible for defining the primary key.

Best practices when defining the primary key:

- Do not use the default pseudo column `RowId` as the primary key to deal with transaction sensitive business data. For example, if you delete a row from a table, a database might re-use its `RowId` value to a row inserted later. This may result in serious side effects for a business application.

- Prefer surrogate keys over a composite primary key.

- Do not allow the user to modify primary key fields from UI. Note that the framework uses the primary key to identify the corresponding row in the model. When you change the primary key from the UI, the data displayed in the UI and model go out of synchronization. In ADF 11.1.2.0.0 release, Oracle has added minimal support for allowing primary key modification during entity creation from UI. However, this still does not work for a composite primary key (multiple attributes as a primary key). If the use case demands an update on the primary key, try adding a surrogate key to the table and mark this as the primary key.

To programmatically find the entity object by using the primary key, you can call `findByPrimaryKey()` on the corresponding `EntityDefImpl` as shown in the following code snippet:

```
//This method finds the employee entity instance for
// employee id
private EmployeeEOImpl findEmployeeById(int empId) {
//Find the entity definition from the implementation class

  EntityDefImpl orderDef = EmployeeEOImpl.getDefinitionObject();
//Create the Key object
  Key orderKey = EmployeeEOImpl.createPrimaryKey(new Integer(empId));
//Find and return the desired instance
  return (EmployeeEOImpl)orderDef.findByPrimaryKey
  (getDBTransaction(), orderKey);
}
```

The `findByPrimaryKey` method is called on an entity definition and this will try to find the entity from the entity cache first and if not found it will query the database.

Inheritance hierarchies in entity objects

Though inheritance is a common concept in object oriented programming languages such as Java, relational database management systems do not have this concept in place. As an entity object is considered a Java representation of datasources such as tables, introducing inheritance in an entity object is a bit tricky.

ADF entity objects use a single table per hierarchy approach while implementing multiple inheritances. To make it clear, the datasource for entities in the inheritance hierarchy would be a single table. Child entities can be mapped to extra columns from the same table, if needed. The polymorphic discriminator type is introduced to simulate inheritance hierarchies in entity and view objects. Each entity in the hierarchy will have a different value for each polymorphic discriminator attribute and run time will use this value to identify rows for each entity in the hierarchy.

Creating inheritance hierarchies for entity objects

Building inheritance hierarchies based on a single table is useful if you have database tables that store different kinds of information in rows of the same table, which can be distinguished using a discriminator column. Here is an example:

This example uses the EMPLOYEES table to represent the entity hierarchy. DEPARTMENT_ID (discriminator column) is used to distinguish rows belonging to each entity in the hierarchy:

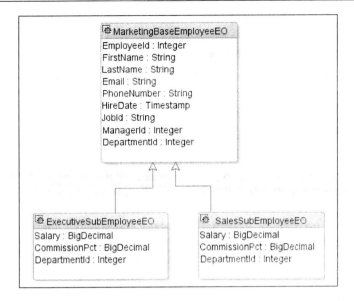

MarketingBaseEmployeeEO is the base entity in the hierarchy. The subtype entity objects used in this example are ExecutiveSubEmployeeEO and SalesEmployeeEO.

To define the base entity object, follow the next steps:

1. Right-click the model project and select **New**. In **New Gallery**, expand **Business Tier**, select **ADF Business Components**, and then select **Entity Object**. Click on **OK** to continue.

2. In the **Create Entity Object** wizard, enter the entity name and package for the entity, and select the schema object.

   For example, enter the entity name as MarketingBaseEmployeeEO and select **EMPLOYEES** as the schema object.

3. On the **Attributes** page, select only those attributes that are relevant to the base entity object.

   This example removes Salary and CommissionPct from the MarketingBaseEmployeeEO.

4. On the **Attribute Settings** page, select the attribute that needs to be marked as a discriminator, and check the **Discriminator** checkbox. You must also supply the default value for the discriminator attribute.

   For example, **MarketingBaseEmployeeEO** marks **DepartmentId** as **Discriminator** and the default value is set to **20**.

5. Click on **Finish** to complete the entity creation.

To define subtype entity objects in the hierarchy, perform the following steps:

1. In **New Gallery**, select **Entity Object** and click on **OK**.

2. In the **Create Entity Object** wizard, enter the entity name and package for the entity, and click on the **Browse** button next to the **Extends** field to select the parent entity for the entity that is being created.

    For example, **SalesSubEmployeeEO** is built by choosing **MarketingBaseEmployeeEO** as parent.

3. On the **Attributes** page, select the attributes that you want to include in the subtype. Note that IDE, by default, will not display attributes from the table, which is already present in the parent entity. To override the attributes present in the parent entity, click on the **Override** button and choose the desired attributes. You must override the discriminator column from the parent entity, as the child entity has to supply a distinct default value for the discriminator column.

4. On the **Attribute Settings** page, select the discriminator attribute and change the **Default Value** field to provide a distinct default value to the entity subtype being created.

    For example, for **SalesSubEmployeeEO**, the default value for **DepartmentId** is set as **80**.

5. Click on **Finish** to complete the entity creation.

You can follow the preceding steps for generating entity objects in any hierarchy. The story is not complete yet. We will discuss how to build a view object for entity objects participating in inheritance hierarchy in the section entitled *Inheritance hierarchies in view objects* in *Chapter 4, Introducing View Objects*.

When you execute a view object built by using an entity, which acts as a base entity in the hierarchy, the framework will not try to add any special WHERE clause to reflect the discriminator attribute values of the entity object. The filtering based on the discriminatory attributes happens later in the execution cycle when the view rows are being created from the result set. Those rows, which satisfy the discriminator attribute values, will only be present in the final row set.

While finding entities in a hierarchy by using primary key, if you also want to include subtypes in search, use the findByPKExtended() method from the EntityDefImpl class:

```
EntityImpl empEOImpl =              empBaseEODef.findByPKExtended
(getDBTransaction(), empIdKey, true);
```

Updatability of entity attributes

If you do not want an attribute to always be updatable, you can use the **Updatable** property to control when the value of a given attribute can be updated. The **Updatable** property is displayed as a drop-down list in the **Details** tab on the **Attributes** page. The possible values are **Never**, **While New**, and **Always**.

- **Never**: An attribute is never updatable. You will use this property to prevent an update on an attribute, unconditionally. For example, if an entity object has some derived attributes, whose values are calculated from other attributes present in the row, you should mark the updatable property as **Never** to prevent unwanted updates.

- **While New**: An attribute is updatable, if the entity object is newly created and the changes (transaction) are not committed to the database. Once the changes are committed, the attribute becomes read only. This property is useful if you want the client to update attributes only during the creation of rows and not after that. For example, if an entity object has some attributes for capturing the name of the user who created the row, you can set the **Updatable** property as **While New** to prevent subsequent updates on this field.

- **Always**: An attribute is always updatable. This is the default setting for an attribute.

Refreshing attributes on posting changes to the database

If certain columns in your table are populated through database trigger or stored procedure when the data is posted to the database, it is necessary to refresh the corresponding entity object attributes with values from the database after posting data to the database. You can turn on **Refresh on Insert** or **Refresh on Update** for such attributes and the rest will be taken care of by the framework.

To turn on the **Refresh on Insert** or **Refresh on Update** options, open the entity in the overview editor, select the attribute that needs to refreshed, and then select the desired refresh option in **Property Inspector**. The framework will update the refresh enabled attributes on the database post operation.

For example, if you have set **Refresh on Update** for `DepartmentId` in `DepartmentEO`, when the modified data is posted to the database the framework will modify the `UPDATE` statement, as shown in the following code snippet, to return `DEPARTMENT_ID` from the database. Once this statement is executed, the framework will populate `DepartmentId` with values returned from the database.

```
BEGIN UPDATE DEPARTMENTS Departments SET DEPARTMENT_NAME=:1 WHERE
DEPARTMENT_ID=:2 RETURNING DEPARTMENT_ID INTO :3; END;
```

The attribute's refresh properties are available only with Oracle database. If your application uses a different database, these properties may not work.

Marking an attribute as mandatory

This option marks the attribute as a mandatory one and this will be enforced during the entity-level validation.

The **Mandatory** checkbox option is displayed in the **Details** tab of the **Attributes** page in the entity object overview editor.

Checking data inconsistency by using the Change Indicator attribute

When the business components runtime posts changes back to database, the framework will try to ensure that the data update is not on a stale object. This is done by executing the `SELECT` query for the modified entity and comparing the originally retrieved values for all attributes with values from the database. If you do not want the framework to compare all the attributes to detect stale data, you can mark one or more attributes as **Change Indicators** so that the entity runtime will use only those attributes to detect if the row has been modified since the user queried it last time. This concept is explained in detail under the *Concurrent access and locking* section discussed later in this chapter.

The **Change Indicator** checkbox option is available in the **Details** tab of the **Attributes** page in the entity object overview editor.

Queriable attributes

This is a Boolean flag that decides if you can query the attribute. If the value is `true`, attribute will be part of the `SELECT` clause generated by the view objects based on this entity.

The **Queriable** checkbox option is available in the **Details** tab of the **Attributes** page in the entity object overview editor.

Tracking change history

If you need to keep track of auditable business data, such as when an entity was created or modified and by whom, or the number of times the entity has been modified, you can make use of the **Track Change History** option provided by the framework.

To configure the history column, in the editor, choose the attribute that needs to be stored in the history information and then in the Property Inspector, select the appropriate history type by using the **Track Change History** drop-down list. The history attribute value will be populated by the framework before posting data to the database. The following are the history columns provided by the framework out of the box:

- **Created On**: This attribute is populated with the time stamp of when the entity instance was created.
- **Created By**: This attribute is populated with the name of the user who created the entity instance.
- **Modified On**: This attribute is populated with the time stamp of when the entity instance was modified.
- **Modified By**: This attribute is populated with the name of the user who modified the entity instance.

For example, consider a use case where you want to track the last updated date on record. To avail the framework feature for tracking the last updated date, you may need to add a column of type TIMESTAMP in the database table to store the last updated date. Now in your entity object, make sure that the attribute corresponding to this column is mapped to java.sql.Timestamp (or a similar type such as oracle. jbo.domain.Timestamp). Mark this attribute as a history column by selecting **Modified On** by using the **Track Change History** drop-down list. At runtime, when the transaction is committed, the framework will take care of populating this file with the logged-in user name.

If the existing history types are not good enough to meet your use cases, ADF provides a way to add custom history types that can be used by the developers as we discussed earlier. To learn about custom history type creation, refer to the section *Building custom history types* in *Chapter 5, Advanced Concepts on Entity Objects and View Objects*.

Configuring UI hints for an attribute

An entity component has the ability to define control hints on attributes. Control hints are typically used for building a model driven UI. The view layer can automatically display the queried information by using UI hints set for each attribute present in the collection. The UI hints include properties such as display hint, label, tool tip, format type, format, control type, and display height and width.

The UI hints for an attribute are set by using the **UI Hints** tab in the **Attributes** page in the entity object overview editor. Note that when you build a view object by choosing the entity object as the datasource, all the UI hints from the underlying entity object will be copied into the view object. The UI hints defined on a view object can be carried over to the ADF-rich client components through ADF-specific **Expression Language** (**EL**) at runtime. We will cover these items in detail when we discuss building databound web user interfaces in *Chapter 8, Building Databound Web User Interfaces*.

Specifying dependency attributes

If the value of an attribute depends on other attributes in an entity object, whenever driving attribute changes, the dependent attribute value needs to be recalculated. The **Dependencies** setting does this job out of the box. The **Dependencies** tab will help you to add other attributes as dependencies to the selected one. The framework will recalculate the dependent attribute value whenever any attribute in the dependencies list changes.

The dependencies for an attribute are set by using the **Dependencies** tab of the **Attributes** page in the entity object overview editor.

Commonly used properties of an entity object

In the previous section, we discussed how to configure properties for an entity attribute. There are a set of configuration properties available at entity object level as well. These properties are provided to customize the default behavior of an entity, overriding the default settings.

Setting an alternate key for an entity object

An entity may have attributes, which uniquely identify an instance in the collection apart from its primary keys. These attributes qualify for **alternate keys** on entity.

To define an alternate key for an entity object, perform the following steps:

1. Double-click on the entity object to open up the overview editor. Select the **General navigation** tab and expand the **Alternate Keys** section. Click on the green plus icon to define an alternate key.

2. In the pop-up window, enter the name for the alternate key and then select the attributes from the available list, which defines the alternate key. Shuttle them to the selected list. Alternative keys can also be defined by right-clicking on the entity object and then choosing the **New Entity Constraint** option.

The advantages of defining alternate keys are as follows:

- Alternate keys are indexed and are useful for finding the entity instance in the cache by executing `findByAltKey()` on the `EntityDefImpl` class. Here is an example:

```
//Find employee entity definition
EntityDefImpl empEODef = EmployeeEOImpl.getDefinitionObject();
String email= "jobinesh@xyz.zom";
//Email has been defined as alt key on entity
Key emailAltKey = new Key(new Object[] { email });
//Find by alt Key 'EmailAltKey' on employee entity definition
EntityImpl employeeEO = empEODef.findByAltKey(getDBTransaction(),
"EmailAltKey", emailAltKey, false, true);
```

- Alternate key attributes can be used to define the Unique Key Validator for an entity.

Specifying custom properties

This option will help you to define custom properties that the entity object can access at runtime. This is conceptually similar to the properties used in **Property Set** that we discussed earlier in this chapter. But the custom properties defined in entity object are local to the entity object. To define custom properties, perform the following steps:

1. Open the entity object in the overview editor. Click on the **General** tab and expand the **Custom Properties** section.

2. Click on the green plus icon displayed in the **Custom Properties** section and choose the **Translatable** or **Non-translatable** property as appropriate.

If it is a translatable property, the actual definition will be in a localized properties file. All the non-translatable properties will be stored with the attribute definition in the entity object descriptor XML file.

Defining entity association

The **association** describes the relationship in the entity data model. When you define an association, the wizard generates an accessor, which can be used for accessing entities participating in the other side of association, in the entity.

To create an association between entities, perform the following steps:

1. Right-click on the model project where you want to define an association and select **New**.

2. In **New Gallery**, expand **Business Tier**, select **ADF Business Components**, and then select **Association**.

3. On the **Name** page, you can type the package and name for the association and then click on **Next**. On the **Entity Objects** page, you are supposed to specify the cardinality for the association, and for the source and destination entity attributes, which form the association.

4. Clicking on **Next**, the **Association Properties** page will be displayed, where you can decide whether the association needs to be unidirectional or bidirectional. If you select the checkbox to expose the accessor in source and destination entities, the association becomes bidirectional, otherwise association turns into unidirectional.

5. Click on **Next** and then click on **Finish the wizard**.

The following are the different types of associations based on the cardinality of the relation:

- **One to One**: An entity instance is associated to a single instance of another entity

- **One to Many**: An entity instance is associated to multiple instances on another entity

- **Many to One**: Multiple instances of an entity are associated to one instance of another entity

- **Many to Many**: Multiple instances are participating in the association at both the ends

While defining association by using the IDE, you may notice multiple cardinality options in the dialog window. Though the list contains many options, runtime will end up in generating one from the four categories of associations (that we just discussed) in all cases. The following table lists the mapping between association types and various cardinalities used in the association.

Association types	Cardinality in association
One to Many	0...1 to *
	1 to *
One to One	0...1 to 0...1
	0...1 to 1
	1 to 0...1
Many to One	* to 1
	* to 0...1
Many to Many	* to *

To programmatically access the destination entities, you can use the association accessor generated on entity implementation class, as shown in the following code snippet:

```
EntityDefImpl deptEODef = DeptEOImpl.getDefinitionObject();
//Find Creates the Key to find Department
Key deptIdKey = DeptEOImpl.createPrimaryKey(new Integer(deptId));
//Find the Department entity using deptId
DeptEOImpl deptEOImpl = (DeptEOImpl)departmentEODef.findByPrimaryKey(g
etDBTransaction(), deptIdKey);

//Access Employees for this depertament using association
//accessor getEmpEO() generated on DeptEOImplclass
RowIterator rowIter= DeptEOImpl.getEmpEO();
while(rowIter.hasNext()){
  Row row=rowIter.next();
  //Row represent Emp entity instance
  //Business logic goes here
}
```

When you access the destination entities by using the association accessor attribute, the behind the scenes framework uses the association definition to form the WHERE clause and sets the bind variable with values from the source entity, and executes the SELECT query with the WHERE clause to retrieve destination entities.

Composition association

Association type, which we discussed in the previous section, relates source with destination entities where both parties can exist independent of each other. However, this may not be true for all relations. For example, consider the relation between car and engine, where the engine cannot exist without the car. If the container is destroyed, normally every instance that it contains is destroyed as well. This is called **composition association**.

To mark an association as composition association, select the **Composition Association** option in the **Association Properties** page in the overview editor window.

Properties of composition association

When you define association, the overview editor window will display the **Behavior** tab as shown in the following screenshot:

The properties available under the **Behavior** tab are as follows:

- **Use Database Key Constraints**: This property does not have any ADF runtime implementation. It is used to create the foreign key constraints in the database when you generate the database table from entity objects, which participate in association.

- **Implement Cascade Delete**: This option will allow you to unconditionally delete the composed entities together with composing entities. If this is deselected, runtime will not allow the deletion of a parent entity if it has any child entities. Use this feature if you do not want child entities to exist on removal of parent entity.

- **Optimize for Database Cascade Delete**: This option will act as hints for the runtime to optimize the deletion of detailed entities participating in the association. If this option is selected, when you delete the parent, detailed entities will not trigger an individual DELETE command. Your database should have the ON DELETE CASCADE constraint specified to take care of the deletion of entries from the child tale. This feature is useful when you do not want to replicate the database constraints in the middle tier. This approach makes sense, if there is less chance for the application to migrate to a different database (or to a different datasource) in future.

- **Cascade Update Key Attributes**: This option will automatically update foreign keys in the child entities when the primary key in the parent tale is changed. Enable this option if the application allows the user to edit the foreign key in the parent row.

- **Update Top-level History Columns**: This option will trigger the history column (**Modified On** or **Modified By**) update on the parent when the child is removed, modified, or added. This feature is useful if you are working on transaction-sensitive applications where you may need to update the history columns in the parent row when any changes in the child rows are posted to the database. This history column update for the parent row is triggered with this setting even if there is no change in the parent row attributes.

- **Lock Level**: This option will issue a lock on the composing parent entity whenever the composed child entity is locked during the data update. The following are the various lock levels that you can choose from:

  - **None**: No locking is issued on the parent when the framework acquires a lock on the child entity (destination).

  - **Lock Container**: This option locks the immediate parent entity (source entity in the association definition) when the framework acquires a lock on the child entity (destination entity in the association definition).

  - **Lock Top-level Container**: Framework locks the topmost entity object in the composition association hierarchy when the framework acquires a lock on the child (destination) entity object. The logic to lock the top level container walks up the association hierarchy and stops either at the top level or when a composition association that has the **Lock Top-level Container** flag turned off is found.

Retaining the association accessor row set

If your code makes multiple calls to the same association accessor attribute while serving a request, you can try fine-tuning the execution by opting for retaining the association accessor row set. This option is available in the entity object overview editor under **General** in the **Tuning** section.

When you set the retain association accessor row set on parent, the framework will execute the query to fetch the child row set for the very first access by using the accessor attribute and the same row set will be re-used for subsequent accesses. As the child row sets are retained in this case, the client may need to call `reset()` to reset the previous iterator state:

```
RowIterator rowIter= DeptEOImpl.getEmpEO();
rowIter.reset();
while(rowIter.hasNext()){
  Row row=rowIter.next();
  //Row represent Emp entity instance
}
```

Adding validation

Ensuring the validity of business data is critical for any enterprise application. ADF Business Components are packaged with a set of built-in validation rules. You can even add more rules, if the existing rules do not meet your requirements. For an entity object, validation rules can be defined at two levels as follows:

- **Attribute level validation rule**: The attribute level validation rules will be fired before updating the entity attribute
- **Entity level validation rule**: The entity level validation will be fired either at the row selection changes or when the client commits the transaction

Adding a validation rule to an attribute

To add a validation rule to an attribute, follow the next steps:

1. Double-click on the desired entity object to open up the overview editor and then click on the **Business Rules** tab. To add the validation rule, right-click on the attribute and select **New Validator**.

2. In the **Add Attribute Rule** dialog, select the rule type and define the rule.

3. The **Validation Execution** tab in the dialog window will allow the developer to set some condition for executing the validation.

4. The validation error level such as **Error** or **Informational Warning**, and error messages are set by using the **Failure Handling** tab. Error messages can take parameters whose values can be supplied by using the Groovy expression. When you enter the token into the text of the error message — delimited by curly braces (for example, {errorParam}) — the **Token Message Expressions** table at the bottom of the dialog displays a row that allows you to enter a Groovy expression for the token. The Groovy expression allows you to refer the underlying model data without really referring the exact instance.

For example, if you enter a failure message for the date field as **{hireDate} should be less than {todaysDate}**, the **Token Message Expression** table displays **hireDate** and **todaysDate** under the **Message Token** column as shown in the following screenshot:

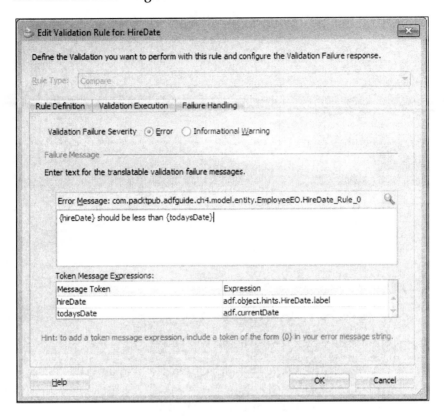

The **Expression** column in the **Token Message Expression** table takes the Groovy expressions, which will be evaluated to the actual values at runtime. For instance, in this example, the **Expression** field for **todaysDate** contains a predefined Groovy syntax to refer to the current date, which is **adf.currentDate**.

To learn more about the Groovy support, refer to the Oracle white paper *Introduction to Groovy Support in JDeveloper and Oracle ADF 11g*, which is available online at http://www.oracle.com/technetwork/developer-tools/jdev/introduction-to-groovy-128837.pdf.

If you need to provide specific validation implementation apart from the built-in rules, select **Method** as **Rule Type** in the **Add Validation Rule** dialog window. This action will generate a method in your entity object class. The methods take the following signature:

```
public boolean validateXXX(String  attributeValue)
```

The methods take the new attribute value as a parameter and return a Boolean flag. As this method is invoked before setting the value as an attribute, your validate logic is expected to treat the method parameter as a new value for the attribute. The following example validates the name field and returns a Boolean flag:

```
/**
 * Validation method for Name. Return false if name is null or
empty string
 */
public boolean validateName(String name) {
    if (name != null && name.trim().length() == 0) {
        Return false;
    }
    return true;
}
```

Adding a validation rule to an entity object

To add a validation rule to an entity, double-click on the desired entity object to open up the overview editor and then click on the **Business Rules** tab. To add the validation rule, right-click on **Entity Validators** and select **New Validator**. In the **Add Attribute Rule** dialog, select the desired rule type from the list and finish the rule definition as we did for the attribute level validation.

As we have discussed under the attribute level validation, custom methods can be used to validate your entity as well. When you select **Method** as **Rule Type** in the **Add Validation Rule** dialog window, the wizard will generate a method with the following signature in your Entity Object class:

```
public boolean validateXXX(ArrayList ctxList)
```

Unlike attribute level validation, entity level validations will be triggered after the model update, but before posting data to database. So, your validate method can read entity attributes by assuming that they are holding the latest data.

Transaction level validation

You can defer the execution of certain validation rule types such as Key Exists and Method validations to transaction level (data control) by selecting the **Defer execution to Transaction Level** option displayed under the **Validation Execution** tab. You may need to keep in mind that transaction level validation does not really defer until you commit a transaction. For a web application, as the application module instances are getting recycled, runtime will call `validate()` on the data control while posting data to the server. This call in turn will trigger both entity level and transaction level validations. However, for a validation cycle, validations defined at transaction level will be triggered only once for an entity type. In other words, it is not triggered for each modified instance in the entity cache.

Defining a custom validation rule

To create a custom validation rule, right-click on the model project where you want to define the validation rule and select **New**. In **New Gallery**, expand **Business Tier**, select **ADF Business Components**, and then select **Validation Rule**. In **Create Validation Class** enter the class name, package, and the rule's display name. JDeveloper will display the custom validation rule along with the standard rules when you choose to define validations for an entity.

Concurrent access and locking

When many users work on the same business data simultaneously, it is necessary to ensure that the concurrent business transactions do not overwrite the other user's changes inadvertently. Locking is a way to do this. ADF Business Components supports locking out of the box. In this section, we will see how the locking is handled in an ADF application and possible locking modes as well.

Configuring Locking Mode for an ADF application

The `jbo.locking.mode` configuration property controls how entities are locked. This property is configurable from two places:

- **Per application module level**: Open the application modules in the editor and then select the desired configuration. Click on the yellow edit icon to open up the **Edit configuration** dialog box. Click on the **Properties** tab and modify `jbo.locking.mode` to the desired value.

- **Application level**: Double-click on the `adf-config.xml` file in the ADF META-INF folder in the **Application Resources** under the **Descriptors** panel view in **Application Navigator**. Click on the **Business Components** tab on the **adf-config.xml** editor window and set **Locking Mode** appropriately.

Supported values for `jbo.locking.mode` are as follows:

- **None**: This implies the case where no locking is done when the user updates a row.

- **Pessimistic**: The pessimistic locking mode will try to lock an entity instance in advance before allowing any changes by explicitly firing SELECT FOR UPDATE on the underlying database row, and the row will remain locked till you commit the transactions. This is not recommended for a web application in optimistic mode, because during recycling of application modules framework will issue a rollback on JDBC connection and potentially client may loss all the lock associated with database connection.

- **Optimistic**: The optimistic locking mode will try to lock the entity before posting modified data to the database, followed by a check for stale data.

- **Optupdate**: The optupdate locking mode will not issue lock on the row, it will just see if all row attributes that are participating in the update have the latest value from the database table.

To understand the concept of different locking modes further, let us take a look at the following code snippet and analyze how the framework handles locking for different locking modes.

```
//Find the employee entity using ID
EmployeeEOImpl empEO= findEmployeeById(1000) ;
//Modifies the entity name
empEO.setName("John");
//Commit the transaction
getTransaction ().commit();
```

The following table illustrates how the locking behavior varies with locking mode for the preceding code snippet:

Business logic	Locking behavior
`empEO.setName("John");`	When an attribute is modified, the framework will check the locking mode to take appropriate actions. If the locking mode is `pessimitic`, ADF Business Components runtime performs the following steps: • Executes `SELECT FOR UPDATE NOWAIT` on the underlying database row to acquire lock. • Checks if the originally retrieved values of the entity attributes are the same as the values in the database. If the entity has any attribute marked as change indicators, the stale data check is done only for those attributes. • The framework will not attempt to lock the row for other locking modes during this stage.

`getTransaction().`
`postChanges();`
 	
or
 	
`getTransaction().commit();`
	If the locking mode is `optimistic` or `optupdate`, the concurrency handling happens at this stage.
	
	If the lock mode is `optimistic`, the ADF Business Components runtime performs the following steps:
	
	• Executes `SELECT FOR UPDATE` on the row for the entity to acquire lock.
	
	• Checks if the originally retrieved values of the attributes are the same as the values in the database. If the entity has any attribute marked as change indicators, the stale data check is done only for those attributes.
	
	If the lock mode is `optupdate`, the framework does not explicitly lock any database row. ADF Business Components runtime generates `UPDATE` with the `WHERE` clause to ensure that the update is not happening on stale data. The `WHERE` clause checks whether the originally retrieved values of the attributes are the same as the values in the database or not. Similar to the optimistic locking mode, if the entity has any attribute marked as change indicators, the stale data check is done only for those attributes.

Securing entity objects

ADF entity objects are security-enabled components. You can restrict the action of an entity by specifying the permission map.

To add the permission, double-click on the entity to display the overview editor. Click on the **General navigation** tab, expand the **Security** section, and select the desired operation—read, update, or remove. These operations are defined by the `oracle.adf.share.security.authorization.EntityPermission` class and will be used by the ADF security to authenticate the user. To test the functionality of the class, application should be secured with ADF security. We will revisit this topic with examples when we discuss ADF security in *Chapter 14, Securing Fusion Web Applications*.

Enabling a batch update in an entity object

The batch update facility allows multiple update operations to be submitted to a datasource for processing at once. If a use case demands an update on multiple instances of the same entity in a single transaction, the update batching can be turned on for the entity. This feature works with Oracle database.

To enable update batching on an entity, click on the **General** tab in the overview editor, expand the **Tuning** section, check the **Use Update Batching** checkbox, and specify the appropriate threshold.

 Please be warned that entity refresh features such as **Refresh on Update** and **Refresh on Insert** may not work in batch update mode.

Working with entity objects

We have covered the basic lessons on entity objects in earlier sections of this chapter. It is time for us to put all the pieces together to understand the working of entity objects.

Programmatically creating an entity instance

The following example will help you to understand the create functionality on an entity object. This example assumes that you have already generated an entity object from the EMPLOYEES table and also generated Java classes for the entity object and entity definition. In this example, we create an instance of an employee entity object, populate the attribute values, and finally post the changes to the database by committing the transaction. This method is defined in the application module implementation class.

```
//Application Module

public class HRServiceAppModuleImpl extends ApplicationModuleImpl
implements HRServiceAppModule {

public EmployeeEOImpl createEmployee() {
  //Get the EmployeeEODefImpl which is the
  //java repsentstaion of EmployeeEO.xml
  EmployeeEODefImpl employeeEODefImpl =
  (EmployeeEODefImpl)EmployeeEOImpl.getDefinitionObject();
  //Create the entiy instance in the current transaction
  EmployeeEOImpl newEmployee =
  (EmployeeEOImpl)employeeEODefImpl.createInstance2
  (this.getDBTransaction(), null);
  //EmployeeEO uses EmployeeID as PK

  //EmployeeId is the PK
  newEmployee.setEmployeeId(1000);
  newEmployee.setFirstName("Jobinesh");
  newEmployee.setLastName("Purushothaman");
  newEmployee.setDepartmentId(10);
  newEmployee.setEmail("JOBINESH@XYZ.COM");
  newEmployee.setHireDate(new
  Timestamp(System.currentTimeMillis()));
  newEmployee.setJobId("IT_PROG");
  try {
  //Commit the transaction
    getDBTransaction().commit();
  } catch (JboException ex) {
    //If commit fails, then roll back the entire transaction
    getDBTransaction().rollback();
    throw ex;
  }
    return newEmployee;
  }
// Other methods go here
}
```

As this is our first attempt to programmatically create an entity instance, let us explore the underlying execution path to get a better understanding of these APIs.

The first line in the `createEmployee()` method obtains `EmployeeEODefImpl` by invoking `getDefinitionObject()` on the `EmployeeEOImpl` class. When you call `getDefinitionObject()` on an entity class, the framework reads the corresponding entity XML metadata file and generates the Java representation for the metadata. The next line in the preceding code snippet creates an entity instance. Though this line looks simple, it performs a lot of tasks for you behind the scenes. Default values of attributes are initialized at this step. The entity object's state is set as `Initialized`. An entity in the `Initialized` state will not participate in the transaction.

The entity instance is added to the entity cache once the primary key is populated. When you set any attribute value, the entity's state transitions into `NEW` and will be added to the transaction. Once all the required attributes are populated, the program calls `commit()` on `DBTransaction`, which triggers `postChanges()` on the entity object, followed by actual commit operation at database connection level.

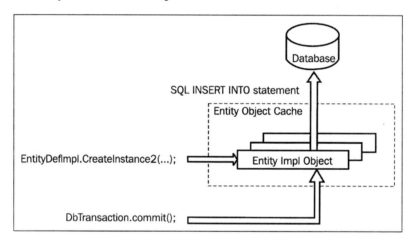

A detailed discussion on the transaction commit cycle for an entity is given in the next section.

Entity object in a transaction post cycle

Let us now examine the find and update functionalities on an entity object. Take a look at the following code snippet, which may help you to understand the APIs to be used. This code is copied from an application module method:

```
//Get the Entity Definition
EntityDefImpl empEODef = EmpEOImpl.getDefinitionObject();
//Generate Key using empId parameter
Key empIdKey = EmpEOImpl.createPrimaryKey(new Integer(empId));
//Find Emp entity using Key
EmpEOImpl empEO= (EmpEOImpl) empEODef.findByPrimaryKey(getDBTransacti
on(), empIdKey);
```

```
//Update the  attribute
empEO.setFirstName("Jobinesh");
//Commit transaction
getDBTransaction().commit();
```

The following diagram shows the sequence of interactions between the entity
object, transaction manager, and datasource when you execute the find and
update functionalities on an entity:

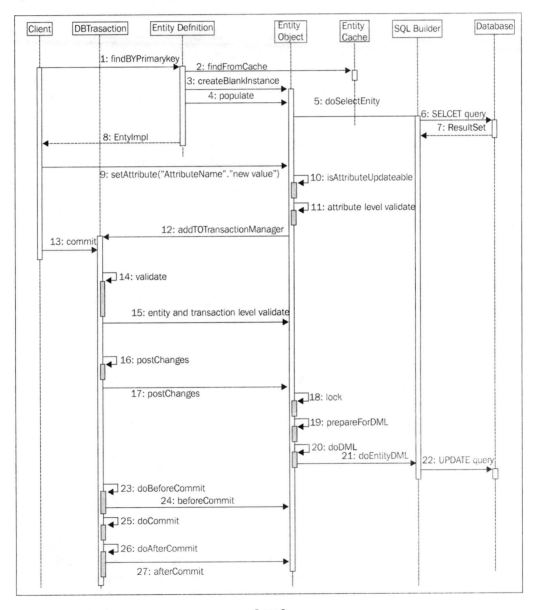

The client retrieves the entity object, calling `findByPrimaryKey()` on an entity definition by passing a key object. First, the framework will check the entity cache for the entity, and if not found, the `SQL SELECT` query will be fired to read the row from the database. An example is as follows:

```
SELECT DEPARTMENT_ID, DEPARTMENT_NAME, MANAGER_ID, LOCATION_ID FROM
DEPARTMENTS DepartmentEO WHERE DEPARTMENT_ID=:1
Where binding parameter 1: 10
```

 Native SQL generation for ADF business components is done by the `SQLBuilder implementation` class. Runtime picks up the right implementation based on the value set for the `jbo.SQLBuilder` property. This property can be either set globally by using `adf-config.xml` or per application module by using the `bc4j.xcfg` file.

The entity cache will be updated with the retrieved entity instance and the status will be marked as `Unmodified`. The client receives the retrieved instance.

In the next step in this example, the client updates an attribute by calling setter on the entity instance. Before allowing the change, the framework will check if the update is permitted on this attribute. If the attribute value is modifiable, the new value will be validated and passed on to the entity. The entity status is transitioned into `Modified`.

The transaction manager comes into the picture at this stage. `oracle.jbo.server.DBTransactionImpl2` is the default configured transaction manager for business components. `DBTransactionImpl` maintains three lists to carry out the transaction commit cycle:

- **Validation listener list**: This list contains entities for validation
- **Transaction post listener list**: This list keeps dirty entities which need to be posted to the database
- **Transaction listener list**: This list contains application modules and entities, which want to listen to the transaction commit phase

The modified entity instance will be added to all these three lists.

When the program commits the transaction later, the entity object will go through the following stages:

1. The transaction manager validates all the entries from the validation listener list by calling `validate()` on each listener, which includes dirty entities as well. This will validate all the entity level validations that you have added.

2. Once the entire validation is successful, the next phase is posting data to the database. The transaction manager iterates through the transaction post listener list and calls `postChanges()` on each item. The data post for an entity happens in multiple steps:

    ○ **Lock the entity**: Locking algorithm is decided based on the `jbo.locking.mode` property configured for the application module. All our discussion in this section is based on optimistic locking mode, which is the default locking mode set for a fusion web application.

      The `lock()` method on the entity locks the current instance and fires the SELECT FOR UPDATE query to lock the database row. If this entity is participating in any composition association, the composing entities will also get locked.

    ○ **Prepare the entity for DML**: The `prepareForDML()` method is called on the entity and it performs all the preparation prior to posting data to the database. This includes updating history columns and other custom updates, if any.

    ○ **Post data to database**: The `doDML()` method generates appropriate native SQL statement to perform INSERT, UPDATE, or DELETE processing for the row.

3. Once the data is posted to the database, the next phase is to commit the transaction. The transaction manager will invoke `beforeCommit()` on each element in the transaction listener list. Then it commits the transaction and if successful, `afterCommit()` is called on each item in the transaction listener list. The entity object's state will be reset back to Unmodified in the `afterCommit()` method.

Summary

In this chapter, you learned general concepts behind an entity object, its architecture, and configurations. We discussed the following items:

- Visual and declarative development of entity objects
- Commonly used properties of entity objects
- Entity object life cycle

But there is more to come on entity objects. We will be covering more advanced examples on entities in *Chapter 5, Advanced Concepts on Entity Objects and View Objects*.

4

Introducing View Object

In the last chapter we learned about the ADF Business Components, which is responsible for posting changes to the database, namely the ADF entity object. In this chapter, we will discuss the ADF view object, which is in charge of reading and shaping the data for presenting it to the client. This chapter explains the architecture of a view object, its usage, and runtime behavior.

In this chapter we will cover the following topics:

- Concepts and architecture
- Core features of ADF view objects
- Developing view objects
- Working with view objects

Introduction

An **ADF view object** is a business component that reads data from the datasource, shapes the data to be used by clients, and controls the updates on the data. In today's world, vast majority of the enterprise application uses a database as their primary mechanism to store data. In a typical database-centric ADF application, a view object implements the logic for reading database tables through SQL query, and contains the logic for building the collection of rows that can be used by the client. It also controls the data update by delegating the calls to underlying entities.

Concepts and architecture

A view object abstracts the raw JDBC APIs to read data from the database and encapsulates the logic for managing the result set. The ADF view object has a very flexible and layered architecture, which improves the extensibility of the system.

Ingredients of a view object

This is in continuation of our discussion on the constituents of a view object in *Chapter 2, Introduction to ADF Business Components*. In this section, we will revisit the same topic to analyze the concepts in depth. The following diagram represents the runtime artifacts of a view object that help the view object to carry out the task at different stages of the query execution life cycle:

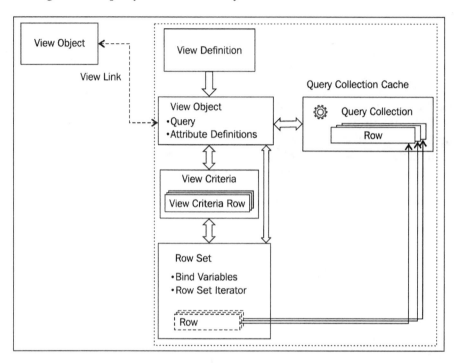

An ADF view object is composed of the following components:

- View definition XML file: This is the view object descriptor XML file, which holds metadata definitions. The metadata includes the following:

  - The SQL SELECT statement used in the view object

  - Bind parameter definitions used in the SQL SELECT statement

  - Attribute definition describing each column returned by the query—this includes UI-related metadata, such as UI Hints and UI Categories for attributes

  - Entity usage information (if there is entity backup for the view object)

- Metadata definition for **list of values** (**LOV**) and view criteria (query)
- View accessor definition for accessing other view objects
- Business rules

- **View definition**: This is the runtime Java class representation for the view definition XML file. The default view definition class used by the ADF Business Components' runtime is `oracle.jbo.server.ViewDefImpl`, which can be extended to provide custom functionalities, if needed.

- **View object**: This class represents a view object instance. The view object instance manages the query execution at runtime. The default view object class used by the ADF Business Components' runtime is `oracle.jbo.server.ViewObjectImpl`. Developers can extend this class to add custom functionalities, if needed.

- **View criteria**: View criteria will let you define filter conditions for attributes in a view object, which will be used at runtime to filter the query result. This implementation takes the form of a query-by-example approach, which allows the end user to supply values for attributes of the target view object in order to form the desired search condition.

- **Bind variables**: These are placeholder variables in a SQL statement used in a view object. These variables will be replaced with the valid ones before executing the query.

- **View accessor**: This acts as a gateway for a view object to access another view object. This is used in validation and LOV definitions.

A view object uses the following framework components to set up the infrastructure for query execution and managing the result set:

- **Row**: A row represents an element in the collection that is a result from a query on a view object.

- **Row set**: View object uses row sets to manage the collection of rows from a query. The framework will create a different row set when the same view object is used as a mechanism to query the datasource in different contexts. Some of these areas act as query for list of values implementation and query for child collection in master-child tree structure. Parameterized conditions used for finding the row sets are maintained at each row set level.

- **Row set iterator**: This enables the client to traverse the row set and work with individual items. A client can create one or more row set iterators to enumerate through the rows.

- **Query collection**: A query collection contains the rows used in a view object. A view object instance may maintain multiple query collection, depending on the row filter (a data structure holding bind variable values) used by different row sets to execute query. Note that a row or row set does not store any data within it, rather they use query collection object for storing rows.

- **View link**: View link connects two view objects, typically used for implementing master-child relationships.

Core features of ADF view objects

The following are the important offerings from the view object:

- Visual and declarative development
- Read-only and updatable view objects
- Automated master-child co-ordination
- Domain-driven development
- Query-by-example support
- Caching of result set
- Out-of-the-box pagination support
- Built-in CRUD operations
- Polymorphic view objects
- Declarative settings for fine-tuning runtime performance
- Customizable framework components
- Scalable architecture through out-of-the-box support for activation and passivation cycles

Developing view objects

In this section, we will learn about building and configuring view objects, using JDeveloper IDE. This section mainly focuses on declarative development aspects.

Creating view objects

JDeveloper provides multiple options to build view objects. These options are as follows:

- **Using the Create Business Components from Tables option**: This option allows you to build multiple view objects and underlying entity objects in one go.

To use this option, right-click on the model project and select **New**. In **New Gallery**, expand **Business Tier**, select **ADF Business Components**, and then select **Create Business Components from Tables**. Then follow the steps in the **Create Business Components from Tables** dialog window. This option will help you to define entity objects, view objects, and the application module in a single go. We have discussed this approach in *Chapter 2*, *Introduction to ADF Business Components* under the section entitled *Building a simple business service*.

- **Using Create View Object wizard**: This option allows you to create one view object at a time. This is discussed in the following section.

Using the Create View Object wizard

To build a view object by using the Create View Object wizard, follow these steps:

1. Right-click on the model project where you want to generate view object and select **New**.

2. In **New Gallery**, expand **Business Tier**, select **ADF Business Components**, and then select **View Object**, which will open the **Create View Object** wizard.

3. The first page in the **Create View Object** wizard allows you to enter the view object name and package name. It also provides options to build view objects from the following database source types:

    ° **Entity object**: An entity-based view object is the right choice when the client needs to update the data. In this case, the view object acts as a mechanism for querying the datasource. The actual data is stored, using the entity object instances.

    ° **SQL query**: A SQL-based view object is a read-only view object, which is built using an explicitly specified SQL query.

    ° **Programmatic**: If the default implementations of view objects are not enough to meet the requirement for querying some specific datasources such as third-party services or non-database data stores, you can go for a programmatic view object. The view object's runtime behavior is controlled by using handwritten code by overriding the standard call back methods. This is also useful if you need to query by using database objects such as stored procedures, which are not supported by default by the view object component.

- ° **Static list**: A static list datasource-based view object is useful if the view object needs to act as value holder for a set of non-critical business data, which does not change at runtime. For example, if you need to display the colors of a rainbow as a drop-down list in UI, you can create a static list-based view object containing all the seven colors and build the UI based on this view object.

Creating a view object with entity usage mapping

The next steps in the wizard's dialog vary with the datasource that you have selected in the first steps of the Create View Object wizard. If you chose entity objects, the wizard dialog will display the following steps:

1. If you chose entity object as datasource in the first page of the **Create View Object** wizard, you will see the **Entity Objects** page in the next step. In the **Entity Objects** page, you can specify one or more entity usages by shuttling the entities from the **Available** to the **Selected** list. The first entity object that you select is known as **primary entity usage** and the rest in the selected list are secondary entity usages.

   If you select a secondary entity usage in the preceding step, you must complete the following configurations.

   Select an association for the secondary entity usage from the drop-down list. Based on the association definition, the editor window will populate source entity usage. Now you need to select the suitable join type such as **inner join, left outer join**, or **right outer join**.

   You can also specify the **Updatable, Reference**, and **Delete Participant** properties for entity usages:

   - ° **Updatable**: This property decides if the entity object attributes can be modified through view object. By default, the first entity object is updatable and subsequent ones are read-only.
   - ° **Reference**: Select this option if you want the information from this entity object to be treated as read-only reference information in this view object. Attribute values are dynamically fetched from the entity cache when a joining key attribute changes.

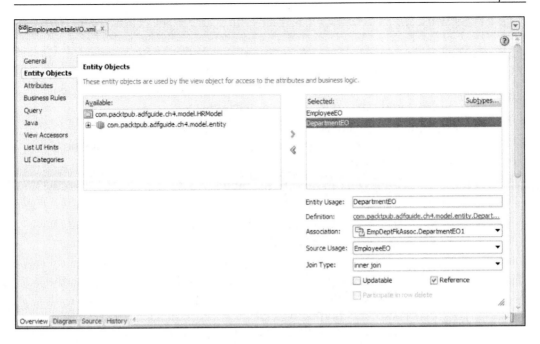

For example, take a view object called **EmployeeDetailsVO**, with **EmployeeEO** and **DepartmentEO** entity usages. These entities are associated through the `DepartmentId` attribute, which is available in both the entities. If the `DepartmentEO` is marked as a Reference, modifying the `EmployeeEO::DepartmentId` attribute in the view object from 10 to 20 changes the department that the current employee works in, and framework automatically retrieves the proper department name into the current view. .

○ **Participate in Row Delete**: This property decides if the removal of row in a view object will result in deletion of the entity instance participating in the view object row. Select this option when you have defined the secondary entity usage as **Updatable** and your use case demands the action of removing rows in the UI to delete the participating secondary entity object as well. This option is enabled for the primary entity usage by default.

Once you selected entity objects and associated properties, click Next to continue the wizard.

2. The **Attributes** page in the wizard will allow you to select attributes for the view object by shuttling the attributes from the **Available** to the **Selected** list. You can optionally select individual attributes in the **Selected** list, and change the attribute names or define new attributes by clicking on the **New** button available on the same page. Once you are happy with the changes, click on **Next** to display the **Attribute Settings** page.

3. The **Attribute Settings** page will allow you to alter the view object attribute properties copied from the corresponding entity object usage. Click on **Next** to display the **Query** page.

4. In the **Query** page, you can modify the mode of the view object. The possible options are as follows:

    ° **Normal**: This is the default mode for a view object, which will allow you to edit only the WHERE clause for the query.

    ° **Expert**: When you enable the **Expert** mode, the wizard will allow you to edit the entire query. If you need any assistance in defining the query, click on **Query Builder** to open up the SQL statement editor. This editor may help you to visually build the query by selecting tables, columns, and other common SQL clauses. However, you should be careful when you work in **Expert** mode as with this mode IDE provides limited attribute mapping assistance for any altered SELECT clause.

    ° **Declarative**: In the **Declarative** SQL mode, the view object will formulate its SQL statements at runtime based on the columns selected by the client for display. More on declarative view objects is discussed in the next section.

    The wizard will also allow you to specify the Order By clause, using this screen. You can either directly include the ORDER BY clause in the corresponding field or click on the **Edit** icon to do this visually, using an editor.

5. You can either finish the **Create View Object** wizard at this stage or continue the same to perform a few more optional configuration tasks. If you continue with the wizard by clicking on **Next**, you will get a screen to define the bind variable. Note that bind variables are variables that are used in place of dynamic input values in a SQL statement. We will discuss this soon in the section entitled *Querying datasource using view object*.

6. If you proceed further, the next page in the wizard will allow you to generate Java classes for view object components.

7. The next page is the **Application Module** page, which will allow you to attach the newly created view with an application module. As we will be discussing bind variables and Java implementation later in the chapter, we are not focusing much on these options at this stage.

Creating a view object with SQL query

This section will teach you how to build a view object by choosing SQL query as the datasource. To create a view object from SQL query, follow the steps listed here:

1. Right-click on the desired model project and select **New**. In the **New Gallery** dialog, expand **Business Tier** and select **ADF Business Components | View Object**.

2. Choose **SQL Query** as the datasource in the first page of the **Create View Object** wizard. Enter the package and name for the view object. Then click on **Next**.

3. In the **Query** page, enter the appropriate SQL SELECT statement. If you are not comfortable with building a SQL query, you can avail the visual tool support for generating a query by clicking on **Query Builder**. Click on **Next** to continue.

4. In the **Bind Variable** page, define the bind variable that your query uses (if any). Click on **Next** to continue.

5. The **Attribute Mapping** page displays the mapping between query columns and attribute names. You can optionally edit the mapping in this screen. Click on **Next** to continue.

6. The **Attributes** screen displays all the attributes generated from the query. You can optionally add new transient attributes in this page.

7. The next page displays the **Attribute Settings** options for each attribute in the view object. You can modify the attribute definition as appropriate.

8. On continuing the wizard, you will see the Java page that will allow you to generate Java classes. You can do this later as well; we will discuss this concept shortly.

9. The next page will list the application module that you have in the project. Select the **Add to Application Module** option if you want to expose the view object to be used by the client. Click on **Finish** to complete the creation of the view objects.

Creating a view object with static list

This section will briefly teach you how to build a view object by choosing static list as the datasource. Here are the steps:

1. Right-click on the desired model project and select **New**. In the **New Gallery** dialog, expand **Business Tier** and select **ADF Business Components | View Object**.

2. Choose **Static List** as the datasource in the first page of the **Create View Object** wizard. Enter the package and name for the view object, and click on **Next** to continue.

3. In the **Attributes** page, enter the attribute names and click on **Next** to continue.

4. In the **Attribute Settings** page, override the default properties for the attributes, as appropriate. Make sure at least one attribute is marked as **Key Attribute** for the view object. Click on **Next** to continue.

5. In the **Static List** page, enter static values for the attributes and click on **Next** to continue.

6. In the **Application Module** page, choose **Add to Application Module** for exposing this view to the client. Click on **Finish** to generate the view object.

Creating a programmatic view object

In this wizard, the basic steps for building the template for a programmatic view object are the same as those we have discussed for creating a view object with a static list, with few exceptions. When you finish generating a programmatic view object, IDE generates Java implementation for the view object where you can add custom logic for handling the life cycle. As this requires a thorough understanding of the view object implementation, we will defer this discussion until *Chapter 5, Advanced Concepts on Entity Objects and View Objects*. For details, see the section *Building programmatically managed view objects* in *Chapter 5, Advanced Concepts on Entity Objects and View Objects*.

Creating a declarative SQL mode view object

While discussing the **Create View Object** wizard, we had a glance at the possible SQL modes for a view object in the query page of the wizard. Let us revisit this topic to discuss the declarative SQL mode in detail.

A declarative SQL mode view object will formulate its SQL statements at runtime based on the columns selected by the client for display. A declarative view object will simplify the query in two steps:

- Removing the attributes in the SELECT list, which are not selected by the client
- Removing tables in the FROM clause — if the pruning rules allow this

There are two approaches to define a declarative view object:

- When you create a view object by selecting an entity object as the datasource, the **Query** page in the wizard will help you to set the **Declarative** mode for the view object.
- Alternatively, if you have already generated an entity-based view object, double-click on the view object to display the overview editor. In the overview editor window, click on the **Query** tab and then click on the **Edit SQL Query** icon to display the **Edit Query** dialog window. In the **Edit Query** dialog window, select the **Query** node and then select the **Declarative** mode in the drop-down list.

A detailed discussion on creating declarative SQL mode view objects is available in *Oracle Fusion Middleware Fusion Developer's Guide* under the topic *Working with View Objects in Declarative SQL Mode*. To access the documentation visit http://www.oracle.com/technetwork/developer-tools/jdev/documentation/index.html and navigate to **Oracle JDeveloper and ADF Documentation Library | Fusion Developer's Guide**. Use the search option to find specific topics.

While using declarative view objects, there are certain points that you need to keep in mind:

- Only entity-based view objects can be turned into declarative mode
- Primary key attributes will always be in the SQL SELECT statement generated at runtime.
- Attributes, which need to be conditionally excluded from the SQL SELECT statement, should have **Selected** in the **Query** (which is mapped to the attribute IsSelected in the view object XML) property set to false. In other words, if you leave the default value of true for the selected property, this forces the attribute to always appear in the query. You can edit this value through the **Property Inspector** window for the attribute.

- If an attribute is configured to depend upon other attributes, the driving attributes will be automatically selected whenever the dependent attribute is part of the selected attribute list.

- If a view object is based on multiple entity object usages (built by choosing multiple entities), the following things can be true:

    ° The table corresponding to the primary entity usage will always be part of the join in the query

    ° The table corresponding to secondary (non-primary) entity usage will be part of the join query, if it has at least one attribute in the selected list

    ° The primary key attribute of a table corresponding to an entity usage will be automatically added to the selected list, if that table is part of the join query

    ° The table corresponding to an entity usage will be automatically added to the join query, if an applied view criteria or a sort criteria clause refers an attribute from this entity usage

Optionally generating Java classes for a view object

When you build a view object, JDeveloper generates a view object XML file to store the metadata, by default. This metadata will be used at runtime to instantiate the view object instances, using default framework classes. If you want to customize the default behavior of framework classes or add custom business logic, you will need to generate Java classes and override default callback methods, as we did for entity objects in the previous chapter.

To generate Java classes for a view object, double-click on the view object to display the overview editor. In the overview editor, go to the **Java** tab and click on **Edit Java Options** icon. In the **Select Java Options** dialog, select the types of Java classes that you want to generate.

- **View object class**: This class is customized to add business methods and to override the default lifecycle of view object instances. For example, to build programmatic a view object, you must generate a view object class for the desired view object and override the lifecycle call back methods to hook the custom logic.

- **View row class**: This class represents a row in the result collection in a view object. If you want to modify the default read and write operations for specific attributes, this is the class you need to extend. For example, if you have any transient attributes defined in the view object whose value is derived from other attributes in the row, you can override the `get<AttributeName>` method and add the logic over there.

- **View object definition class**: This class manages the view definition implementation and controls view row creations. You may rarely customize this class to override the properties at runtime. For example, if you want to modify the properties or attributes of a view object at runtime, you can override the `resolveDefObject()` method in the `oracle.jbo.server.ViewDefImpl` class and add custom logic for altering the definition before returning to the caller.

- **Service data object (SDO) class**: This is useful if you want to expose the view object as a web service abstracting the data of the view object. This is typically used in service-oriented architecture when you need to expose functionalities of a view object as web service. The SDO standardizes the way that data structures are passed between Java and XML.

A detailed discussion on service-enabling of ADF Business Components falls outside the scope of this book. To learn more on generating web service interfaces for the application module, refer to the topic *Integrating Service-Enabled Application Modules* in *Oracle Fusion Middleware Fusion Developer's Guide for Oracle Application Development Framework*. To access the documentation go to `http://www.oracle.com/technetwork/developer-tools/jdev/documentation/index.html` and navigate to **Oracle JDeveloper and ADF Documentation Library | Fusion Developer's Guide**. Use the search option to find specific topics.

Commonly used properties of view objects

The vast majority of the attribute properties that we see for a view object are inherited from the underlying entity object or from the database dictionary. When you generate a view object from an entity object, the view object is copied and added to the view definition XML file.

In this section, we will skip those properties, which we have discussed for entity objects, to avoid repetition and to make our discussions more productive. However, we will discuss some properties, which need special attention in the context of view objects.

To see a detailed discussion on the attribute properties of a view object which are copied from the underlying entity object, refer back to the *Commonly used properties of an entity attribute* section in *Chapter 3, Introducing Entity Object*.

Annotate attributes using UI hints

View object supports control hints on attributes that describe how the attribute needs to be displayed in the UI. UI hints are typically used for annotating attributes, which can be leveraged in building a model-driven UI. Here are the details of its usage:

- IDE uses UI hints to infer the component type for each attribute during design time. For example, when you drop a collection onto a page, IDE uses UI hints to come up with appropriate component tags for each attribute.

- ADF framework automatically makes use of the UI hints added to an attribute while rendering it using dynamic model-driven UI components such as query, dynamic form, dynamic table, and model LOV. To use UI hints with static UI components such as input fields or actionable components, you should bind the property of the UI component with the appropriate UI hints through **expression language (EL)**. The following **Java Server Faces (JSF)** code snippet illustrates how EL expressions help you to bind component properties, such as label, columns, maximum length, and so on, with the appropriate UI hints defined for the underlying attribute in a view object:

```
<af:inputText value="#{bindings.DepartmentId.inputValue}"
  label="#{bindings.DeptVO.hints.DepartmentId.label}"
  required="#{bindings.DeptVO.hints.
  DepartmentId.mandatory}"
  columns="#{bindings.DeptVO.hints.
  DepartmentId.displayWidth}"
  maximumLength="#{bindings.DeptVO.hints.
  DepartmentId.precision}
  shortDesc="#{bindings.DeptVO.hints.
  DepartmentId.tooltip}"
  id="it1">
  <af:convertNumber groupingUsed="false"
  pattern="#{bindings.DeptVO.hints.
  DepartmentId.format}"/>
</af:inputText>
```

To specify UI hints for an attribute, open the view object in the overview editor. In the **Attributes** page, select the desired attribute, click on the **UI Hints** tab, and specify the hints as appropriate.

Let us take a quick look at the commonly used UI hints for an attribute:

- **Display Hint**: This hint decides whether the attribute will be displayed or not at runtime.

- **Label**: This stores the label for the attribute.

- **Tooltip**: This stores the tooltip for the attribute.

- **Format Type and Format**: **Format Type** specifies the formatter to be used for the attribute, such as date, number, and so on, depending upon the datatype. **Format** specifies the format mask to be used for the attribute when displayed in UI.

- **Control Type**: This field stores the control type for the attribute. This is used by the IDE to generate an appropriate component tag for the attributes when you design the page by dropping the collection. ADF runtime also uses this property to decide the control type while rendering the collection using dynamic model-driven UI components.

- **Display Width**: This specifies the number of characters shown on the UI control.

- **Display Height**: This specifies the number of character rows of the UI control that displays the attribute.

- **Category and Field Order**: **Category** is used to categorize (group) the attributes when displayed in dynamic model-driven UI components such as query, quick query, and dynamic form. **Field Order** specifies the order in which attributes are displayed in a category at runtime.

- **Auto Submit**: This automatically submits the value to the server on tabbing out from UI control.

 We will cover more detailed examples on UI hints in *Chapter 8, Building Data Bound Web User Interfaces*.

Adding business rules

Generally, you may not define business rules on a view object, rather you may use an entity object for holding all business rules. Now, you may ask what if a view object contains attributes that are not backed up by the entity object. This section provides a solution for such use cases.

View objects can also hold transient attributes as entity objects. ADF allows you to set business rules on updatable transient attributes in a view object. To define a validation on a transient attribute in a view object, select the view object in the overview editor and then select the transient attribute on which you want to define validation. Right-click on the desired transient attribute and then select **New Validator** to open up the dialog for adding a validation rule. The usage of the **Add Validaton Rule** wizard dialog is the same as that that we discussed in *Chapter 3, Introducing Entity Object* in the section entitled *Adding validation*.

In real-life applications, you may rarely define updatable transient attributes on a view object. If you find a need to define updatable transient attributes on a view object, check the feasibility of defining it on the underlying entity object, and then use it from the view object as appropriate. This may help you to post the modified value to the appropriate datasource at the right time during the transaction commit cycle. Remember that it is the entity object that participates in the transaction post cycle, not the view object.

Working with view objects

We learned the basic lessons on view objects and their declarative configuration options in the last section. In fact, a view object offers a lot more. In the coming sections, we will explore the common utility services offered by a view object and common usage patterns along with a lot of code samples.

List of values

The **list of values (LOV)** component will allow a business user to select a value for a field on UI from a pre-populated list. Enabling LOV for a view object attribute is easy and straightforward.

Configuring the list of values

To define the LOV, decide the list datasource first. For example, in a classic Department-Employee example, if you want to display the departments' list for the department attribute in an employee row, the Department table is the datasource. As the ADF Business Components uses the view object to query the datasource, we will be defining (or choosing an existing) view object to query the datasource for the LOV as the first step. Once the datasource view object is in place, you can configure the LOV as discussed here:

1. To configure LOV, double-click on the view object in the model project that contains the attribute you wish to enable for LOV. In the overview editor, select the **Attributes** tab and then select the attribute that you wish to configure for LOV. Select the **List of Values** tab and click on the green plus icon to add the list of values to display in the **Create List of Values** dialog window.

2. The next step is to define a mechanism to access the LOV datasource view object from the base view where you define the LOV. ADF view objects use view accessor definition for accessing other view objects which are found in the projects class path.

3. In the **Create List of Values** dialog window, enter the LOV name and then click on the green plus icon to create a new view accessor for the list datasource view object. In the **Create View Accessor** window, select the view object that will act as the source for the LOV and shuttle that to the **View Accessor** list, and optionally modify **Accessor Name**. Click on **OK** to save the view accessor definition. If you have already generated a view accessor for the target view object, you can skip the view accessor definition task and instead continue with the next step.

4. In the **Create List of Values** dialog window, expand **List Data Source** and select the view accessor that you have created. Then select **List Attribute** (list return value) from the LOV data source view object, which will be mapped to the LOV-enabled attribute on the base view object. If the attribute names are the same in the LOV source view object and base view object, the editor creates a default mapping between them. You can add more return values mapping between the attributes in the base view object and the LOV datasource view object by clicking on the **Create return attribute map** icon displayed in the **List Return Values** table.

5. To choose the LOV display type, click on the **UI Hints** tab and then select **Default List Type**. You can optionally configure other properties, which affect the LOV display at runtime. Click on **OK** to save the changes.

More advanced topics on LOVs such as building cascading LOVs, LOV switching, and programmatic examples will be discussed in *Chapter 5, Advanced Concepts on Entity Objects and View Objects*.

Linking two view objects

You can link one view object to another view object to form a master details hierarchy of any complexity. To defined a view link, follow these steps:

1. Right-click on the project in which you want to create the view object and choose **New**. In **New Gallery**, expand **Business Tier**, select **ADF Business Components**, and then select **View Link**.

2. In the **Create View Link** dialog window, enter the package and view link name on the **Name** page, and click on **Next**. On the **View Object** page, select the cardinality for the relationship, and then add the source and destination view object attributes, which form the relation. If the source and destination view objects are based on entity objects and there exists an association between the entity objects, you can define view links by choosing the existing associations.

3. Click on **Next**; the **View Link Properties** page will be displayed, where you can decide whether the view link needs to be unidirectional or bidirectional. If you select the checkbox to expose the accessor in source and destination view object, the view link becomes bidirectional. By default it is unidirectional. This allows the current row of the source to access related rows in the destination view object. Optionally, you can override the accessor names in the view objects' implementation classes. The accessor attributes let you programmatically access the destination view object. Click on **Next** and then click on **Finish** to end the wizard.

Where clause and Reverse Where clause

In general, when you access a child view object by traversing the child view accessor attribute defined in the parent view, the framework will append the WHERE clause to the query in the child view object with attributes derived from the view link definition to identify the child rows. If you want to override the default WHERE clause generated by the view link definition, while traversing through accessor attributes, you can make use of the Where and Reverse Where options available on the view link. The Where attribute is a custom WHERE clause that will be used as part of the query that is executed when navigating from source to destination. For example, if you try to access Employee details by using the Department-Employee view link, the query becomes:

```
SELECT ...   FROM EMPLOYEES EmployeeEO WHERE   (Where)
```

The `WhereReverse` attribute is a custom `WHERE` clause that will be used as part of the query that is executed when navigating from destination to source, so the query becomes:

```
SELECT ...  FROM DEPARTMENTS DepartmentEO WHERE (Reverse Where)
```

Inheritance hierarchies in view objects

The ADF Business Components framework supports inheritance in view objects irrespective of the underlying datasource. However, there are subtle differences between inheritances in view objects based on polymorphic entity usages and the rest. This is discussed in the following section.

Inheritance hierarchies in view objects with non-polymorphic entity usage

When you create a view object by using the editor, the **Name** page in the **Create View Object** window will allow you to extend the new view object from an existing view object. If the view objects that you have selected as a base for extending do not contain any polymorphic entity usage, the extended view object will have the following properties:

- The new extended view object will inherit all the metadata definitions from the base view object, which includes attribute definitions, query, view criteria, bind variables, view accessor, and view link definitions.

- The extended view object can optionally override the query and bind variable values, and add extra bind variables, view criteria, and view links.

- Overriding the attributes and methods from the Java implementations of an extended view object follows the rules in Java language.

Inheritance hierarchies in view objects with polymorphic entity usage

If the base view object that you are going to choose is based on polymorphic entity usages, JDeveloper will allow you to select subtypes of entities from the entity hierarchy in the entity usage mapping. A polymorphic view object refers to a view object, which has the ability to process properties and functions differently by dynamically linking the matching entity object usages in the hierarchy based on the polymorphic discriminator value. The polymorphic discriminator value set for the entities will be used to qualify each row retrieved from the datasource for the final row set.

Step-by-step instructions for defining view objects with polymorphic entity usage is discussed in *Oracle Fusion Middleware Fusion Developer's Guide* under the topic *How to Create a View Object with a Polymorphic Entity Usage*, which is available as part of the Oracle JDeveloper and ADF Documentation Library. To access the documentation go to `http://www.oracle.com/technetwork/developer-tools/jdev/documentation/index.html`, choose **Oracle JDeveloper and ADF Documentation Library | Fusion Developer's Guide**. Use the search option to find specific topics.

When you use a polymorphic view object to create a row, the framework will delegate the call to create a row for the corresponding entity usage, which is evaluated based on the value set for the polymorphic discriminator attribute. For example, consider employees in a marketing department with two subgroups — marketing executives and sales. Let us see how a polymorphic view object can be used to implement this employee inheritance hierarchy.

We will start with polymorphic entity objects. In this example, `MarketingEmployeeGenericEO` is a base entity with `DepartmentId` as the polymorphic discriminator attribute. Entity objects `ExecutiveEmployeeEO` and `SalesEmployeeEO` are subtypes in the inheritance hierarchy:

- `MarketingEmployeeGenericEO` (DepartmentId=20)
- `ExecutiveEmployeeExEO` (DepartmentId=80)
- `SalesEmployeeExEO` (DepartmentId=90)

The following diagram depicts the entity objects hierarchy and the view objects:

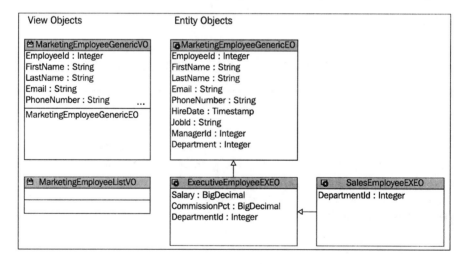

`MarketingEmployeeGenericVO` is based on `MarketingEmployeeGenericEO`.
The view object `MarketingEmployeeListVO` is a polymorphic view object, which
is extended from `MarketingEmployeeGenericVO`. The `ExecutiveEmployeeExEO`
and `SalesEmployeeExEO` entity objects are selected as subtypes in the entity usage
section for `MarketingEmployeeListVO`. A polymorphic `MarketingEmployeeListVO`
means that it will pick up a different entity usage instance to perform the operation
based on the context set by the discriminator attribute value. Let us take a look at
an example.

If you call `createAndInitRow()` on `MarketingEmployeeListVO` with
`DepartmentId=90`, as shown in the following example, the framework will
resolve the underlying entity object as `SalesEmployeeEO` by using the
discriminator attribute value and will invoke the `create(AttributeList
nameValuePair)` method on it.

```
//In application module implementation class
public void createOnPolymorphicVO(){
    Row row=null;
    NameValuePairs nvp=null;
    //Get the polymorphic VO
    MarketingEmployeeListVOImpl vo =
        (MarketingEmployeeListVOImpl)
    getMarketingEmployeeList();    nvp = new NameValuePairs();
    nvp.setAttribute("DepartmentId", "90");
    //VO delegates the createAndInitRow() call to
    //SalesEmployeeExEO as DepartmentId=90
    row=vo.createAndInitRow(nvp);
    nvp = new NameValuePairs();
    nvp.setAttribute("DepartmentId", "80");
    //Vo delgates the createAndInitRow() call to
    //ExecutiveEmployeeExEO as DepartmentId=80
    row=vo.createAndInitRow(nvp);
}
```

Querying the datasource by using a view object

A typical enterprise application may need to query the datasource with various
search conditions independent of the underlying storage medium. Sometimes
applications may even need to filter the rows in the memory. An ADF view object
has declarative support for defining the query with various search conditions and
search modes. In this section, we will take a quick tour on the features provided by
the view object to query the datasource and for managing the result set along with
code samples.

Specifying the query mode for a view object

Let us start our tour with discussing various query modes supported by view objects.
A view object's query mode selects the datasource that will be used to populate the
row set. The query modes for a view object are as follows:

- **Scan database tables**: In this mode, the query is fired against the database.
  This is the default query mode for a view object.

- **Scan view rows**: In this mode, the view object queries the rows that are
  already present in the query collection. In other words, when you use the
  scan view rows mode, you need to have first queried the rows into the view
  row cache (query collection).

- **Scan entity cache**: This mode is applicable only to entity-based view objects.
  In this mode, the rows in the entity cache are queried to build the row set.
  Unlike scan view rows mode, this mode scans through the entity cache. Note
  that all the view objects that are backed up by the same entity objects end up
  using the same entity cache in a transaction. This implies that the scan entity
  cache mode scans through all the rows that were queried into the entity
  cache by multiple view objects.

The following example illustrates the usage of query mode in a typical business logic
implementation. This example first fires the query against the database to read all
employee rows, and then reads all rows returned by the query. Then to further refine
the result, the program changes the query mode to entity cache and fires the query
against the entity cache to find out employee rows whose last name starts with the
letter *P*. The query mode that you set on a view object is sticky and will remain until
you set a new or original query mode.

```
// In ApplicationModuleImpl

public void changingQueryModeDynamically() {
//Possible view object modes are
  //1. ViewObject.QUERY_MODE_SCAN_DATABASE_TABLES
  //2. ViewObject.QUERY_MODE_SCAN_VIEW_ROWS
  //3. ViewObject.QUERY_MODE_SCAN_ENTITY_ROWS

  //Get the view object
  ViewObject vo = findViewObject("EmployeeDetails");
  //Fires query against database(default query mode)
  vo.executeQuery();
  //Rest of the business logic goes here..
  //This e.g just prints all rows
  //In real life application, you can process the rows here
  while (vo.hasNext()) {
```

```
    Row r = vo.next();
    String email = (String)r.getAttribute("Email");
    System.out.println("Employee with email -" + email);
}
//Now find all employees whose last name start with 'P'
//This is done against the rows in the cache(no DB hit)
vo.setQueryMode(ViewObject.QUERY_MODE_SCAN_ENTITY_ROWS);
ViewCriteria vc = vo.createViewCriteria();
ViewCriteriaRow vcr1 = vc.createViewCriteriaRow();
vcr1.setAttribute("LastName", "LIKE 'P%'");
vc.setCriteriaMode(ViewCriteria.CRITERIA_MODE_CACHE);
vc.add(vcr1);
vo.applyViewCriteria(vc);
vo.executeQuery();


}
```

You can either use the query modes individually on a view object or combine multiple query modes, using Java logical operator (mode1 | mode2). Here is an example:

```
// Defined In custom ApplicationModuleImpl
public void queryUsingMulitpleQueryModes(){
  //Find the view object
  ViewObject employeeVO = findViewObject("EmployeeDetails");
  //Combine both database mode and entity cache query mode
  employeeVO.setQueryMode(
    ViewObject.QUERY_MODE_SCAN_DATABASE_TABLES |
    ViewObject.QUERY_MODE_SCAN_ENTITY_ROWS);
  //Execute query
  employeeVO.executeQuery();
  // Business logic to manipulate row goes here
}
```

Runtime uses the following execution order when the view object has multiple query modes set:

1. Scan through view rows (if specified).
2. Scan through entity cache (if specified).
3. Scan through database tables (if specified).

You cannot use expert mode view objects in the in-memory query mode such as scan the view rows or scan the entity cache. This is because the framework does not replicate all the search capabilities from the database in the middle tier, which is not efficient as well. However, the framework supports the in-memory filtering if the view object is based on multiple entity usages that are connected through association or if the search condition is set through the in-memory mode view criteria.

Adding WHERE clause to a view object

You can restrict the number of records returned by a view object by appending search conditions to the query. This can be done either at design time through a static WHERE clause or by programmatically appending a condition at runtime.

Appending the WHERE clause at design time

To append the WHERE clause to a query in a view object, follow these steps:

1. Double-click on the view object to display the overview editor. Click on the **Query** tab in the overview editor and click on the **Edit SQL Query** icon to display the **Edit Query** dialog window.

2. In the **Edit Query** window, enter the appropriate WHERE clause. If the WHERE clause contains parameters whose values may change each time, it is recommended to introduce bind variables in the SQL query.

3. To define bind variables, select the **Bind Variables** node in the **Edit Query** window and click on **New**. Modify the default variable name and the type that is set by the editor to reflect the bind variable name. Also modify the type used in the query. Optionally, you can set the default value in the **Value** field, which can be either a literal or an expression.

Appending the WHERE clause at runtime

To append the WHERE clause at runtime, call setWhereClause() on the view object. If the WHERE clause contains bind variables that have been added at runtime, call defineNamedWhereClauseParam to define the same. Here is an example:

```
//This is in application module implementation class

public void executeEmployeeDetailsVOWithBindVar(){
    ViewObject vo = findViewObject("EmployeeDetails");
    //Append WHERE cluase
    vo.setWhereClause("FirstName = :bindVarFirstName");
```

```
    //Define the bind variable
    vo.defineNamedWhereClauseParam("bindVarFirstName", null,
        null);
    //Set the bind param value
    vo.setNamedWhereClauseParam("bindVarFirstName","Tom");
    vo.executeQuery();
}
```

Using bind variables

Bind variables are variables that are used in place of dynamic input values in a SQL statement. This has the effect of sending exactly the same SQL statement to the database every time the query is executed. JDeveloper allows you to define bind variables through multiple editor windows to ease your job. If you edit an existing query or view criteria to add a bind variable, you can see an option to define bind variables in these editor windows. The **Query** tab in the overview editor of a view object also has support for defining bind variables.

If the bind variable appears in the query at design time, while defining the bind variable you will need to mark it as **Required**. An example may be a static WHERE clause with bind variables added to the query at design time.

If the bind variable appears in the query conditionally, the corresponding bind variables are supposed to be marked as optional (uncheck the **Required** flag). An example is bind variables used in a view criteria.

Programmatically specifying the value for bind variables

There are multiple ways to supply bind variable values for a view object. You must know what means what when you build business components. Here are the details:

- **Using** setNamedWhereClauseParam() **on the view object**: This method sets the value on the default row set of the view object instance. In other words, this does not affect the secondary row sets that you or the system generates. Here is an example:

```
//In application module implementation class

public Row findEmployeeForEmpId(Integer empId){
    ViewObject employeeVO = findViewObject("Employees");
    //Define WHERE clause
    String whereClause = "EmployeeEO.EMPLOYEE_ID = :empId";
    employeeVO.setWhereClause(whereClause);
```

```
employeeVO.setNamedWhereClauseParam("empId", empId);
employeeVO.executeQuery();
return employeeVO.first();
}
```

- **Using** `setVariableValue()` **on** `VariableValueManager`: The variable value manager manages named variables and their values for the view object instance. If the bind variable values have not been set on the bind variables by explicitly calling `setNamedWhereClauseParam()`, the bind variable value set may reflect across all row sets by calling `setVariableValue()` on `VariableValueManager`. This is because the call to `setNamedWhereClauseParam()` on a row set takes precedence over the variable value manager's copy of bind variable value. Here is an example:

```
//In application module implementation class

public void findEmployeeForEmplId(Integer empId){
  ViewObject employeeVO =findViewObject("Employees");
  VariableValueManager vm =
    employeeVO.ensureVariableManager();
  vm.setVariableValue("empId", empId);
  employeeVO.executeQuery();
}
```

- **Using** `setWhereClauseParam()` **on the view object**: You can use this method for view objects with the binding style of Oracle Positional or JDBC Positional. This is typically used when you work with non-Oracle databases where you cannot use named bind variables.

```
//In application module implementation class

public Row findEmployeeForEmpId(Integer empId){
  //Define WHERE clause with JDB style bind var :NNN
  String whereClause = "EmployeeEO.EMPLOYEE_ID = :1";
  ViewObject employeeVO =findViewObject("Employees");
  employeeVO.setWhereClause(whereClause);
  employeeVO.setWhereClauseParam(1,empId);
  employeeVO.executeQuery();
  return employeeVO.first();
}
```

Changing the query of a view object at runtime

A view object will allow you to modify the design-time SQL query at runtime. If you are modifying the query of the view object, which is bound to some non-dynamic UI elements on a web page, make sure the new query that you set for the view object returns the same attribute definitions as in the original case. This feature is useful when you need to use the same UI to display data from different datasources (database tables) depending on the context of the usage. Before you alter the query dynamically, make sure you close all existing row sets that are using the existing query. The following code snippet illustrates how you can modify the query on a view at runtime:

```
/**
 * This is a custom method defined in an application module.
 * It sets the query on a view object at runtime
 */
public void modifyQueryDynamically(ViewObjectImpl voImpl, String
newQueryString) {
    // FULLSQL_MODE_AUGMENTATION flag that tells framework that
    // you want to keep the query set through setQuery() for
    // the rest of the execution using this view object
    voImpl.setFullSqlMode(voImpl.FULLSQL_MODE_AUGMENTATION);
    closeAllRowsets(voImpl);
    //clear the previous WHERE clause and parameters
    voImpl.setWhereClause(null);
    voImpl.setWhereClauseParams(null);
    //Query can be set fully in expert mode
    voImpl.setQuery(newQueryString);

}

/**
 * Close all row set when query changes
 * to avoid the orphan Rowset
 */
public void closeAllRowsets(ViewObject vo) {
    RowSet[] rowSets = vo.getRowSets();

    if (rowSets == null || rowSets.length == 0) {
        return;
    }
    for (RowSet rowSet : rowSets) {
        rowSet.closeRowSet();
    }
}
```

Programmatically sorting view object rows

To sort the rows in a view object at runtime, you can use the following APIs depending upon whether the attribute is a transient type or persistent:

- Use the setSortBy() method to sort transient attributes, which will take attribute names with the desc or asc clause. Next time when the client executes the view object, the framework sorts the columns in memory. This is done in memory and has a performance impact for a large number of rows. So, avoid using it for persistent attributes. Here is an example:

```
//In a method defined in application module implementation
//class

ViewObject vo = findViewObject("EmployeeDetails");
//FullName is a transient attribute
vo.setSortBy("FullName desc");
vo.executeQuery();
```

- Use the setOrderByClause() method to sort columns from the database table (persistent attributes). Next time when the client executes a view object, the view object translates this sorting clause into an appropriate format to use it for ordering the rows depending on the SQL mode.

```
//In a method defined in application module implementation
//class

ViewObject vo = findViewObject("EmployeeDetails");
vo.setOrderByClause("EmployeeEO.FIRST_NAME ASC");
vo.executeQuery();
```

In-memory filtering of row sets

So far in our discussion of view objects, we have been talking about different approaches for executing a query. Most of our code samples use a database as a datasource. This may not always be the case. A rich enterprise application should have the infrastructure for supporting the query on unposted data as well. This is highly desirable when you build a rich internet application where a specific business transaction may span across multiple requests. An ADF view object has facilities to filter data in memory, as discussed in the following sections.

In-memory filtering with RowMatch

The oracle.jbo.RowMatch class will help you to filter the rows in a view object from in-memory. The RowMatch class can be used either standalone or along with a view object to filter the rows.

The following example illustrates the standalone usage of RowMatch to check if an individual row qualifies as a specific condition:

```
//In a method defined in application module implementation
//class

//Get row to be checked from employee view object
ViewObject vo = findViewObject("EmployeeDetails");
Row row =  vo.getCurrentRow();
//Set the condition for in memory filtering
RowMatch rm = new RowMatch("FirstName = 'William'");
// alternatively use  rm.setWhereClause( condition );
if (rm.rowQualifies(row)) {
//Row exists with William as first name
}
```

The following example illustrates the usage of RowMatch to filter a row set in a view object:

```
//In a method defined in application module implementation
//class

//Get employee view object
ViewObject vo = findViewObject("EmployeeDetails");
//Set the condition for in memory filtering
RowMatch rm = new RowMatch("FirstName like 'J%'");
vo.setRowMatch(rm);
vo.executeQuery();
```

You can also use bind variables in the expression set for RowMatch. When RowMatch is used for a view object, the view object's variable manager will supply the bind variable value.

```
//In a method defined in application module implementation
//class

//Get employee view object
ViewObject vo = findViewObject("EmployeeDetails");
RowMatch rm = new RowMatch("LastName = :bvLastName");
vo.getVariableManager().setVariableValue("bvLastName", "Grant");
```

If `RowMatch` is being used standalone to test an individual row, the owner of the row will manage the bind variable value. Here is an example:

```
//In a method defined in application module implementation
//class

//Get row to be checked from employee view object
ViewObject vo = findViewObject("EmployeeDetails");
Row row = vo.getCurrentRow();
RowMatch rm = new RowMatch("FirstName = :bvFirstName");
ViewObject ownerVO=(ViewObject)row.getStructureDef();
ownerVO.getVariableManager().setVariableValue
    ("bvFirstName", "William");
Row row=getRow
if(rm.rowQualifies(row)) {
//Row exists with William as last name
}
```

You can use basic SQL functions while coding for in-memory filtering, using `RowMatch`. It supports the following SQL functions:

SQL function	Operation
UPPER	Uppercases the string
TO_CHAR	Converts a number or date to a string
TO_DATE	Converts a string to a date
TO_TIMESTAMP	Converts a string to a timestamp
ABS	Returns absolute value
SIGN	If the number is positive returns +1 If the number is negative returns -1 else returns 0
DECODE	Provides the functionality of the IF-THEN-ELSE statement
MOD	Returns the remainder of "m" divided by "n"

Here is an example for `RowMatch` with SQL function:

```
RowMatch rm = new RowMatch("UPPER(FirstName) = UPPER(:bvFirstName)");
```

The following are the SQL operators supported by in-memory filtering with RowMatch:

Operator	Operations
=, < >, <, <=, >, >=, LIKE, and BETWEEN	Comparison
NOT	Negation
AND	Conjunction
OR	Dejection

 Don't use RowMatch if you have the option to filter the values at database level. In-memory filtering is much slower than filtering done at the database layer.

In-memory filtering by overriding rowQualifies() in ViewObjectImpl

If your view object needs to proactively perform in-memory filtering when rows are read from datasource or cache, you can override the rowQualifies(ViewRowImpl vr) method on ViewObjectImpl. This method is invoked on new view rows as well as view rows coming from the query to see if the view row should be added to the query collection.

The following example uses this feature to implement soft deletion. When a row is deleted from the UI, the program sets StatusFlag to DELETE, without removing the row. To hide the row from appearing in the collection used in the UI, this example overrides rowQualifies(). This overridden method disqualifies all the rows with StatusFlag set to DELETE from adding into the query collection.

```
//In view object implementation
@Override
protected boolean rowQualifies(ViewRowImpl vr) {
  //Omit the rows from row set whose StatusFlag= 'DELETE'
  Object attrValue =vr.getAttribute("StatusFlag");
  if (attrValue != null) {
    if ("DELETE".equals(attrValue))
      return false;
    else
      return true;
  }
  return super.rowQualifies(vr);
}
```

You can also use view criteria with the in-memory query execution mode to perform in-memory filtering on row sets. This is discussed in the following section.

View criteria

The **view criteria** definition contains the filter information for the rows of a view object. It comprises view criteria rows and view criteria items, which will be used to form the WHERE clause at runtime. This is useful if you want to optionally filter the rows at runtime against the database, in-memory, or both.

Here are the steps to define the view criteria on a view object:

1. Click on the **Query** tab in the overview editor and then expand the **View Criteria** section. Click on the green plus icon to create new view criteria.

2. In the **Create View Criteria** dialog window, enter **View Criteria Name**, select **Query Execution Mode**, and then add **View Criteria Items**. Each view criteria item contains **Attribute**, **Operator**, **Operand Type**, and optionally default operand value. You can optionally specify the required field validation too.

3. The **UI Hints** tab on the **Create View Criteria** dialog window will help you to set the control hints for the criteria item. These control hints will be used by the UI components, such as af:query and af:quickQuery, to render their fields at runtime.

>
> To learn more about the options for creating view criteria, refer to *Chapter 5, Defining SQL Queries Using View Objects* in *Oracle Fusion Middleware Fusion Developer's Guide for Oracle Application Development Framework.* To access the documentation go to http://www.oracle.com/technetwork/developer-tools/jdev/documentation/index.html, choose **Oracle JDeveloper**, and navigate to **ADF Documentation Library | Fusion Developer's Guide**. Use the search option to find specific topics.

Architecture of view criteria

A view criteria can include multiple view criteria or view criteria rows linked by various criteria conjunction types such as AND, OR, and UNION. Each view criteria row can optionally include multiple view criteria items.

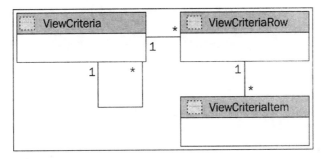

The query execution mode that you set for the view criteria decides the source to read rows:

- **Database**: In this mode view criteria is used for database query. This is the default mode. You can use the `ViewCriteria.CRITERIA_MODE_QUERY` constant to refer this mode programmatically.

- **In-memory**: In this mode, view criteria is used for in-memory filtering. You can use the `ViewCriteria.CRITERIA_MODE_CACHE` constant to refer this mode programmatically.

- **Both (database and in-memory)**: In this mode, view criteria is used for a database query first and then for in-memory row filtering. You can combine the `ViewCriteria.CRITERIA_MODE_QUERY` and `ViewCriteria.CRITERIA_MODE_CACHE` constants in order to refer this mode programmatically:

```
ViewCriteria.CRITERIA_MODE_QUERY | ViewCriteria.CRITERIA_MODE_
CACHE
```

View objects even help you with APIs to build view criteria dynamically. Here is a simple example:

```
//In application module implementation class

public void executeEmployeeVOWithDynamicVC(){
    //Get the desired view object
    ViewObject vo = findViewObject("EmployeeDetails");
    //Build View Criteria first
    ViewCriteria vc = vo.createViewCriteria();
    //Create View Criteria Row
    ViewCriteriaRow vcr = vc.createViewCriteriaRow();
    //Set the QBE
```

```
            vcr.setAttribute("FirstName","LIKE 'J%'");
            //Optionally override the default criteria mode-Database
            vc.setCriteriaMode(ViewCriteria.CRITERIA_MODE_QUERY |
                ViewCriteria.CRITERIA_MODE_CACHE);
            //Add View Criteria Row
            vc.add(vcr);
            //Execute Query, Framework will generate a WHERE clause
            //for the above VC as
            //SELECT … FROM … WHERE EmployeeEO.LAST_NAME LIKE
            //:vc_temp_1
            vo.executeQuery();
        }
```

 View criteria with in-memory execution mode supports all the SQL operators discussed under RowMatch.

You can even use bind variables in view criteria items while creating view criteria through code. When you use a bind variable, you pass a strong message about the exact parameter type to framework. This is very essential when the native SQL needs to offer special handling for datatypes such as date and time and numeric values. The bind variable API also gives you an option to set attribute hints, which will be consumed by query components to render the corresponding field on UI. Here is an example for creating view criteria with a bind variable:

```
/**
 * This method creates view criteria programmatically and
 * returns it to the caller.
 * This is defined inside EmployeeViewObjectImpl.
 */
public ViewCriteria CreateVCForEmpName(){
    //Get the  VariableValueManager who is responsible for
    //managing bind vairbales
    VariableValueManager vvm =ensureVariableManager();
    //Create View Criteria
    ViewCriteria vc =createViewCriteria();
    ViewCriteriaRow vcr = vc.createViewCriteriaRow();
    //Create View Criteria Item and set operator
    ViewCriteriaItem vci = vcr.ensureCriteriaItem("FirstName");
    vci.setOperator(JboCompOper.OPER_LIKE);
    vci.setRequired(ViewCriteriaItem.VCITEM_REQUIRED);
    //Define bind variable and init properties
    VariableImpl fstNameVar = (VariableImpl)vvm.
        addVariable("dynamicBindVarAttribute");
```

```
fstNameVar.setJavaType(String.class);
fstNameVar.setMandatory(true);
fstNameVar.setUpdateableFlag(Variable.UPDATEABLE);
fstNameVar.setVariableKind(
    Variable.VAR_KIND_VIEW_CRITERIA_PARAM);
fstNameVar.setProperty(
    AttributeHints.ATTRIBUTE_DISPLAY_HINT,
    AttributeHints.ATTRIBUTE_DISPLAY_HINT_HIDE);
//Add bind variable to VC Item as value
vci.setValue(0, ":dynamicBindVarAttribute");
vci.setIsBindVarValue(0, true);
//Initialize bind variable value
vvm.setVariableValue(fstNameVar, "A%");
//Insert View Criteria Row to VC
vc.insertRow(vcr);
return vc;
}
```

Once you have applied the view criteria to a view object, it will be stuck there till you remove the same from the applied list. To remove an applied view criteria, use the API shown in the following example:

```
//In application module implementation class

public void unApplyVC(String viewCriteriaCNameToBeRemoved){
    //Get Employee view object
    ViewObjectImpl vo = (ViewObjectImpl)findViewObject
        ("EmployeeDetails");
    vo.removeApplyViewCriteriaName
        (viewCriteriaCNameToBeRemoved);
}
```

You can alter the existing view criteria definitions dynamically through code as shown in the following example. If you want to persist the changes made on a view criteria, call saveState() on the ViewCriteria object. The following example updates an existing view criteria to add a new condition, and persists all the changes by calling saveState() on view criteria:

```
//In application module implementation class

public void alterVCAndSaveState(){
    //Get Employee view object
    ViewObject vo = findViewObject("EmployeeDetails");
    ViewCriteriaManager vcm = vo.getViewCriteriaManager();
    //Get an existing VC
```

```
          ViewCriteria vc = vcm.getViewCriteria
              ("EmployeeDetailsVC");
          //Add new condition to VC
          ViewCriteriaRow vcr = vc.createViewCriteriaRow();
          vcr.setAttribute("EmployeeId","IN (1000,2000)");
          vc.add(vcr);
          //Persist the changes
          vc.saveState();
      }
```

When multiple ViewCriteriaRow objects are added to ViewCriteria, you can
specify whether the conditions generated by ViewCriteriaRow should be combined
using the logical operator AND or OR with the existing conditions (WHERE clause).
You can do this through the setConjunction() method. You can use conjunction
constants from ViewCriteriaRow to specify the desired logical operator. Multiple
conjunction constants are combined through bit-wise OR operator. The following
example illustrates how to combine multiple view criteria rows to achieve a WHERE
clause as WHERE (((EmployeeEO.JOB_ID LIKE :vc_temp_1)) AND (NOT (
(EmployeeEO.DEPARTMENT_ID = :vc_temp_2)))):

```
    // Show employees with JobId=IT_PROG and DepartmentId <> 60

    public void applyVCRowWithConjunction(){
        //Get employee view object
        ViewObject vo = findViewObject("EmployeeDetails");

        ViewCriteria vc = vo.createViewCriteria();
        ViewCriteriaRow vcRow1 = vc.createViewCriteriaRow();
        vcRow1.setAttribute("JobId", "IT_PROG");
        vc.addElement(vcRow1);

        ViewCriteriaRow vcRow2 = vc.createViewCriteriaRow();
        vcRow2.setAttribute("DepartmentId", "= 10");
        vcRow2.setConjunction(ViewCriteriaRow.VC_CONJ_AND |
        ViewCriteriaRow.VC_CONJ_NOT);
        vc.addElement(vcRow2);
        vo.applyViewCriteria(vc);
        vo.executeQuery();
    }
```

Multiple view criteria can be combined by using the UNION operator or you can do
this in SQL. The following example illustrates how you can apply the UNION operator
on two view criteria's:

```
    //In application module implementation class

    //Get employee view object
    ViewObject vo = findViewObject("EmployeeDetails");
    vcu = vo.createViewCriteria();
```

```
vcm = vo.getViewCriteriaManager();
vcu.setConjunction(ViewCriteria.VC_CONJ_UNION);
//Add first VC
vcu.add(vcm.getViewCriteria("JobCriteria"));
//Add next VC
vcu.add(vcm.getViewCriteria("SalCriteria"));
vo.applyViewCriteria(vcu);
vo.executeQuery();
```

To access bind variables programmatically from a view object, always route your request through variable value manager. Note that a UI search form (af:query) built by dropping ViewCriteria accesses the bind variable values through the variable value manager of the view object. So this approach also helps you to initialize the bind variable value displayed in af:query, if required. Here is an example:

```
//This is in application module impl.
public void initEmpNameInVC(){
    ViewObject vo = findViewObject("EmployeeDetails");
    //Get variable value manager
    VariableValueManager vvm = vo.ensureVariableManager();
    String bvEmployeeName=vvm.getVariableValue("bvEmpName");
    //Assign value to bind variable
    String empName="Chinmay";
    vvm.setVariableValue("bvEmpName", empName);
}
```

By default, when you execute a view object with specific conditions, the framework overrides the default row set to store the result. Sometimes you may want to extract rows from the default row set in memory without overriding the default row set. In other words, search in memory without affecting the default row set of a view object. You can do this by calling findByViewCriteria() on view object. The following example uses this API to perform filtering of country names in memory. Note that query mode for view criteria is set as ViewCriteria.CRITERIA_MODE_CACHE.

```
public RowSet searchInMemoryWithoutAffectingDefaultRowset() {
    ViewObject vo = findViewObject("Countries");
    vo.executeQuery();
        showRows(vo, "Print All Rows");
    //Define VC for in-memroy filtering
    ViewCriteria countryStartsWithA = vo.
        createViewCriteria();
    countryStartsWithA.setCriteriaMode(
        ViewCriteria.CRITERIA_MODE_CACHE);
    //Criteria for finding country names with letter A
    ViewCriteriaRow vcr1 = countryStartsWithA.
        createViewCriteriaRow();
    vcr1.setAttribute("CountryName", "LIKE A%");
    countryStartsWithA.add(vcr1);
    //Set In memory VC mode
```

```
countryStartsWithA.setCriteriaMode(
    ViewCriteria.CRITERIA_MODE_CACHE);
//Perfrom in-memory filtering
//and get result in new row set
RowSet rs = (RowSet)vo.findByViewCriteria(
    countryStartsWithA, -1,
    ViewObject.QUERY_MODE_SCAN_VIEW_ROWS);
return rs;

}
```

Effective dated view objects

This topic is in continuation with what we discussed under the topic *Effective dated entity object* in *Chapter 3, Introducing Entity Object*. Effective-date-enabled view objects are useful to limit the row set returned by a view object based on the value set for the property `ApplicationModule.EFF_DT_PROPERTY_STR`.

To define an effective dated view object, you should define an effective dated entity object first as we discussed in *Chapter 3, Introducing Entity Objects*. Once your effective dated entity object is in place, define a view object based on the date effective entity. When you run the effective dated view object, the framework will append the WHERE clause with the BETWEEN clause to enable date effective filtering. For example, if you have marked the attributes `StartDate` and `EndDate` in `JobHistoryEO` as effective start date and end date, the framework will append the WHERE clause — for the date effective `JobHistoryVO` at runtime — as follows:

```
SELECT JobHistoryEO.EMPLOYEE_ID, JobHistoryEO.START_DATE,
JobHistoryEO.END_DATE WHERE (:SysEffectiveDateBindVar BETWEEN
JobHistoryEO.START_DATE AND JobHistoryEO.END_DATE)
```

The framework will use value set for the property EFF_DT_PROPERTY_
STR in the application module to supply the value for the bind variable
SysEffectiveDateBindVar at runtime. The default value is the current date. You
can set EFF_DT_PROPERTY_STR as shown in the following example. The client can
invoke the method with appropriate effective date value.

```
// A method in HRServiceAppModuleImpl.java
//This method initializes effecitvedate with the value passed // by
the client
public void initEffectiveDate(Date effectiveDate) {
  //Set the AM property
  setProperty(ApplicationModule.EFF_DT_PROPERTY_STR,
  (effectiveDate == null) ? new Date("2008-16-10") :
  effectiveDate);

}
```

Using alternate keys in a view object

In the last chapter on entity objects, we learned that alternate keys allow us to define unique keys that can be used for the fast look up of specific entity rows. If you want to enable search based on alternate key for a view object, you will have to define alternate keys at the view object level too. This feature is available only for entity-based view objects and the underlying entity should have an alternate key defined before starting the alternate key definition for the view object.

To define an alternate key for a view object, click on the **General** tab in the overview editor of a view object and expand the **Alternate Keys** section. Click on the green plus icon to add an alternate key and then enter a name in the **Alternate Key Name** field. Now you need to select the existing alternate key definitions from the entity object usages, as appropriate. Click on **OK** to save the changes.

The following example illustrates how you can make use of alternate keys to find view rows.

The following code snippet illustrates the usage of alternate keys for finding rows in a view object. Note that when you search using alternate keys, the framework first checks whether the row is available in the entity cache, and if not found, the search is performed against the database.

```
//In application module implementation class
public void findByAlKey(){
    ViewObject vo =findViewObject("EmployeeDeptDetails");
    //EmployeeDeptDetailVO has two entity objects EmpEO and
    //DeptEO. The alt key EmpDeptAltKey is defined on
    //EmployeeDeptDetailVO by selecting alt keys from both the
    // EO
    Key empDeptAltKey = new Key(new Object[] { "JWHALEN",
    "Administration" });
    //findByAltKey() has the following method signature :
    //findByAltKey(String keyName, Key key, int maxNumOfRows,
    //boolean skipWhere)
    RowIterator iter = vo.findByAltKey("EmpDeptAltKey",
    empDeptAltKey, -1, false);
}
```

Using findByKey() on view objects

View objects based on multiple entity usages have the ability to find view rows by using keys from the entity usages. It follows these conditions:

- The attribute values, which form the key, should be marked as the key attributes in the view object.

- If the secondary entity usage has multiple attributes as a primary key and you want to include keys from the secondary entity usage in the findByKey() call, you will need to make sure that all the primary key attributes in the secondary entity object are marked as key attributes in the view object.

- findByKey() will allow you to search based on partial keys. However, the keys that you are passing as an argument are assumed to be in the same order as they are defined in the view object. If you want to perform a partial key search by skipping some keys, make sure you are handling them properly by passing null values to keep in the order as they appear in the view object. Here is an example for a key with null arguments:

  For example, consider a business scenario where you need to search for a specific employee row and update the salary details. When you implement such use cases, you may always consider using findByKey() on view object. This call will try to read the cached entity row first, and will hit database only if the row is not yet queried. The following code snippet illustrates the search, using findByKey() on the view object :

```
//In application module implementation class

public  Row[] findEmpByKey(Integer empId, Integer deptId) {
  // EmployeeDeptDetails has EmployeeEO and DepartmentEO
  // as entity usages
  ViewObject vo = findViewObject("EmployeeDeptDetails");
  //EmployeeId is PK in EmployeeEO and DepartmentId
  //is PK in EmployeeEO
  //Both these attributes are makrked as Keys in the
  //EmployeeDeptDetailsVO

  Key key = new Key(new Object[] { empId, deptId });
  //-1 implies return all matching rows
  Row row[] = vo.findByKey(key, -1);
  return row;
}
```

Creating new rows through the view object

Create a new view row by calling `createRow()` on the view object as shown in the following code snippet:

```
/**The createCountry is a custom method defined in application
 * module implementation class.
 */
 public void createCountry() {
 //Get the view object
 ViewObject countries = findViewObject("CountryVO");
 // Create a row and fill in the columns.
 Row row = countries.createRow();
 row.setAttribute("CountryId", "IN");
 row.setAttribute("RegionId", 3);
 //Insert row in to the default row set
 countries.insertRow(row);
 }
```

You can also use `createAndInitRow(AttributeList initVals)` on the view object to create a new view row. This API allows you to initialize the row with an attribute list. Note that this is primarily designed for initializing entity objects in the context of composition association and inheritance hierarchy. More specifically, you can call this API while creating child entity objects participating in a composition association in order to initialize it with foreign key attribute values. This is also used for initializing discriminator attributes for entity objects participating in an inheritance hierarchy. Note that when you use this method on a view object based on multiple entity usages, the framework will not consider attributes (other than association and discriminator columns) supplied for secondary entities through the input list while creating a new view row. The following section contains an example for the `createAndInitRow()` API usage in the context of composition association.

Creating child rows in composition association

Creating a new child row is a bit tricky when the master-child entity association type is composition. When you mark an association between master and child entity objects as composition, the framework takes the necessary steps to ensure that the child entity object row does not exist without the master entity row. If you try to create a new child row by calling `createRow()` on the view object, the framework will throw the `oracle.jbo.InvalidOwnerException: JBO-25030: Failed to find or invalidate owning entity` exception.

There are two possible ways to create child entity rows in this case:

- Find the master row by using `findByKey()` or calling `executeQuery()` with a proper condition and then get the `RowIterator` for the child collection by accessing the view link accessor attribute. Now you can use the child `RowIterator` to call `createRow()` for creating the child row. The following code snippet illustrates the creation of the child entity row for the Country-Location composition association:

```
//In application module implementation class
/**
 * This custom method defined in application module
 * creates child location rows for a master
 * country entity through accessor iterator
 */
public  void createChildRowsThruIter() {
   //Find the parent view object
     ViewObject countries = findViewObject("Countries");
     //IN is the Key value for a specific Country row
     Key key = new Key(new Object[] { "IN" });
     //Find the country for 'IN', maxNumOfRows=1
     Row rows[] = countries.findByKey(key, 1);
     //Access the RowIterator for Location
     RowIterator locIter = (RowIterator)rows[0].
getAttribute("LocationVO");
     //Create and init location row
     Row row = locIter.createRow();
     row.setAttribute("LocationId", 2200);
     row.setAttribute("City", "Bangalore");
     locIter.insertRow(row);
}
```

- Alternatively, you can directly create a new row in the child view object, using `createAndInitRow()` by passing an appropriately constructed instance of `oracle.jbo.NameValuePairs`, which includes the foreign key attribute that provides the context for a child row. Here is an example:

```
//In application module implementation class

/**
 * This custom method defined in application module
 * creates child location rows for a master
 * country entity using createAndInitRow()
 */
public void createChildRowsThruNameValuePairs() {
   ViewObject locations = findViewObject("Locations");
   //Initialize Attributes and Values
   String[] attributes = new String[] { "CountryId" };
```

```
    Object[] values = new Object[] { "IN" };
    //Pass the foreign key value for Country while
    //initializing new location row
    Row locRow = locations.createAndInitRow(new
      NameValuePairs(attributes, values));
    //Set other attributes
    locRow.setAttribute("LocationId", 2200);
    locRow.setAttribute("City", "Bangalore");
    locations.insertRow(locRow);
}
```

View link consistency

ADF view objects allow you to create multiple view objects on the same entity object. Though this looks simple, things become slightly complex when you manipulate rows through different view objects. A framework may need to ensure that all the view objects based on the same entity display the same data for the user session. In this section, we will learn a mechanism used by ADF Business Components to ensure consistency across view objects based on the same entity object.

To keep our discussion simple, let us take two view objects, DepartmentDetailVO and DepartmentSummaryVO, built using same entity object, DepartmentEO. Suppose you are creating a new row through DepartmentDetailVO. Once you commit the changes to the database, on next query execution, this new row will be available for all view objects that are based on DepartmentEO. What if your business user wants the new row to be available for DepartmentSummaryVO before committing the changes to the database? Well, this feature is available out of the box with view objects. This feature is known as **view link consistency**. View link consistency allows all view objects based on the same entity objects to display the newly created entity row through any of the view objects. Let us take a closer look at this feature.

Configuring view link consistency

You can control the view link consistency at application module level through the property jbo.viewlink.consistent. To edit this property, double-click on the application module in the model project to display the overview editor. Go to the **Configuration** page and then choose the desired configuration to edit. In the **Edit Configuration** dialog, select the **Properties** tab, and scroll to the **jbo.viewlink. consistent** property to select the desired value. The possible values are as follows:

- DEFAULT: This value means, for single entity usage, that view link consistency is enabled.

For multiple entity usages,

- ○ If all secondary entity usages are marked as contributing reference information, view link consistency is enabled.

- ○ If any secondary entity usage is marked as not being a reference, view link consistency is disabled.

- `true`: View link consistency is enabled in all cases.

- `false`: View link consistency is disabled in all cases.

If you want to enable or disable view link consistency for a specific view object, override the `create()` method in the view object implementation class and call `setAssociationConsistent(boolean)` as shown in the following code snippet:

```
//In view object implementation class
protected void create() {
    super.create();
    //Pass true to enable view link consistency.
    //Pass false to disable view link consistency.
    setAssociationConsistent(true);
}
```

It is not mandatory to have the view link consistency feature enabled for all view objects. If your application does not need this feature for certain view objects, you can turn it off programmatically by passing `false` to the `setAssociationConsistent()` call.

 View link consistency is enabled only for view objects based on entity objects.

How view link consistency works

Let us understand the working of view link consistency with an example. Consider two view objects, `DepartmentDetailVO` and `DepartmentSummaryVO`, built using the same entity object, `DepartmentEO`. When you create a new row on `DepartmentDetailVO`, the call creates a new `DepartmentEO` instance. When you set a primary key for the new row, the entity instance will be added to the entity cache. This action fires an event by indicating that a new row has been created and all other view objects that are backed up by `DepartmentEO` receive this event. If view link consistency is enabled, the view object will walk through its entire query collections (`oracle.jbo.server.QueryCollection`) and start processing the new row for each query collection object.

While processing the new row for the query collection, the view objects check if the row already exists in the collection. If the query collection does not have any view row for the new entity instance, a new view row is created. However, the new row is added only after the following check.

The view object's `rowQualifies()` method and `RowMatch` are applied to the new view row to see if the row qualifies to be in this query collection. If the in-memory filtering succeeds, the new row is finally inserted into the query collection. The insertion location for the new row in the row set varies based on the state of the view object. There are two possible scenarios:

- Consider two entity-based view objects backed up by the same entity object. When a new row is created in a row set for one of the view objects, the framework sends a message to the second view object, indicating the creation of a new row. If the second view object has view link consistency enabled, a copy of the new row is added to the bottom of second view object's row set.

- If a view object has view link consistency enabled, when you call the `executeQuery()` method, any qualifying new rows are added to the top of the row set before the queried rows from the database. This typically happens if view link consistency was disabled for a view when the new row was added to the entity cache through another view object. Later, when you enable view link consistency programmatically and call the `executeQuery()` method, framework uses this rule for adding the matching new rows.

Why does view link consistency fail when you add a dynamic WHERE clause?

When you call `setWhereClause()` on a view object to set a WHERE clause at runtime, the view link consistency feature will be disabled for that view object. This is because the framework may not be able to use the complex WHERE clause conditions to filter the rows in memory. However, you can work around this scenario by providing a custom `RowMatch` object to qualify new rows for adding to the row set and making a call to `setAssociationConsistent(true)` after `setWhereClause()` on the view object.

The following is an example that illustrates this idea. This example uses two view objects, EmployeeVO and EmployeeInDeptVO—both are based on EmployeeEO. EmployeeVO lists all employee rows, whereas EmployeeInDeptVO lists rows from Admin department alone. By default, the view link consistency is enabled for these two view objects. Due to this, when you create a new row in EmployeeVO, it will be reflected in EmployeeInDeptVO as well. However, if you add a WHERE clause dynamically to EmployeeInDeptVO, the framework disables view link consistency and the new row created through EmployeeVO will no longer appear in EmployeeInDeptVO.

A possible solution for this use case is to explicitly call setAssociationConsistent(true) on EmployeeInDeptVO after calling setWhereClause(). You can add a RowMatch object to empInDeptVO in order to filter the unposted (new) rows in memory. The following code snippet from an application module implementation class illustrates this concept:

```
//This is a custom method is defined in application module
//class
public void exampleForVLConsistencyEnablement(){

  //Get the EmployeesInAdminDept view object
  ViewObject empInDeptVO = findViewObject
    ("EmployeesInAdminDept");
  //The below call disables view link consistency
  empInDeptVO.setWhereClause
    (" EmployeeEO.LAST_NAME = :bvLastName ");
  empInDeptVO.defineNamedWhereClauseParam
    ("bvLastName", null, null);

  //Set the condition for in memory filtering which is
  //needed to filter out unwanted new rows
  //when you expliclty enable view link consistency
  //by calling setAssociationConsistent(true)
  RowMatch rm = new RowMatch("LastName = :bvLastName");
  empInDeptVO.setRowMatch(rm);
  empInDeptVO.getVariableManager().setVariableValue
    ("bvLastName", "Purushothaman");

  //Re-enable the view link consistency
  empInDeptVO.setAssociationConsistent(true);

  //Get the employee view object
  ViewObject employeeVO = findViewObject("Employees");
  Row row =employeeVO.createRow();
  employeeVO.insertRow(row);
```

```
row.setAttribute("EmployeeId", 24170);
row.setAttribute("FirstName", "Jobinesh");
row.setAttribute("LastName", "Purushothaman");
row.setAttribute("Email", "jobinesh@xyz.com");
row.setAttribute("HireDate",
  new oracle.jbo.domain.Date().timestampValue() );
row.setAttribute("JobId", "AD_PRES");

empInDeptVO.executeQuery();
//Along with rows from database, empInDeptVO
//will have new row as well
System.out.println("Count "+
  empInDeptVO.getEstimatedRowCount());

}
```

What happens when you execute a view object?

In *Chapter 2, Introduction to ADF Business Components,* you were introduced to the collaboration of business components during a call to executeQuery() on a view object. In this section, we will take a detailed look at the execution plan for the following code snippet to understand the concepts better. The view object used in this example uses the default tuning settings. Data fetch mode is set as fetch as needed (which is the default).

```
//In application module implementation class
public void executeEmployeeVO(){
    //Get employee view object
    ViewObject vo = findViewObject("EmployeeDetails");
    //Execute employee view object
    vo.executeQuery();

    //Fetch rows from the ResultSet
    while (vo.hasNext()) {
        Row row = vo.next();
        //Work with empRow
    }
}
```

To keep it simple, we are splitting this discussion into two parts. In the first part, we will analyze the basic query execution for retrieving the result set from datasource. In the second part, we will analyze the iteration over the result set.

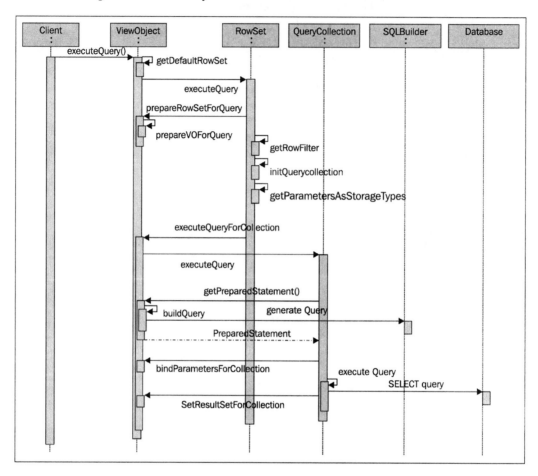

When a client calls `executeQuery()` on a view object, the framework will try to get the default row set if it is already present. If this is the very first execution, a new row set will be created and assigned to the view object. Once the row set is in place, the view object will delegate the call to the default row set for further action. At this stage, the row set engages the view object in the execution cycle by invoking the call back on view object instance `prepareRowSetForQuery(ViewRowSetImpl vrs)`. This callback method can be overridden to alter the default query or to assign additional bind variable values to the current row set at runtime, right before the query execution.

The `prepareRowSetForQuery()` method in the view object in turn will invoke `prepareVOForQuery()`. As the name suggests, this method prepares the view object instance for query. Then, row set will look for any bind parameter values in the query and if found, it will prepare an array of bind parameters. Row set uses a data structure known as row filter to hold this bind parameter array.

There may be multiple query collections for a view object—each holding rows for a unique row filter object (search conditions). Row set will try to identify an existing query collection by comparing the row filter values. If no query collection exists, a new instance is created and associated to the row set.

The next step is to build a parameter storage array, extracting the bind variable values defined for the view object instance. This array of bind parameter values will be used later in the execution cycle to supply the bind variable values appearing in the query. Once the basic preparation for query execution is over, the actual work horse is put into action—query collection.

Row set delegates the remaining tasks to query collection by invoking `executeQuery()` on it. Query collection will start the actual execution by invoking the call back `executeQueryForCollection(Object qc, Object[] params, int noUserParams)` method on the view object. This method can be overridden if you want to skip the default execution path in order to read data from alternate datasources. Query collection asks the view object for JDBC `PreparedStatement` for firing the SQL `SELECT` query. In response to this call, view object reads the relevant metadata and uses the native query builder to generate the native SQL query and returns it to the caller. The bind parameter values are set by the `bindParametersF orCollection(QueryCollection qc, Object params[], PreparedStatement stmt)` method in the view object.

Once all is set, query collection executes `PreparedStatement` and stores the result set for further action.

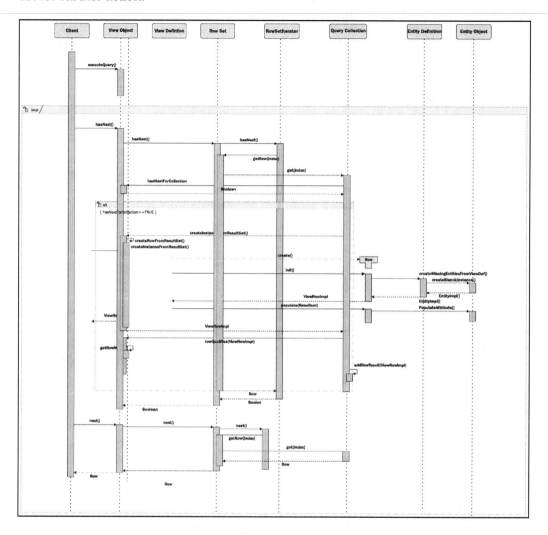

When a client starts iteration on the row set by calling `hasNext()` on the view object, the call reaches the row set iterator. Row set iterator will calculate the current row index and will call `getRow()` on row set. Row set delegates the call to query collection. Query collection will read the result set to check if it has any rows to process by calling `hasNextForCollection(Object qc)`. If this call returns `true`, query collection will issue a call back method `createRowFromResultSet(Object qc, ResultSet resultSet)` on the view object to create a row for holding the result.

The next step is to start the new row creation. The view object delegates the row creation job to the view object dentition object. The view object definition object creates a new row and initializes the row with the right storage mechanism. If the view object is based on updatable entity objects, blank entity instances will be created to back up the view row. For read-only or non-entity-based view objects, query collection will use a thin storage known as **view row storage**. Once the data storage is ready, the framework will populate the view row with attribute values from the result set. The newly created row will be added finally to the query collection after executing the in-memory criteria (if any) set on the view object.

When the client calls `vo.next()`, the call reaches query collection, and it returns the row which is added in the last step.

The preceding steps are repeated till client finishes the iteration. Note that data read sequences vary based on data fetch mode set for the view object. If the view object is configured to fetch all the rows at once, data retrieval from the database occurs as part of the query execution itself, without any need of explicit request from the client for the row set.

Summary

In this chapter, we discussed the general concepts behind view object, its architecture, and configurations. More specifically we discussed:

- Core features
- Defining and configuring view objects
- How to use view objects to query datasources in real life
- Runtime behavior of view objects

The story on view objects is not over yet. More exciting things are in queue. We will be covering more advanced concepts and examples on view objects in *Chapter 5, Advanced Concepts on Entity Objects and View Objects*.

5

Advanced Concepts on Entity Objects and View Objects

In the previous chapters we have discussed the entity objects, view objects, and their basic functionalities. This chapter will take you deeper into the internals of view objects and entity objects. In this chapter we will focus on the advanced concepts of these components along with code samples.

This chapter includes the following sections:

- Taking a closer look at entity objects
    - i.   Lifecycle of an entity object
    - ii. Some generic usage patterns with examples
- Taking a closer look at view objects
    - i.   Lifecycle of a view object
    - ii. Some generic usage patterns with examples
- Building business components dynamically

Taking a closer look at entity objects

We have discussed the basics of entity objects in *Chapter 2, Introduction to ADF Business Components*. It is now time for us to understand the concepts better. We will need to take a deep dive into entity objects in this section. Take a deep breath and prepare yourself.

Lifecycle of an entity object

In this section, we will learn what happens to the state of an entity object when you, as a developer, create, update or delete an entity instance, and commit the transaction later.

When a client starts a new business transaction or commits a business transaction, entity objects go through certain stages in the lifecycle. Let us explore the different states of an entity row when it participates in a typical business transaction.

- **Create a new entity row**: Consider the following code snippet that creates a department entity row:

```
//In application module implementation class
public void createDeptEntity() {

    //Get entity definition object
    EntityDefImpl departmentEODef = DepartmentEOImpl.
getDefinitionObject();

    //Create the blank entity instance,
    DepartmentEOImpl newDept =
        (DepartmentEOImpl)departmentEODef.createInstance2
        (this.getDBTransaction(), null);
    //newDept status is STATUS_NEW now

    newDept.setDepartmentId(1000);
    // newDept status is STATUS_NEW now
}
```

When you create an instance of an entity object by using the `createInsta nce2(DBTransaction,AttributeList)` method on the entity definition, its state is **New**. Entity objects in the New state will qualify in order to participate in the transaction.

- **Find and update an entity row**: Consider the following code snippet that finds an existing department entity row and updates it:

```
//In application module implementation class
public void findAndUpdateDeptEntity(Integer deptId) {
  //Create Key
  Key key = DepartmentEOImpl.createPrimaryKey(deptId);
  //Find the entity row
  DepartmentEOImpl deptRow =
        (DepartmentEOImpl)DepartmentEOImpl.
            getDefinitionObject().
                findByPrimaryKey(getDBTransaction(), key);
  //deptRow status is STATUS_UNMODIFIED now

  deptRow.setDepartmentName("IT Admin");
  //deptRow status become STATUS_MODIFIED now
  }
```

When a client invokes finder methods on an entity definition or on an entity based view object, the framework creates entity rows for each row from the database. The state of these entity rows will be marked as **Unmodified.** Later when the client modifies some attributes, the state is transitioned to **Modified** and they become eligible to participate in the transaction.

- **Remove an entity row**: Consider the following code snippet that finds a department entity row and removes it:

```
//In application module implementation class
public void findAndRemoveDeptEntity(Integer deptId) {
  //Create Key
  Key key = DepartmentEOImpl.createPrimaryKey(deptId);
  //Find the entity row
  DepartmentEOImpl deptRow =
      (DepartmentEOImpl)DepartmentEOImpl.
            getDefinitionObject().findByPrimaryKey
                (getDBTransaction(), key);
  //deptRow status is STATUS_UNMODIFIED now
  deptRow.remove();
  //deptRow status become STATUS_DELETED now
}
```

When a client calls the remove method on an entity object, entity state becomes **Deleted** and it will be added to the transaction cycle.

- **Commit the transaction:** The ADF framework commits the transaction when the client calls commit on the transaction object. An example is given as follows:

```
//In application module implementation class
public void commitTransaction(){
   getDBTransaction().commit();
}
```

The transaction commit cycle takes place in two phases, posting changes to the database and then committing the database transaction. On successful commit to the database, all the entities in the state New and Modified will be transitioned to Unmodified, and Deleted entity rows will be transitioned to the Dead state.

The following diagram depicts the entity row status at various stages of a business transaction:

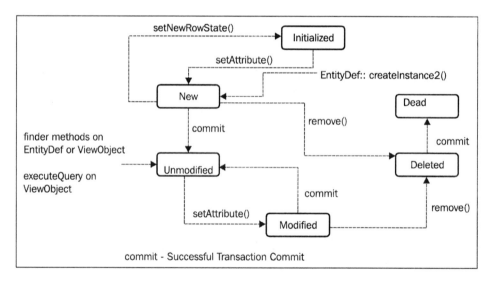

Reading the current state of an entity row

You can use the getEntityState() and the getPostState() methods on an entity object to access the current state of an entity row. These APIs are useful if you need to determine the status of the entity instance in your business logic and take actions accordingly.

- The getEntityState() method gives you the current state of an entity row with regard to the transaction

- The getPostState() method gives you the current state of an entity row with regard to the database

Once you post the changes to the database (without committing the transaction), this method behaves differently from getEntityState(). For example, when you create a new entity row, both getEntityState() and getPostState() on the entity row returns Entity.STATUS_NEW. If you post the new entity row (without committing the transaction) the getEntityState() returns Entity.STATUS_NEW and getPostState() returns Entity.STATUS_UNMODIFIED. Once the transaction is committed, both the calls return Entity.STATUS_UNMODIFIED. This is illustrated in the following code snippet:

```
//In application module implementation class
public void checkingEntityStates() {
  //Get defnition object
  EntityDefImpl departmentEODef = DepartmentEOImpl.
getDefinitionObject();
  //Create the entiy instance in the current transaction
  DepartmentEOImpl newDept1 =
       (DepartmentEOImpl)departmentEODef.
           createInstance2(this.getDBTransaction(), null);
  newDept1.setDepartmentId(1000);
  newDept1.setDepartmentName("IT Strategy");
  //newDept1.getPostState() - NEW
  //newDept1.getEntityState() - NEW

   //Post changes to DB
  getDBTransaction().postChanges();
  //newDept1.getPostState() - UNMODIFIED
  //newDept1.getEntityState() - NEW

   //Commit the Transaction
  getDBTransaction().commit();
  //newDept1.getPostState() - UNMODIFIED
  //newDept1.getEntityState() - UNMODIFIED

}
```

When you remove a new entity instance by calling remove() on it, getEntityState() returns Entity.STATUS_NEW because the entity instance is still new for the ongoing transaction. The getPostState() returns Entity.STATUS_DEAD.

When you remove an existing entity instance by calling remove() on it, both getEntityState() and getPostState() returns Entity.STATUS_DELETED. If you post the deleted entity row (without committing the transaction) the getEntityState() returns Entity.STATUS_DELETED and getPostState() returns Entity.STATUS_DEAD. Once the transaction is committed, both the calls return Entity.STATUS_DEAD.

Reading the originally retrieved attribute value

There are use cases where you may want to read the originally retrieved values of the entity attributes in your business logic. For example, while updating the salary for an employee, you may want to validate whether the difference between the original and revised salary is within the allowed range.

If you need to read the originally retrieved value for an attribute in an entity, you can use either of the following:

- Call getAttribute(attrIndex, EntityImpl.ORIGINAL_VERSION) on an entity object. An example is shown as follows:

```
//In EmployeeEOImpl class
/**
 * Validation method for Salary hike.
 */
public boolean validateSalaryHike(BigDecimal newSalary) {
  //Gets the attribute index for'Salary'
  int attribIndex = EmployeeEOImpl.SALARY;
  //Read originally retrieved value of 'Salary'
  BigDecimal originalSlary = (BigDecimal)getAttribute(attribIndex,
EntityImpl.ORIGINAL_VERSION);
  //returns false if the revised slary is less
  if (newSalary.compareTo(originalSlary) > 0)
    return true;
  else
    return false;
}
```

- Call getPostedAttribute(int attribIndex) on an entity object. This is a protected method in the EntityImpl class, and cannot be accessed by a client unless you expose it through an overridden public method through a subclass.

Retrieving all entity instances in the cache

You can retrieve all entity instances in the cache for a specific definition, including the deleted entity rows, using the method `getAllEntityInstancesIterator()` on the entity definition instance. The following example illustrates the usage of this API. This example finds deleted instances of the `model.entity.DepartmentEO` entity type and returns the list to the caller. The returned list can be used by the client for summarizing the number of rows deleted by the business user.

```
//In application module implementation class
/**
 * Return the list of deleted department rows
 * @return
 */
public ArrayList<Entity> findDeletedEmployees() {
  //Get an iterator for stepping through instances
  //of Entities of specific type
  //Iterator iterator
  EntityDefImpl.findDefObject("model.entity.DepartmentEO").
    getAllEntityInstancesIterator(getDBTransaction());
  ArrayList<Entity> deletedList = new ArrayList<Entity>();
  //Steps through each instance in cache
  //and indentify the deleted rows
  while (iterator.hasNext()) {
    EntityImpl eo = (EntityImpl)iterator.next();
    if (eo.getEntityState() == Entity.STATUS_DELETED) {
      deletedList.add(eo);
    }
  }
  return deletedList;
}
```

Lifecycle callback methods of an entity object

An ADF entity object includes a variety of callback methods for monitoring changes in the lifecycle of entity rows. These callback methods are defined on the base entity object implementation class (`oracle.jbo.server.EntityImpl`) which can be overridden to add your custom logic, if needed. To customize the default behaviour of an entity object, it is worth knowing these lifecycle callback methods and the sequence in which they are called during the entity lifecycle. This section discusses this topic.

The following diagram depicts the sequence of a lifecycle callback for an entity object; right from the entity row creation to the commitment of the transaction.

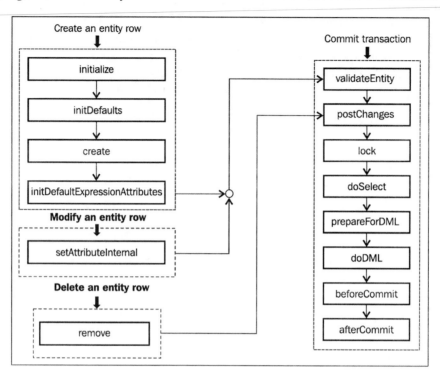

Let us discuss these methods in detail.

What happens when a new entity instance is created?

When a client creates a new entity row, the framework invokes the following methods on the entity instance to initialize the entity row. The methods are listed in the sequence as they are invoked at runtime.

- `EntityImpl::initialize()`: When you create a new entity instance, under the cover, the framework performs the basic initialization tasks for the new instance. After running the mandatory initialization activities, the framework invokes `initialize()` on the entity instance. You can override this method if you want to add initialization logic for the new entity row that needs to be executed early in the lifecycle, even before the framework starts defaulting attribute values.

- `EntityImpl::initDefaults()`: This method initializes default values for a newly created entity row using the default **static** value settings from the entity definition. The defaulting attribute values using Groovy expressions are handled later in the cycle by the `initDefaultExpressionAttributes()` method.

  This is also invoked when the client calls `refresh(int refMode)` on a new entity row to undo the changes. We will discuss more about `EntityImpl::refresh(int)` later, under the section entitled *Refreshing entity rows, forgetting the changes*.

- `EntityImpl:: create(AttributeList nameValuePair)`: This method takes an attribute list for initializing the newly created row. The framework uses this method to pass foreign key values to the newly created child entity row if it is part of composition association. You can override this method to supply default values to attributes while creating a new entity row. For example, developers typically override this method to add custom logic to initialize a primary key with a value from the database sequence. The following is an example that initialized the `EmployeeId` attribute with a value from the database sequence:

```
//In EmployeeEOImpl(entity implementation class)
@Override
public void create(AttributeList attributeList) {
   super.create(attributeList);
   SequenceImpl seq = new SequenceImpl
     ("EMP_TABLE_SEQ", getDBTransaction());
   Integer seqNextval = seq.getSequenceNumber().intValue();
   setEmployeeId(seqNextval);
}
```

- `EntityImpl::initDefaultExpressionAttributes(AttributeList nameValuePair)`: This method initializes an entity row with values evaluated from expressions that are defined on the attributes. Remember that all the static value defaulting is handled in `EntityImpl::initDefaults()`.

  You should override this method for programmatically setting default values for attributes or for executing some initialization code, which you want to fire when the row is first created, as well as when a modified row is refreshed back to initialized status by calling `refresh(int refMode)` on it. As the method `initDefaultExpressionAttributes()` is invoked towards the end of the initialization cycle after executing the `initDefaults` and `create` methods, this is the safest place to add any custom logic for programmatically setting the default attribute values.

What is the right method to programmatically initialize attributes in an entity object?

The right place to add your programmatic logic for initializing entity attributes is in the overridden `initDefaultExpressionAttrib utes(AttributeList nameValuePair)` method in your entity implementation class. This has the following advantages:

- This method is invoked after `initDefaults()`. Note that `initDefaults()` handles defaulting static values while `initDefaultExpressionAttributes()` handles defaulting dynamic Groovy expression default values. So your initialization logic can safely refer the attributes initialized through both Groovy and static values.

- Another advantage is that when you revert a new row back to the Initialized state by calling `refresh(int refMode)` on it, the entity object's `initDefaultExpressionAttributes()` method is invoked, but not its `create()` method. On a related note, when you call `refresh()` on a new row to revert the changes done on attributes, make sure you are not passing REFRESH_REMOVE_NEW_ROWS or REFRESH_FORGET_NEW_ ROWS to the `refresh()` method.

See the section *Refreshing entity rows, forgetting the changes* for more details on the refresh flags.

What happens when an entity instance is modified or removed?

Once the basic initialization is done, an entity row is sent back to the client for use. The following methods are invoked for an entity row in response to the update by the client:

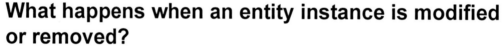

- `EntityImpl::setAttributeInternal(int index, Object val)`: This method is the global entry point for all attribute updates for an entity row. This method is called to set an attribute value after validating the value against declarative validators set for that attribute. The framework adds the entity row to the current transaction whenever the client modifies any values. If you need a quick brush-up on declarative validation support for entities, refer back to the section entitled *Adding validation* in *Chapter 3, Entity Objects*.

- `EntityImpl::remove()`: This method is invoked when a client calls `remove()` on an entity instance. The framework marks the row for deletion and adds it to the transaction listener list. You can override this method to add your own business logic for the remove operation. The following example overrides the `remove()` method to add some custom business checks before allowing the removal of the row:

```
public class EmployeeEOImpl extends EntityImpl {
//Other methods go here

//The remove() method is overridden to check whether
//the row is in use by other applications
@Override

public void remove() {
   if (isInUseByOtherApps())
     super.remove();
   else
     throw new JboException(
            "Row is in use by another system");
  }
}
```

What happens when the transaction is committed?

Modifying an entity row, or removing an existing row will mark the current transaction as dirty and the affected rows will be added to the transaction's pending change list. Later when a client commits the transaction, the framework invokes the following methods on entity instances from the pending changes list to post changes to the database.

- `EntityImpl::validateEntity()`: This method validates the current entity row as well as all the child entities linked through composition association. This method is triggered by the framework for row currency (current row) change and for committing the transaction. You may rarely override this method in order to control the execution of entity validation. Note that ADF provides better declarative mechanisms to control the validation execution for an entity object, which is explained in *Chapter 3, Entity Objects*, in the section entitled *Adding validation*.

- `EntityImpl::postChanges(TransactionEvent e)`: This method controls the data post cycle for the current entity row as well as for all child entity rows linked through a composition association. Depending on the state of this entity object, this method calls the following operations in sequence to carry out the transaction post cycle: `lock`, `preprareForDML`, and `doDML`.

  - `EntityImpl::lock()`: This method locks the row by calling `doSelect(lock)` with the lock flag set to true. If the row is new or already locked by this entity object, or if the transaction's locking mode is `None`, then this method does not do anything at runtime.

  - `EntityImpl::doSelect(boolean lock)`: This method performs **SELECT** or **SELECT FOR UPDATE** processing for the current row depending upon the lock flag value. This method is invoked by the framework in the following scenarios:

    i. When the framework calls `lock()` on the current row, this method is invoked with the lock flag set as true. In the rest of the cases, that we discussed below, the lock flag would be false.

    ii. When a client calls `findByPrimaryKey` on an entity definition to find a specific entity row.

    iii. When a client calls `findByKey()` on a view object.

    iv. When a client tries to read an attribute which is missing from the entity cache.

    v. When a client tries to update an attribute which is missing from the entity cache.

    vi. When a client calls `refresh()` on a row to refresh with the database.

  - `EntityImpl::prepareForDML(int operation, TransactionEvent e)`: As the name suggests, this method is invoked before posting changes to the database which allows subclasses to modify any attributes on this entity before posting changes to the database.

    - In the case of batch mode, the modified entities in a transaction are posted in two steps. In the first step, the transaction manager notifies all entities with `prepareForDML()` so that entities can make changes to any attributes, take for example, a history column that needs to be updated right before a database update occurs. Then the `doDML()` is called on the entities to execute the **DML** statements.

- ◦ In the case of non-batch mode, the transaction manager invokes the postChanges() method on the entity. The postChanges() in turn invokes prepareForDML() followed by doDML(). If you want to assign programmatic defaults for entity object attribute values before a row is saved, override the prepareForDML() method and call the appropriate attribute setter methods to populate the derived attribute values.

  - ◦ EntityImpl::doDML(int operation, TransactionEvent e): This method performs insert, update, and delete processing for the row. This uses appropriate SQL builder implementation for building the java.sql.PreparedStatement. For insert and update operations, the DML statement will only set the values that have been modified for this transaction. Other attributes do not participate in the DML. Once PreparedStatement is generated for the entity row, the next step is to bind the PreparedStatement with values to be inserted or updated. After everything is set, this method executes the JDBC statement. This method can be overridden to provide custom logic for processing modified entity rows. For example, if you want an entity object to update a non-database data source, then you should override this method and provide the necessary implementation.

- EntityImpl::beforeCommit(TransactionEvent e): This method is invoked on each entity row participating in the transaction after the changes have been posted to the database, but before committing the transaction to the database. This method can be overridden to invoke stored procedures based on business validation logic or a similar mechanism which requires updated data in the database.

 If the overridden beforeCommit() logic throws a ValidationException when you commit the transaction, then it is recommended to set the jbo.txn. handleafterpostexc property to true in the application module configuration. This property tells the framework to automatically handle the rolling back of the other entity objects that may have already successfully posted to the database (but not yet committed).

- EntityImpl::afterCommit(TransactionEvent e): This method is invoked on each entity row in the transaction's pending changes list after the changes have been successfully committed to the database. This method can be overridden to perform custom processing such as sending a notification or triggering another service on a successful commit of a row to the database.

Building programmatically managed entity objects

When you build database-centric ADF applications, the out of the box features offered by entity objects really eases the implementation. However, there are business use case scenarios where these applications may need to read and write data using non-conventional data sources such as web services or third party APIs. If you want to use ADF entity objects for the purpose of updating data from alternative data sources, you will need to build programmatic entity objects by overriding lifecycle callback methods. In this section, we will take a look at the implementation of a programmatic entity object.

To build a programmatically managed entity object, perform the following steps:

1. Right-click on the model project and select **New | New Entity Object**.

2. In the **Create Entity Object** wizard, enter the name and package for the entity.

3. Select the data source as **Database Schema Object** and deselect the **Existing Objects** option. Click on **Next** to continue. If the IDE asks if you want to use the entity object's name as the name of the schema object, click on **NO** and proceed.

4. In the **Attributes** page, enter the attribute definitions and click on **Next**.

5. In the **Java** page of the **Create Entity Object** wizard, select the option to **Generate Entity Object** class and include the **Accessors** and **Data Manipulation Methods** for the entity object class. Click on **Finish** to generate the entity definition. Select the **Java** implementation for the entity in the model project, and override the lifecycle callback methods as we discussed earlier.

The following example illustrates a programmatically managed entity object implementation class that uses stored procedures to post changes to the database. This example overrides doSelect(boolean lock) and doDML(int operation, TransactionEvent e) methods from the base EntityImpl. The reason for selecting these methods is that these are the two methods which interact with the database. As we discussed earlier, doSelect() is invoked when the framework tries to lock an entity row before posting changes to the database, and also when a client calls the finder method for reading an entity row using key attributes. The method doDML() is invoked to post changes to the database during the transaction post cycle.

```
//Programmatically managed entity implementation
//It uses PLSQL procedure for Insert, Update and Delete
public class DepartmentProgrammaticEOImpl extends EntityImpl{
```

```
/**
 * Override the default doSelect processing
 * to invoke an appropriate stored procedure
 * instead of performing the default one.
 * @param lock
 */
@Override
protected void doSelect(boolean lock) {
  if (lock) {
    callLockProcedureAndCheckForRowInconsistency();
  } else {
    callSelectProcedure();
  }
}


/**
 * Custom DML update/insert/delete logic here.
 * @param operation the operation type
 * @param e the transaction event
 */
@Override
protected void doDML(int operation, TransactionEvent e) {
  /**
   * Call appropriate stored proc, checking operation flag set for
entity tow
   */
  if (operation == DML_INSERT)
      //This method invokes PLSQL procedure for Insertion
    callInsertProcedure(e);
  else if (operation == DML_UPDATE)
      //This method invokes PLSQL procedure for Update
    callUpdateProcedure(e);
  else if (operation == DML_DELETE)
      //This method invokes PLSQL procedure for Delete
    callDeleteProcedure(e);
 }

//Other methods and variables go here
}
```

We are not giving the full source code of the programmatically managed entity object here. The working examples for programmatic entity objects can be found in the example code that we mentioned at the beginning of this book, in the *Preface* section. To access the programmatic entity object sample in the example code, open the `ADFDevGuideCh5HRModel` workspace in JDeveloper and look for `DepartmentProgrammaticEO` in the `Model` project.

Generating a database independent unique ID

You can use database sequences to automatically generate primary key values for a newly created entity row. This works for most of the applications. However, if you are looking for a database independent mechanism to generate unique IDs across different databases, then you can use the unique ID generation feature provided by ADF middle tier.

How does unique ID sequencing work

The unique ID generation mechanism provided by ADF is facilitated by `oracle.jbo.server.uniqueid.RowIdAM`, a row ID generator application module that comes with the framework. The `RowIdAM` uses a database table `S_ROW_ID` to track the unique identifier values. When a client asks for a unique ID, the `RowIdAM` checks the cache and returns the next identifier value from the cache, if it is available. Otherwise, a database query is fired to fetch the identifier value. The generator logic looks for the `NEXT_ID` column in the `S_ROW_ID` table, which contains the value of the next available identifier. After returning an identifier, the `NEXT_ID` column value is incremented.

Using middle tier generated unique keys

To use middle tier generated unique keys for primary keys, run the following script that is found in your JDeveloper installation on a database to generate the required database objects:

```
<JDeveloperHome>/oracle_common/modules/oracle.adf.model_11.1.1/bin/
bc4jUniqueId.sql
```

Once the database is set up with the required object, go to the **Application Resources** panel in the **Application Navigator** window and define a new database connection named `ROWIDAM_DB` and point it to the database where you ran the SQL script in the previous step.

To assign the default value for a numeric primary key attribute, select the entity objects in the overview editor and then select the attribute. Expand the **Value** tab in the property inspector window, select **Expression** as the default value type and then enter the following Groovy expression as the default value: `oracle.jbo.server. uniqueid.UniqueIdHelper.nextId`.

 The unique ID returned by the expression `oracle.jbo. server.uniqueid.UniqueIdHelper.nextId` is of type `java.math.BigDecimal`.

If you want to force the unique ID mechanism to use a custom data source name instead of the default name (`ROWIDAM_DB`), then add the following property initializing logic in a static initialization block somewhere in the application where it will be called before any unique ID is requested. Alternatively, you can use a `ServletContextListener` for executing this initialization block.

```
if (PropertyDefaultContext.getInstance().getDirect(
PropertyMetadata.ENV_ROWID_AM_DS_NAME.pName) == null){
    PropertyDefaultContext.getInstance().setDirect(
    PropertyMetadata.ENV_ROWID_AM_DS_NAME.pName,
    "java:comp/env/jdbc/YourDatasourceDS");
}
```

You can set the previous property using a Java system property named `jbo.rowid_am_datasource_name`, where its value is the name of a JNDI JDBC data source, for example, `jdbc/YourDatasourceDS` or `java:comp/env/jdbc/YourDatasourceDS`.

Refreshing entity rows, forgetting the changes

When you work on *undo* features for an enterprise application, a very common requirement may be the ability to roll back changes performed on a specific set of rows without rolling back the entire transaction. The ADF entity object comes with out of the box support for such use cases.

You can call `refresh(int refreshFlag)` on an entity row to restore the entity-mapped attributes to original values. The refresh behaviour of this method is controlled by the flag or combination of flags passed as a parameter to this method. The refresh flags available in the `Row` interface are as follows:

- `REFRESH_WITH_DB_FORGET_CHANGES`: The latest data from the database replaces the data in the row regardless of the changes done on the row. The newly created rows are reverted back to blank by default. If this flag is used in combination with `REFRESH_REMOVE_NEW_ROWS`, then new rows are removed.

- `REFRESH_WITH_DB_ONLY_IF_UNCHANGED`: The latest data from the database replaces data in the unmodified row, leaving the modified or the new row as it is. If this flag is used in combination with `REFRESH_REMOVE_NEW_ROWS`, then the new rows are removed.

- `REFRESH_UNDO_CHANGES`: The latest data from the database replaces data in the unmodified row. The modified rows' attribute values are reverted back to their original values at the beginning of the current transaction. The newly created rows revert back to blank by default. If this flag is used in combination with `REFRESH_REMOVE_NEW_ROWS`, then new rows are removed. When in the `REFRESH_UNDO_CHANGES` mode, the entity row remains in its previous state even after it is refreshed.

The following flags are typically used in combination with the previously discussed flags:

- `REFRESH_REMOVE_NEW_ROWS`: The new rows are removed during refresh. Typically this flag is used in combination with other refresh flags using a bitwise OR operator.

- `REFRESH_FORGET_NEW_ROWS`: The new rows are dead during refresh. Typically, this flag is used in combination with other refresh flags using a bitwise OR operator.

- `REFRESH_CONTAINEES`: This mode causes a `refresh(int refreshFlag)` call on its child entity rows with the same refresh flags. Typically, this flag is used in combination with other refresh flags using a bitwise OR operator.

For example, consider the following code snippet. This method reverts the department row and its child employee rows to the initial state by calling `refresh()` with the following flag combination: `Row.REFRESH_WITH_DB_FORGET_CHANGES` and `Row.REFRESH_CONTAINEES`.

```
//In application module implementation class
/**
 * This method revert department row and its containees
 * to initial state
```

```
 * @param deptId
 */
public void revertDepartmentRowAndContainees(int deptId) {
  ViewObject vo = findViewObject("Departments");
  Key k = new Key(new Object[] { deptId });
  //Return the the element matches with Key
  Row deptRow = vo.findByKey(k, 1)[0];
  //Revert dept row and it's child employee rows
  deptRow.refresh(Row.REFRESH_WITH_DB_FORGET_CHANGES | Row.REFRESH_
CONTAINEES);
}
```

Building custom history types

While discussing entity objects in *Chapter 3, Entity Objects*, we had a glance at the history types shipped with JDeveloper. Though the default types offered by ADF are good enough to meet most of the generic requirements, sometimes you will need to create custom history types to track specific changes in your business data. In this section, you will learn to create custom history types and their usage. Note that the creation of custom history types involves the following three parts:

- Building a custom history type
- Implementing logic in the desired entity implementation class for returning an appropriate value for the history type
- Assigning the history type to the desired attribute in the entity definition

To create a history type, perform the following steps:

1. Go to the main menu, select **Tools | Preferences**. In the **Preferences** dialog window, expand the **ADF Business Components** section and then select **History Types**.

2. On the **History Type** page, select **New**. In the **New History Type** dialog window, enter **History Type Id** and **Display String** for the new history type. The **Type Id** must be an integer between 11 and 126. Click on **OK** to save the definition.

3. Once the basic configuration is done, open the entity implementation class for which you want to use the new history type, and provide implementation for the new history type by overriding the method `getHistoryContextForA ttribute(AttributeDefImpl attr)` in the entity implementation class. The framework will call this method to get the value for the history type enabled attributes before posting changes to the database.

4. The last step is to mark the desired attribute in the entity object as a history type. To do this, select the desired attribute in the overview editor of the entity object and choose the custom history type that you defined using the **Track Change History** drop-down list. Save the changes.

For example, consider an airline reservation system that tracks bookings done by a booking agent along with the city where the agent is operating. Instead of asking the booking agent to enter the city for each booking he or she makes, let us make the application to do this job. To do this, build a new history type, `LoggedInCity` as we discussed earlier. Now select the entity object that posts booking data to the database. This example uses the **BookingEO** entity object for handling booking transactions. Along with booking data, it contains an attribute to hold the agent city name. Open the Java implementation class for the **BookingEO** entity and override the `getHistoryContextForAttribute()` method.

The following code snippet illustrates the implementation of the method `getHistoryContextForAttribute` for the `LoggedInCity` history type. Note that the value set for `LOGGED_IN_CITY_HISTORY_TYPE` must be the same as the **Type Id** that you specified while creating the history type.

```
//In Entity Implementation class

// Type Id for LoggedInCity history type
public final int LOGGED_IN_CITY_HISTORY_TYPE = 11;

@Override
protected Object getHistoryContextForAttribute(AttributeDefImpl attr)
{
//Custom history type, which return logged in city
//for the user
   if (attr.getHistoryKind() == LOGGED_IN_CITY_HISTORY_TYPE) {

//return business city for the logged in user
//The following logic assumes the user profile object is
// holding city information for the user.
      return ADFContext.getCurrent().
            getSecurityContext().getUserProfile().
            getBusinessCity();
   }
   return super.getHistoryContextForAttribute(attr);
}
```

As the last step in this example, select the `City` attribute in the **BookingEO** and mark it as the **LoggedInCity** history type. To do this, select the attribute in the overview editor. In the **Details** tab, click on the **Track Change History** drop-down list and choose **LoggedInCity**.

During runtime, when you commit the transaction or post changes to the database, the framework will invoke the overridden `getHistoryContextForAttribute()` method and will use the return value in order to populate the history enabled attributes as appropriate.

Taking a closer look at view objects

In this section, we will explore the advanced concepts in view objects and features that have not been discussed in *Chapter 4, Introducing View Objects*. We will start by discussing lifecycle callback methods for a view object. As we move forward in this section, we will discuss some advanced usage patterns for view objects with examples.

Lifecycle callback methods of a view object

The ADF view object component includes a variety of callback methods for executing the query and for managing the result set. These callback methods are defined on the base view object implementation class which can be optionally overridden to add custom logic. The following diagram depicts the sequence of the lifecycle callback for a view object.

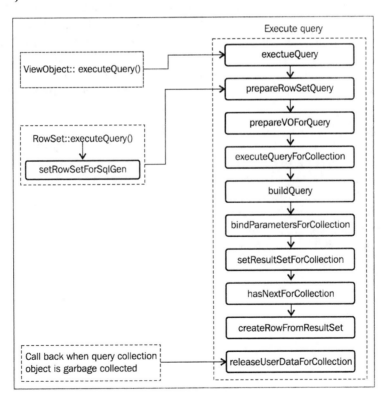

What happens when a client invokes executeQuery() on a view object instance?

When a client invokes executeQuery() on the view object the following methods defined on the view object are engaged at various stages of query execution:

- ViewObjectImpl::executeQuery(): This method is invoked when a client calls executeQuery() on the view object. This method in turn engages the default row set for the view object in the query execution cycle, and delegates the call for further processing.

- ViewObjectImpl::prepareRowSetForQuery(ViewRowSetImpl vrs): This method prepares the row set for query execution. If you need to assign bind variable values or modify the WHERE clause conditionally, just before executing the query for a specific row set, then this is the method where you can hook your custom code. This method also gets executed before the count query methods such as getQueryHitCount() and getCappedQueryHitCount(). The count queries are typically used by UI components such as tables or tree tables to size their scroll bar.

- ViewObjectImpl::prepareVOForQuery(): This method prepares the view object for build queries. If you need to assign bind variable values or modify the WHERE clause conditionally, just before executing the query for a view object, then this is the method where you can hook your custom code. This method is called from prepareRowSetForQuery(). Logically, you will override this method if you want to alter the query or to set bind variable values at the view object level, which needs to be reflected in all containing row sets.

- ViewObjectImpl::executeQueryForCollection(Object qc, Object[] params, int noUserParams): This method is invoked right before the row set starts executing the query. If this method is overridden, the custom logic will be applied to all row sets owned by this view object. In contrast, if the user overrides the view object's executeQuery(), then the custom logic in it applies only when the user calls executeQuery() on the view object. In other words, if a client calls executeQuery() on secondary row sets, then the framework will not engage the executeQuery() method during query executions.

Note that you should not use the `ViewObjectImpl::` `executeQueryForCollection()` method to alter the bind variable value or modify queries at runtime, instead you must use either `prepareRowSetForQuery()` or `prepareVOForQuery()` for the same. This is because the framework extracts the bind variable values before calling `executeQueryForCollection()` at runtime, and also this method will never get engaged with count queries such as `getQueryHitCount()` and `getCappedQueryHitCount()`. So your custom logic will not be considered in count queries.

- `ViewObjectImpl::buildQuery (int noUserParams, boolean forRowCount)`: This method builds the native SQL statement. A view object's query statement is normally built from various clauses, such as SELECT, FROM, WHERE, and ORDER BY that you set for a view object. However, an application can bypass this mechanism either by supplying a user defined query at design time and selecting an expert mode for the view object or by calling `setQuery()` on a view object instance at runtime. While generating the query, the framework also provides database specific interpretation for range paging, view criteria, and effective dated attributes.

- `ViewObjectImpl::bindParametersForCollection(QueryCollection qc, Object[] params, PreparedStatement stm)`: This method binds parameter values for the SQL statement at runtime. This includes bind parameters appearing in the query statement as well as the range paging parameters supplied by the framework.

- `ViewObjectImpl::setResultSetForCollection(Object qc, ResultSet rs)`: This method is responsible for storing results of query execution for further processing. By default, the result set is stored in the corresponding query collection object.

- `ViewObjectImpl::hasNextForCollection(Object qc)`: This method is invoked when a client starts to iterate over the rows set by calling `hasNext()` on the row set iterator. This method returns `true` if there are more rows in the query result.

- `ViewObjectImpl::createRowFromResultSet(Object iqc, ResultSet resultSet)`: This method creates a view row instance from the query result. The new view rows are created when the client traverses through the result set.

- `ViewObjectImpl::releaseUserDataForCollection (Object qc, Object data)`: This is a callback method which can be overridden to add some resource cleanup. Runtime invokes this method when the query collection object for the row set is garbage collected.

Note that these methods are invoked in the same sequence as previously listed, during the query execution of a view object.

Count queries in a view object

A view object also exposes APIs to find total records returned by the query. This is used by many clients in different scenarios. For example, when a web page displays data from a view object through a UI table component, the table component may issue a count query to size its scroll bar. The view object exposes multiple methods for finding the row count. Let us take a quick look at these before winding up our discussion on lifecycle methods for a view object.

- `ViewObjectImpl::getRowCount()`: This method fetches all the rows from the database and then counts each row to find the total row count. This has a performance overhead if the rows are large in number.

- `ViewObjectImpl::getQueryHitCount(ViewRowSetImpl viewRowSet)`: This method executes the count query on the database to return the row count for each invocation by the client.

- `ViewObjectImpl::getEstimatedRowCount()`: This method finds the row count by calling `getQueryHitCount()` for the first invocation. Once the row count is read from the database, the framework keeps the estimated row count up-to-date as rows are inserted and removed. So the second call from the client does not result in a fresh database query. This is preferred over the first two methods to find the total number of rows.

- `ViewObjectImpl::getCappedQueryHitCount(ViewRowSetImpl viewRowSet, oracle.jbo.Row[] masterRows, long oldCap, long cap)`: The count query could be very expensive in some scenarios, for example, if the number of records in the database is huge. This method provides a cap argument to the count query so that the count query generated at runtime has a special clause to limit the number of rows scanned.

Building programmatically managed view objects

If your view objects need to read data from a custom data source, and you still want to leverage the declarative features offered by view objects then you can build a programmatic view object by overriding the default lifecycle callback method for populating the row set with data from the custom data source.

To learn more about building programmatic view objects, refer to the topic *Using Programmatic View Objects for Alternative Data Sources* in *Oracle Fusion Middleware Fusion Developer's Guide for Oracle Application Development Framework*. To access the documentation go to `http://www.oracle.com/technetwork/developer-tools/jdev/documentation/index.html` and navigate to **Oracle JDeveloper and ADF Documentation Library | Fusion Developer's Guide**. Use the **Search** option to find specific topics.

To build a programmatic view object, you are supposed to override the following lifecycle callback methods in the corresponding view object implementation java class: `executeQueryForCollection`, `hasNextForCollection`, `createRowFromResultSet`, `getQueryHitCount`, `getCappedQueryHitCount`, and `releaseUserDataForCollection`. As we have discussed these methods in the last section, we are not repeating the same here.

Working examples for the programmatic view object can be found in the example code that we mentioned at the beginning of this book, in the *Preface* section. To access the programmatic view object sample in the example code, open the `ADFDevGuideCh5HRModel` workspace in JDeveloper and look for `DepartmentProgrammaticVO` in the `Model` project.

Another example that uses a programmatic view object backed up by a programmatic entity object can be found in the `ProgrammaticallyManagedBCSample` folder. This uses a simple Java class as the data source. To access the source, open the `ProgrammaticallyManagedBCSample` workspace in JDeveloper and look for `ProgrammaticallyManagedEmployeeEO` and `ProgrammaticallyManagedEmployeeVO` in the `Model` project.

Intercepting query generation for view criteria

The view object allows you to hook custom codes to intercept the default query generation logic at runtime for applied view criteria. There are multiple ways to hook your query customization logic, as follows:

- Using a custom view criteria adapter for the view object
- **Overriding** `getViewCriteriaClause(boolean forQuery)` or `getCriteriaItemClause(ViewCriteriaItem vci)` in the view object implementation class

Let us take a closer look at these techniques.

Using a custom view criteria adapter

You may use this feature to override the default SQL WHERE clause generation logic provided by the framework for the view criteria applied on a view object. When you execute a view object after applying one or more view criteria, the framework uses oracle.jbo.server.CriteriaAdapterImpl to interpret the applied view criteria and convert them to WHERE clauses at runtime. You can subclass CriteriaAdapterImpl to return a customized WHERE clause. The following code snippet illustrates a custom CustomCriteriaAdapter implementation. This example generates a special WHERE clause fragment for view criteria with the name INTERNAL_ SECURITY_VC. This approach is commonly used for adding custom security clauses to the view objects.

```
//Custom CriteriaAdapter implementation
public class CustomCriteriaAdapterImpl extends
    CriteriaAdapterImpl implements CriteriaAdapter {

    @Override
    public String getCriteriaClause(ViewCriteria criteria) {
        String clause = super.getCriteriaClause(criteria);
        String vcName = criteria.getName();
        //INTERNAL_SECURITY_VC' is a custom marker VC
        //without any rows
        //This method generates '1<>1' clause if the user
        //is not logged in and '1=1' in all other cases
        if (vcName.startsWith("INTERNAL_SECURITY_VC") &&
            !criteria.isCriteriaForRowMatch()) {
            String secPredicate = getDataSecurityWhereClause
                (criteria);
            return secPredicate;
        }
        return clause;
    }

    private String getDataSecurityWhereClause(ViewCriteria criteria) {
        if (ADFContext.getCurrent().
            getSecurityContext().isAuthenticated())
            return "1 = 1";
        else
            return "1 <> 1";
    }

}
```

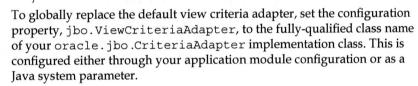

To return your own `oracle.jbo.CriteriaAdapter` implementation, override the `getCriteriaAdapter()` method in the view object implementation class and return the desired `CriteriaAdapter` implementation as shown in the following example:

```
//In view object implementation class

@Override
public CriteriaAdapter getCriteriaAdapter() {

// CustomCriteriaAdapterImpl extends
CriteriaAdapterImpl
  CustomCriteriaAdapterImpl customCriteriaAdapterImpl =
new CustomCriteriaAdapterImpl();
  return customCriteriaAdapterImpl;
}
```

To globally replace the default view criteria adapter, set the configuration property, `jbo.ViewCriteriaAdapter`, to the fully-qualified class name of your `oracle.jbo.CriteriaAdapter` implementation class. This is configured either through your application module configuration or as a Java system parameter.

Overriding getViewCriteriaClause(boolean forQuery) in the view object implementation class

This method builds the WHERE clause expression from the applied view criteria before executing the query. You may override this method if you want to alter the default query generation for a specific view object.

The following example overrides `getViewCriteriaClause` to set the UpperColumns flag for all view criteria that are applied on a view object. If this flag is true, the UPPER SQL operator will be applied to all CHAR/VARCHAR columns when the SQL WHERE clause is generated.

```
//In view object implementation class
/**
 * getViewCriteriaClause will be invoked for both database
 * query and in memory query mode. While overriding
 * developer will need to take care of this point.
 */
@Override
public String getViewCriteriaClause(boolean forQuery) {

//Identifies the applied view criteria for the current
```

```
  //execution mode and call setUpperColumns on each VC
    ViewCriteria[] vcs =
        getApplyViewCriterias(forQuery ? ViewCriteria.CRITERIA_MODE_QUERY
  : ViewCriteria.CRITERIA_MODE_CACHE);
    if (vcs != null && vcs.length > 0) {
      for (ViewCriteria vc : vcs) {
        if (!vc.isUpperColumns()) {
          vc.setUpperColumns(true);
        }
      }
    } return super.getViewCriteriaClause(forQuery);
}
```

Overriding getCriterialtemClause(ViewCriterialtem vci) in the view object implementation class

This method gets engaged when the framework tries to interpret each view criteria item present in the view criteria for building the WHERE clause fragments. This method can be overridden to return the custom WHERE clause fragments for a specific ViewCriteriaItem.

The following example overrides getCriteriaItemClause() for generating a special WHERE clause fragment for the DepartmentName view criteria item present in the DepartmentVC view criteria. The overridden method returns matching department rows as well as rows with null department names. The WHERE clause returned by this method looks like the following:

```
(( DeptEO.DEPARTMENT_NAME = :bindVarDeptNames ) OR ( DeptEO.
DEPARTMENT_NAME  IS NULL))

//In the view object implementation class
/**
 * getCriteriaItemClause is invoked for both database query
 * and in memory query mode. While overriding developer
 * will need to take care of this point.
 */

@Override
public String getCriteriaItemClause(ViewCriteriaItem vci) {
// This method generates custom WHERE clause for search
// on DepartmentName to return the matching columns as well
// NULL columns
  if (vci.getAttributeDef().getName().
      equals("DepartmentName") &&
      vci.getViewCriteria().getName().
```

```
        contains("DepartmentVC") &&
          hasBindVarValue(vci.getViewCriteria(),
            "bindVarDeptNames")) {
    String attrName = null;
      //Handle database query and in-memory query separately
    if (vci.getViewCriteria().isCriteriaForQuery()) {
      return getItemClauseForDatabaseUse(vci);
    } else {
      return getItemClauseForInMemoryUse(vci);
    }
  }
  return super.getCriteriaItemClause(vci);
}

/**
 * Custom WHERE clause fragment for database query
 */
protected String getItemClauseForDatabaseUse(ViewCriteriaItem vci) {
  String attrName = this.getEntityDef(0).getAliasName() +
      ".DEPARTMENT_NAME";
  return "((" + attrName + " = :bindVarDeptNames ) OR (" + attrName +
" IS NULL))";
}

protected String getItemClauseForInMemoryUse(ViewCriteriaItem vci) {
  String attrName = "DepartmentName";
  return "((" + attrName + " = :bindVarDeptNames ) OR (" + attrName +
" IS NULL))";
}

/**
 * Custom WHERE clause fragment for in-memory query
 */
private boolean hasBindVarValue(ViewCriteria vc, String varName) {
  VariableValueManager varValueMgr = vc.
      ensureVariableManager();
  return varValueMgr.hasVariableValue(varName);


}
```

Tips on overriding getViewCriteriaClause() and getCriteriaItemClause() in the view object implementation

The following tips may prove helpful when overriding `getViewCriteriaClause()` and `getCriteriaItemClause()` in a view object implementation:

- The view criteria callbacks `getCriteriaItemClause` and `getViewCriteriaClause` will be invoked only when the framework tries to build the WHERE clause for the very first execution of the query, or when the view criteria structure changes later which may affect the WHERE clause fragments. In all other cases, the framework reuses the already built WHERE clause. If you need to trigger the custom logic for each query execution, then hook your code by overriding `prepareRowSetForQuery()` in the view object implementation class. This is explained in the next section.

- When you override `getCriteriaItemClause()` and `getViewCriteriaClause()`, make sure the overridden method has logic for handling both the query on the database as well as in-memory. When a transient criteria item is present in the view criteria, the binding layer sets the criteria mode to both database and in-memory. When the model layer builds the clause, it does two passes, first as database and then as in-memory. The in-memory clause is evaluated after the rows are fetched. If the overridden method returns null or does not handle the in-memory filtering properly, then the rows fetched from first pass are disqualified and removed from the row set.

- When you check for specific view criteria names from these methods, check if the view criteria name contains a specific name (e.g `if(vcName.contains("SomeVCName")) {...}`) instead of applying an equality check. This is because when a view criteria is used for LOV filtering or in other internal processes, the framework creates a copy of the view criteria and sets a unique name by prefixing an internal text along with the criteria name. The previous suggestion will make your logic work in all scenarios.

Customizing the query at runtime

In the previous section, we have discussed various methods to customize the query generation for the view criteria applied on a view object. What if you want to alter the query or supply bind variable values at runtime for every query execution, irrespective of the applied view criteria. In this section, we will explore a couple of solutions for such scenarios.

Customizing the query for a row set

You can override prepareRowSetForQuery(ViewRowSetImpl vrs) in the view object implementation class to dynamically alter the query for a row set. This method is invoked when a client calls executeQuery() and count queries such as getQueryHitCount() and getCappedQueryHitCount() on a row set. This method can be overridden to programmatically assign bind variable values or to modify the WHERE clause, right before the query execution.

In the following example, we are setting the value for a bind variable value :bindVarDeptId if the query is executed for default row set of a view object.

```
//In view object implementation
public void prepareRowSetForQuery(ViewRowSetImpl vrs) {
  //Set the value for bind variable ':bindVarDeptId' only
//for default row set
  if(vrs.isDefaultRowSet()){
    vrs.setNamedWhereClauseParam(  "bindVarDeptId", getUserDeptId());
  }
  super.prepareRowSetForQuery(vrs);


}
```

Customizing the query for a view object

In previous section, we were talking about API for customizing the query for a specific row set in a view object. What if you want to alter the query at view object level so that changes would be available for all containing row sets? This section answers this question.

You can override the prepareVOForQuery() in the view object implementation class to dynamically alter the query set on a view object. This method is invoked during the query execution lifecycle of a view object. More precisely, this is called from the prepareRowSetForQuery() method that we discussed in the previous section.

Override this method to assign bind variable values or to modify the WHERE clause for a view object right on the fly just before the query execution. Note that when you alter the query for the view object instance, it will affect all containing row sets.

The following example appends the view criteria with the name LOC_CRITERIA to the view object on the fly in order to retrieve departments belonging to the logged-in user's location.

```
//In view object implementation class
@Override
public void prepareVOForQuery() {
```

```
super.prepareVOForQuery();
//Check if the LOC_CRITERIA is already applied on the VO
 //If yes, returns from this method
String[] vcnames = getViewCriteriaManager().
    getApplyViewCriteriaNames();
 if (vcnames != null){
  for (String name : vcnames) {
   if (name.equals("LOC_CRITERIA")) {
    return;
   }
  }
 }
 // The following code create LOC_CRITERIA
 //and applies it to the VO.
 //This view criteria hold a condition to read
 //department rows from logged-in user's location
ViewCriteria vc = createViewCriteria();
vc.setName("LOC_CRITERIA");
vc.setConjunction(ViewCriteria.VC_CONJ_AND);
ViewCriteriaRow vcr = vc.createViewCriteriaRow();
vc.insertRow(vcr);
ViewCriteriaItem vci =
    vcr.ensureCriteriaItem("LocationId");
vci.setOperator("=");
ViewCriteriaItemValue vciv = vci.getValues().get(0);
 //getLoggedInLocId() returns logged in user's location
vciv.setValue(getLoggedInLocId());
applyViewCriteria(vc, true);
}
```

Passing parameters to a SQL IN clause using oracle.jbo.domain.Array

Oracle ADF Business Components support passing arguments to a SQL IN clause using the `oracle.jbo.domain.Array` domain type. Of course, you can build the IN clause dynamically with comma delimited arguments. However, this is not considered as best practice from the performance angle. Passing values through a bind parameter improves the performance of query execution by avoiding the repeated parsing of the SQL. Let us explore a couple of implementations where `oracle.jbo.domain.Array` is used for passing multiple arguments to an IN clause.

Using oracle.jbo.domain.Array as a NamedWhereClauseParam value

The following example illustrates the usage of `oracle.jbo.domain.Array` for passing the parameter values to a SQL IN clause present in a SELECT statement. While initializing a bind variable of type `oracle.jbo.Array`, it is required to set up the proper context for the Array object that you are supplying as a value. Specifically, you must describe the column type and element type for the Array object when it is used as a bind variable value. The following are the details:

- The column type represents the database object name used for holding values from `oracle.jbo.Array`. Typically this would be a database **table** object. An example is given as follows:

  ```
  CREATE OR REPLACE TYPE "CHARTABLETYPE" AS TABLE OF VARCHAR2
  (4000);
  ```

- The element type represents the data type for Array members.

The following code method defined in an application module implementation illustrates the usage of `oracle.jbo.Array` as a bind variable value. The method `findDepartmentsForDepartmentNames(..)` used in this example appends SQL's WHERE clause that takes an Array typed named parameter to department view object. The Array object is used for passing departments' names to the query. You may also notice the code for setting context for the Array object in the method `getValueAsArray()`:

```
//In view object implementation class

/**
 * Finds the department rows for array of department names
 * @param deptNamesArray
 */
public void findDepartmentsForDepartmnetNames(String[] deptNamesArray)
{
  ViewObjectImpl deptVOImpl = getDepartments();
  //Define named parameter
  deptVOImpl.defineNamedWhereClauseParam("ArrayOfDeptNames", null,
null);
  //Set the Where clause that takes 'Array' typed
  //named parameter
  deptVOImpl.setWhereClause("DepartmentEO.DEPARTMENT_NAME MEMBER OF
CAST(:ArrayOfDeptNames AS CHARTABLETYPE)");
  //Set the parameter value
  deptVOImpl.setNamedWhereClauseParam("ArrayOfDeptNames", getValueAsAr
ray(deptNamesArray));
```

```
      deptVOImpl.executeQuery();
}

/**
 * This method converts string array to
 * oracle.jbo.domain.Array
 * @param deptArray
 * @return
 */
public Array getValueAsArray(String[] deptArray) {
  Array arr = null;
  try {

    arr = new Array(deptArray);
    HashMap context = new HashMap();
     //CHARTABLETYPE is DB object table of varchar2(4000)
     context.put(DomainContext.ELEMENT_SQL_NAME,
       "CHARTABLETYPE");
     context.put(DomainContext.ELEMENT_TYPE, String.class);
    arr.setContext(null, null, context);
  } catch (Exception ex) {
    ex.printStackTrace();
  }
  return arr;
}
```

Using oracle.jbo.domain.Array as a bind variable value for a view criteria item

The bind variable of type `oracle.jbo.domain.Array` can be used along with a view criteria item from a view criteria for passing multiple parameter values to the SQL WHERE clause fragments generated at runtime. However, as the usage of the Array object is not generic by nature, the default WHERE clause fragment generated by the framework for a view criteria item might not meet our requirement. Now, the solution is to override the default logic for generating a SQL WHERE clause fragment for a view criteria item by subclassing the view object implementation class.

To use the `oracle.jbo.domain.Array` parameter type for a view criteria item, you will need to perform the following steps on the view object:

1. Define a bind variable of the type `oracle.jbo.domain.Array`. When defining a bind variable, select the type as **Array**. In the property inspector window, set **Column Type** as the database object name that you defined for holding values from `oracle.jbo.Array`, and **Element Type** as the item type that you store in the Array object. The following screenshot displays this setting:

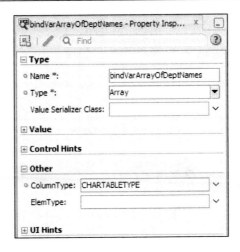

The **CHARTABLETYPE** used in this example is defined in the database as follows:

```
CREATE OR REPLACE TYPE  "CHARTABLETYPE"  AS TABLE OF
VARCHAR2(4000);
```

2. Create or edit the view criteria and specify the **Array** type bind variable as parameter for the desired view criteria item which is supposed to take multiple parameter values.

3. Generate the view object implementation Java class for the view object, if it does not exist. Open the view object implementation class and override the `getCriteriaItemClause(ViewCriteriaItem vci)` method to return the customized WHERE clause fragment which takes an Array typed bind variable as discussed in the following example.

The following example illustrates the usage of an Array typed bind variable parameter `bindVarArrayOfDeptNames` to pass the array of string values to the WHERE clause fragment for the criteria item `DepartmentName`.

```
//In view object implementation class
/**
 * Interpret the given ViewCriteriaItem and generate
 * a where clause fragment that takes Array typed bindvariable
 * @param vci
 * @return
 */
@Override
public String getCriteriaItemClause(ViewCriteriaItem vci) {
//Check for view criteria and view criteria item that needs
//special treatment to handle Array typed bind variable
```

```
          if (vci.getAttributeDef().
              getName().equals("DepartmentName") &&
               vci.getViewCriteria().getName().
                 contains("DepartmentVC")) {
      //Handle database query and in-memory query separately
          if (vci.getViewCriteria().
                   getRootViewCriteria().isCriteriaForQuery()) {
            return getINClauseForDatabaseUse(vci);
          } else {
            return getINClauseForCache(vci);
          }
        } else {
          return super.getCriteriaItemClause(vci);
        }

      }

      /**
       * Generates WHERE clause with Array for database query
       * @param vci
       * @return
       */
      protected String getINClauseForDatabaseUse(ViewCriteriaItem vci) {

        String whereCluase = "1=1";
        if (getbindVarArrayOfDeptNames() != null) {

          whereCluase =
              this.getEntityDef(0).getAliasName()
                + ".DEPARTMENT_NAME MEMBER OF "
                + "CAST(:bindVarArrayOfDeptNames AS CHARTABLETYPE)";
        }
        return whereCluase;
      }

      /**
       * Generates search clause for in memory query
       * @param vci
       * @return
       */
      protected String getINClauseForCache(ViewCriteriaItem vci) {
        String whereCluase = "1=1";
        return whereCluase;
      }
```

```
/**
 * Returns the variable value for bindVarArrayOfDeptNames.
 * return variable value for bindVarArrayOfDeptNames
 */
public Array getbindVarArrayOfDeptNames() {
  return (Array)ensureVariableManager().
    getVariableValue("bindVarArrayOfDeptNames");
}
```

The following method defined in an application module implementation illustrates how a client can use the view criteria that we defined in the previous example to filter rows returned by a view object:

```
//In application module implementation class
/**
 * Finds the department rows using VC for array of department
 * names
 * @param deptNamesArray
 */
public void findDepartmentsForDepartmnetNamesUsingVC(String[]
deptNamesArray) {
  ViewObjectImpl deptVOImpl = getDepartments();
  ViewCriteria deptVC = deptVOImpl.getViewCriteria("Department
VC");
  VariableValueManager vvm = deptVC.ensureVariableManager();
//The source for method getValueAsArray() is available
//in the previous example under 'Using oracle.jbo.domain.Array //
as a NamedWhereClauseParam value'
  Array arr = getValueAsArray(new
        String[]{"Administration","Marketing"});
  vvm.setVariableValue("bindVarArrayOfDeptNames", arr);
  deptVOImpl.applyViewCriteria(deptVC);
  deptVOImpl.executeQuery();
}
```

Defining a cascading list of values

We have learned the basic lessons on **list of values (LOV)** in *Chapter 4, Introducing View Objects*. While discussing the basics in the previous chapter, we deferred a couple of advanced concepts on LOV. It is time for us to explore them in detail.

In some scenarios, the list of values displayed for an LOV enabled attribute may change with the value specified for one or more attributes on the same row. In other words, the LOV needs to be refreshed whenever the value for dependency attributes change. The ADF Business Component framework supports such LOV definitions through a special type known as the **Cascading** (or **Dependent**) **LOV**.

Let us take an example to understand this concept better. Suppose you are working on a data model as shown in the following diagram:

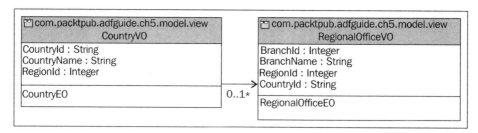

In this example, the regional office view object (**RegionalOfficeVO**) contains information about the branches in a country, and the country view object (**CountryVO**) stores a list of country names along with the region where each country belongs to. The use case requirement is to enable LOV for the **Countryid** attribute. This can be achieved by using **CountryVO** as the data source for the LOV and then following the normal LOV dentition technique that we learned in *Chapter 4, Introducing View Objects*. What if the customer wants to filter the **CountryName** attribute displayed in the LOV based on the **RegionId** attribute? In other words the country LOV UI components need to display countries belonging to a specific region alone at runtime. We may need to go for the dependent LOV technique for such cases. Let us see how to implement this in our example. In this example we will enable the `region` dependent LOV for the column **CountryId** in **RegionOfficeVO**. The initial steps for defining the cascading LOV are the same as for defining a normal LOV. We need to decide on the data source for the LOV, which is **CountryVO** in this example. The LOV enabled for **CountryId** in **RegionOfficeVO** is expected to display only those countries belonging to a specific region. We need to add a named view criteria on the LOV source view object as the next step to filter country details based on the **RegionId** set for the row.

To define the named view criteria on **CountryVO**, perform the following steps:

1. Double-click on the **CountryVO** view object to display the overview editor. In the overview editor, select the **Query** tab and click on the green plus icon to **create new view criteria**.

2. In the **Create View Criteria** dialog window, enter the view criteria name and then click on the **Add Item** button.

3. In the **Criteria Item** section, select the **RegionId** attribute and then select **Bind Variable** as the value for the operand field. To define a bind variable click on the green plus icon next to the **Parameter** field. In the **Bind Variable** window, enter the name and type for the bind variable. Once you finish defining the bind variable, the **Create View Criteria** window may look like the following screenshot. Click on **OK** to save changes.

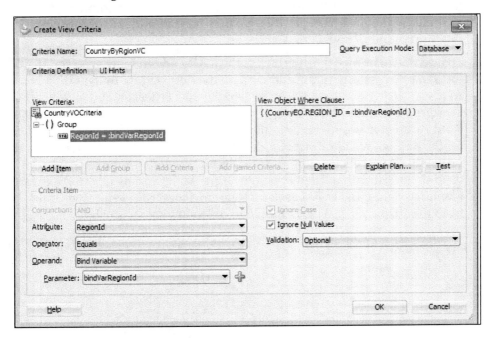

We have now added the required search condition on the data source view object. Next is to use this view object to enable the LOV on the **CountryId** attribute in **RegionalOfficeVO**.

To enable the cascading LOV for **CountryId** in **RegionalOfficeVO**, perform the following steps:

1. Double-click on **RegionalOfficeVO** to display the overview editor. In the overview editor, select the **CountryId** attribute, the attribute on which you want to enable the LOV, and then select the **List of Values** tab.

2. Click on the green plus icon displayed in the toolbar section of the **List of Values** table to add the LOV. In the **Create List of Values** dialog window, enter the **List of Values Name** and then proceed to define a data source for the LOV.

3. To link the data source for the LOV, click on the green plus icon button next to the **List Data Source** drop-down list. In the **View Accessor** dialog window, select the source view object for the LOV and shuttle that to the **View Accessors** list displayed on the right. In our example, we will select **CountryVO** and shuttle that to the right. The basic view accessor is in place, but this is not enough for us to define the cascading or dependent LOV. In our example, the LOV is supposed to display the list of countries for a specific region in a row. For this, we may need to add an appropriate filtering condition on the view accessor.

4. To add this filtering condition, select the newly added view accessor in the **View Accessor** window and click on the **Edit** button. In the **Edit View Accessor** dialog window, select the named view criteria that you defined on **CountryVO** to filter the country list and shuttle that to the **Selected** list. The **Bind Parameter Values** section displays the bind parameter that you defined for the data source view object. Select the bind parameter used in the selected view criteria and click on the **Value** column. The value column displays a drop-down list with a list of attributes from the base view object. As we are planning to filter the LOV based on **RegionId** for a row, select **RegionId** from the attribute list. This is shown in the following screenshot:

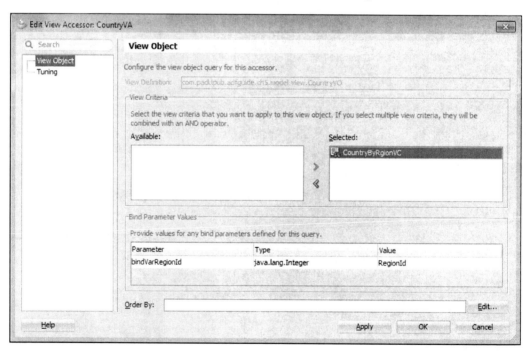

5. Click on **OK** to save and dispose the window. Click on **OK** in the **View Accessor** dialog window to save the definition. Now we are back on the **Create List of Values** dialog window. The rest of the steps are the same as for defining a normal LOV.

6. In the **Create List of Values** dialog window, expand the **List Data Source** and select the view accessor you created. Then select the **List Attribute** (list return value) from the LOV data source view object. This value will be copied to an LOV enabled attribute on the base view object upon selecting the value from the LOV at runtime. If the attribute names are the same in the LOV source view object and base view object, then the editor creates a default mapping between them. You can add more return values mapping between attributes in the base view object and the LOV data source view object by clicking on the green plus icon displayed in the **List Return Values** table.

7. To choose the LOV display type, click on the **UI Hints** tab and then select the **Default List Type**. You can optionally configure other properties which may affect the LOV display at runtime. Click on **OK** to save and dispose off the dialog.

8. Once you defined a cascading LOV, you will have to tell the framework when the LOV needs to be refreshed, apart from its default execution. In our example, the LOV query needs to be fired whenever the **RegionId** changes. To achieve this, select the **Attributes** tab in the overview editor for **RegionalOfficeVO** and then select the attribute for which a cascading LOV is defined. And then go to the **Dependencies** tab and shuttle the attribute that drives the values displayed in LOV and shuttle that to the **Selected** list. To display the countries for a selected **RegionId**, we need to shuttle **RegionId** to the **Selected** list.

Switching the LOV at runtime

In the last section we discussed the dependent LOV, where the list of values refreshes for each row in the collection depending upon the dependent attribute values. We are continuing our discussion on LOV with a different use case in this section. There are some business cases where you may need to dynamically switch the data source (source view object) used for the LOV based on specific conditions. For example, consider an employee data capture UI which displays employee attributes such as first name and salary, and department. The LOV is enabled for the department. The business requirement is that depending on the logged-in user role, LOV should query different database tables to display the departments. Oracle ADF supports such use case scenarios by allowing you to define multiple LOVs for an attribute. The framework uses a **switcher** attribute to decide the ID of the LOV that needs to be shown at runtime. Typically a transient attribute is marked as the LOV switcher, whose value is evaluated to one of the LOV IDs defined on the attribute.

The following are the high-level steps for enabling multiple LOVs on an attribute in a view object:

1. Open up the desired view object in the overview editor. Go to the **Attributes** page and select the attribute on which you want to define multiple LOVs.

2. Select the **List of Values** tab. Now you can add multiple LOVs (as required by your business use case) for the selected attribute by clicking on the green plus icon displayed on the toolbar section of the **List of Values** table. We are not repeating the steps for defining the LOV in this section. If you need a quick brush up, refer back to the topic *Configuring Lists of Values* in *Chapter 4, Introducing View Objects*. When you add a second LOV, you may notice two drop-down lists in the screen, namely **List Type UI Hint** and **List of Values Switcher**. Select the desired UI hints for the LOV using **List Type UI Hint**. Do not select **List of Values Switcher** during this step; we will revisit this screen after defining a transient attribute, which is explained in the following steps.

3. Now you may need to help the framework by providing logic for choosing the appropriate LOV at runtime. The framework chooses the LOV ID by evaluating a transient attribute (which needs to be marked as the LOV switcher) present on the row.

4. To define a transient attribute, select the **Attributes** tab in the overview editor for a view object and click on the green plus icon to add new attributes. Make sure the **Transient** radio button is selected for the new attribute in its **Details** tab. In the property inspector, expand the **Value** section and select **Value** type as **Expression** and then enter the Groovy expression which evaluates to the LOV ID to be used at runtime. For example, suppose that the LOV IDs defined for the `departmentId` attribute are **AdminDeptLOV** and **GenericDeptLOV**. The following Groovy expression returns **AdminDeptLOV** if the logged in user belongs to the Admin group, and **GenericDeptLOV** in all other cases.

```
securityContext.userInRole['Admin']?"AdminDeptLOV":
"GenericDeptLOV"
```

5. The last step is to mark the transient attribute that you defined in the previous step as an LOV switcher. To do this, select the multiple LOV enabled attribute in the **Attributes** table and choose the **List of Values** tab. Click on the **List of Values Switcher** drop-down and then select the appropriate transient attribute that you defined in step 4.

Reading and writing XML data

The ADF view object has support for writing queried data into XML format and for reading XML documents in order to apply changes to data. You will be using `writeXML()` and `readXML()` methods defined on the view object implementation class for the purpose of achieving the previously mentioned functionalities.

- `writeXML()`: This produces an XML document for rows in a view object row set. You may use this API to export data from the database in the XML format in a language-neutral way for use by third party systems.

- `readXML()`: This processes all rows from an incoming XML document. This is useful to update the data with an incoming XML document.

To learn more about presenting data using XML, see the topic *Reading and Writing XML* in *Oracle Fusion Middleware Fusion Developer's Guide for Oracle Application Development Framework*. To access the documentation go to http://www.oracle.com/technetwork/developer-tools/jdev/documentation/index.html and choose **Oracle JDeveloper and ADF Documentation Library | Fusion Developer's Guide**. Use the **Search** option to find specific topics.

The following examples illustrate the usage of `readXML()` and `writeXML()` methods on a view object and on a row in a view object.

- **Using `writeXML()` on a row object**: This example finds the row with `departmentId = 10` and writes the contents of the row into XML by calling `writeXML(depthCount, options)` on the `oracle.jbo.Row` object. The `depthCount` parameter in the `writeXML()` call represents what level system should traverse the rows in the view object hierarchy while creating the node structure. For example, `depthCount = -1` indicates that the row object should render all child rows by traversing all the view links.

```
public void writeAllRowsAsXML(ApplicationModule am) throws
IOException {

    ViewObject vo = am.findViewObject("Departments");
    //Find the department row with Key=10
    Key k = new Key(new Object[] { 10 });
    Row deptRow = vo.findByKey(k, 1)[0];
    //Traverse all view links and produce XML for all
    //child rows
    Node node = deptRow.writeXML(-1, XMLInterface.XML_OPT_ALL_ROWS);
    //Print the XML
    ((XMLNode)node).print(System.out);
}
```

- **Using** `writeXML()` **on a view object**: This example renders all rows from a view object in XML by calling `writeXML()` on the view object. The usage is the same as that we discussed for a view row.

  While writing rows into XML, you can refine the rows by supplying a hash map that contains the names of the desired view object and its attributes. In this case, the framework will export only those rows that match the supplied view object names and attributes. You will use the overridden `writeXML(long options, HashMap voAttrRules)` API for such cases. An example is as follows:

```
public void writeSelectiveRowsAsXML(ApplicationModule am) throws
IOException {

    ViewObject vo = am.findViewObject("Departments");
    //Render only those view objects and attributes
    //present in the viewDefMap
    HashMap viewDefMap = new HashMap();
    viewDefMap.put("model.view.DepartmentVO",
        new String[] { "DepartmentId", "DepartmentName" });
    Node node = vo.writeXML(-1, viewDefMap);
    //Print the XML
    ((XMLNode)node).print(System.out);

}
```

- **Using** `readXML()` **on a view object**: You can call the `readXML()` API on a view object class to read in the data from the incoming XML. When you call `readXML()` on a view object passing an XML filename, the framework will read the XML content and will take the following actions for each node present in the XML:

  ○ Update existing view rows attribute values from XML.

  ○ Create a new row, if the row that you supplied in the XML has not been retrieved by calling `findByKey()`. If the primary key for the new row is populated using DB Sequence or Groovy expression, remove that attribute from the XML. ADF runtime will take care of populating these attribute values.

  ○ Deletes the view row if the corresponding XML element has `bc4j-action='remove'`.

For example consider the following input XML file that contains the Department and Employee details. The Department view object is linked to the Employee view object through the view link accessor, and **EmployeeVO** is the name of the accessor attribute. The `readXML()` API on the view object expects input XML format in the same format as that produced by a call to `writeXML()` on the same view object.

```xml
<?xml version="1.0" encoding="windows-1252" ?>
<DepartmentVO>
    <DepartmentVORow>
<!--Update the DepartmentName to Marketing, Id=10 is in DB -->
        <DepartmentId>10</DepartmentId>
        <DepartmentName>Marketing</DepartmentName>
        <ManagerId>200</ManagerId>
        <LocationId>1800</LocationId>
        <EmployeeVO>
            <EmployeeVORow>
<!--Add a new employee row, Id=1001 is not in DB ->
                <EmployeeId>1001</EmployeeId>
                <FirstName>Jobinesh</FirstName>
                <LastName>Purushothaman</LastName>
                <Email>jobinesh@gmail.com</Email>
                <HireDate>2010-05-14</HireDate>
                <JobId>AD_ASST</JobId>
                <ManagerId>200</ManagerId>
                <DepartmentId>10</DepartmentId>
            </EmployeeVORow>
        </EmployeeVO>
    </DepartmentVORow>
    <DepartmentVORow bc4j-action='remove'> <!-- Remove the row for
DepartmentId= 40 -->
        <DepartmentId>40</DepartmentId>
    </DepartmentVORow>
```

You can input this XML to the `readXML()` API on a view object to apply changes to the appropriate rows in the view object. The following method illustrates this feature:

```java
/**
 * This method reads rows from XML
 */
public void readRowsFromXML(ApplicationModule am) throws IOException {

    ViewObject vo = am.findViewObject("Departments");
    try {
        //Perform insert, update, delete based on the data read
```

```
      //from dept.xml. The dept.xmlis given at the beginning
        //of this example.
      Element xmlToRead = getInsertUpdateDeleteXMLGram
                              ("dept.xml");
      vo.readXML(xmlToRead, -1);
    } catch (Exception ex) {
      //Handle Exception
      ex.printStackTrace();
    }
  }


/**
  * Helper method for reading XML data
  */
private Element getInsertUpdateDeleteXMLGram(String xmlurl) throws
XMLParseException, SAXException, IOException {
    URL xmlURL = CRUDXMLTestClient.class.getResource(xmlurl);
    DOMParser dp = new DOMParser();
    dp.parse(xmlURL);
    return dp.getDocument().getDocumentElement();
}
```

Advanced data type techniques

We have discussed the common data types used by business components in *Chapter 3, Entity Objects*, under the section *Attribute types*. Apart from the out of the box data types, ADF allows you to define custom data types to handle custom object types used in the database or to extend the functionalities provided by existing data types. In this section, we will discuss ADF support for building custom data types, and then we will discuss some special data types such as the **Binary Large Object** (**BLOB**) and the **Character Large Object** (**CLOB**) which may require a special mention on their usage.

Building custom data types using domain type

ADF allows you to customize the data types used for attributes in a business component by defining custom domain types. You can either extend the existing data types such as String, Integer, and Date, or build new domain types to represent a custom data structure such as **Oracle Object type** used in the database.

Oracle object types are user-defined types which consist of one or more basic types. It provides higher-level ways to organize and access data in the database.

Let us define a domain type for a custom Oracle object type. The object type used in this example is as follows:

```
CREATE OR REPLACE TYPE ADDRESS_DETAIL AS OBJECT (CITY
VARCHAR2(100), COUNTRY VARCHAR2(100));
```

Once you defined the previously mentioned object type in the database, you will need to build a custom domain type to use the same from business components.

To define a domain type for the ADDRESS_DETAIL object type, perform the following steps:

1. Right-click on the Model project and select **New Domain**.

2. In the **Create Domain** dialog window, enter the domain name and package. As we are building a domain for the oracle object type, select **Domain** for an **Oracle Object Type** option. From the **Available Types** list, select the desired object type. In this example, we will select the **ADDRESS_DETAIL** object which is present in the database.

3. Continue the wizard. The **Settings** page will allow you to modify the attribute definitions, if required. This example does not need any change in the system generates properties. Click on **Finish**.

When you finish generating the domain type, JDeveloper will create an XML definition to hold the metadata for the domain type and a corresponding Java class.

Later when you generate business components by selecting a database table which uses ADDRESS_DETAIL as one of the columns, JDeveloper will automatically map the ADDRESS_DETAIL column type to the custom domain Java type that you defined.

You can even set the attribute types of entity objects or view objects explicitly to the custom domain you generated. To do this, select the desired attribute in the **Attributes** tab for an entity object or view object, and then select the desired **Type** in the property inspector.

To display the attributes which use custom domain types in the ADF **Faces** pages, you will need to create custom JSF converters. This takes care of the encoding and decoding of the domain type when displayed in UI. We will cover this topic in *Chapter 8, Building Data Bound Web User Interfaces*.

Working with BLOB and CLOB data types

The **BLOB** data type is used for storing large binary data, in a database table, such as images, audio, or other multimedia objects. The **CLOB** data type is used to store large texts with a special sense to handle the character set used for the text. If an application uses Oracle database, then ADF Business Components can use `oracle.jbo.domain.BlobDomain` and `oracle.jbo.domain.ClobDomain` data types to represent BLOB and CLOB types in the middle tier. In this section, we will explore examples on updating BLOB and CLOB columns.

The following example demonstrates the usage of `oracle.jbo.domain.ClobDomain` for inserting large text files into the database table through the **FileStorageVO** view object. This example uses the following entity and view objects:

- **FileStorageEO**: This is the entity object used in this example for uploading binary content to the database. The **FileContent** attribute as the name suggest stores the contents of the file and is of the type `oracle.jbo.domain.ClobDomain`.

- **FileStorageVO**: This is a view object backed up by **FileStorageEO**.

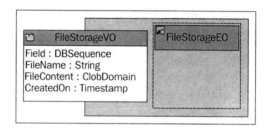

The following code snippet illustrates the APIs to be used for creating `ClobDomain` from `java.io.InputStream`. Note that, in real life implementation, code for creating `ClobDomain` should ideally be placed in the client tier (for example, managed bean in JSF), and you can pass the `ClobDomain` object to the appropriate application module method for inserting into a database. To keep things simple, this example creates the `ClobDomin` in the application module itself. The method `demoCLOBInsert()` takes the filename and `InputStream` as a parameter which is used for creating a `ClobDomain` object.

```
//In application module implementation class

public class HRServiceAppModuleImpl extends
    ApplicationModuleImpl implements HRServiceAppModule{

// Other AM methods go here...

/**
```

```
 * This method inserts file content in to DB using
 * ClobDomain
 * @param filename
 * @param fileInputStream
 */
public void demoCLOBInsert(String filename, InputStream
fileInputStream) {
  try {
     //Get the view object
    ViewObjectImpl fileStrorages = getFilesStorageVO();
    FileStorageVORowImpl newRow =
         (FileStorageVORowImpl)fileStrorages.createRow();
    fileStrorages.insertRow(newRow);
    //Set the ClobDomain conent
    newRow.setFileContent
         (newClobDomainForInputStream(fileInputStream));
    newRow.setFileName(filename);
      //Commit transaction
    getDBTransaction().commit();
  } catch (Exception ex) {
    ex.printStackTrace();
  }
}


/**
 * Generates ClobDomain from InputStream
 */
private ClobDomain newClobDomainForInputStream(InputStream in) throws
SQLException, IOException {
  ClobDomain b = new ClobDomain();
  Writer out = b.getCharacterOutputStream();
  writeInputStreamToWriter(in, out);
  in.close();
  out.close();
  return b;
}


/**
 * Helper method to write to ClobDomain's OutputStream
 */
private static void writeInputStreamToWriter(InputStream in,
    Writer out) throws IOException {
    InputStreamReader isr = new InputStreamReader(in);
    char[] buffer = new char[8192];
```

```
    int charsRead = 0;
    while ((charsRead = isr.read(buffer, 0, 8192)) != -1) {
    out.write(buffer, 0, charsRead);
  }
 }

}
```

The following example demonstrates the usage of `oracle.jbo.domain.BlobDomain`
for inserting binary files into the database table through the **FileStorageVO**
view object.

```
//In application module implementation class

public class HRServiceAppModuleImpl extends
    ApplicationModuleImpl implements HRServiceAppModule{
// Other AM methods go here...

/**
* This method inserts the binary content in to DB
* @param fileName
* @param fileInputStream
*/
public void demoBLOBInsert(String fileName, InputStream
fileInputStream) {
   //Get the view object
   ViewObjectImpl fileStrorages = getBinaryFilesStorage();
   FileStorageVORowImpl newRow =
       (FileStorageVORowImpl)fileStrorages.createRow();
   fileStrorages.insertRow(newRow);
  //Set the BlobDomain content
  newRow.setFileContent
       (newBlobDomainForInputStream(fileInputStream));
  newRow.setFileName(fileName);
  getDBTransaction().commit();
}
/**
 * Generates BlobDomain from InputStream
 */
private BlobDomain newBlobDomainForInputStream(InputStream in) throws
SQLException, IOException {
  BlobDomain b = new BlobDomain();
  OutputStream out = b.getBinaryOutputStream();
  writeInputStreamToOutputStream(in, out);
  in.close();
  out.close();
```

```
    return b;
}
/**
 * Helper method to write to BlobDomain's OutputStream
 */

private static void writeInputStreamToOutputStream(InputStream in,
OutputStream out) throws IOException {
  byte[] buffer = new byte[8192];
  int bytesRead = 0;
  while ((bytesRead = in.read(buffer, 0, 8192)) != -1) {
    out.write(buffer, 0, bytesRead);
  }
}
}
```

A working example of using `oracle.jbo.domain.ClobDomain` for storing uploaded text files can be found in the example code that we mentioned at the beginning of this book, under Preface section. To access the `ClobDomain` example, open the `ADFDevGuideCh5HRModel` workspace in JDeveloper and look for `clobDomainExample.jsf` in the `ViewController` project.

BLOB and CLOB support for alternate databases

If your application uses a non-Oracle database, then you can use `java.sql.Clob` and `java.sql.Blob` attribute types in the entity objects and view objects to represent CLOB and BLOB database table columns. The `java.sql.Clob` and `java.sql.Blob` are interfaces; the actual implementation classes used by ADF runtime for these interfaces are:

- `oracle.jbo.domain.generic.GenericClob`
- `oracle.jbo.domain.generic.GenericBlob`

If you are developing against a non-Oracle database, select **SQL92** for the SQL platform and **Java Data Type Map** when you initialize the business component project by defining the database connection.

Building business components dynamically

The ADF Business Component framework allows you to programmatically define entity objects and view objects at runtime. This feature is useful when you need to deal with a highly dynamic business model where the same web UI may need to query or update different data sources depending upon the current user profile or other settings.

Building dynamic entity objects and view objects

ADF entity objects and view objects expose APIs for building definitions at runtime. Let us learn these APIs through an example.

In this example, we are programmatically building an entity object and a view object on the fly. As mentioned earlier, you may go for such implementations when you need to build highly dynamic pages whose display content and the underlying data source changes dynamically.

> Note that we are not discussing how to build a dynamic UI in this chapter. The techniques for building a dynamic model and UI are discussed in the Appendix *A* section of this book with an end-to-end example. You can download the Appendix from the Packt website link that we mentioned at the beginning of this book, in the *Preface* section.

Let us take a quick look at the methods and APIs used in this example:

- `buildDynamicDeptViewCompAndAddtoAM()`: This is the entry point for this example. This method generates an entity object based on the DEPARTMENTS table and then creates a view object based on this entity object. The dynamic view object is exposed through the application module for use by the client.

- `buildDeptEntitySessionDef()`: This method creates an entity definition object (EntityDefImpl), sets the DEPARTMENTS table as the data source, and then adds attributes as appropriate. Before returning the definition object to the caller, this method registers the new definition object with the definition manager used by the ADF Business Components' runtime.

- `buildDeptViewSessionDef()`: This method creates a view definition from the dynamically generated entity definition object and registers it with the definition manager used by the ADF Business Components' runtime.

- `addViewToPdefApplicationModule()`: This method adds a dynamically generated view object to the application module.

This example under the cover uses **MDS (Meta Data Services)** to store the personalized definitions for the dynamic business components that we create on the fly. So if you want to try out a similar example, you may need to configure an MDS persistent store in your application. This example uses the following configuration in `adf/META-INF/adf-config.xml`:

```
<adf-mds-config xmlns="http://xmlns.oracle.com/adf/mds/config">
<mds-config version="11.1.1.000" xmlns="http://xmlns.oracle.com/mds/
config">
<persistence-config>
  <metadata-namespaces>
    <namespace path="/sessiondef"
        metadata-store-usage="mdsRepos"/>
    <namespace path="/persdef"
        metadata-store-usage="mdsRepos"/>
    <namespace path="/xliffBundles"
        metadata-store-usage="mdsRepos"/>
  </metadata-namespaces>
  <metadata-store-usages>
    <metadata-store-usage id="mdsRepos"
        deploy-target="true" default-cust-store="true"/>
  </metadata-store-usages>
</persistence-config>
<cust-config>
  <match path="/">
    <customization-class
        name="oracle.adf.share.config.SiteCC"/>
  </match>
</cust-config>
</mds-config>
</adf-mds-config>
```

In order for personalization of business components to work, you must have a valid `<cust-config>` entry in `adf-config.xml`.

The sample application module methods for building programmatic entity and view objects are as follows:

```
//In application module implementation class
public class HRServiceAppModuleImpl extends
    ApplicationModuleImpl implements HRServiceAppModule {
```

```
private static final String DYNAMIC_DETP_VO_INSTANCE =
"DynamicDeptVO";
/**
  * This method defined in the application module
  * generates dynamic entity definition and view object
  * definition for DEPARTTMENTS table and add it to AM instance
  */
public void buildDynamicDeptViewCompAndAddtoAM() {
  //Check if view definition exists for
   //DYNAMIC_DETP_VO_INSTANCE
  ViewObject internalDynamicVO = findViewObject
       (DYNAMIC_DETP_VO_INSTANCE);
  if (internalDynamicVO != null) {
     return;
  }
  //Build entity definition
  EntityDefImpl deptEntDef = buildDeptEntitySessionDef();
  //Build view object definition
  ViewDefImpl viewDef = buildDeptViewSessionDef(deptEntDef);
  //Add view object to application module
  addViewToPdefApplicationModule(viewDef);
 }
//Other method definitions go here...
 }
```

The method body for `buildDeptEntitySessionDef()` and `buildDeptViewSessionDef(EntityDefImpl)` are explained in detail, in the following step-by-step instructions.

Steps for building entity definition at runtime

The following are the steps for building a typical entity definition at runtime:

1. Create `oracle.jbo.server.EntityDefImpl` with `DEF_SCOPE_SESSION`. All the entity definitions created at runtime should be marked as session scope.

2. Specify a unique name for the newly created entity definition by calling `EntityDefImpl::setFullName(String name)`. You can use the full name to find the definition object later.

3. Specify a name for the definition object by calling `EntityDefImpl::setName(String name)`. You can skip this step if the name is set while creating the definition object in step1.

4. Set the alias name for the entity definition by invoking `EntityDefImpl:
   :setAliasName(String s)`, which will be used by the framework while
   generating a query at runtime.

5. Set the name of the database source table by calling
   `EntityDefImpl::setSource(String source)`.

6. Set the name of the database source type (such as table, view, and so on) by
   calling `EntityDefImpl::setSourceType(String sourceType)`.

7. Add the attributes to the entity definition by invoking `addAttribute(String
   attrName, String columnName, Class javaType, boolean
   isPrimaryKey, boolean isDiscriminator, boolean isPersistent)` on
   `EntityDefImpl`.

8. Resolve the entity definition before use by the client by calling `EntityDefIm
   pl::resolveDefObject()`. When you call this API, the framework performs
   the validation and resolution of various part of the definition.

9. Write the definition to an XML outputs stream by calling `EntityDefImpl::w
   riteXMLContents()`.

10. Save the definition to XML by calling `EntityDefImpl::saveXMLContents()`.

These steps are clearly marked in the following code snippet to make it easier for you
to understand:

```
//In HRServiceAppModuleImpl class ...
/**
 * Build entity definition for DEPARTMENTS table
 * @return
 */
private EntityDefImpl buildDeptEntitySessionDef() {
  //Step1: Build the entity definition object.
  //All definitions created at runtime
  //should be marked as session scope.
  EntityDefImpl entDef =
    new EntityDefImpl(
        oracle.jbo.server.EntityDefImpl.DEF_SCOPE_SESSION,
        "DynamicDeptEntityDef");
  //Step 2: Set the full name for the entity definition
  entDef.setFullName(entDef.getBasePackage() + ".dynamic." +
      entDef.getName());

  //Step 3: Sets the name for entity definition
  entDef.setName(entDef.getName());

  //Step 4: Sets the alias which is used in query
```

```
            entDef.setAliasName(entDef.getName());

        //Step 5: Set the database table name
        entDef.setSource("DEPARTMENTS");
         //Step 6: Set the database source type
        entDef.setSourceType(EntityDefImpl.DBOBJ_TYPE_TABLE );
        //Step 7:Add the attributes
        entDef.addAttribute("DepartmentId", "DEPARTMENT_ID",
            Integer.class, true, false, true);
        entDef.addAttribute("DepartmentName", "DEPARTMENT_NAME",
            String.class, false, false, true);
        entDef.addAttribute("ManagerId", "MANAGER_ID",
            Integer.class, false, false, true);
        //Step 8:Resolves entity definition and
        //validates it before this definition object can be used.
        entDef.resolveDefObject();


        //Step 9: Write the definition to XML stream
        entDef.writeXMLContents();
        //Step 10:Save the XML file
        entDef.saveXMLContents();

        return entDef;
    }
```

Steps for building a view definition with entity usage at runtime

The following are steps for building a typical view definition based on entity usage at runtime:

1. Create `oracle.jbo.server.ViewDefImpl` with `DEF_SCOPE_SESSION`. All the view definitions created at runtime should be marked as session scope.

2. Specify a unique name for the newly created view definition by calling `ViewDefImpl::setFullName(String name)`. You can use the full name to find the definition object later.

3. Specify the access mode and other configuration required for the view object definition.

4. Add the entity usage by calling `addEntityUsage(String usageName,` `String entityDefName, boolean referenceOnly, boolean readOnly)` on `ViewDefImpl`. This specifies the entity objects that back up the view object at runtime.

5. Specify attributes for the view object. This example calls `addAllEntityAttributes(String entityUsageName)` to include all the attributes from an entity definition.

6. Resolves the view definition before use by the client, by calling `ViewDefImpl::resolveDefObject()`. This call resolves the attribute definitions with its entity bases.

7. Write the definition to an XML output stream by calling `ViewDefImpl::writeXMLContents()`.

8. Save the definition to XML by calling `ViewDefImpl::saveXMLContents()`.

The previous steps are marked in the following code snippet to make it clearer for you:

```
//In HRServiceAppModuleImpl class ...

/**
 * Build view definition from the EntityDefImpl
 * @param entityDef
 * @return
 */
private ViewDefImpl buildDeptViewSessionDef(EntityDefImpl entityDef) {
  //Step 1:Define the ViewDefImpl. All definitions created at

  // runtime should be marked as session scope.
  ViewDefImpl viewDef =
     new oracle.jbo.server.ViewDefImpl(
        oracle.jbo.server.ViewDefImpl.DEF_SCOPE_SESSION,
       "DynamicDeptViewDef");
  //Step 2: Sets the full name for the view definition
  viewDef.setFullName(viewDef.getBasePackage() + ".dynamic."
        + viewDef.getName());
   //Step 3: Sets the access mode and generic configurations
  viewDef.setUseGlueCode(false);
viewDef.setIterMode(RowIterator.ITER_MODE_LAST_PAGE_FULL);
  viewDef.setBindingStyle(
        SQLBuilder.BINDING_STYLE_ORACLE_NAME);
  viewDef.setSelectClauseFlags(
        ViewDefImpl.CLAUSE_GENERATE_RT);
  viewDef.setFromClauseFlags(ViewDefImpl.CLAUSE_GENERATE_RT);
```

```
    //Step 4:Add entity usage
viewDef.addEntityUsage("DynamicDeptUsage",
      entityDef.getFullName(), false, false);
    //Step 5:Add all attributes from entity
viewDef.addAllEntityAttributes("DynamicDeptUsage");
/**
  *Step 6: It resolves attribute definitions
  * with its entity bases.
  */
viewDef.resolveDefObject();

    //Step 7: Write to XML Stream viewDef.writeXMLContents();
    //Step 8: Save to XML file
viewDef.saveXMLContents();

    return viewDef;
}
```

Note that while building the view dentition or entity definition at runtime, they must go through resolveDefObject(), writeXMLContents(), and saveXMLContents() calls before it can be used by the runtime.

Once the entity definition and view definition objects are in place, the last step in this exercise is to add the view object that we generated in the previous step to the desired application module. This is shown in the following code snippet. This example uses a personalization definition of the application module to store the changes. The personalized business components are explained in the next section.

```
/**
  * Adds the view definition to application module
  * @param viewDef
  */
private void addViewToPdefApplicationModule(ViewDefImpl viewDef) {
//This example uses the PDefApplicationModule object which
//is a personalization definitions of AM. This is explained in
// next section - Personalized Business Components .
//If you don't need to persist the dynamically added
//view object across sessions, then you can bypass the
// PDefApplicationModule and directly invoke
// createViewObject() available on application module
// for creating VO. If you do so, these changes will be
//available only for the current user session.

  oracle.jbo.server.PDefApplicationModule pDefAM =
    oracle.jbo.server.PDefApplicationModule.findDefObject
```

```
                (getDefFullName());

    if (pDefAM == null) {
      pDefAM = new oracle.jbo.server.PDefApplicationModule();
      pDefAM.setFullName(getDefFullName());
    }

    pDefAM.setEditable(true);
    pDefAM.createViewObject(DYNAMIC_DETP_VO_INSTANCE,
        viewDef.getFullName());
     //Apply changes to PDef object of AM
    pDefAM.applyPersonalization(this);
     //Write the PDef to XML
    pDefAM.writeXMLContents();
    pDefAM.saveXMLContents();
   }

//Other methods go here...
  }
```

You can find the previous sample in the example code that we
mentioned at the beginning of this book, in the *Preface* section. To access
this example, open the ADFDevGuideCh5HRModel workspace in
JDeveloper and look for the HRServiceAppModuleImpl class in the
Model project.

Personalized business components

Oracle ADF Business Components use personalization definition objects to
customize the business component definitions at runtime. ADF uses oracle.jbo.
server.PDefEntityObject, oracle.jbo.server.PDefViewObject, and oracle.
jbo.server.PDefApplicationModule to store the runtime customization for
an entity object, view objects, and application modules respectively. When the
framework loads the application module definition, view definition, or entity
definition, it checks whether there is a corresponding personalization definition
object present and, if present, *wears* the **PDef** like a transparent overcoat on top of all
of the existing features of that object. It provides a context on which to pin additional
attributes and validators. The end user sees a definition that is the union of the base
definition plus the additional personalization. The runtime changes are stored in
the Meta Data Service (MDS) store. All the structural changes are stored at site level,
reflecting changes across all user sessions.

In other words, for personalization to work adf-config.xml should have
<cust-config> entry in adf-config.xml under the **MDS configuration** section.
In the last example, we have used oracle.jbo.server.PDefApplicationModule
which falls in the personalized component category.

> For details about MDS, see *Customizing Applications with MDS*
> in *Oracle Fusion Middleware Fusion Developer's Guide for Oracle
> Application*. To access the documentation online go to http://
> www.oracle.com/technetwork/developer-tools/jdev/
> documentation/index.html and choose **Oracle JDeveloper and
> ADF Documentation Library | Fusion Developer's Guide**. Use the
> **Search** option to find specific topics.

The following example illustrates how you can use PDefViewObject to alter a
view definition that we created at runtime in the previous section. The following
example adds a new attribute LocationId to the DynamicDeptViewDef, if the
existing definition object is not containing it. The changes are then saved to a
PDefViewObject.

```
//In application module implementation class
private static final String ATTRIB_LOC_ID = "LocationId";

private boolean addLocAttributeToDeptView() {
    //Step 1- Find PDefViewObject for
    //'sessiondef.dynamic.DynamicDeptViewDef'
    ViewDefImpl viewDef = ViewDefImpl.findDefObject
        ("sessiondef.dynamic.DynamicDeptViewDef");
    PDefViewObject pDefVO = (PDefViewObject)viewDef.
        getPersDef();
    //Step 2- No personalization exist, then create
    // a new PDefViewObject
    if (pDefVO == null) {
      pDefVO = new PDefViewObject();
      pDefVO.setFullName(viewDef.getFullName());
    }
    //Step 3- check if ATTRIB_LOC_ID exist in the defnition
    if (pDefVO.getAttributeIndexOf(ATTRIB_LOC_ID) != -1) {
      return false;
    }
    //Step 4- If no definition exist for ATTRIB_LOC_ID, then
    // create it and add it to PDefViewObject
    pDefVO.setEditable(true);
    pDefVO.addEntityAttribute(ATTRIB_LOC_ID,
```

```
    "DynamicDeptUsage", ATTRIB_LOC_ID, true);
  //Apply changes to PDef object for the VO
pDefVO.applyPersonalization(findViewObject(
    DYNAMIC_DETP_VO_INSTANCE));
  //Save changes to XML
pDefVO.writeXMLContents();
pDefVO.saveXMLContents();
return true;
}
```

Summary

In this chapter we have explored the advanced concepts on entity objects and view objects. Specifically, we discussed the lifecycle of both entity objects and view objects, and then went through a bunch of generic usage patterns for these components with examples. We concluded this chapter with an example to programmatically build business components at runtime.

As we progress with other layers in the ADF framework in the coming chapters, we will discuss more and more advanced features. The fine-tuning parameters available for business components will be discussed in *Chapter 12, Oracle ADF Best Practices*. In the next chapter, you will learn about the ADF application module, the service layer for the business components' stack.

6

Introducing
the Application Module

In the previous chapters we have discussed the business components that build the data model for your application. Now the question that you may have in your mind is, how does Oracle ADF expose that data model and business methods to the client for use? Before answering this question let us take a step back and see what is missing from the picture, as we put all the pieces together from our discussion so far. One thing you may surely notice is that we have not yet discussed about a service layer which act as an interfacing layer for the business model implementation. In this chapter, we will learn about the application module component, the service layer for the business components stack. We will be discussing the following topics:

- Concepts and architecture
- Core features of an application module
- Defining an application module
- Sharing of application module data
- Nesting application modules
- Working with an application module

Introduction

In simple words, an **application module** is a logical unit of work for an application. However in reality it does a lot more. Being the client facing layer of the business components stack, an application module does all the generic book keeping activities involved in executing view objects or business methods, such as acquiring the database connection, transaction management, user session tracking, and maintaining the state of the service invocations. And it was all done without sacrificing the scalability of your system. We will start our discussion with the basic concepts of the application modules, and as we proceed further we will be discussing more advanced concepts.

Concepts and architecture

The application module is a modular container of the view object instances, view links, business methods, and other child application modules. As any other framework components in the ADF Business Components stack, the application module also follows a highly extensible structure by design.

Ingredients of an application module

This is in continuation of the basic things we discussed in *Chapter 2, Introduction to ADF Business Components.*An application module comprises of the following components:

- **Application module XML metadata file**: This is the application module descriptor file holding metadata definitions. The metadata includes exposed business methods and data models for use, by clients, such as view objects and associated view criteria, master-child view, objects connected through view links, and nested application modules.

- **Application module definition**: This is the runtime Java class representation of the application module XML metadata file. The default base class for storing the application module definition is `oracle.jbo.server.ApplicationModuleDefImpl` which can be extended to add custom functionalities if needed. This class stores the runtime metadata for application modules read from the corresponding XML file.

- **Application module implementation**: This class represents an application module instance generated by runtime to serve a request from the client. The default base class used for representing an application module instance is `oracle.jbo.server.ApplicationModuleImpl.` You will subclass this class to define the custom business logic that must execute in the application's middle tier.

- `bc4j.xcfg`: This file contains metadata for all the application modules present in the same Java package for a project. This file is located in the `Common` subdirectory relative to the path where the application module's XML component definition is located. An application module's runtime behaviour is controlled by the configuration properties present in this file. The properties stored in this file include the JDBC data source name, application module pooling configurations, database specific configurations, locking mode, and so on.

The following diagram illustrates the ingredient of an application module. You may notice additional framework components such as Application Pool and Connection Strategy in the diagram. These items are discussed in the next section.

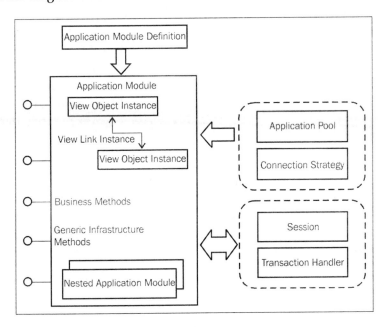

Additional core components

When we talk about application modules, the story is incomplete without referring to core components used by the framework to control the runtime behaviour of application module instances. The following is the list of core components:

- **Application Pool**: The application pool is responsible for managing the instance's pool for a specific application module. The default implementation class used by runtime is `oracle.jbo.common.ampool.ApplicationPoolImpl`. However, you can configure an application module to use the customized application pool implementation by setting the `PoolClassName` property pointing to the fully qualified custom class name in the corresponding `bc4j.xcfg` file.

- **Connection Strategy**: Application pool makes use of this component for creating new application module instances and also for connecting an application module with a data source. The default implementation used by the runtime is `oracle.jbo.common.ampool.DefaultConnectionStrategy`. To provide a custom connection strategy class, override the `jbo.ampool.connectionstrategyclass` property in the `bc4j.xcfg` file by setting it to the fully qualified name of the custom connection strategy class.

- **Session**: The session object stores the session context for the client. A session object is instantiated for each root application module when the application module is activated. The default session implementation class is `oracle.jbo.server.SessionImpl`. To provide a customized session implementation class, override the `SessionClass` property in the `bc4j.xcfg` file by setting it to the fully qualified name of the custom session class.

- **Transaction Handler**: This handles the database transaction associated with the user session. To override the default transaction handler (`oracle.jbo.server.DefaultTxnHandlerImpl`), you will have to implement `oracle.jbo.server.TransactionHandlerFactory` that returns a custom `oracle.jbo.server TransactionHandler` implementation.

  To make the application module to use your custom `TransactionHandlerFactory`, customize the `oracle.jbo.server.SessionImpl` by overriding the `SessionImpl::getTransactionHandlerFactory()` method to return the custom `TransactionHandlerFactory` implementation that you created.

You may rarely customize the default implementations supplied by the framework for these components. However there are some exceptional cases. One such scenario is building application modules without using a database. This case arises when your application module contains only programmatic entity objects and/or view objects which do not use databases as their data source. The steps for building an application module with no database connection are explained in the Appendix titled *More on ADF Business Components and Fusion Page Runtime* of this book. You can download the Appendix from the Packt website link that we mentioned at the beginning of this book, in the *Preface* section.

The core features of an application module

The following are the important offerings from the application module component:

- Visual and declarative development.

- Improved modularity support for the business services.

- Out of the box support for basic infrastructure services required for an enterprise application. The list includes management of user sessions, business transactions, database connections, and concurrent access.

- Support to nest multiple application modules to build composite services.

- Declarative settings to fine-tune runtime performance.

- Runtime monitoring and tuning support.

- Scalable architecture through out of the box support for instance pooling.

- Cluster aware components which ensure the high availability for the system.

- Ability to expose the service methods as web services for use by heterogeneous clients.

Defining an application module

In this section we will learn about building and configuring an application module using JDeveloper IDE. This section mainly focuses on declarative development aspects.

Creating application modules

To define an application module, perform the following steps:

1. Right-click on the model project and select **New Application Module**. In the **Create Application Module** dialog window, enter a package name and application module name. Then click on **Next**.

2. On the **Data Model** page, select the view object you want to expose for use by the client from **the Available View Objects** list and shuttle it to the **Data Model** list. Optionally, you can rename the view object instance in the **Data Model** list to make it more readable. Click on **Next**.

3. On the **Application Module** page, select the existing application module in the **Available** list and shuttle it to the **Selected** list to use it in the current application module. Optionally, you can rename the application module object instance in the **Data Model** list. The application module you added is nested under the root application module.

4. On the **Java** page, you can optionally generate Java classes.

5. Click on **Finish** to save the changes and generate the application module definition.

Optionally generating Java classes for an application module

When you generate an application module, by default, the IDE creates an XML file for storing the metadata for the component. If you want to add custom business methods or want to customize the default behaviour of the application module component, you will need to generate Java classes and add your custom code.

To generate Java classes for an application module, double-click on the application module object to display the overview editor. In the overview editor, go to **Java** tab and click on the **Edit** icon. In the **Select Java Options** dialog, select the types of Java classes you want to generate. The possible options are as follows:

- **Application Module Class**: This class represents an application module instance. You may generate an application module class to add custom business methods for use by the client or to override default lifecycle callback methods in order to meet your use case requirements.

- **Application Module Definition Class**: This class stores the runtime metadata for an application module. You may rarely customize the default application module definition class.

Adding hierarchical view object instances to an application module

The ADF application module has out of the box support for enabling master detail coordination between hierarchical view object instances in the data model linked through view links.

To enable active master detail coordination in the data model, perform the following steps:

1. Double-click the application module to open in the overview editor. Select the **Data Model** page in the overview editor and then expand the view object instances section.

2. In the **Available View Objects** list, locate the view object hierarchies that you want to expose to the client for use. Select the master view object in the **Available View Objects** list and add that instance to the **Data Model** list. Leave the newly created master view instance selected so that we can add child view object instances.

3. To add the detail (child) instance to the master instance, shuttle the desired detail view object to the **Data Model** list below the selected master view instance, as shown in the following screenshot:

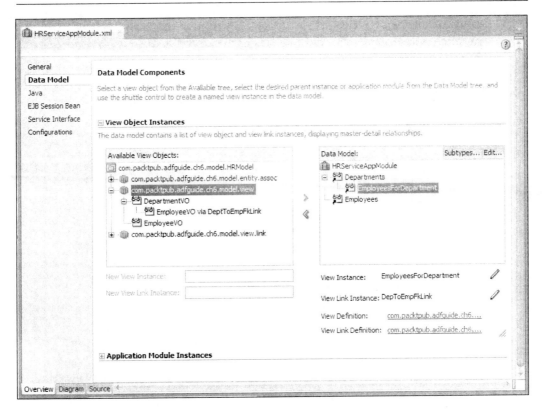

The previous steps can be repeated for building a data model of any complex hierarchy.

Overriding the default properties of an application module

While the default configuration parameter values for the application modules may be good enough for most of the generic use cases, you are free to override the specific configuration parameters based on the usage pattern of individual application modules.

To configure the application module properties, perform the following steps:

1. Double-click the desired application module in the model project. In the overview editor, select the **Configurations** tab.

2. The configuration table will display **Local, Shared**, and any custom configurations present in the `bc4j.xcfg` file for the selected application module. Select the desired configuration and then click on the **Edit** icon.

3. In the **Edit Configuration** window dialog, edit the desired properties and once you are happy with the changes click on **OK** to save the modified values.

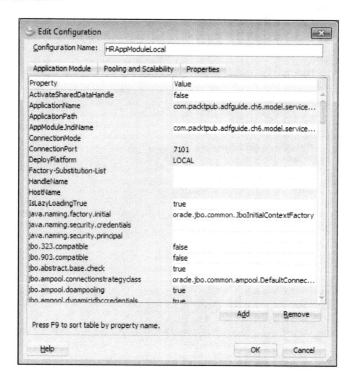

An enterprise application typically may have many application modules. Configuring or overriding the properties for each of these application modules is not an easy task. To make your life easier, ADF allows you to manage the *commonly used* properties for the application modules present in an application using the adf-config.xml file. This file is located in the <application_folder>\.adf\ META-INF folder. The configuration present in adf-config.xml will override the individual application module properties.

Commonly used application module configuration properties

The following table displays the most commonly used properties for an application module:

Property	Description	Default Value
`jbo.ampool.initpoolsize`	The number of application module instances created when the pool is initialized.	0
`jbo.ampool.minavailablesize`	The minimum number of available application module instances that the pool monitor should leave in the pool during the resource cleanup operation.	5
`jbo.ampool.timetolive`	How long to wait before the application module in the pool becomes a candidate for removal.	3600000 ms
`jbo.dofailover`	Enable eager passivation of the pending transaction state each time an application module is released to the pool in managed release (stateful) mode. This needs to be turned ON for high availability.	false
`jbo.max.cursors`	The maximum number of cursors the business components may have open. The framework will clean up free JDBC statements as the number of cursors approaches this number.	50
`jbo.load.components.lazily`	Determines whether to load components definitions lazily.	false
`jbo.recyclethreshold`	Maximum number of application module instances that attempt to preserve session affinity for the next request.	10

Property	Description	Default Value
jbo.txn.disconnect_level	This mode controls how the application module is disconnected from the client at the end of a request, typically used in conjunction with connection pooling. If jbo.txn.disconnect_level = 0, then the framework removes the view object and its row set when the application module is disconnected from the client and recreates the same for next request. If jbo.txn.disconnect_level = 1, then the framework stores the state of the view object and row set in memory closing the corresponding JDBC objects, which is faster and recommended. In other words jbo.txn.disconnect_level = 1 instructs the framework to manage the partially fetched JDBC ResultSets in memory rather than passivating their state.	0

To know more about the application module configuration parameters, refer to the topic *Tuning Application Module Pools and Connection Pools* in *Oracle Fusion Middleware Fusion Developer's Guide for Oracle Application Development Framework*. To access the documentation go to http://www.oracle.com/technetwork/developer-tools/jdev/documentation/index.html and choose **Oracle JDeveloper and ADF Documentation Library | Fusion Developer's Guide**. Use the **Search** option to find specific topics.

Modifying the JDBC data source name for an application module

You can alter the JDBC connection type or JDBC data source name specified for an application module at any point in time during development. To alter the database connection properties, perform the following steps:

1. Double-click the desired application module in the model project to open up the overview editor and then select the **Configurations** tab.

2. In the **Configurations** tab, select the desired configuration and click on the **Edit** icon.

3. In the **Edit Configuration** window dialog, select the **Application Module** tab. This page allows you to change the JDBC **Datasource Name** used in the application module. For example, the following screenshot displays the JDBC Datasource name specified for the **HRAppModule** application module. This page also allows you to edit the **Connection Type** (JDBC URL or JDBC Datasource) used in the application module.

4. Make changes as appropriate and click on **OK** to save the modified value.

Overriding properties for a view object instance

An application module allows you to declaratively apply view criteria on a few selected view object instances present in the application module. The editor also helps you to override certain tuning properties for the view object instances.

Declaratively applying view criteria to a view object instance

JDeveloper will help you to apply view criteria to a view object instance that you added to the data model in an application module. All the query execution through this view object instance will have this view criteria appended.

To customize a view object instance added to an application module, perform the following steps:

1. Double-click the application module in the model project.

2. In the overview editor, select the **Data Model** navigation tab. On the **Data Model Components** page, select the desired view object instance in the data model list and click on the **Edit** button.

3. In the **Edit View Instance** dialog window, select the view criteria that you defined in the view object definition and shuttle that to the **Selected** list. The **Bind Parameter Values** section will display the bind parameters defined on the view object. If the view criteria that you selected use bind variables, then optionally you can set the value using Groovy expression.

4. In the **Edit View Instance** dialog window, select the **Tuning** option in the left panel to override the tuning parameters for the currently selected view object instance.

5. Click on **OK** to save changes.

At runtime, the framework will automatically apply this view criteria usage to the view object instance.

Sharing of application module data

An enterprise application often uses seed data as master data in business data capture screens. An example might be, the use of currency codes in a list of values components displayed in various data capture screens. As the seeded data changes very rarely in the lifespan of an application, it makes sense to cache the data and share it across multiple user sessions or share it across requests for a specific session.

The ADF Business Component framework allows you to cache the query results of a view object using a **shared application module**. An application module can be shared either at *application level,* allowing all user sessions to access the same instance, or shared at user *session level* allowing a user session to share the same application module instance added under a distinct root application module. In the case of session level sharing, the framework will not share the data from a session scoped shared application module between different root application modules. The following section explains how you can use JDeveloper to build shared application modules declaratively:

1. To create a shared application module instance, right-click on the model project, in which you want to create the shared application module and choose **Project Properties**.

2. In the **Project Properties** window, expand the **ADF Business Components** node and select **Application Module Instances**. On the **ADF Business Components** section, select one of the following tabs:

   i. The **Application** tab: If you want to share the application module at application level.

   ii. The **Session** tab: If you want to share the application module at user session level for a specific root application module.

3. Once you select the scope for sharing the application module, select the desired application module in the **Available Application Module** list and shuttle that to the **Application Module Instances** list. Give a logically and meaningful unique **Instance Name** for the newly added application module as shown in the following screenshot. Click on **OK** to save the changes.

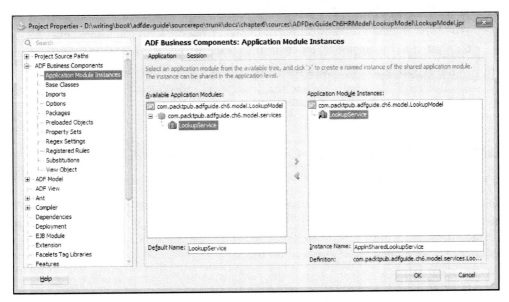

When you define a shared application module, the JDeveloper IDE updates the `<ModelProject>.jpx` file with a new `<AppModuleUsage>` entry. To view this entry in the editor, open the `<ModelProject>.jpx` file in the overview editor and select **AppModules** tab. You can see the new application module usages that you added as shown in the following screenshot:

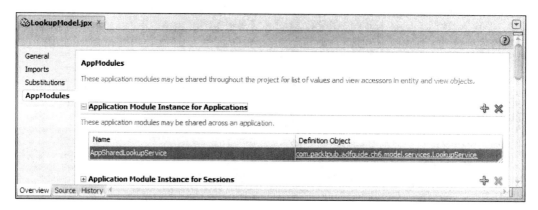

An alternative option to define a shared application module

You can also use the overview editor of the model project file to define the shared application module. To do this, perform the following steps:

1. Open the desired `<ModelProject>.jpx` in the overview editor and then select the **ApplModules** tab.

2. To define shared application module instances, click on the green plus icon displayed in the appropriate section (**Applications** or **Sessions**).

3. In the **Application Module Instances** dialog, select the desired application module from the available list and shuttle it to the right. Click on **OK** to save changes and dispose of the dialog.

Runtime behaviour of shared application modules

A **Session scoped shared application module** is created as a nested application module under the root application module at runtime. Its data is shared only within the same application module hierarchy where it has been added. In other words, it is not shared across distinct root application modules.

An **Application scoped shared application module** is shared across sessions. A view object in an application scoped shared application module uses multiple iterators on top of a single row set for serving multiple clients. If the query used in the view object is parameterized, then multiple row sets are generated based on the bind parameter values supplied by the client. These row sets are cached by individual query collection objects with unique bind variable combinations. For example, an employee view object instance from a shared application module creates a query collection pool named `<SharedApplicationModuleName>.<ViewObjectName>`, which holds the view object's query collections. If the employee view object has the query `SELECT Emp.EMPLOYEE_ID, Emp.FIRST_NAME, Emp.DEPARTMENT_ID FROM EMPLOYEES Emp WHERE Emp.DEPARTMENT_ID = :deptIdBindVar` and is executed with four different bind variable values, say 10, 20, 30, and 40, then four query collections will be created in the view object.

Query execution for a shared view object

When you call `executeQuery()` on a view object that is added to a shared application module, the framework will delegate the call to `refreshCollection(Row[] masterRows, boolean resetIter, boolean fillUpRange)` to reuse the possibly existing query collection. If you really want to re-execute a shared view object without re using the cached query collection, then you may want to call `forceExecuteQueryOfSharedVO()` on the view object, as follows:

```
ViewObjectImpl vo = (ViewObjectImpl)
findViewObject("Departments");

vo.forceExecuteQueryOfSharedVO();
```

Shared query collection cache management

The query collections in a non-shared application module are weakly referenced. On the other hand, the shared query collections, which reside in the shared application modules, are stored in query collection pools and are strongly referenced. Consequently, they may stick around for the lifetime of **JVM (Java Virtual Machine)** and may even outgrow the heap if left unchecked. This section describes how the shared query collections are managed by the business components runtime.

The ADF Business Components framework removes the unwanted query collections based on a maximum idle time setting. This feature limits the growth of the cache and removes unused query collections from the memory space. You can override the default values for the maximum idle time for the shared query collection and the sleep period for its pool monitor using the configuration parameters listed in the following table:

Property	Description	Default Value (in Milliseconds)
jbo.qcpool.maxinactiveage	The maximum amount of time (ms) that a shared query collection may remain unused before it is removed from the pool.	1800000
jbo.qcpool.monitorsleepinterval	The time (ms) that the shared query collection pool monitor should sleep between pool checks	900000

The maximum weight of the query collection pool

After removing expired query collections, the pool monitor checks to see if the total number of rows in a view object (from all query collection instances) exceeds the specified maximum weight. If so, the query collections are removed in **Least Recently Used (LRU)** basis until the weight falls below the limit. The default value for maximum weight is -1; no limit is placed on the weight. To set a maximum weight allowed in all the query collection pools, you can specify a positive long value for the jbo.qcpool.maxweight property in your application module configuration.

To set a maximum weight for a particular view object, you will override the method, initSharedQCPoolProperties(), from the corresponding ViewObjectImpl class as follows:

```
//In view object implementation class
protected void initSharedQCPoolProperties(QCPoolProperties qcProp){
    qcProp.setMaxWeight(10000);
}
```

Query collection weight

As explained earlier, the default weight of a query collection is the fetched row size. The weight can be customized for a view object by overriding `getQueryCollectionWeight(QueryCollection)` from the corresponding view object implementation class as follows:

```
//In view object implementation class
protected double getQueryCollectionWeight(QueryCollection qc){
    double weight;
    weight = super.getQueryCollectionWeight(qc);
    // your algorithm...
    return weight;
}
```

When a pool monitor wakes up after the time specified in `jbo.ampool.monitorsleepinterval` to do cleanup work, it will attempt to remove an application module only if the minimum available size (`jbo.ampool.minavailablesize`) is less than the current number of instances. So, for example, if you want all the shared application module instances to be removed whose inactive age is older than specified, then the minimum available size should be set to `0`.

Although both conditions (minimum available size and maximum inactive usage) are met, the application module will not get removed if a session is referencing it. The session must get invalidated via either timeout or explicit logout.

The root application modules with the same `jbo.shared.txn` property value string will share the same database connection and entity cache. This property is originally designed for shared application modules to make them reuse the database connection and entity cacheby keeping same string value for the `jbo.shared.txn` property. This optimizes the resource usage for the shared application modules. Note that, connection pooling is disabled for the shared application modules by design.

Consuming a shared application module

This section discusses declarative solutions for accessing shared application modules from a client.

Accessing view objects defined in a shared application module through a view accessor

In a real life scenario, can may build a separate project to hold shared application modules, which contains objects such as view objects and entity objects. Other projects can consume the shared components as an ADF library. Let us take a quick look at such usages.

To consume a view object defined in a shared application module, you will need to do the following:

- Package the project that holds the shared components (the shared application module) as an ADF Library JAR

- To consume this Library from another project, add it as a dependent to the consumer project and reuse the components

We are not discussing the detailed steps of how to package an ADF project as ADF Library JAR and how to consume it from another project in this section. If you are not familiar with this concept, refer to the topic *Reusing Application Components* in *Oracle Fusion Middleware Fusion Developer's Guide for Oracle Application Development Framework*. To access the documentation go to http://www.oracle.com/technetwork/developer-tools/jdev/documentation/index.html and choose **Oracle JDeveloper and ADF Documentation Library | Fusion Developer's Guide**. Use the **Search** option to find specific topics.

The high level steps for sharing an application module as an ADF Library JAR are as follows:

1. Package the project that contains the shared application module as an ADF Library JAR file.

2. Add the ADF Library JAR to the consumer project.

3. This example demonstrates how to consume the shared view object through a view accessor from a client project. You can later use this view accessor for defining the LOV or for defining validation. In the consumer model project, double-click the entity object or view object on which you want to define the view accessor.

4. In the overview editor, select the view accessor navigation tab and click on the green plus icon to create the new view accessor.

5. In the **View Accessors** dialog, select the desired view instance name from the shared application module node and shuttle it to the **View Accessors** list. This is shown in the following screenshot:

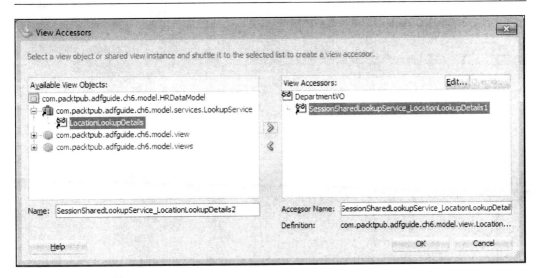

6. Click on **OK** to save changes.

When you define a view accessor for accessing a *shared* view object exposed through a shared application module, JDeveloper generates the view accessor entry in the base view object XML file with two special items in the configurations, namely **AMUsageName** and **ViewInstanceName**. The **AMUsageName** represents the name that we specified while defining the shared application module and **ViewInstanceName** represents the view object instance name exposed though the shared application module. This is used by the framework to identify the right application module usage and view object instance when the client code accesses the view accessor at runtime. For example, the following XML code snippet from a view object illustrates the view accessor definition that uses the **LocationLookupDetails** view object instance from a session shared application module usage with the name **SessionSharedLookupService**.

```
<ViewAccessor
Name="SessionSharedLookupService_LocationLookupDetails1"
ViewObjectName=
"com.packtpub.adfguide.ch6.model.view.LocationLookupVO"
AMUsageName="SessionSharedLookupService"
ViewInstanceName="LocationLookupDetails"
RowLevelBinds="true"/>
```

Associating view criteria with shared application module instances

To append view criteria to view object instances added into a shared application module, edit the view object instance from the overview editor for the application module. In the **Edit View Instance** window, select the desired view criteria and shuttle that to the right. This topic is discussed in detail in the section entitled, *Declaratively applying view criteria to a view object instance*.

Nesting application modules

Application modules are designed to support modularity. In general, an ADF application may have multiple application modules, each exposing services for a specific business use case or workflow. If a specific application module wants to consume services exposed by another one or if a client wants to consume services from multiple application modules, then you will have to build composite services by nesting desired application modules under a root application module. Composing services by nesting the desired application module under a root application module is known as **application module nesting**.

To nest an application module under a root application module, in the model project, double-click on the application module which you want to act as a root application module. Select the **Data Model** tab in the overview editor.

In the **Data Model Components** page, expand the **Application Module Instances** section. Select the application module that you want to nest from the **Available** list and shuttle that to the right. Optionally, you can modify the default name set for a new application module instance to improve the readability.

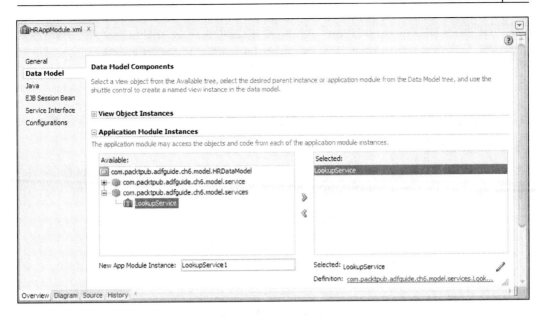

All nested application modules will participate in the root application module's transaction at runtime, and will share the same database connection and a single set of entity caches with the root application module. A nested application module cannot see the instances of any other application modules that might be nested under the same root at the same level. The following diagram depicts the high-level architecture of a root application module and the nested application modules within it.

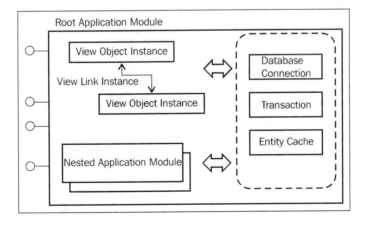

When the application modules are nested, the root application module's configuration overrides the configuration parameters specified for nested application modules.

Accessing a nested application module from the parent

You can use the `findApplicationModule()` method on the parent application module to find the nested application module. An example is as follows:

```
//In application module implementation class
/**
 * Container's getter for Child ApplicationModule
 * @return DummyAppModule1
 */
public ApplicationModuleImpl getMychildAppModule() {
    return (ApplicationModuleImpl)findApplicationModule("MychildAppModu
le");
}
```

Refer to the API documentation for the `findApplicationModule(String amName)` method on the `oracle.jbo.server.ApplicationModuleImpl` class to learn about the multi-part name support to search for more deeply nested child components.

To find the root application module, use `getRootApplicationModule()` on the current application module:

```
//In nested application module implementation class
ApplicationModule rootAM = this.getRootApplicationModule();
```

Working with an application module

So far our discussions were more focused on the various declarative configuration options available for an application module. In this section, we will be discussing programmatic options and APIs available on an application module to deal with more complex business use cases.

Exposing the business service method through data control

If the declarative features are not enough to meet the use cases, then you can add custom business methods in the middle tier. ADF has design time support for exposing custom business methods from both view object and application module implementation classes through data control for use by the client.

To expose the methods defined in the application module (or view object) implementation class through data control, perform the following steps:

1. Double-click on the application module (or view object) in the model project.

2. In the overview editor, select the **Java** tab. On the **Java Classes** page click on the yellow edit icon corresponding to the **Client Interface** section.

3. In the **Edit Client Interface** window, select the desired method from the **Available** list and shuttle that to the right.

   The exposed methods will be available in the data control panel as shown in the following screenshot. The exposed methods can be dragged and dropped on a page at design time or can be invoked programmatically from Java code using the binding API which we will learn in *Chapter 7, Binding Business Services with User Interface*.

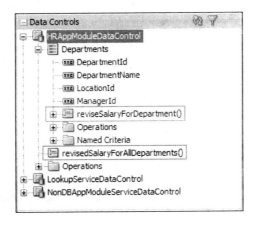

Where do you write custom business logic in a fusion web application?

Although the ADF Business Components framework along with JDeveloper IDE will help you to declaratively build basic business logic for your application, in some cases, based on the complexity of use cases, you will have to go beyond the declarative capabilities and write custom business methods for use by the client. There are multiple places where you can write your custom logic, as follows:

- **Entity Implementation Class**: This class can contain custom business logic that you may want to be executed at different stages of an entity instance.

- **View Object Implementation Class**: You can use this class to code business logic that you may want to be executed at different stages of data retrieval process. The business methods in the view object implementation can also be exposed through data control for use by the client.

- **View Row Implementation Class**: You will use this class to add your custom logic when a specific attribute is read from a data source or modified by the client.

- **Application Module Implementation Class**: This class acts as a service layer for your system. This class can be extended to add the following:

  i. Custom business service methods that can be exposed through data control.

  ii. Custom business logic that you may want to be executed at different stages of an application module lifecycle.

Both view objects and application modules can expose business methods through the data control panel for use. Logically, you will use view object implementation for writing a custom business method, if the business method deals with that specific view object alone and does not need to interact with any other view objects or entity objects in the module. You will use application module implementation for writing custom logic for all other cases.

Invoking an application module from a Java client

If you want to invoke an application module from a Java client, then you will have to use the `createRootApplicationModule()` method available in the `oracle.jbo.client.Configuration` class. Once the processing is done call `releaseRootApplicationModule()` in the `Configuration` class passing the application module instance. The following is an example:

```
//In the client class
public void invokeAM(){

String amDef =
    "com.packtpub.model.service.HRServiceAppModule";
String config = "HRServiceAppModuleLocal";
HRServiceAppModuleImpl am =null;

try{

  // creates or acquires an AM instance from the pool using
  // the specified configuration.
  am = (HRServiceAppModuleImpl)
      Configuration.createRootApplicationModule(amDef,
          config);
  //Invoke business methods on AM
  am.doSomething();

}finally{

  //Release the specified AM
  //true for the second parameter removes the
   //application module,
  //'false' causes to check in application module
   //instance to the pool for future use
  if(am != null)
    Configuration.releaseRootApplicationModule(am, true);
 }

}
```

Invoking a shared application module from a Java client

When you work on a shared application module in a multithreaded environment, you will have to use thread safe APIs for creating an application module from a Java client. The following is an example:

```
//In the client class
public void invokeSharedAM(){

String amDef =
    "com.packtpub.model.service.HRServiceAppModule";
String config = "HRServiceAppModuleShared";
ApplicationModuleHandle handle = null;

try{

   //Returns an application module handle.
   //The handle is then used to obtain an AM instance
  handle = Configuration.
           createRootApplicationModuleHandle(amDef, config);
  ApplicationModule am = handle.useApplicationModule();
   //Invoke business methods on AM
   am.doSomething();

}finally{
   // Releases the application module associated with
   // the handle created from
   // createRootApplicationModuleHandle()
   // 'false' causes to retain the application module
  if(handle!= null)
     Configuration.releaseRootApplicationModuleHandle
       (handle,false);
 }
}
```

What you may need to know about programmatically releasing an application module?

When you call the following APIs on the `Configuration` class for releasing an application module after use, the `boolean remove` flag decides whether to retain the state of the application module for later use by the same client or remove the application module instance after its release. If the remove flag is `false`, then the application module is checked into the pool without resetting the state. However the state will be reset later, if a different client (Session) grabs this instance for use. Note that when a client calls `Configuration::createRootApplicationModule(...)`, there is no way for the framework to track the caller. In such a case, the session affinity concept will not work.

- `Configuration.releaseRootApplicationModule(ApplicationModule appModule, boolean remove)`
- `Configuration.releaseRootApplicationModuleHandle(ApplicationModuleHandle handle, boolean remove)`

What happens when a client creates an application module instance?

It is always interesting to know what happens under the cover when a client calls `createRootApplicationModule` on `Configuration` to grab an application module instance. The following code snippet creates an application module using an application module definition and configuration files:

```
//In the client class
String amDef = "com.packtpub.model.service.HRServiceAppModule";
String config = "HRServiceAppModuleLocal";
ApplicationModule am = Configuration.createRootApplicationModule(amD
ef, config);
```

Let's take a look at the underlying execution path when a client tries to grab an application module instance. The following sequence diagram illustrates the sequence of actions and collaboration between various framework components when an application module is checked out from the pool to serve a new client:

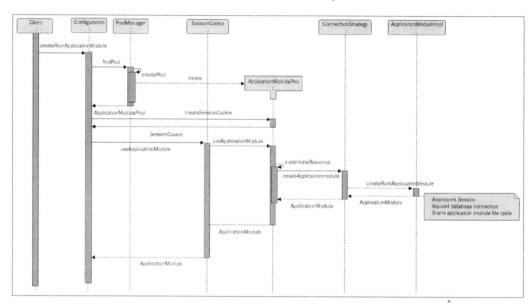

When a client invokes `createRootApplicationModule(String qualifiedAMDefName, String configName)` on the **Configuration** class, the first task is to find or create the appropriate **ApplicationPool** that is responsible for checking out (or pooling) the application module instance from the pool. The **Configuration** class then requests a **SessionCookie** object, while passing application pool instances as parameter. The session cookies are used by the framework to identify unique client sessions across server requests and server instances. The basic context for checking out an application module instance is in place by now.

The next step is to check out the application module instance from the pool. The **Configuration** class triggers the check out process by calling `useApplicationModule()` on a session cookie object. The call is then delegated to the application pool instance. Before starting the check out process, the application pool will check to see if the session cookie is already referencing an application module instance of the type requested by the client and if available, then the referenced instance will be given back to the caller and the rest of the steps in the check-out process will be skipped.

If there is no application module instance available in the checked out state for the client, then the application pool instance will load the associated **ConnectionStrategy** class which is responsible for the application module creation and database connection for use. A server side session implementation will be created at this stage to hold the session specific information such as user locale, transaction handler, environment details, and security context. The session object is instantiated for each root application module when the application module is activated. If there is no free instance available in the pool and the pool size is allowed to grow further, then a new instance of the application module is created to serve the client request. The framework prepares the checked out instance ready for use by calling basic lifecycle methods to restore the previous transaction state (if any) before returning the same to the caller.

The lifecycle of an application module

An application module plays a very crucial rule in deciding the scalability and health of your ADF application. If you want to override the lifecycle methods of an application module to change the default behaviour or to add extra functionalities, it is essential to know what happens under the covers when an instance is checked out from the pool to serve a request. Let us take a look at the details of an application module lifecycle.

When a client requests an application module, the framework will try to identify an instance to serve the new request using the following algorithm:

- Application module pooling logic will try to identify the client using the Session Cookie that is carried along with the request. If it is a web client, a session cookie is generated from the session identifier information present in the `HttpRequest` object.

- If this is the first request from the client, then the default application module pool implementation will try to allocate an available unreferenced instance from the pool to the client. If this is not the first time that the client has requested an application module, then application module pool will try to identify the instance used previously and will allocate the same if it is available.

- If all the instances in the pool are in use and the numbers of instances in the pool are fewer than the maximum pool size and the recycle threshold for the application module pool is not reached, then the application module pool will create a new instance and allocate the same to the client.

- If the pool size is equal to the maximum pool size or recycle threshold is reached and there are idle instances available in the pool, then the application module pool chooses the least recently used one from the pool, passivate its state, and activate the same for servicing the current request.

- If all instances are in use and the pool size is equal to the maximum pool then the resource application module pool will throw a check-out failure exception to the caller.

After identifying the application module instance to serve a client request, the framework will take it through the predefined phases to prepare it for use. The following lifecycle callback methods defined on the application module are engaged (in the same order as listed) when an instance is checked out and allocated for use by a client. You can override these methods in your application module implementation class based on the use case.

- `ApplicationModuleImpl::activate(Session session)`: This method is invoked by the framework when a root application module is created. This method can be overridden to add custom logic for initializing resources or setting up the context at the root level.

- `ApplicationModuleImpl::applyPersonalization()`: This method is responsible for applying the personalized definition (customization) added for the component. Refer to the topic *Personalized Business Components* in *Chapter 5, Advanced Concepts on Entity Objects and View Objects*, to brush up the memory.

- `ApplicationModuleImpl::afterConnect()`: This is invoked after the application module database connection has been established. This method may be overridden by applications to perform application module initialization which requires database access.

- `ApplicationModuleImpl::prepareApplicationModuleSession(Session session)`: This method prepares the application module session. This method can be overridden to initialize the application module session that should not be re-executed when the application module is reconnected.

- `ApplicationModuleImpl::prepareSession(Session session)`: The `prepareSession(Session session)` is invoked when an application module is first created, and each time when an application instance is associated with a user session. The application module is assumed to be in connected state at this stage. This can be overridden to initialize the database state as well the application state for the user session.

- `ApplicationModuleImpl::prepareForActivation(Element amNode)`: This method is called at the beginning of the activation cycle. You will override this method if you want to add custom activation logic that needs to be executed before the activation of view objects, or child application modules.

- `ApplicationModuleImpl::activateState(Element parent)`: The `activateState(Element parent)` is called towards the end of the activation cycle, after all the view object instances have been activated. This method can be overridden to add custom activation logic or to retrieve custom data from an XML node under the given parent element.

- `ApplicationModuleImpl::afterActivation(int activationMode)`: This method is called after activating the application module and its child components.

- `ApplicationModuleImpl::activateConnectionState(Element parent)`: The `activateConnectionState(Element parent)` is invoked at the end of activation cycle as well as when an application module is reconnected with a user session. Generally, developers may override this method to use custom approaches for restoring state information. However, this is not going to limit you in using the standard approach for restoring the state by reading the parent elements passed as an input parameter into this method. If no child nodes were added during `pssivateConnectionState(Document doc, Element parent)`, then the parent node would be null.

After serving the request for the client, towards the end of the request cycle, the framework will check in the application module instance back to the pool. The release mode property (`RELEASE_MODE`) set for the application module configuration decides how this instance needs to be released back to the pool. The possible options are as follows:

- **Stateful**: This is the default release mode (also known as the **managed** mode). In this mode, the application module pool will allocate the same instance of the application module for the same data control if it is available at the moment. If the previously used application module is busy or unavailable, then a different application module will activate this data control's state. The previous state of business components will be restored when the framework uses a new application module instance to serve an existing client.

- **Stateless**: This mode is also known as **unmanaged** mode. In this mode no state is preserved across requests from the same client. This is more of a performant than the other two modes because of its stateless nature, however this may not be an ideal option if the transaction state spans across multiple requests.

- **Reserved**: This guarantees that the application module will remain sticky for a data control (client) and the same instance will be available throughout the session. This is not recommended for a web application as it adversely affects the scalability of the system.

Passivation activation of application modules

When an application module pool does not find any unreferenced entity instances to serve a new request, the framework will check to see if the number of application module instances in the pool which were released in the managed state has reached the recycle threshold value. If the recycle threshold is reached, then the framework will look for the least recently used (LRU) instance in the pool and will allocate it to the current requestor. While doing so, it will passivate the chosen application module instance. The framework passivates both transactional data and non-transactional data attached to the application module. This list includes dirty entity rows, current state of view objects such as current rows, applied view criteria, bind variables, passivate enabled transient attributes, page ranging parameters, row set state, query set at runtime, and dynamic structural changes performed on business components. The state to be passivated is converted into XML and saved in a passivation store which could be either a local file system or a database configured using the property jbo.passivationstore in the bc4j.xcfg file. Once the passivation is over, the framework will activate new client states on the allocated application module instance. The activation mechanism restores the state from the passivation store.

Programmatic passivation and activation of custom data

The following example illustrates programmatic approach to passivate and activate custom data present in an application module. This example overrides the passivatesState(Document, Element) and activatesState(Element) methods in an application module to make the regionId data available for the client even after the passivation and activation cycle of the application module.

```
//In application module implementation class
/**
 * Overridden framework method to passivate user data
 * in XML format by appending to the parent node
 */
@Override
public void passivateState(Document doc, Element parent) {
   //This code snippet stores the data in USERDATA node
  Element nodeUserData = doc.createElement("USERDATA");
  nodeUserData.setAttribute("KEY", USER_REGION);
  nodeUserData.setAttribute("VALUE",
      getRegionId().toString());
  parent.appendChild(nodeUserData);
  super.passivateState(doc, parent);
}
```

```
/**
 * Overridden framework method to activate user data from
 * XML snapshot, stored during passivation
 */
@Override
public void activateState(Element parent) {
    //This code snippet reads the data stored in USERDATA node
  if (parent != null) {
    NodeList nl = parent.getElementsByTagName("USERDATA");
    for (int i = 0; i < nl.getLength(); i++) {

      Element e = (Element)nl.item(i);
      String key = e.getAttribute("KEY");
      String value = e.getAttribute("VALUE");
      setRegionId(new Integer(value));
      break;
    }
  }
  super.activateState(parent);
}
// regionId is made activation safe in this e.g
private Integer regionId = null;

private Integer getRegionId() {
  return regionId;
}

private void setRegionId(Integer regionId) {
  this.regionId = regionId;
}
```

Storing business data at user session level

When you build rich enterprise applications, it is a very common requirement to
have a mechanism to store some business specific data for a user session. Let's take
a look at some possible options for storing session data in the business service layer
without sacrificing the flexibility of the system.

Using a transient view object

A **transient view object** contains only transient attributes, whose values are
populated programmatically. This can be used to store user session specific
business data which needs to be accessed from the view layer or from other
business components.

The steps for building a transient view object is more or less the same for a normal view object that we learned about in *Chapter 4, Introducing View Object,* with few exceptions, discussed as follows.

To create a transient view object, build a view object by selecting the programmatic data source. When you add attributes, make sure all the attributes are marked as updatable and at least one attribute is marked as a key attribute. Generate the implementation class for the view object and override the `beforeRollback(Trans actionEvent)` and `afterRollback(TransactionEvent)` methods with an empty method body. This will help you to avoid losing the data you stored in the transient view object during transaction rollback and application module recycling.

As the transient view object is used as a data holder, there is no need to query the data source at any point. To disable any queries on the view object, select the **General** page of the overview editor. Expand the **Tuning** section, and in the **Retrieve from Database** group box, select the **No Rows** option.

You will have to make sure that the transient view object that you use for holding the session data is passivation safe. Transient view object attributes are not passivated by default, as the attribute values can be easily recreated during activation. However, this theory may not be valid if you use a transient view object as a value holder for your session data, because in this case we do not keep track of the data source once the transient view object is populated, and there is no way to recreate these attribute values during activation. In such cases, we have to enable the default passivation support for view objects provided by the framework.

To enable passivation support, double-click on a view object to open it in the overview editor. On the **General** page, expand the **Tuning** section and select the **Passivate State** checkbox which will passivate the view object state, such as bind variable values and current row. To enable passivation support for all transient attributes, select the **Including All Transient Attributes** checkbox displayed as a child to the **Passivate** flag.

Alternatively, you can individually set the passivation state for transient view object attributes. To do this, on the **Attributes** page, select the transient attribute you want to passivate and in the **Details** tab, select the **Passivate** checkbox.

Using a user session data map

Another option for keeping session data is to make use of a *user data map* from the session object in an application module. A session object is instantiated for each root application module when the application module is activated. The following code snippet is from an application module:

```
//In application module implementation class

public void updateSessionWithRegionId(Integer regionId){
    Hashtable userdata = getSession().getUserData();
    userdata.put("USER_REGION", regionId);
}
```

The same can be accessed through Groovy expression as follows:

```
adf.userSession.userData.USER_REGION
```

The above mentioned Groovy expression is useful when you want to initialize a bind variable with some session level information set by the client, or if you need to set the value from the user session data map for a transient attribute.

Using a client bound session map object

If you have some legacy web client code which uses `javax.servlet.http.HttpSession` for storing session scoped business data, then the same can be accessed from your business components using the `oracle.adf.share.ADFContext` class as shown in the following code snippet:

```
ADFContext adfContext = ADFContext.getCurrent();
Map httpSessionMap = adfContext.getSessionScope();
```

However, you should be very judicious while using ADFContext to refer to client bound session objects because these objects may be missing when you run unit tests in the standalone mode; also, it may not be available for non web-based clients.

Using JDBC APIs in an application module

Although the declarative features of ADF business components will help you to query database tables and update rows, in specific cases you will have to use raw JDBC APIs by passing the declarative features while dealing with database objects. An example is to call a stored procedure from custom business logic implementation for performing specific tasks. The `oracle.jbo.server.DBTransaction` implementation class exposes APIs for dealing with row JDBC APIs. This class encapsulates database connections and transaction contexts. Let us take a look at some examples on using JDBC APIs exposed through `DBTransaction`.

The following custom method defined in an application module illustrates the usage of the `java.sql.CallableStatement` statement for executing a stored procedure in a data base.

```
//In application module implementation class

/**
 * Find department details using department id. This method
 * uses CallableStatement for executing stored procedure.
 * @param departmentId
 */
public void findDepartmentById(Integer departmentId) throws
SQLException {
  String stmt =
      "call departments_api.select_department(?,?,?,?)";
  // Create a CallableStatement for invoking stored procedure
  CallableStatement cs =
      getDBTransaction().createCallableStatement(stmt, 0);
  try {
    // Register the OUT parameters and types
    cs.registerOutParameter(2, Types.VARCHAR);
    cs.registerOutParameter(3, Types.NUMERIC);
    cs.registerOutParameter(4, Types.NUMERIC);
    //Register IN parameter
    cs.setObject(1, departmentId);
    // Execute the statement
    cs.executeQuery();
    // Retrieve the column values
    String deptName = cs.getString(2);
    BigDecimal managerId = cs.getBigDecimal(3);
    BigDecimal locId = cs.getBigDecimal(4);
    // Add your code here for further processing
  } finally {
    if (cs != null) {
      //Closing the statement
      cs.close();
    }
  }
}
```

The following custom method defined in an application module illustrates the usage of `java.sql.PreparedStatement` for executing a SQL statement:

```java
/**
 * Finds employee id using email id. This method uses
 * PreparedStatement for executing SQL
 * @param email
 * @return
 * @throws SQLException
 */
public Long findEmployeeIdByEmail(String email) throws SQLException {
  Long empId = null;
  ResultSet rs = null;
  PreparedStatement stmnt = null;
  try {
    int noRowsPrefetch = 1;
    String query = "SELECT Emp.EMPLOYEE_ID FROM EMPLOYEES"
                        + " Emp WHERE Emp.EMAIL = ?";
     //Create a PreparedStatement for SQL call
    stmnt = getDBTransaction().
          createPreparedStatement(query, noRowsPrefetch);
     //Set the inpute parameter
    stmnt.setObject(1, email);
    rs = stmnt.executeQuery();
    if (rs.next()) {
      empId = rs.getLong(1);
    }
  } finally {
     //Close the result set
    if (rs != null) {
      rs.close();
    }
     //Close the statement
    if (stmnt != null) {
      stmnt.close();
    }
  }
  return empId;
}
```

The following methods defined in the application module commits and rolls back the current transaction:

```
//In application module implementation class
/**
 * Commit the transaction
 */
public void commitTransaction() {
  getDBTransaction().commit();
}
/**
 * Rollback the transaction
 */
public void rollbackTransaction() {
  getDBTransaction().rollback();
}
```

Using save points for undo operations

An application module enables you to create save points within a transaction that can be *rolled back to* without affecting any work done in the transaction before the save point was created. These save points are within transaction scope only, and will be removed when transaction commit or rollback occurs. The following custom application module implementation uses passivateStateForUndo(String id, byte[] clientData, int flags) and activateStateForUndo(String id, int flags) methods defined in ApplicationModuleImpl to illustrate the usage of this feature.

```
public class HRAppModuleImpl extends ApplicationModuleImpl
    implements HRAppModule {
  // other code goes here...
  /**
    *This method save the state of application module and
    * return save point id.
    */
  public String passivateStateForUndo(String savePointId) {
    String savePoint = super.passivateStateForUndo(
          savePointId, null, PASSIVATE_UNDO_FLAG);
    return savePoint;
  }
  /**
    * This method restores the state to the stave point
    */
  public void activateStateForUndo(String savePointId) {
```

```
        super.activateStateForUndo(savePointId,
            ACTIVATE_UNDO_FLAG);
    }


}
```

Client side code for creating save points and restoring the same using the above defined methods in the application module are as follows:

```
    HRServiceAppModul hrAMImpl = getHRServiceAppModul();
    boolean rollBackToSavePoint=false;
    //Create save point
    String spId = hrAMImpl.passivateStateForUndo(null);
    //your business logic goes here
    //.............
    //Some operation fails, rollBackToSavePoint becomes true
    rollBackToSavePoint = hrAMImpl.updateEmployeeData();
    //Restore save point for undo operation
    if(rollBackToSavePoint){
        hrAMImpl.activateStateForUndo(spId);
    }
```

Programmatically configuring an application module

An application module's properties are configured at design time using the corresponding bc4j.xcfg. Sometimes you will need to go beyond the design time properties, and programmatically supply configuration parameters based on various runtime parameters. An application module has support supplying configuration parameters at runtime. Configuration properties can be set programmatically by creating a Java class that implements the oracle.jbo.common.ampool. EnvInfoProvider interface.

You can configure the application module to use the custom EnvInfoProvider class by setting the fully qualified EnvInfoProvider implementation class as the value for the jbo.envinfoprovider property by using the application module configuration editor (in the **Property** tab). The framework will use this class to read overridden configuration parameter values while initializing an application module. If you are not familiar with the application module configuration editor, refer back to the topic *Overriding the default properties of an application module* in this chapter.

The following example illustrates the usage of the custom `EnvInfoProvider` class for setting the data source name onto an application module on the fly. This example reads the data source name from http session data.

```java
//Custom EnvInfoProvider implementation class

/**
 * Dynamic EnvInfoProvider for an application module
 */
public class DynamicEnvInfoProvider implements EnvInfoProvider {
    /**
     * This method gets engaged when invoked by the
     * ApplicationPool
     * to acquire dynamic application context before the
     * applicationModule lifecycle event starts
     */
    public Object getInfo(String infoType, Object env) {
        if (EnvInfoProvider.
            INFO_TYPE_JDBC_PROPERTIES.equals(infoType)) {
          //Read data source name from Http Session through
          //ADFContext
           Map session = ADFContext.getCurrent().
               getSessionScope();
           Object dsName = session.get
               (Configuration.JDBC_DS_NAME);
           //Update the data source property

           if (dsName != null) {
               if (((Hashtable)env).
                   containsKey(Configuration.JDBC_DS_NAME)) {
                       ((Hashtable)env).
                       put(Configuration.JDBC_DS_NAME,
                                        (String)dsName);
               }
           }
        }
        return null;
    }
    //Other methods goes here
}
```

Programmatically building a master-child view object

We have discussed an example for programmatically building entity objects and view objects at runtime in *Chapter 5, Advanced Concepts on Entity Objects and View Objects,* under the topic *Building business components dynamically.* We are revisiting a similar topic with a slightly different use case. In the previous example, we were discussing dynamic view objects built on top of dynamic entity objects. In this section, we are going to see an example for programmatically creating SQL query based view objects with master-child coordination enabled.

The following example defines two SQL query based view objects, DynamicDeptVO and DynamicEmpVO, and DynamicDeptEmpViewLink view link between them to enable master-child synchronization. This example can be used as reference for building a master-child UI at runtime.

```
//In application module implementation class
public void createMasterChildViewObjects() {
   // Create a new "model.views.DynamicDeptVO" view definition
   ViewDefImpl deptViewDef = new ViewDefImpl(
         "model.views.DynamicDeptVO");
   // Define the names and types of the view attributes
   deptViewDef.addViewAttribute("DepartmentId",
         "DEPARTMENT_ID", Integer.class);
   deptViewDef.addViewAttribute("DepartmentName",
         "DEPARTMENT_NAME", String.class);
   // Define the SQL query that this view object will perform
   deptViewDef.setQuery("SELECT Dept.DEPARTMENT_ID,  Dept.DEPARTMENT_
NAME FROM DEPARTMENTS Dept");
   deptViewDef.setFullSql(true);
   deptViewDef.setBindingStyle(
         SQLBuilder.BINDING_STYLE_ORACLE_NAME);
   deptViewDef.resolveDefObject();
   // Create an instance of the new view definition,
   // named "DynamicDepartments"
   ViewObject deptView = createViewObject(
         "DynamicDepartments", deptViewDef);
   // Create a new "model.views.DynamicEmpVO" view definition
   ViewDefImpl empViewDef = new ViewDefImpl
      ("model.views.DynamicEmpVO");
   // Define the names and types of the view attributes
   empViewDef.addViewAttribute("EmployeeId",
         "EMPLOYEE_ID", Integer.class);
```

```
empViewDef.addViewAttribute("FirstName",
    "FIRST_NAME", String.class);
empViewDef.addViewAttribute("LastName",
    "LAST_NAME", String.class);
empViewDef.addViewAttribute("DepartmentId",
    "DEPARTMENT_ID", Integer.class);
 // Define the SQL query that this view object will perform
empViewDef.setQuery("SELECT Emp.EMPLOYEE_ID, Emp.FIRST_NAME, Emp.
LAST_NAME, Emp.DEPARTMENT_ID FROM EMPLOYEES Emp");
empViewDef.setFullSql(true);
empViewDef.setBindingStyle(
    SQLBuilder.BINDING_STYLE_ORACLE_NAME);
empViewDef.resolveDefObject();
 // Create an instance of the new view definition,
 //named "DynamicEmployees"
ViewObject empView = createViewObject(
    "DynamicEmployees", empViewDef);
 // Create a view link between these two new view instances
ViewLink empsInDepartment =
  createViewLinkBetweenViewObjects(
    "DynamicDeptEmpViewLink",
    "EmployeesInDepartment",
  deptView, new AttributeDef[] {
    deptView.findAttributeDef("DepartmentId") },
    empView, new AttributeDef[] {
        empView.findAttributeDef("DepartmentId") },
    DEPARTMENT_ID = :Bind_DepartmentId");
}
```

Using ADF Business Components with Java EE components

You will have to mix and match various technologies while building complex business models for an application. This is very essential when you are integrating services exposed by multiple applications, or when you build next generation applications reusing services exposed by the legacy systems.

The following example illustrates a stateless session bean method that invokes business methods from an application module. This example updates the DEPARTMENT database table through Java Persistence APIs in the session EJB bean, and passes the details about this operation to an application module method in order to update the DEPARTMENT_AUDIT table. Both EJB and the application module share the same XA data source enabling two-phase commit for the database transaction. If you see the following method, you may notice that the client does not call commit on an application module, rather it only calls postChanges() on DBTransaction to post changes without committing the database transaction. The commit is triggered finally from the EJB method when it calls commit on the javax.transaction. UserTransaction object.

```
//In SessionEJB implementation class

@Stateless(name = "SessionEJB", mappedName = "DemoSessionEJB")
@TransactionManagement(TransactionManagementType.BEAN)
@TransactionAttribute(TransactionAttributeType.REQUIRED)
public class SessionEJBBean implements SessionEJB, SessionEJBLocal {
    @PersistenceContext(unitName = "EJBModel")
    private EntityManager em;
    @Resource
    SessionContext sessionContext;
  public Departments mergeDepartments(Departments departments) {
    AuditAppModule am = null;
    try {
      UserTransaction userTxn = sessionContext.
            getUserTransaction();
//Start user transaction in session EJB bean
      userTxn.begin();
//Merge changes in session EJB Bean
      departments = em.merge(departments);

//Invoke audit routine in application module(AM)
      HashMap dataForAduit = new HashMap();
      dataForAduit.put(DepartmentsAuditImpl.DEPARTMENTID,
            new oracle.jbo.domain.Number(
                      departments.getDepartmentId()));
      dataForAduit.put(DepartmentsAuditImpl.DEPARTMENTNAME,
          departments.getDepartmentName());

      String amDef = "model.audit.AuditAppModule";
      String config = "AppModuleLocal";
```

```
//Create AM instance
     am = (AuditAppModule)Configuration.
             createRootApplicationModule(amDef, config);

//Pass data to AM method to update desired database tables
     am.createDepartmentsAudit(dataForAduit);
//Post Changes to DB without committing transaction
     am.getDBTransaction().postChanges();

//Commit the transaction in EJB, which will commit transaction
//in AM as well, because both use same XA Datasource
     userTxn.commit();
   } catch (Exception ex) {
   ex.printStackTrace();
   } finally {
   if (am != null)
      Configuration.releaseRootApplicationModule(
          am, false);
   }
   return departments;
}
```

Summary

In this chapter we learned about the generic concepts of application modules and their architecture and configuration. We also discussed many examples for using application modules. With this chapter, your understanding of business component fundamentals should be complete. Note that we will be revisiting the fine-tuning parameters available for application modules in *Chapter 12, Oracle ADF Best Practices,* with real life use cases.

In the coming chapters our focus will be more towards consuming the services exposed by the business components from the UI.

7
Binding Business Services with the User Interface

In the previous chapters, we discussed about the business service implementation by using ADF Business Components. In this chapter, you will learn to bind the user interface for the data model built from ADF Business Components. We will discuss the following topics in this chapter:

- Binding model data with user interfaces
- Building a simple data bound web page
- What happens when you drop a data collection on a page?
- Browsing through page definition files
- What happens when you access a fusion web page?
- Invoking an application module from a Java servlet
- Adding custom phase listeners

Introduction

The great advantage of using the ADF framework is its declarative support for building a **user interface (UI)** for business services. The ADF data binding layer enables you to build a UI for a data model through a visual and declarative programming model. The ADF data binding layer offers data binding support and out-of-the-box infrastructure for common UI functionalities such as navigation over rows, range fetching, built-in CRUD operations, and state management. If you want to go beyond the declarative features by overriding the default behavior of specific functionalities, you can use the ADF binding APIs provided by the framework.

The ADF binding layer is also referred to as the **ADF Model (ADFm)** and the two words are used interchangeably in this book.

Binding model data with user interfaces

Presenting business data to end users without sacrificing the usability and scalability of the system is very important for any enterprise application. When you wire data from the business services implementation to the UI, in general, there are two tasks involved:

- **Invoking business services for data**: Typical implementation may contain some infrastructure code to invoke business services for data access. The service invocation code may vary with technology used for building business services.

- **Binding the data with UI components**: Once the business data is read, the application should populate data on the UI without losing the meaning.

The ADF model performs the preceding tasks in a more generic way by abstracting the infrastructure code required for service invocation and data binding from developers. ADF uses the following concepts to bind the UI with the data model:

- **Data control**: Data control acts as a proxy cum adaptor implementation for the business services. In other words, data control invokes business services and returns the result wrapped in a generic data structure to be used by the binding layer. Data control usage varies with the technology used for building business services. The most commonly used data controls include the following:
    - **ADF Business Components Data Control**: This is used with ADF Business Components.
    - **JavaBean Data Control**: This is used to access data from the **Plain Old Java Object (POJO)** class.
    - **EJB Data Control**: This is used to access data from the EJB Session Bean.
    - **URL Service Data Control**: This is used to consume the data stream from a specified URL. They are non-updatable by nature.
    - **Web Service Data Control**: This is used to access data from the **Web Services Description Language (WSDL)** for a web service.
    - **JMX Data Control**: This is used to access **Java Management Extensions (JMX)** MBeans from an MBean Server.

o **Placeholder data control**: Placeholder data control is useful to mimic the model data when you choose to build the UI before the actual model. Later this can be replaced with the real data control when it becomes available.

Note that the above list contains only commonly used data controls. In real life application development, you may see more data control implementations, each dealing with a specific service implementation such as Oracle Essbase, **Business Activity Monitoring (BAM)**, or **Universal Content Management (UCM)**.

- **Declarative data binding**: Declarative data bindings abstract the details of accessing data from data collections in a data control and the details of invoking its operations. The framework uses different data binding definitions based on the underlying data model for each UI component. Value bindings will be populated at runtime whenever they are referenced by the components through EL expression.

The following diagram represents the layered architecture of the ADF Model. You will notice that the ADF framework uses the ADF binding layer (ADF Model) for accessing the data exposed by the business services. The ADF binding layer deploys different data controls based on the technology used for building business services.

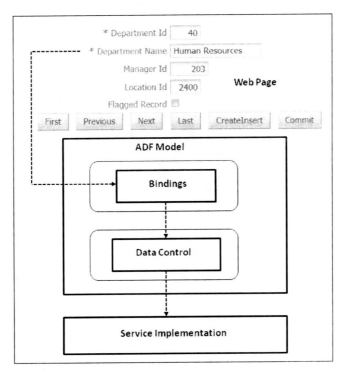

Building a simple data bound web page

Let us build a simple data bound web UI to get a feel for the visual and declarative development experience offered by the JDeveloper IDE along with Oracle ADF framework. During this exercise, we will also take a look at the metadata files generated by the IDE to be used by the runtime.

To build a fusion web application workspace, follow these steps:

1. Create a fusion web application by selecting the **New Application** option within the application navigator tab in the JDeveloper.

2. This will display the **New Gallery** dialog window with a set of predefined templates targeting various technologies. For ADF web applications, select the **Fusion Web Application** template and click on **OK**.

3. Enter the application package prefix as `com.packtpub.adfguide.ch7`. On the next page, enter the model project name as `HRDataModel`.

4. Click on **Finish** to save the changes.

As we have already discussed about the generation of business components (entity object, view object, and application module) in the previous chapters, we are skipping the step for business component creation. This example uses entity objects and view objects built using the `DEPARTMENTS` and `EMPLOYEES` tables from the `HR` schema. If you need a quick brush-up on generating business components, refer to the topic *Building a simple business service* in *Chapter 2, Introduction to ADF Business Components*.

Once you generate an application module along with the desired data model, the same will be exposed in the **Data Controls** panel. The following screenshot displays the **Data Controls** panel, exposing the data model used for our current example. It exposes the **Departments** and **Employees** view object instances to be used by the client.

To build a web page, perform the following steps:

1. Right-click on the **ViewController** project and select **New | Page**.

2. In the **Create JSF Page** dialog window, enter a logically meaningful name for the page and select the document type as **Facelet**. In the **Page Layout** tab, select the **Create Blank Page** option and click on **OK** to save changes.

When you work on real life applications, you can create a custom page template and use the same for building web pages.

 To learn more about Page Templates and ADF Faces Components, refer to *Oracle Fusion Middleware Web User Interface Developer's Guide for Oracle Application Development Framework*. To access the documentation go to `http://www.oracle.com/technetwork/developer-tools/jdev/documentation/index.html`. Navigate to **Oracle JDeveloper and ADF Documentation Library** and then choose **Web User Interface Developer's Guide**. Use the search option to find specific topics.

You can use the drag-and-drop offerings from JDeveloper to visually lay out controls on a page. For example, to build a UI table displaying data collection from the **Departments** database table, you just need to drag the instance of the **Departments** view instance from the **Data Controls** panel and drop on the page by choosing the desired display component available in the context menu. In this example, we have used the **ADF Form** component along with navigation controls for displaying the collection returned by the **Departments** view instance:

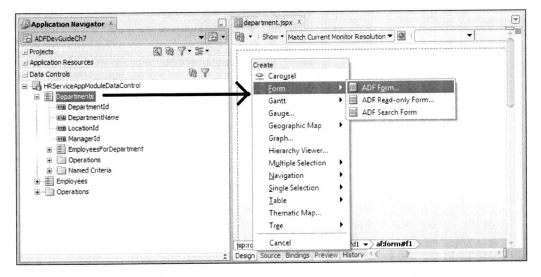

The preceding steps are enough to make your page work. To run the page, right-click on the page and select **Run**.

If you are a beginner to ADF, you may have many questions in your mind by this time—is a view object instance a data collection? What happens when a data collection is dropped on a page? What happens under the covers when we run a data bound page? Stay tuned, the rest of this chapter will answer all these queries.

Is a view object really a data collection?

This may be the first question that you may ask when you start using view object instances exposed through the data control panel for building a UI.

Yes, the view object instance is a data collection (row set) in itself. To understand this point let us take a step back and take a closer look at the structure of the view object. The following class diagram represents the `oracle.jbo.server.ViewObjectImpl` class and its associated infrastructure classes namely `oracle.jbo.server.ViewRowSetImpl` and `oracle.jbo.server.ViewRowSetIteratorImpl`.

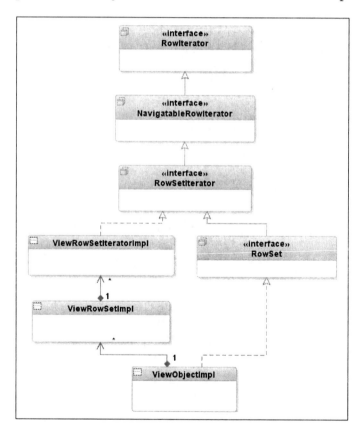

The following list discusses the roles of each class in brief from the above diagram:

- A view object (`oracle.jbo.server.ViewObjectImpl`) contains logic for controlling the query execution.

- A view object uses a row set class (`oracle.jbo.server.ViewRowSetImpl`) to manage the collections of view rows read from a query. A view object may have multiple row sets—a default (primary) row set and secondary row sets. When the client calls `executeQuery()` on `ViewObjectImpl`, the default row set is refreshed to hold the query result.

- `RowSet` uses an internal row set iterator (`oracle.jbo.server.ViewRowSetIteratorImpl`) class to iterate over the collection. This saves you from calling a different API to find the iterator object for the row set.

The above classes are the real work horses, which manage the view row collection when you execute a view object and iterate over rows from a query. If you see the class diagram for the view object that we discussed a while ago, you may notice that the `ViewObjectImpl` class itself implements the `RowSet` interface. Wondering why? This is done to improve the usability of the view object so that you really do not need to use a separate collection class for reading the queried rows and for iterating over them as well. In fact, the default view object implementation class (`ViewObjectImpl`) does not really provide complete method body implementations for the `RowSet` interfaces. The methods implementing the `RowSet` interface in a `ViewObjectImpl` simply delegate all the calls to an internal default row set implementation object (`ViewRowSetImpl`). This implementation gives the feel of data collection for a view object class and this is the reason why you are able to iterate over a view object instance, using Iterator APIs. An example is here:

```
//In application module implementation class

Public void readEmployeeRows(){
//Get the view object,
//execute it and iterate over the rows
  ViewObject employeeVO= getEmployees();
  employeeVO.executeQuery();
  while (employeeVO.hasNext()) {
    Row row = employeeVO.next();
    //Business logic goes here
  }
}
```

What happens when we drop a data collection on a page?

When we drag a view object instance (data collection) from the **Data Controls** panel and drop it on a page, JDeveloper IDE creates (or updates, if existing) binding metadata XML files for holding binding definitions. IDE performs the following tasks:

- IDE adds ADF Faces Components to the JSF page. Common attributes of the UI components are defaulted by using the attribute definitions present in the model, referred through **Expression Language** (EL).

 Expression Language is used to access underlying the model component in the ADF Faces pages. To learn general concepts on Expression Language, go to http://java.sun.com/products/jsp/reference/techart/unifiedEL.html.

- It creates DataBindings.cpx if it is not found in the default view package under the ADFm source directory. The default location of the ADF model source is the adfmsrc folder located under the view project.

- It creates adfm.xml if it is not found in the META-INF folder under the adfmsrc directory. This is considered as a registry of all metadata registries used by the view project. When IDE creates a data binding cpx file (DataBindings.cpx), an entry is made in adfm.xml to keep track of all the cpx files present in a web application.

- It creates the page definition XML (<PageName>PageDef.xml) file if it is not already present for the page. This is located in the pageDefs folder under the view project package, which is found under the adfmsrc directory. This file contains the binding metadata for each data bound UI element present on the page. When IDE creates a page definition file for the JSF page, it also adds a mapping entry between the JSF and page definition file in the DataBindings.cpx file.

- It adds the required library dependencies to the view project.

- It updates web.xml to add runtime configurations such as ADFBindingFilter, which is required by the ADF Faces Components runtime.

The following diagram illustrates how a UI component is EL-wired to the attribute definition present in a view object. The page definition file for the web page contains metadata for identifying the data collection (view object instance) for an attribute. The ADF binding layer uses detailed configurations present in `DataBindings.cpx` to load the right application module usage for the client. The view usage entry present in the application module tells about the view object instance that backs the data collection displayed in the UI.

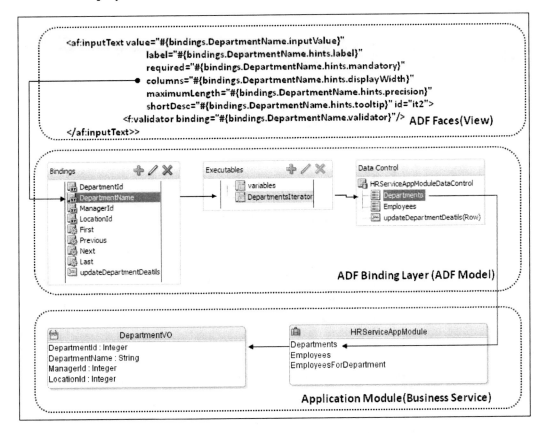

Taking a closer look at the ADF Model metadata files

This is in continuation with the discussion from the last section. In this section, we will take a closer look at the metadata files used by ADF to wire the UI with business services. An Oracle Fusion web application uses various metadata XML files to configure the runtime behavior of the system.

The following diagram represents the metadata XML files used for a Fusion web application:

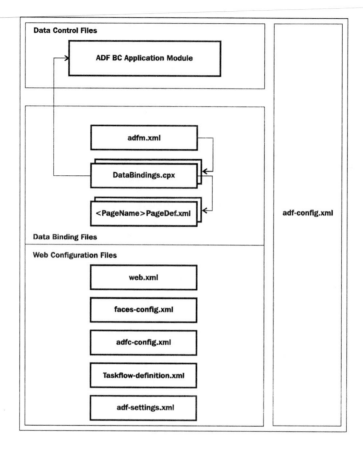

Let us take a look at the important metadata files used by the ADF Model layer.

adfm.xml

The adfm.xml file is a registry of registries used by the framework to quickly find all metadata registry files used at runtime. This registry XML file records four types of metadata files:

- Data binding registry (DataBindings.cpx)
- Data control registry (DataControls.dcx)
- Business component service registry (bc4j.xcfg)
- Business component project registry (<ModelProject>.jpx)

When you generate data binding or data control, the `adfm.xml` file immediately records corresponding `.cpx` and `.dcx` file entries. However, ADF Business Components registry files, such as `.jpx` and `.xcfg` files, are not recorded in the `adfm.xml` file in real time. The `.jpx` and `.xcfg` files are updated only after a compile and/or deployment. In effect, during design time, your application source may not have the correct version of `adfm.xml` — only the final artifact generated for deployment will have the correct version with all entries. Here is a sample `adfm.xml` file that contains entries for the metadata files used in an application. Note that this sample is copied from the final artifact — you may not see `bc4j.xcfg` and `<ModelProject>.jpx` entries in `adfm.xml` during design time:

```
<?xml version = '1.0' encoding = 'UTF-8'?>
<MetadataDirectory xmlns="http://xmlns.oracle.com/adfm/metainf"
version="11.1.1.0.0">
   <DataBindingRegistry
   path="com/packtpub/adfguide/ch7/view/DataBindings.cpx"/>
   <BusinessComponentServiceRegistry
   path="com/packtpub/adfguide/model/service/common/bc4j.xcfg"/>
   <BusinessComponentProjectRegistry
   path="com/packtpub/adfguide/model/HRDataModel.jpx"/>
</MetadataDirectory>
```

DataBindings.cpx

The `DataBindings.cpx` file defines the runtime binding context for the entire application. This file contains mapping between page and page definition files, and metadata definition for the data control usage. For example, the following `DataBindings.cpx` file displays the mapping between the `dept.jsf` and `view.pageDefs.deptPageDef` files. The data control usage `AppModuleDataControl` listed in this `.cpx` file contains metadata for invoking the underlying application module.

Page Mappings	
path	usageId
/dept.jsf	view_deptPageDef

Page Definition Usages	
id	path
view_deptPageDef	view.pageDefs.deptPageDef

Data Control Usages
id
AppModuleDataControl

When you generate a deployable artifact (JAR file) for the view projects, the
`DataBindings.cpx` file will be stored in a default package folder from the
root without the `adfmsrc` folder.

> Note that if you have multiple view controller projects in your Fusion
> web application, make sure each project follows different package names.
> This ensures that, at runtime, `DataBindings.cpx` from one project does
> not override an other one with the same package name.

adf-config.xml

The `adf-config.xml` file provides a central metadata file to manage
application-wide configuration data. This file is located in `<Application>/.
adf/META-INF/adf-config.xml` and there should be only one such file in the
application. When you deploy an ADF application as EAR, `adf-config.xml` will
be available at the `ear` class loader level — hence available to all modules contained
in that application. This file is designed to contain application level configuration
that can be set at deployment time and changed at runtime.

The application's `adf-config.xml` contains the following configuration entries:

- MDS configuration
- `ResourceBundle` override information
- Security context
- Application UID

The `oracle.adf.share.ADFConfig` class represents the runtime representation
of the `adf-config.xml` file. `ADFConfig` is a customizable document and it uses
the **metadata service (MDS)** to persist customizations. Updates to `ADFConfig`
are checked and updated, if needed, at the start of each HTTP request.

> The schema for `adf-config.xml` can be found in the `adf-share-
> support.jar` file as `oracle/adf/share/config/schema/
> config.xsd`. The `adf-share-support.jar` file is located in the
> `<JDeveloper_Home>/oracle_common/modules/oracle.adf.
> share_xx.x.x` folder.

adf-settings.xml

ADF Settings is designed to store project-level or library-level settings for view layers such as ADF Faces help providers, phase listeners, MDS web-app prefix, and web cache configuration information. You cannot alter the configuration settings for this file during or after application deployment. This file is located in the `<application>\<ViewController>\src\META-INF` directory.

Browsing through the page definition file

We have already discussed the creation of the page dentition file when dropping data collection on a page. The following screenshot displays a typical page definition file in the structure window of JDeveloper:

In this section, we will analyze the different entries in a page definition file and their usage at runtime.

Parameters

The `<parameters>` section in the page definition file allows you to define parameter binding objects that other bindings or UI components can refer. In real life, you may use this section to define parameters whose value is referenced from multiple places in a page definition file.

Executables

The `<executables>` section defines executable items that get executed during the ADF page lifecycle. Note that the data collections used in the page are refreshed through appropriate executable binding entries. The following are the executable binding objects supported by the framework:

- **Iterator**: The `<iterator>` section binds to an iterator object that iterates over the data collection exposed through data control. An example for a data collection is a view object instance in the data control panel. The iterator binding definition decides how and when to refresh the attached data collection during a page lifecycle.

- **Method iterator**: The `<methodIterator>` section binds to an iterator object that iterates over the data collection returned from a custom method exposed through data control.

- **Variable iterator**: The `<variableIterator>` section binds to an iterator object that exposes all the variables in the page definition, which other bindings can reference. Variable iterators include method parameters and scalar return values of custom methods exposed through data control.

- **Invoke action**: The `<invokeAction>` section binds to a built-in action or method action binding present in the binding section of the page definition file. This is useful if you want to execute a method action during the lifecycle of a page for each request from the browser.

  You should keep the following points in mind while using this binding in the application:

  - `invokeAction` is executed for each request from the web client. Use the appropriate `Refresh` property for the `invokeAction` binding to decide the lifecycle phase at which the binding is refreshed.

  - If the method contains page initialization logic and it is supposed to be executed only once during the page load, check the feasibility of using a method call activity in the navigation flow definition (bounded or unbounded task flow XML file), before the page renders, to invoke the method instead of using `invokeAction`. If method call activity is not a viable option for you, make sure that the framework is not triggering the `invokeAction` executable multiple times during the page lifecycle by adding the appropriate `refreshCondition`.

- **Page**: The `<page>` binding is used to refresh the data binding for the page template. This entry will appear only if the current page is built by choosing a data bound page template. The page binding executable is refreshed during the Prepare Model phase. During this phase, the binding container for the template is created based on the template's page definition file, and it is added to the binding context.

- **Search region**: `<searchRegion>` defines the executable binding definition for the query component and **Query By Example (QBE)** criteria that appears on a UI table. This binds the named view criteria to the iterator for data collection.

- **Task flow**: `<taskFlow>` defines the binding for the task flow that is embedded in a region. During the page lifecycle, the framework instantiates the binding container for a region's task flow.

- **Multitask flow**: `<multiTaskFlow>` defines the binding for an unknown number of task flows whose IDs are decided at runtime. This is useful when you have a page that contains an unknown number of regions. An example is the dynamic `panelTabbed` component where each tab is a region, whose contents are decided at runtime.

Bindings

The bindings section in a page definition file defines value bindings as well as action bindings for a web page. Value bindings bind the UI with the attribute value returned by an iterator, and action bindings bind component actions (events) with operations from the underlying data model exposed through data control. ADF supports the following binding types:

- **Action**: The `<action>` binding defines bindings for built-in operations on the row iterator object as well as on data control.

- **Method action**: The `<methodAction>` binding defines bindings for custom methods exposed through data control.

- **Attribute value**: The `<attributeValues>` binding defines the binding for accessing attribute values of the currently selected row in a data collection. Note that attribute binding is accessed through the iterator executable.

- **Boolean value**: The `<button>` binding (also known as Boolean binding) defines the bindings for attribute types whose value takes the form of checked or unchecked states.

- **Data visualization components bindings**: ADF provides data binding supports for the following graph types:
    - Map
    - Gantt
    - Gauge
    - Graph
    - PivotTable

- **List**: The `<list>` binding defines the bindings for list of items. The list binding definition can refer to the model-driven list, static list, or dynamic list. ADF also supports a variant of list binding, the `<listOfValues>` binding, which offers more options on the UI such as lazy loading, search and select, and range fetching.

- **Tree bindings**: The `<tree>` binding defines the binding for nested data collections that are used for populating hierarchical UI components such as trees and hierarchy viewer components. The tree binding even works for single-level collections as well. When you drag-and-drop a collection as a table, JDeveloper generates tree binding although the data collection is not hierarchical.

- **Table binding**: The `<table>` binding defines the binding for a single-level collection of data.

In the next chapters, we will learn more about each of these binding entries and their properties.

Using the binding editor

When you build the UI by dropping the data collection from the **Data Control** panel, JDeveloper generates necessary bindings behind the scenes. This feature helps you to build basic data bound pages, and mostly you do not really need to create bindings explicitly. However, if required, you are allowed to explicitly define bindings or edit the existing definitions.

To define bindings, open the page definition file in the overview editor and select the **Bindings and Executables** tab. You can find options to create, edit, or delete the control binding entries in the **Bindings** panel. Similarly, to manually edit executable bindings, use the edit options in the **Executables** panel. If required, use **Property Inspector** to override the properties of the bindings or executables definitions.

To define parameters used in a page, use the **Parameters** tab in the overview editor.

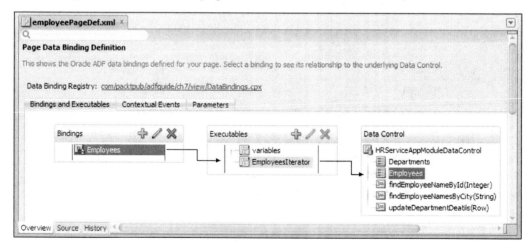

A detailed discussion on page definition binding entries can be found under the topic *Oracle ADF XML Files* in the **Appendices** section in *Fusion Developer's Guide for Oracle Application Development Framework*. To access the documentation go to http://www.oracle.com/technetwork/ developer-tools/jdev/documentation/index.html. Navigate to **Oracle JDeveloper | ADF Documentation Library** and choose **Fusion Developer's Guide**.

Programmatically accessing page binding elements

Although declarative data binding support provided by the framework is good enough for most of the use cases, there may be some scenarios where you may want to go beyond the declarative features to achieve the desired functionality such as performing some pre-processing before invoking method binding, accessing model attribute binding values from Java classes, or programmatically refreshing the data collection. You will have to use ADF Model APIs for such use cases. This section discusses about using ADF Model APIs for accessing page definition binding entries from the Java code.

Accessing binding container

The `BindingContainer` class represents Java representation of the page definition file. You may need to access the binding container object to read the bindings or executable entries present in the page definition XML at runtime. For example, to programmatically execute a method exposed through data control from your managed bean code or to refresh an iterator object bound to a view object instance, you must get the binding container object first. The following code snippet illustrates how you can programmatically access the current binding container object:

```
//In managed bean class
/**
 * This method returns BindingContainer for the current page
 * @return
 */
public BindingContainer getBindingContainer() {
    // BindingContext is a container object that holds a list
    // of available
    // data controls and data binding objects. It is the Java
    // representation of all cpx files marked in your
    //adfm.xml file
```

```
BindingContext bindingContext = BindingContext.
    getCurrent();
return bindingContext.getCurrentBindingsEntry();
}
```

Programmatically accessing the parameter binding

You can define parameters by choosing the **Parameters** tab in the overview editor of a page definition file. Consider the following parameter definition present in the page definition file:

```
<pageDefinition...>
  <parameters>
    <parameter id="DeptIdParam" value=
    "${viewScope.deptId != null ? viewScope.deptId : 10 }"
    evaluate="inPrepareModel"/>
  </parameters>
  ...
</pageDefinition>
```

In some scenarios, you may need to read this parameter value from the Java code in order to pass this value to a business method or to third-party service APIs. The following code snippet illustrates how you can access the parameter binding definition from Java code, using ADF binding API:

```
//In managed bean class

//Gets Binding Container
BindingContainer bc = getBindingContainer();
Map map= bc.getParametersMap();
Long    deptIdParam =(Long )
    ((DCParameter )map.get("DeptIdParam")).getValue();
```

Programmatically executing method action binding

Consider the following custom method definition in the application module implementation class, which is exposed through data control to be used by the client.

```
public Row updateDepartmentDeatils(Row departmentRow)
```

When you drop this method on to a page as a command button, IDE generates a `<methodAction>` binding as shown in the following code snippet:

```
<pageDefinition...>
...
  <bindings>
    <methodAction id="updateDepartmentDeatils"
    InstanceName="data.HRServiceAppModuleDataControl.dataProvider"
      DataControl="HRServiceAppModuleDataControl"
      RequiresUpdateModel="true" Action="invokeMethod"
      MethodName="updateDepartmentDeatils"
      IsViewObjectMethod="false"
      ReturnName="data.HRServiceAppModuleDataControl.
      methodResults.updateDepartmentDeatils_
      HRServiceAppModuleDataControl_dataProvider_
      updateDepartmentDeatils_result">
      <NamedData NDName="departmentRow"
      NDValue="#{bindings.DepartmentsIterator.currentRow}"
    </methodAction>
  </bindings>
</pageDefinition>
```

This can be wired to actionable UI components, using EL expression. What if you want to execute this method from your managed bean code along with some client-side business logic? The following example illustrates the usage of ADF binding APIs for accessing `methodAction` or action binding, and executing the same. Note that this example uses the preceding method action binding to access the `updateDepartmentDeatils(Row)` method in the application module.

```
//In managed bean class
public void updateDepartmentRow(Row currentDeptRow){
  //Gets Binding Container
  BindingContainer bc = getBindingContainer();
  //Gets the Method Action binding with the given name.
  OperationBinding opb =
    bc.getOperationBinding("updateDepartmentDeatils");
  //Pass the Parameters
  opb.getParamsMap().put("departmentRow", currentDeptRow);
//Execute the method and store returned value in
//return Value variable
  Object returnValue = opb.execute();
  //Any exception is thrown by the method?
  if (opb.getErrors().isEmpty()) {
  //No exception, Operation is success
  } else {
```

```
    //Exception is thrown from the method, handle it here
    //OperationBinding::getErrors() return list of JboException
    List errorList = opb.getErrors();
       //Alternative path 'on error' go here
    }
}
```

Accessing the list control binding

When you drop a view object instance with an LOV-enabled attribute on to a page as an ADF Form, JDeveloper generates list binding for the LOV-enabled attribute as shown in the following code snippet:

```
<pageDefinition...>
...
  <bindings>
    <list IterBinding="EmployeesIterator" StaticList="false"
    Uses="LOV_DepartmentId" id="DepartmentId"
    DTSupportsMRU="false" SelectItemValueMode="ListObject"/>
  </bindings>
</pageDefinition>
```

You can make use of appropriate ADF binding classes for accessing list binding used by the LOV component in the UI. The following code snippet illustrates the usage of ADF binding APIs for accessing list binding. This example reads the list binding object and finds the selected item in it:

```
//In managed bean class
public Integer getSelectedDepartmentId(){
    BindingContainer bc = getBindingContainer();
    //Get the list binding object
    JUCtrlListBinding lb = (JUCtrlListBinding)bc.
        getControlBinding("DepartmentId");
    //Get the selected row
    Row selectedRow = (Row)lb.getSelectedValue();
    //Read the desired attribute from the row.
    Integer deptId= (Integer)selectedRow.
        getAttribute("DepartmentId");
    return deptId;
}
```

Accessing the attribute binding

When you drop a view object as an ADF Form on to a page, IDE generates an attribute value binding for each attribute displayed in the UI. The following is an example:

```
<pageDefinition...>
...
  <bindings>
    <attributeValues IterBinding="DepartmentsIterator"
      id=" DepartmentId">
      <AttrNames>
        <Item Value="DepartmentId"/>
      </AttrNames>
    </attributeValues>
  </bindings>
</pageDefinition>
```

To access the attribute value from the client side, you can use the attribute binding class. The following example illustrates the usage of ADF binding APIs for accessing attribute binding:

```
//In managed bean class
public Integer getDeptAttributeValue(){
  BindingContainer bc= getBindingContainer();
  //Access Attribute binding for DepartmentId
  AttributeBinding departmentIdBinding =
    (AttributeBinding)bc.getControlBinding("DepartmentId") ;
  Integer deptId=(Integer)departmentIdBinding.getInputValue();
  return deptId;
}
```

Accessing the iterator binding and associated view object

The JDeveloper IDE generates an iterator binding definition in the page definition file when you drop a data collection from the data control panel on to a page. The iterator binding decides when to execute the underlying view object for populating the data bound UI components. Here is an example:

```
<pageDefinition ...>
  <executables>
    <iterator Binds="Departments" RangeSize="25"
    DataControl="HRServiceAppModuleDataControl"
    id="DepartmentsIterator" ChangeEventPolicy="ppr"/>
  </executables>
...
</pageDefinition>
```

In some use cases, you may need to access the iterator binding object from the client-side code in order to programmatically execute the underlying view object or to get the currently displayed row. The following example illustrates the usage of ADF binding APIs for accessing the iterator binding. This example executes the iterator programmatically:

```
//In managed bean class
public void refreshIterator() {

    //Gets Binding Container
    DCBindingContainer bc = (DCBindingContainer)
        getBindingContainer();
    //Gets the Iterator binding.
    DCIteratorBinding iteratorBinding = bc.
        findIteratorBinding("DepartmentsIterator");
    //Execute VO query by executing iterator
    iteratorBinding.executeQuery();
    //To gets the underlying view object for the itertaor
    //ViewObject vo = iteratorBinding.getViewObject();

}
```

What happens when you access a Fusion web page?

The ADF Faces is extended from JSF technology with improved usability. When a client requests a page, the framework executes standard JSF lifecycle phases along with an extended ADF page lifecycle. In this section, we will discuss the sequence of ADF page lifecycle phases that starts when a request comes on the server and continues until the page is returned to the client.

When a user tries to access a data bound ADF Faces page, the basic flow of processing the web page request on an application server is as follows:

1. When a client (for example, a web browser) requests a page, the web server inspects the application name present in the URL and delegates the request to the appropriate web application deployed on the server. Once the request is routed to the target application, that application takes over the request processing job. A Fusion web application uses the Faces Servlet (`javax. faces.webapp.FacesServlet`) to control the processing of a request. This is enforced through the following servlet mapping entry in the `web.xml` file:

```
<servlet-mapping>
    <servlet-name>Faces Servlet</servlet-name>
    <url-pattern>/faces/*</url-pattern>
</servlet-mapping>
```

The above entry tells the server to use the Faces Servlet for URLs, which follow the `/faces/*` pattern. This basic configuration is good enough to make a typical JSF page to work. The ADF Faces framework is extended from JSF with extra features such as declarative data bindings and an enhanced security model that calls for pre-processing the request in order to initialize the binding context and perform a security check before transferring the control to the Faces Servlet. This is achieved through adding servlet filters for the Faces Servlet. You will find the following filters in a typical ADF Faces application's `web.xml`:

- ○ JPS filter: This filter is used to set up the **Oracle Platform Security Services (OPSS)** policy provider. This filter intercepts each request and challenges the user for authentication. It is important that the first filter definition in the `web.xml` file should be the JPS filter.

- ○ **Trinidad filter**: This ensures that Trinidad is properly initialized by establishing a `RequestContext` object. This filter also processes file uploads.

- ○ **ADF Binding filter**: This is used to pre-process any HTTP requests that may require access to the binding context.

While we discuss the page lifecycle, in the previous list our focus is the ADF binding filter, which pre-processes the current request to use ADF binding features.

2. When the request reaches `ADFBindingFilter`, it looks for the ADF binding context in the HTTP session, and if it is not yet present, initializes it for the first time. The ADF binding context contains data binding metadata, such as page definition usages and data control usages for the application. `ADFBindingFilter` performs the following tasks on a high level:

- ○ Finds the name of the binding context metadata file(the `.cpx` extension file), reads the entries, and generates binding context

- ○ Creates `SessionContext`, if it's not existing

- ○ Sets up the error handler

- ○ Sets up locale

- ○ Creates the binding container for the page

- ○ Finds or constructs an instance of each data control present in the binding container for the requested page

The ADFBindingFilter object invokes the beginRequest() method on each data control participating in the request in order to prepare it for action. If the page uses ADF Business Components, this method checks out the application module from the pool.

3. The ADFBindingFilter returns the control to the runtime after setting up the binding context, and the control reaches the Faces Servlet if there are no more filters in the chain. The Faces Servlet is responsible for orchestrating the standard processing phases of each request.

   Faces Servlet by design follows an extensible architecture. It allows you to configure a custom lifecycle implementation for the JSF pages by overriding the default lifecycle-factory entry in the faces-config.xml file. Customized javax.faces.lifecycle.LifecycleFactory can be coded to return custom lifecycle implementation. The ADF framework makes use of this feature to return an ADF-flavored LifecycleImpl class that extends the standard JSF lifecycle to add the extra functionalities required by ADF. Here is an example for a custom lifecycle factory configuration entry in the faces-config.xml file:

```
<factory>
<lifecycle-factory>
oracle.adfinternal.view.faces.lifecycle.LifecycleFactoryImpl
</lifecycle-factory>
< /factory>
```

   Once the request reaches the Faces Servlet, it takes over the control and performs a basic initialization task before starting the lifecycle for the page. It creates the FacesContext object that contains all of the per-request state information related to the processing of a single JavaServer Faces request and then delegates the call to the lifecycle implementation class (oracle.adfinternal.view.faces.lifecycle.LifecycleImpl) returned by the overridden LifecycleFactory implementation class. The lifecycle implementation class starts the ADF page lifecycle phases.

4. The LifecycleImpl class executes the JSF lifecycle for the requested page, and for each JSF phase, it invokes the beforePhase(PhaseEvent) and afterPhase(PhaseEvent) methods defined on ADFPhaseListener—a PhaseListener implementation used by the framework. The ADFPhaseListener governs the extended ADF lifecycle phases for the page. Behind the scenes, the framework deploys a separate PagePhaseListener for each task. PagePhaseListener will be executed by ADFPhaseListener at each stage of the lifecycle. This makes the framework more extensible.

The following diagram shows the details of how the JSF, ADF Faces, and ADF Model phases integrate in the lifecycle of a page request:

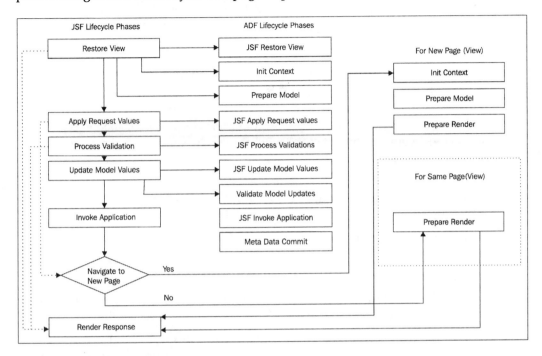

We are not discussing the core JSF lifecycle in detail in this book. To learn more on this topic, please refer to the *The Lifecycle of a JavaServer Faces Application* section in *The Java EE 6 Tutorial*, which is available online at `http://docs.oracle.com/javaee/6/tutorial/doc/bnaqq.html`.

Phases in the data bound ADF Faces page lifecycle are as follows:

- **Restore view**: The component tree for the view of the requested page is either newly built or restored. The framework attempts to restore the component tree if the view has been already processed and the component tree is available in the `FacesContext` object. If this is a new request, the JSF implementation creates an empty view (`UIViewRoot`) during this phase and the components are added to the tree during the render response phase.

- **JSF restore view**: This phase is extended from the restore view phase in the JSF lifecycle. Custom phase listeners can listen on the `before` and `after` events of this phase, to perform extra processing, if any. As mentioned earlier, the framework deploys a set of internal ADF page I ifecycle listeners to carry out extra tasks during the page lifecycle. During the `before` phase event for the JSF restore view, `UpdateBindingListener` (an internal ADF page lifecycle listener) initializes the binding container object by calling `findBindingContainerByPath()` on the `BindingContext` object, which finds the page definition file that matches the URL and builds the binding container for the page. The ADF Controller uses listeners for the `before` and `after` events of this phase to synchronize the server-side state with the request. The page flow scope is available at the end of this phase.

- **Initialize context**: The binding container is initialized during this phase, which includes registering the custom input handler for specific types and setting up the caching mode for the error handler.

- **Prepare model**: During the Prepare model phase, the framework does the following:

  ○ Page parameters defined in the page definition are evaluated.

  ○ If a task flow binding with parameters exists in the page definition, parameters are evaluated and are passed into the task flow.

  ○ For any executables entry, whose refresh property is set to `prepareModel`, is executed. This leads to execution of the underlying datasource available on the data control. For example, if an executable iterator entry is bound to a view object instance, refreshing the property of the iterator in turn will execute the corresponding view object instance. This explains how the page binding reads the data from the datasource when a page loads.

  ○ If the page has been created by using a template that uses ADF binding, the binding container for the page template is initialized during this phase.

  ○ The task flow executable binding is executed during this phase.

  If this is the initial request for the page, the lifecycle skips the process validations, update model values, and invoke application phases and jumps to the render response phase. The next phase continues for postback requests.

- **Apply request values**: After restoring the component tree, each component in the tree extracts new values from the request parameters, converts them to the desired form, and stores those values locally. If the conversion of the value fails, an error message is queued on `FacesContext`.

If the component's immediate attribute is set to `true`, the validation, conversion, and events associated with the component are processed during this phase. For immediate components, the lifecycle skips the process validations, update model values, and invoke application phases and jumps to the render response phase.

 To learn more about the `immediate="true"` settings for UI components, visit `https://cwiki.apache.org/confluence/display/MYFACES/How+the+immediate+attribute+works`.

- **JSF apply request values**: This is extended from the apply request values phase in the JSF lifecycle, allowing registered page phase listeners to listen for the `before` and `after` phase events of this phase.

- **Process validations**: During this phase, local values of components are validated by processing all validators registered on the component. If there are errors, an error message is queued on the `FacesContext` object and the lifecycle jumps to the render response phase.

- **JSF process validations**: This is extended from the process validations values phase in the JSF lifecycle, allowing registered page phase listeners to listen for the `before` and `after` phase events of this phase.

- **Update model values**: During this phase, the component's validated local values are moved to corresponding server-side properties. If the value of an updatable component is bound to a managed bean property, the local value is copied to the corresponding managed bean property. If the value of an updatable component is bound to the attribute in an iterator, the corresponding iterator is refreshed first (if the refresh is deferred and `refreshCondition` is evaluated to `true`), and then the local value of the component is copied to the corresponding attribute. This will call setter on the corresponding attribute in the view row implementation class, which in turn calls setter on underlying entity implementation (if exists).

  Before updating the actual data storage (for example, the entity object), the framework will process all the validations defined on the attribute and on successful validation, the value is copied to the underlying data storage and the control proceeds to the next phase. If the validation fails, the lifecycle jumps to the render response phase. Exceptions are caught by the binding container and cached for display during the render response phase.

- **JSF update model values**: This phase is extended from the update model values phase in the JSF lifecycle, allowing registered page phase listeners to listen for the `before` and `after` phase events of this phase.

- **Validate model updates**: The validation defined on the underlying entity object (validation added through the entity validators) is processed during this phase. Exceptions are caught by the binding container and cached for displaying during the render response phase.

- **Invoke application**: During this phase, application events are invoked. For example, if you have specified any action event for a `command` button, it is processed in this phase. If navigation is specified for the action, navigation to a different view happens at the end of this phase.

- **JSF invoke application**: This phase is extended from the invoke application phase in the JSF lifecycle, allowing registered page phase listeners to listen for the `before` and `after` phase events of this phase.

- **Metadata commit**: This is executed after the invoke application phase. During this phase, changes to runtime metadata are committed to the data store, which is configured using MDS.

  If the navigation occurs in the invoke application lifecycle, the following phases are executed for a new view:

  - ○ **Initialize context**: The page definition file for the new view is initialized in this phase

  - ○ **Prepare model**: Model for the new view is prepared and initialized in this phase

- **Prepare render**: During this phase, the binding container is refreshed to reflect the changes performed in the previous phases. Iterators whose `refresh` property is set to `renderModel`, are refreshed during this phase.

- **Render response**: The page is built during this phase. If this is the initial request for the page, the component tree for the page is built during this phase and appended to `UIViewRoot`. Once the tree is built, each component is asked to write its value into the response object and the state of the response is saved either on the client or server, based on the configuration.

  ADF Faces has data streaming support for certain components such as tables, trees, tree tables, and data visualization components, where the data fetch for these components happens in another request, after rendering the page. The framework executes only the render response phase for data streaming requests.

- **JSF render response**: This phase provides the `before` and `after` phase events for the render response phase.

  At the end of the render response phase, the user sees the resulting page in the browser.

To learn more about the JSF lifecycle and extended ADF Faces lifecycle, refer to the topic *Using the JSF Lifecycle with ADF Faces* in *Oracle Fusion Middleware Web User Interface Developer's Guide for Oracle Application Development Framework*. To access the documentation go to `http://www.oracle.com/technetwork/developer-tools/jdev/documentation/index.html`. Choose **Oracle JDeveloper** and navigate to **ADF Documentation Library | Web User Interface Developer's Guide**. Use the search option to find specific topics.

Invoking an application module from a Java servlet

We have discussed the basic configurations and metadata files required for running an ADF web application. This is very easy if you build an application by choosing a Fusion web application template. JDeveloper will take care of managing all the metadata files-dependent libraries.

What if you want to call services exposed by an application module from a non-ADF web application?

There are two approaches:

- Using `Configuration::createRootApplicationModule(String qualifiedAMDefName, String configName)` to create an appropriate application module instance, and then calling desired methods on it
- Using ADF Model APIs for accessing business methods exposed through data control

These approaches are discussed in the following sections.

Using Configuration::createRootApplicationM odule() in HttpServlet

You can call `createRootApplicationModule()` on the `Configuration` class to instantiate an application module in a `Servlet` class. While doing so, make sure you do the following configuration as well.

Configure `oracle.adf.share.http.ServletADFFilter` in the `web.xml` file to ensure the proper initialization of `oracle.adf.share.ADFContext` while accessing the application module from a non-ADF web application, using the servlet. This filter reads the configuration from `WEB-INF/adf-config.xml` and initializes the `ADFContext` object. However, applications using `ADFBindingFilter` can skip this filter, as this is already taken care of by the binding filter.

The following code snippet illustrates the APIs to be used in `HttpServlet`, to create an application module and release it towards the end of the request:

```
/**
 *Process the HTTP doGet request.
 */
public void doGet(HttpServletRequest request, HttpServletResponse
response) throws ServletException, IOException {
  HRServiceAppModuleImpl am=null;
  try{
    String amDef =
      "com.packtpub.model.service.HRServiceAppModule";
    String config = "HRServiceAppModuleLocal";
    //Creates AM instance
    am = (HRServiceAppModuleImpl) Configuration.
      createRootApplicationModule(amDef, config);
    //Call desired methods defined on am
      am.runSalaryRevisionReoutine();
      //Business logic goes here.......
  }catch(Excpetion ex){
    //Handle Error
  }finally{
    //Release am instance at the end of request
    if(am !=n ull){
    Configuration.releaseRootApplicationModule
      (am, false);
    }
  }
}
```

Using ADF binding APIs in an HttpServlet

You can use ADF binding APIs for accessing underlying business service implementation even outside the context of a Fusion web application. As we have discussed earlier, the ADF binding layer makes use of metadata XML files for holding binding information. To use a binding API from a non-ADF web application, you may need to manually create the adfm.xml, DataBindigs.cpx, and pageDef.xml files in the respective folders and then use ADF binding APIs from a servlet (or any other Java class) for accessing a data collection exposed through data control. Alternatively, to avoid the manual error, you can create a dummy project with a page and necessary method bindings, and copy the generated adfmsrc folder containing the metadata files to your non-ADF web project. The following screenshot displays a non-ADF web project with a Servlet class and hand-coded ADF binding metadata files:

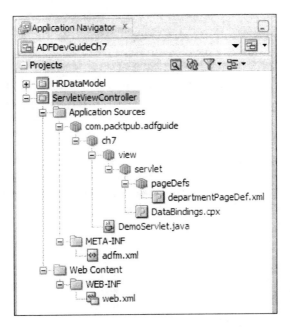

This example uses the following configurations in web.xml. ADFBindingFilter is configured to intercept all URL requests with the /adf/* URL pattern. This filter initializes the binding context before transferring control to DemoServlet used in this example:

```
<web-app ...>
  <filter>
      <filter-name>adfBindings</filter-name>
      <filter-class>oracle.adf.model.servlet.
      ADFBindingFilter</filter-class>
  </filter>
```

```
<filter-mapping>
    <filter-name>adfBindings</filter-name>
    <url-pattern>/adf/*</url-pattern>
</filter-mapping>
<servlet>
    <servlet-name>DemoServlet</servlet-name>
    <servlet-class>com.packtpub.adfguide.ch7.
    DemoServlet</servlet-class>
</servlet>
<servlet-mapping>
    <servlet-name>DemoServlet</servlet-name>
    <url-pattern>/adf/DemoServlet</url-pattern>
</servlet-mapping>
</web-app>
```

The following code snippet illustrates the usage of ADF binding APIs for accessing the row set through the table binding definition present in a page definition. As there are no automated ADF page lifecycles involved for a servlet, you will have to programmatically build the binding container by passing the page definition usage ID mapped in the `DataBindings.cpx` file and refresh it before accessing the bindings.

```
//In custom HttpServletclass
/**
 *Process the HTTP doGet request.
 */
public void doGet(HttpServletRequest request, HttpServletResponse
response) throws ServletException, IOException {
  BindingContext bindingContext = null;
  try {
    bindingContext = BindingContext.getCurrent();
    String CONTENT_TYPE = "text/html; charset=windows-1252";
    response.setContentType(CONTENT_TYPE);
    PrintWriter out = response.getWriter();
    out.println("<html>");
    out.println("<head><title>Demo</title></head>");
    out.println("<body>");
      //Get DataControlFrame
    DataControlFrameImpl dcframe = (DataControlFrameImpl)
      BindingContext.getCurrent().dataControlFrame();
      //Get desired data control
    DCDataControl dcd = dcframe.findDataControl
      ("HRServiceAppModuleDataControl",
      "HRServiceAppModuleDataControl", true);
      //Get the binding container
```

```
    DCBindingContainer dcBindingContainer =bindingContext.
      findBindingContainer(
      "com_packtpub_adfguide_ch7_view_servlet_departmentPageDef");
      JUCtrlRangeBinding depts = (JUCtrlRangeBinding)
      dcBindingContainer.findCtrlBinding("Departments");
      //Execute(refresh) the underlying view object
      dcBindingContainer.refreshControl();
      //Get the row set
    List<JUCtrlValueBindingRef> deptsList =
      depts.getRangeSet();
      //Iterate over row set
    Iterator deptsIter = deptsList.iterator();
  while (deptsIter.hasNext()) {
      JUCtrlValueBindingRef valueBinding =
        (JUCtrlValueBindingRef)deptsIter.next();
      Row attrs = valueBinding.getRow();
      out.println(attrs.getAttribute("DepartmentName") +
        "<br/>");
    }
    out.println("</body></html>");
    out.close();
  } finally {
    //Clean up code goes here...
      //You can call BindingContext::release();on
      //Session timeout or user logout or from here itself

  }
}
```

A working example illustrating the usage of binding APIs from a non-ADF web application can be found in the example code of this book. To access the example code, open the `ADFDevGuideCh7` work space in JDeveloper and look for the `ServletViewController` project.

Adding custom phase listeners

ADF framework allows you to plug in your custom phase listener implementations for each phase in a page lifecycle. This feature is useful if you want to perform some resource cleanup activities or to enable some security check during the page lifecycle. The custom phase listeners can be registered either for an application or for individual pages.

- To register an application level phase listener, create a class that implements the `oracle.adf.controller.v2.lifecycle.PagePhaseListener` interface. Then register the custom phase listener in `adf-settings.xml`, located under the `META-INF` folder. Create a new file if it is not there by default.

- If you want to register the custom `PagePhaseListener` for a page, specify the custom `PagePhaseListener` implementation as `ControllerClass` in the page definition file.

- If you want more ADF-flavored phase listeners for a page that provides more granular control over ADF phase events, build a class extending `oracle.adf.controller.v2.lifecycle.PageController` and register the same in the page definition file as `ControllerClass`.

> To learn more about Fusion page lifecycle customization, refer to the topic entitled *Customizing the ADF Page Lifecycle* in *Oracle Fusion Middleware Fusion Developer's Guide for Oracle Application Development Framework*. To access the documentation, go to `http://www.oracle.com/technetwork/developer-tools/jdev/documentation/index.html`. Choose **Oracle JDeveloper** and navigate to **ADF Documentation Library | Fusion Developer's Guide**. Use the search option to find specific topics.

Summary

In this chapter, you learned about the ADF data binding framework, and its layered architecture and usage. You also experienced the visual and declarative programming model offered by JDeveloper for building UI for the business services. Towards the end, we discussed the page lifecycle for a Fusion web page and the support for lifecycle customization as well.

The story on ADF data binding features and UI is not over yet. In the next chapter, we will see how to build a data bound web UI, and many more exciting features in this area.

8

Building Data Bound Web User Interfaces

In the previous chapter, you learned the fundamentals of building a UI for business services. This chapter continues our discussion on building a UI, this time covering data bound UI development in detail. You will experience the power of model driven UI development support offered by the Oracle ADF framework along with JDeveloper IDE. We will discuss the following topics in this chapter:

- The art of laying out pages.
- Adding actions to your page
- Building data bound table UIs
- Building data bound master-detail UIs
- Building data bound tree table UIs
- Accessing web tier values from business components
- Building data bound query search forms
- Building data bound multi select lists
- Overriding UI hints in a view object

Introduction

We have discussed visual and declarative development features of ADF for business components in previous chapters. In this chapter we will cover visual and declarative development features of the view layer. The view layer of a Fusion web application is built using ADF Faces which is very rich in features, with a large set of over 150 AJAX enabled UI components. Oracle ADF framework along with JDeveloper IDE provides a very easy way to bind components from the business services to the UI layer using a declarative binding layer approach. We will cover these topics in detail in the coming sections.

The art of laying out pages

The first task in building a web page is to pick up the right layout for placing the UI components. The ADF Faces components stack is rich with a number of layout components which can be used for arranging other UI components on the page. The following table lists commonly used ADF Faces layout components:

Component	Description	Stretched by Parent	Stretch Children
af:panelFormLayout	Arranges items in columns or grids.	No	No
	Places items in fixed, peripheral areas around a central area.	No	No
af: panelStretchLayout	Enables automatic component stretching in your pages. This contains top, bottom, start, center, and end facets to hold child components.	Yes (when dimensionsFrom = parent)	Yes
af:panelSplitter	Enables automatic component stretching in your pages. This divides a region into two parts (the first facet and the second facet) where you can place contents.	Yes (when dimensionsFrom = parent)	Yes
af:panelDashBoard	Arranges child components column-wise.	Yes (when dimensionsFrom = parent)	Yes
af:panelAccordion	Creates collapsible panes.	Yes (when dimensionsFrom = parent)	No
af:panelTabbed	Creates stacked tabs.	Yes (when dimensionsFrom = parent)	No
af:decorativeBox	Provides a decorative box for the child components.	Yes (when dimensionsFrom = parent)	Yes

Component	Description	Stretched by Parent	Stretch Children
`af:panelBox`	Provides a titled box which can contain child components.	Yes	Yes (when `type = stretch`)
`af:showDetail`	Hides and displays groups of content through the toggle icon.	No	No
`af:panelGroupLayout`	Enables automatic scroll bars in your pages, and arranges items horizontally or vertically.	Yes (when `layout = scroll` or `vertical`)	
`af:panelCollection`	Adds menus, toolbars, and status bars to data aggregation components such as tables, trees, and tree tables.	Yes	Yes
`af:panelHeader`	Creates titled sections and subsections.	Yes (when `type = stretch`)	Yes (when `type = stretch`)
`af:panelList`	Creates styled lists and content boxes.	No	No
`af:panelGridLayout`	Arranges components in columns or grids using `af:gridRow` and `af:gridCell`.	Yes (when `dimensionsFrom = parent`)	Yes (When `af:gridCell` is configured for it)
`af:spacer`	Adds a blank space between components.	No	Not a container
`af:separator`	Adds divider line between components.	No	Not a container

To learn more about page layout components, refer to the topic *Organizing Content on Web Pages* in *Oracle Fusion Middleware Web User Interface Developer's Guide for Oracle Application Development Framework*. To access the documentation go to `http://www.oracle.com/technetwork/developer-tools/jdev/documentation/index.html` and choose **Oracle JDeveloper and ADF Documentation Library | Web User Interface Developer's Guide**.

You can also refer the layout basics section in the ADF Faces demo application available online at `http://jdevadf.oracle.com/adf-richclient-demo/faces/feature/layoutBasics.jspx`.

Organizing page contents – a case study

This section discusses the basic steps for designing a typical ADF Faces page. Let us take a screen mock-up, and see how the ADF Faces components can be used to realize such screens in real life. This exercise may give you a feel of sequences of tasks involved in designing real life web pages.

Take a closer look at the following screenshot. How do you proceed if you want to design such a page using ADF Faces?

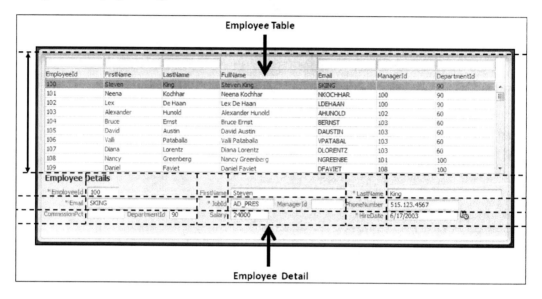

The first step is to identify the top level layout components to organize top level containers. This task is much simpler if you can spend some time analyzing the screen mock-up and understanding the behaviour of each part. A very common approach followed by many developers in this regard is to divide the screen into logical parts and then decide the layout component for each part. For example, if you take a closer look at the previous screenshot, you may find two logical parts in the screen. The first part of the page contains the employee table and the second part contains the employee details parameter form. A second look may reveal that the detail parameter form on the bottom of the page is fixed in size whereas the table on the top is stretched to fit the available window size. You can draw grids over the components to logically partition the screen as shown in the previous screenshot. This makes your life even simpler while choosing layout components.

Once you are done with the logical partitioning of the screen, for the next step, you may need to choose the top level layout component for the page. You can start with the outermost (root level in node hierarchy) layout component and work inwards (leaf levels in node hierarchy) covering all parts in the target page. A possible root layout component that meets the above requirement is af:panelStretchLayout. Note that the term "root layout components" does not refer to the root element in your JSF page, rather it refers the top level container component which is added as a child to the af:form tag. For panelStretchLayout, when you set the height of the top and bottom facets, any contained components are stretched up to fit the specified height, and the remaining portion is allocated to fit the components in the centre facet.

The **facet** for a JSF component represents a named section within the container components. It allows you to add more characteristics to the component. For example, in the case of panelStretchLayout, you can add components that may need to appear in the centre of the container to the center facet as follows:

```
<af:panelStretchLayout id="ps1"><f:facet
name="center"><!-Child components here--> <f:facet></
af:panelStretchLayout>
```

The initial layout structure may look as follows:

```
<af:panelStretchLayout id="ps11" bottomHeight="150px">
  <f:facet name="bottom"/>
  <f:facet name="center"/>
  <f:facet name="start"/>
  <f:facet name="end"/>
  <f:facet name="top"/>
</af:panelStretchLayout>
```

The previous settings for af:panelStretchLayout allocates 150 px height (fixed) to the bottom facet. Now the picture is clearer. You can add the employee details to the bottom facet of panelStretchLayout which takes a fixed height (150 px). The stretchable table can be added to the centre facet. Optionally, you can surround the table with an af:panelcollection component to provide toolbars and menus support for the table components.

The task remaining is identifying an appropriate layout component for the parameter form. The challenge here is the uneven distribution of the UI elements across rows. The `af:panelFormLayout` is the quickest solution to lay out components in a grid. Unfortunately this component lacks support for uneven distribution of child elements across rows. The next possibility is to use `af:panelGridLayout`. This component can be considered as a tabular container which supports uneven distribution of UI controls across rows or columns. It uses `af:gridRow` and `af:gridCell` to arrange components. The `af:gridRow` defines rows for a `af:panelGridLayout` and it is used to arrange `af:gridCell` children for a parent `panelGridLayout` component. The `af:gridCell` allows containing component to span across multiple rows or columns. Apparently the `panelGridLayout` component meets the UI requirements of this example. Refer to the tag documentation to learn more about `af:panelGridLayout` which is available online at `http://jdevadf. oracle.com/adf-richclient-demo/docs/tagdoc/af_panelGridLayout.html`.

The final page structure may look like the following screenshot:

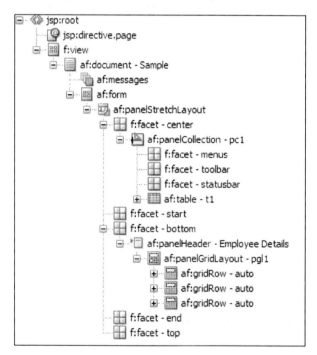

You can find a sample JSF page that uses `af:panelGridLayout` in the example code that we mentioned at the beginning of this book, in the *Preface* section. To access the example code, open the `ADFDevGuideCh8` workspace in `JDeveloper` and look for the `panelGridLayoutSample. jsf` page in the `ViewController` project.

Adding actions to your page

The JSF framework offers an event based programming model that you may see in traditional thick client desktop applications built using Java Swing or similar technology. JSF allows you to execute business logic in response to user actions on the UI component at runtime. These events are broadly termed as **application events**. They are classified further into two categories: action events and value change events. The **action events** are triggered by actionable components, such as command button, and **value change events** are triggered by editable components, such as input field. As ADF Faces is built on top of the JSF framework, ADF Faces inherits the same event model.

You will use ADF Faces command components such as `af:commandButton`, `af:commandLink`, and `af:commandImageLink` to invoke any business service methods or to perform page navigation. You can add custom event handlers for the action components using **action listener** bindings offered by the ADF Faces (JSF) framework. The action listener binding for an action component can be either wired to a managed bean method that takes `javax.faces.event.ActionEvent` as a parameter, or to an operation (custom method or built-in actions method) exposed through data control.

Choosing between the managed bean method and the data control method as event handlers

The managed bean is the code-behind class for an ADF Faces (JSF) page. All your client's specific logic, such as reading a selected row in UI table components, or checking the status of UI components, and so on, should be coded in a managed bean. If you want to programmatically control the behaviour of the UI components or if you want to programmatically retrieve the values from UI components before calling business methods with a click of a button, then such event handlers should be coded in your managed bean.

A data control typically acts as a wrapper over your business service implementation. Ideally business service implementation should be independent of the view layer. If you need to invoke a business method exposed through data control with a click of a button and all the input parameters for this method are readily available or can be derived from the underlying model, then you can directly wire a command button to the data control method.

Using managed bean methods as event handlers

To wire an action component with a method in a managed bean, select the desired component in the UI, go to the property inspector window and scroll to the **ActionListener** property. Select the property menu option (down arrow) for **ActionListener** and select **Edit....** This is shown in the following screenshot:

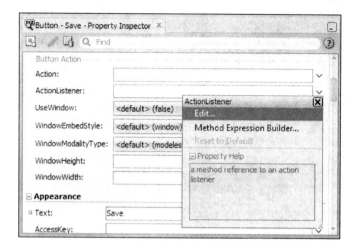

In the **Edit Property** window, specify the bean class and custom event handler method. While specifying the bean class, if you chose to create a new bean for the defining event handler, IDE does the following:

- Creates Java bean class with a method
- Defines an entry for the new bean in `adfc-config.xml` or in the task flow XML file as appropriate
- Generates an EL expression for the binding component `actionListener` attribute in the page with the method in the managed bean

Using data control methods as event handlers

To wire an action component with a method exposed in the **Data Controls** panel, drag the method from the **Data Controls** panel and drop it onto the page as an appropriate UI component such as **ADF Button**, **ADF Link**, and so on. This is displayed in the following screenshot:

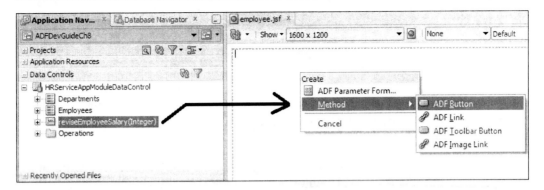

When you drop a method, IDE will prompt you to bind the method either by selecting an existing button or by creating a new button component through the **Method | ADF Button** option in the context menu. Select the appropriate option and finish the menu. If the method that you selected takes parameters, then you will get an **Edit Action Binding** dialog window as shown in the following screenshot:

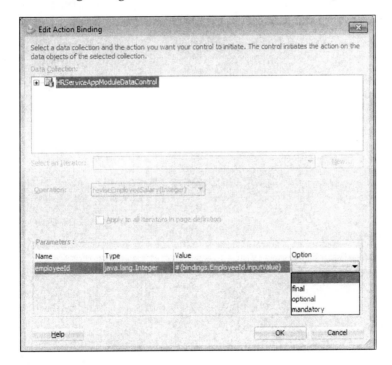

The **Edit Action Binding** dialog allows you to specify values for parameters appearing in the method. The **Value** can be set as an EL expression or static values. If you are setting values through EL, you can optionally avail the **EL Expression Builder** wizard to generate the desired EL, which is available by clicking on a **Value** cell. When you set parameter values, the editor will also allow you to specify parameter evaluation options. The parameter option decides when the binding container should evaluate the value set for the parameter at runtime. The possible parameter options are as follows:

- **final**: This means that the value set for parameters in the binding definition is final, and the framework will not allow clients to override this value. The parameter value **cannot** be passed by the caller when the method is invoked programmatically, for instance while using `oracle.binding.OperationBinding` API for executing an operation.

- **optional**: This allows the caller to optionally override the parameter value set in the binding definition file. The parameter value defined in your binding definition is of least precedence here – just opposite to `final`. This is the default option for a parameter.

- **mandatory**: This option forces the caller to set the parameter value, always. The value specified in the binding definition as an EL expression or a string literal will never be considered if the parameter option specified is `mandatory`.

When you finish dropping a method on the page, IDE creates the following items:

- The IDE creates the `<af:commandButton>` component in the JSF page with the appropriate EL binding for the `actionListener` attribute. For instance, the following JSF code snippet is generated when the **reviseEmployeeSalary** method is dropped on to the page as an **ADF Button**:

```
<af:commandButton actionListener="#{bindings.reviseEmployeeSalary.
execute}"
text="reviseEmployeeSalary"
id="cb5"/>
```

- IDE also generates a `<methodAction>` binding in the page definition file for accessing the method that is dropped from the **Data Controls** panel. This entry is used by the binding framework to invoke the actual method implementation when a user clicks the button at runtime.

  The following is the entry generated in a page definition file when the method **reviseEmployeeSalary** is dropped on to the page:

```
<pageDefinition ... >
  ...
  <bindings>
```

```
    . . .
    <methodAction id="reviseEmployeeSalary"
      RequiresUpdateModel="true" Action="invokeMethod"
      MethodName="reviseEmployeeSalary"
       IsViewObjectMethod="false"
      DataControl="HRServiceAppModuleDataControl"
      InstanceName=
      "data.HRServiceAppModuleDataControl.dataProvider"
    <NamedData NDName="employeeId"
     NDValue="#{bindings.EmployeeId.inputValue}"
     NDType="java.lang.Integer"/>
    </methodAction>
    </bindings>
</pageDefinition>
```

Building data bound table UIs

The table UI is one of the very popular UI components for presenting a collection of rows to end users. In general, displaying data collection on a table UI involves the following tasks:

- Invoking business services for reading data collection
- Populating the UI with retrieved collection

The data bound UI table offered by the Oracle ADF framework does the above tasks out of the box. The steps for building a data bound table are as follows:

1. Drag the view object instance from the **Data Controls** panel and drop it on the visual designer for the page. Doing so displays a context menu with a list of possible UI components to display the data collection.

2. Select **Table | ADF Table** in the context menu.

3. In the **Edit Table Columns** dialog window, specify the **Row Selection**, **Sorting**, and **Filtering** properties. The editor also allows you to add, remove, group, or rearrange columns, and alter the default display label, value binding, and display component for columns. Click on **OK** to save the work.

What happens when you drop a data collection as a table on a page?

When you build a table component by dragging and dropping a data collection on a page, the IDE generates the following:

- Code for `<af:table>` component in the JSF page with all generic properties defaulted with values from model definition through binding EL expressions

- Binding definition for the table in the page definition file. It has two parts:

    1. An executable iterator binding that is responsible for fetching rows displayed in the data bound UI components. The commonly used properties of the iterator bindings are discussed in the next section.

    2. A tree binding definition that describes the attributes of a row present in the collection. Note that the ADF binding framework uses the *tree* binding structure to describe data for a table UI component. This is the reason why you see tree binding here.

The following code snippet from the page definition XML file shows the tree binding definition for the `Departments` collection. This is bound to `af:table` on the UI. The `<nodeDefinition>` that you see in this XML file describes the attributes present in a row.

```
//In page definition XMl file

<pageDefinition ... >
<executables>
 <variableIterator id="variables"/>
 <iterator Binds="Departments" RangeSize="8" DataControl="HRServiceApp
ModuleDataControl" id="DepartmentsIterator"
      ChangeEventPolicy="ppr"/>
</executables>
<bindings>
 <tree IterBinding="DepartmentsIterator" id="Departments">
  <nodeDefinition DefName="com.packtpub.adfguide.ch8.model.view.
DepartmentVO" Name="Departments0">
   <AttrNames>
    <Item Value="DepartmentId"/>
    <Item Value="DepartmentName"/>
    <Item Value="ManagerId"/>
   </AttrNames>
  </nodeDefinition>
 </tree>
</bindings>
</pageDefinition>
```

Commonly used attributes of iterator bindings

The iterator binding in a page definition file is responsible for populating the row set by executing a view object during a page lifecycle. You may not really need to modify the default iterator binding properties in the page definition file for most of the use cases. However, there are some properties which you may want to know, especially when you need to fine-tune default iterator behaviour.

To override the properties of an iterator executable, select the desired executable in the overview editor of the paged definition file and override the properties using the property inspector window as appropriate. The following are the commonly used properties of the iterator binding definition:

- `RangeSize`: This specifies the number of rows in a range (page size) you can use to access a subset of the data objects in the collection. The default value is 25. If you set -1, all rows are read at once.

  For an iterator bound to an `af:table` component, it is recommended to keep the `RangeSize` = `autoHeightRows` property of `af:table` to+ 1 to reduce the number of round trips between the client and the middle tier to fetch rows that fill the view port for the table. The property `autoHeightRows` decides the maximum number of rows for a table component in the viewport, after which a scroll bar is displayed.

- `ChangeEventPolicy`: This specifies the event strategy for the component. The possible values are as follows:

  i. `push`: This is used in **active data streaming** (**ADS**) mode. This setting causes the iterator to refresh when active data is pushed to the client. **Active data** is a continuous stream of changes that is delivered to a client by using a push based mechanism. ADF provides the framework for application developers to configure and use active components to show active data in their applications. To learn more about ADS, refer to the topic *Using the Active Data Service* in *Oracle Fusion Middleware Fusion Developer's Guide for Oracle Application Development Framework*. To access the documentation go to `http://www.oracle.com/technetwork/developer-tools/jdev/documentation/index.html` and choose **Oracle JDeveloper and ADF Documentation Library | Fusion Developer's Guide**. Use the **Search** option to find specific topics.

ii. `ppr`: This is the default `ChangeEventPolicy` value which causes automatic **Partial Page Refresh (PPR)** for all UI components when the associated iterator binding refreshes during a page lifecycle. Partial Page Refresh allows certain components on a page to be refreshed without the need to refresh the entire page. To learn more about PPR in UIs, refer to the topic *Rerendering Partial Page Content* in *Oracle Fusion Middleware Web User Interface Developer's Guide for Oracle Application Development Framework.*

iii. `none`: This flag disables `push` and `ppr` features. During a page lifecycle, the iterator refreshes the data collection based on `refresh` and `refreshConditions` settings.

- `RowCountThreshold`: This property is used for avoiding expensive runaway count queries fired by UI components such as table or tree table. The total row count is used by these components to manage the UI characteristics. For example, the total row count is used by the table or tree table to size the vertical scroll bar displayed on the UI. The framework decides on executing the count query based on the following conditions:

  - if `RowCountThreshold` = 0, executes count query

  - if `RowCountThreshold` < 0, skips count query execution

  - if `RowCountThreshold` > 0, executes count query with `RowCountThreshold` value as upper limit.

  - If the underlying database table has millions of rows, then you can set the `RowCountThreshold` to a positive value in order to avoid a full database table scan. For example, consider the following iterator binding definition present in a page definition file with `RowCountThreshold` = 1000:

    ```
    <iterator Binds="Departments" RangeSize="25"
    RowCountThreshold="1000" DataControl="HRServiceAppModuleData
    Control" id="DepartmentsIterator"/>
    ```

    If the previous iterator is bound to the table UI with a scroll bar, then the count query fired by the framework at runtime will have the `RowCountThreshold` condition appended, as shown here:

    ```
    SELECT count(1) FROM (SELECT DepartmentEO.DEPARTMENT_ID,
    DepartmentEO.DEPARTMENT_NAME,          DepartmentEO.MANAGER_
    ID,          DepartmentEO.LOCATION_ID FROM DEPARTMENTS
    DepartmentEO WHERE ROWNUM <= 1000)
    ```

You may notice that the previous query puts an upper bound (row count threshold) for the SELECT clause which limits the number of rows scanned during execution. This is useful if the table contains millions of rows.

What happens at runtime in a data bound table?

When a data bound table UI renders at runtime, it evaluates the EL expression for value attributes and populates data collection model object with the row set. To render each row, the framework engages corresponding iterator binding objects to traverse over the row set one by one.

Adding edit functionalities for a table

In this section, we will discuss about adding edit functionalities such as create, update, and delete for a data bound table.

Creating a new row

To add the create functionality, perform the following steps:

1. Go to the **Data Controls** panel, select the data collection (view object instance) used for building the table, and expand the **Operations** node.

2. Drag the **CreateInsert** operation and drop it on the page as an action component by choosing the appropriate component displayed in the context menu.

When you drop the built-in operation as a component on a page, IDE generates the corresponding action binding in the page definition file and sets the newly added component as partialTriggers for all the affected components in the JSF page. The property partialTriggers takes the IDs of the components that should trigger a partial update on this component during the post back of the page.

The previous settings are enough for most of the use case to work. However, if the af:table has its editingMode set to clickToEdit, then new rows created at runtime, by clicking on **CreateInsert,** do not become the *active row* by default. This will cause the row level validation to defer till you commit the transaction. Note that in the clickToEdit mode, the framework makes the active row of the table editable and is brought into view. In such cases you must programmatically make a row active by calling the setActiveRowKey() method on the table component.

The editingMode property for an af:table component indicates the mode used for editing the table when it contains editable components. The possible values for this property are clickToEdit and editAll. In the editAll mode, all the editable components are displayed at a time in the table view area. In the clickToEdit mode, a single row is editable at a time. Refer to the tag documentation to learn more, which is available online at http://jdevadf.oracle.com/adf-richclient-demo/docs/tagdoc/af_table.html.

The following example illustrates the usage of setActiveRowKey() for a custom row creation method.

This example EL binds the createInsertAction() method in a managed bean with command button's actionListener property:

```
<af:commandButton  actionListener="#{MyBean.createInsertAction}"
    text="CreateRow" id="cb1"   />
```

The createInsertAction() method definition in the managed bean is as follows:

```
//In managed bean class
public void createInsertAction(ActionEvent actevnt) {
//Call row create routine defined in AM using binding API
  BindingContext bc = BindingContext.getCurrent();
  DCBindingContainer dcb =
    (DCBindingContainer)bc.getCurrentBindingsEntry();
  OperationBinding op = dcb.getOperationBinding
       ("createDeptRow");
  Row row = (Row)op.execute();
  if (op.getErrors().size() == 0) {
   //On success, keep the new row as active
    ArrayList lst = new ArrayList(1);
    lst.add(row.getKey());
    getDataTable().setActiveRowKey(lst);
  }
}
```

The **createDeptRow** operation used in the previous example refers to the following custom method defined in the application module which is exposed through the data control:

```
//In application module implementation class

public Row createDeptRow () {
//Gets Departmentsview object
    ViewObjectImpl vo = getDepartmentsView1();
//Create and insert row
    Row row = vo.createRow();
```

```
        vo.insertRow(row);
        return row;
}
```

Deleting a row

To add a delete functionality, perform the following steps:

1. Go to the **Data Controls** panel and select the data collection used for building the table, then expand the **Operations** node.
2. Drag the **Delete** operation and drop it on the page as an action component by choosing the appropriate component displayed in the context menu.

When you click on the **Delete** button at runtime, the framework will remove the current row from the view object which may in turn call remove on underlying entity objects.

Committing changes

To add the save functionality, drag the **Commit** operation from **Data Controls** and drop it on a page as an action component by choosing the appropriate component displayed in the context menu.

When you click on the **Commit** button at runtime, the framework will call commit on the underlying DBTransaction object which will result in posting changes to the database followed by a commit call on the database connection object level. The APIs used to perform commit from client side code is discussed in *Chapter 7, Binding Business Services with User Interface*, in the section entitled *Accessing the data control frame*.

Programmatically accessing a selected row from a table

While working with a rich UI, you may need to access selected rows of the UI table from a managed bean in response to some user actions. For example, in the employee UI table you may want to check whether the user has selected a "promote employee" checkbox when he or she clicks on the **Process Selected Row** button. The following code snippet illustrates the usage of APIs for reading selected rows from a table:

```
/**
 * This method return selected row for the table
 * @param deptTable - Table bound to the UI
 * @return
 */
public Row getSelectedRow(RichTable deptTable) {
```

```
Row currentRow = null;
RowKeySet selectedRowKeys = deptTable.getSelectedRowKeys();

 //Store original rowKey
Object oldRowKey = deptTable.getRowKey();
try {

  if (selectedRowKeys != null) {
    Iterator iter = selectedRowKeys.iterator();
    if (iter != null && iter.hasNext()) {
      Object rowKey = iter.next();
      //stamp row
      deptTable.setRowKey(rowKey);
      JUCtrlHierNodeBinding rowData =
            (JUCtrlHierNodeBinding)deptTable.
            getRowData();
      //rowData holds current row object,
      //your code to deal with row goes here
      currentRow = rowData.getRow();


    }
  }

} finally {

  //Restore the original rowKey
  deptTable.setRowKey(oldRowKey);
}
return currentRow;
}
```

The API documentation for ADF binding and ADF Faces can be found online. To access the documentation go to http://www.oracle.com/technetwork/developer-tools/jdev/documentation/index.html and choose **Oracle JDeveloper and ADF Documentation Library | ADF Model Java API Reference**. In the same section, follow the ADF Faces Java API reference link for accessing ADF Faces APIs.

Declaratively reading the attribute value from the currently selected row

It is very common that when a row is selected in a table, you may want to update other fields in the UI or call some specific operations with attributes from the selected row. There is an easy way to retrieve the desired attributes for the current row by defining the attribute binding for those attributes.

To define attribute binding, perform the following steps:

1. Double-click on the page definition file to open up the overview editor. Alternatively, if you have the desired JSF page opened in the designer window, then selecting the **Bindings** tab will open the corresponding page definition file editor.

2. Select the **Bindings and Executable** tab and click on the green plus icon to create a control binding icon which will be displayed on the **Bindings** panel.

3. In the **Insert Item** dialog window, select the **Generic Bindings** category (if it is not selected by default) in the drop-down and then select **Attribute values as the item to be created**. Click on **OK** to proceed with the next step. In the **Create Attribute Binding** dialog window, select the desired data source (view object instance) and then the attribute that you want to read from the selected row in the data source.Click on **OK** to dispose of the dialog.

The following is an example for an attribute value binding defined by choosing the **Departments** collection as the data source:

```
//This is in page definition XML file
<attributeValues IterBinding="DepartmentsIterator"
id="DepartmentName">
     <AttrNames>
       <Item Value="DepartmentName"/>
     </AttrNames>
</attributeValues>
```

Once you have defined the attribute bindings, you can refer to them using the binding EL expression from the client. For example, the previous attribute value can be referred to using the ADF binding expression as follows:

```
#{bindings.DepartmentName.inputValue}
```

While referring to the attribute definition present in the page definition file using the EL expression, always append `inputValue` to the binding expression as shown here: `#{bindings.<AttributeName>.inputValue}`. This makes sure that the framework does the formatting of the value using the UI hint pattern present in the view object metadata before returning to the caller.

Building data bound master-detail UIs

A master-detail UI allows you to view data from master and detail collections at the same time. This section discusses declarative support in ADF for building master-detail screens. The task involves two steps as explained in the following section.

Building a master-detail data model

To build a master-detail UI, you will need to have a corresponding data model ready first. If you need a quick brush up on building master-detail data models, refer to the topic *Adding hierarchical view object instances to an application module* in *Chapter 6, Introducing the Application Module*.

Building a master-detail UI

Once the data model is ready, you can proceed to building the UI. To build a master-detail UI, perform the following steps:

1. Go to the **Data Controls** panel, expand the master view object instance and then select the detail view object instance displayed beneath the master view object node.

2. Drag the detail view object instance and drop it on page design window.

3. In the **Create context** menu, select the desired master-detail template.

If the default UI template provided by the IDE does not meet your requirements, then you can separately build the master and detail UI component, explained as follows.

To build a master-detail UI without using the built-in template, drop the master view object instance from the **Data Controls** panel on the page by selecting the desired component. Next, drag the detail view object instance displayed below the master view object instance from the **Data Controls** panel and drop it at the desired area on the page. When you drop the master-details collections on a page, IDE creates necessary bindings and refreshes the settings for the components. You are done!

What happens at runtime in the master-detail UI?

Master-detail coordination is enabled through a view link instance (`ViewLinkUsage`) in the application module that connects the appropriate master and detail view object instances. When you select a master row, the framework eagerly coordinates the detail collection with the master row by re-executing the detail view object. When the detail view object instance executes, the framework appends the SQL WHERE clause from the view link definition to the query with bind values from the new master row.

Building a data bound tree table UI

The tree table displays hierarchical data in tabular form by combining both tree and table UI functionalities in one component. The binding concepts and data model that we discuss for a tree table component in the following section are very generic in nature. These concepts are applicable for other hierarchical components as well such as af:tree and dvt:hierarchyViewer. The following section outlines the basic steps for building a data bound tree table.

Building hierarchical view objects

To build a model bound hierarchical tree table, first you need to have an appropriate hierarchical data model ready. All the view objects participating in the tree hierarchy must be linked through the view link definitions. While defining view links, you must make sure that the child accessor attribute(s) are enabled on all the parent view objects participating in the hierarchy.

The accessors are generated when you define the view links between view objects. For example, take a look at the following screenshot that displays view link properties between **DepartmentVO** and **EmployeeVO**. In the **View Link Properties** editor, the **Generate Accessor** option is enabled for **DepartmentVO** (master view object) with the accessor name as **Employees**. When you expand a specific department node, the framework uses this view link accessor attribute to read the child employee rows. Note that, under the covers, the framework generates an internal view object instance to handle the execution of view link accessors.

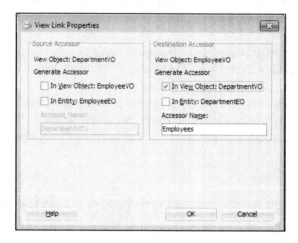

If you need a quick brush up on defining view links, refer to the topic *Linking two view objects* in *Chapter 4, Introducing View Objects*.

The ADF framework uses view link accessor attributes present in the parent view object to read the child collection in order to display tree hierarchies at runtime. The data model hierarchy present in the application module data model does not play any role in displaying data for a model bound tree component.

Creating a tree table UI

To build a tree table UI, perform the following steps:

1. Select the desired data collection (view object instance) in the **Data Controls** panel which represents the root node in the tree hierarchy.

2. Drop the selected view object instance on the page. From the context menu, select **Tree | ADF Tree Table**. Choosing this will display the **Edit Tree Binding** window as shown in the following screenshot:

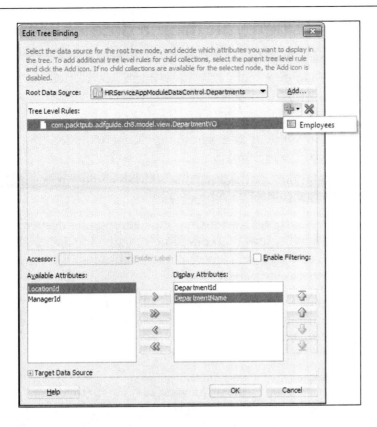

3. In the **Edit Tree Binding** editor, select the desired attributes that you want to display for the root node in the **Available Attributes** list and shuttle them to the **Display Attributes** list. Optionally, you can add basic filtering conditions for each row in the row set by selecting the **Enable Filtering** option.

4. To define the next level of nodes, select the parent node object (view object) in the **Tree Level Rules** list and click on the **Add Rule** icon which will display the accessors defined on the parent view object. For example, the previous screenshot displays **Employees** as an access attribute for **DepartmentVO**. When you select the desired accessor, IDE generates the corresponding child node object under the parent node. Select the display attributes for the child node as you did for the parent node. Repeat the previous steps till you finish defining the tree hierarchy.

5. Click on **OK** to save changes.

What happens when you drop a data collection as a tree table on a page?

When you build a tree table component by dropping a data collection on a page, the IDE generates the following:

- Code for the `<af:treeTable>` component in the JSF page with all generic properties defaulted with values from the model definition (the topmost parent view object definition)

- Binding the definition for the tree table which includes an executable iterator binding and a tree control binding definition

The following example illustrates the tree binding definition for department-employee hierarchy. Only the top level collection is mapped to the executable iterator binding. Child elements are loaded on request through the view link accessor attribute present in the parent view row.

The tree binding contains the node definition for all the node types displayed in the tree. Node definition includes attribute names displayed in the UI and accessors for displaying children from each node.

```
<executables>
  <variableIterator id="variables"/>
  <iterator Binds="Departments" RangeSize="25" DataControl="HRServiceA
ppModuleDataControl" id="DepartmentsIterator"/>
</executables>
<tree IterBinding="DepartmentsIterator" id="Departments">
  <nodeDefinition DefName="com.packtpub.adfguide.ch8.model.view.
DepartmentVO" Name="Departments0">
  <AttrNames>
    <Item Value="DepartmentId"/>
    <Item Value="DepartmentName"/>
  </AttrNames>
  <Accessors>
    <Item Value="Employees"/>
  </Accessors>
  </nodeDefinition>
  <nodeDefinition DefName="com.packtpub.adfguide.ch8.model.view.
EmployeeVO" Name="Departments1">
  <AttrNames>
    <Item Value="EmployeeId"/>
    <Item Value="FirstName"/>
    <Item Value="LastName"/>
     <Item Value="ManagerId"/>
   </AttrNames>
  </nodeDefinition>
</tree>
```

Decorating the tree table UI

When you drop a collection as a tree or tree table on the JSF page, IDE generates the necessary code for displaying a basic `af:treeTable` UI component on the page. For example, the following is the `af:treeTable` code generated by the IDE (by default) when we dropped the department-employee hierarchy model from the **Data Controls** panel on to a JSF page:

```
<af:treeTable value="#{bindings.Departments.treeModel}" var="node"
selectionListener=
            "#{bindings.Departments.treeModel.makeCurrent}"
    rowSelection="single"
    id="resId1" width="300" columnStretching="last">
<f:facet name="nodeStamp">
  <af:column id="c1">
    <af:outputText value="#{node}" id="ot1"/>
  </af:column>
</f:facet>
<f:facet name="pathStamp">
  <af:outputText value="#{node}" id="ot2"/>
</f:facet>
</af:treeTable>
```

You are free to modify the generated component tag to include more attributes or to alter the default layout. This is really required in real life applications as the default UI component tag generated by IDE is very basic. While adding more columns, make sure the corresponding attributes are available in the tree binding definition present in the corresponding page definition XML file.

The following example displays the `af:treeTable` component code with manually added columns. In this example, the `ManagerID` column renders the model driven LOV for `EmployeeVO` node. As the tree table does not really need to display the LOV for the department node, the display of the LOV field is enabled only for the employee node and it is controlled through the following EL expression: `"#{node.hierTypeBinding.viewDefName == 'com.packtpub.adfguide.ch8.model.view.EmployeeVO'}"`.

```
<af:treeTable value="#{bindings.Departments.treeModel}" var="node"
selectionListener=
            "#{bindings.Departments.treeModel.makeCurrent}"
            rowSelection="single"
        id="tt1" binding="#{TreeBean.deptTreeTable}"
            editingMode="clickToEdit">
    <f:facet name="nodeStamp">
      <af:column id="c1">
        <af:inputText value="#{node.DepartmentId}" id="ot1"/>
```

```
        </af:column>
      </f:facet>
      <f:facet name="pathStamp">
        <af:outputText value="#{node}" id="ot2"/>
      </f:facet>
      <af:column headerText="DepartmentName" id="cl1">
        <af:inputText value="#{node.DepartmentName}" id="it1"/>
      </af:column>
      <af:column  headerText="EmployeeId" id="cl2">
        <af:inputText value="#{node.EmployeeId}" id="it2"
autoSubmit="true"/>
      </af:column>
      <af:column headerText="FirstName" id="cl3">
        <af:inputText value="#{node.FirstName}" id="it3"/>
      </af:column>
      <af:column headerText="ManagerID" id="c10">
            <af:inputComboboxListOfValues  rendered=
          "#{node.hierTypeBinding.viewDefName ==
          'com.packtpub.adfguide.ch8.model.view.EmployeeVO'}"
          id="managerIdId"
           popupTitle=
          "Search and Select #{node.bindings.ManagerId.label}"
          value="#{node.bindings.ManagerId.inputValue}"
          model="#{node.bindings.ManagerId.listOfValuesModel}"
          partialTriggers="it4" label="LOV">
            <f:validator
            binding="#{node.bindings.ManagerId.validator}"/>
            <af:convertNumber groupingUsed="false"
            pattern="#{node.bindings.ManagerId.format}"/>
          </af:inputComboboxListOfValues>
        </af:column>
    </af:treeTable>
```

What happens at runtime in a data bound tree table?

When a tree table is displayed, the framework executes the iterator binding for the top level collection during the initial page load. When you expand a parent node, the framework identifies the accessor attribute for the child nodes from the tree binding definition, and then executes the child view object using the accesor attribute in the parent row.

Synchronizing UIs using the target data source

Take a look at the following screenshot. It displays the department-employee tree on the left-hand side and a detailed employee parameter form for the selected tree node on the right-hand side. Whenever an employee node selection changes in the tree, the detailed parameter form on the right-hand side refreshes to reflect the new selection. The tree binding definition has declarative support for building such screens, which may help you to synchronize other parts of the page with the selection of a node in the tree.

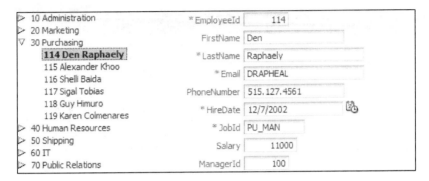

To enable auto-synchronization between iterators of the same type in a page, perform the following steps:

1. Open the page definition file in the overview editor and then select the tree binding whose selection event led to the synchronization of other parts of the page. Click on the **Edit** icon on the **Bindings** panel toolbar.

2. In the **Edit Tree Binding** dialog window, select the desired tree level rule. Expand the **Target Data Source** section displayed at the bottom of the dialog and click on the **EL Picker** button. In the **Variable** dialog, expand the **ADF Bindings | bindings** node and select the desired target iterator which needs to be synchronized with the node selection in the current tree binding.

3. Click on **OK** to save changes.

The following screenshot illustrates the target data source settings for the **EmployeeVO** node in the tree. In this example, **EmployeesIterator** is set as the target data source (target iterator) for the **EmployeeVO** node.

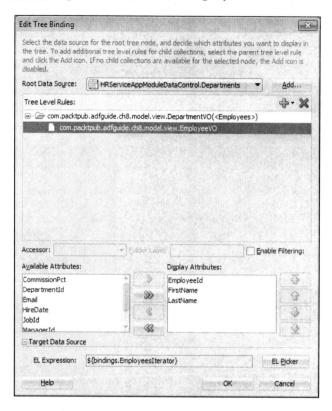

What happens at runtime in the target data source?

Whenever the row selection changes in the source iterator, the binding layer will try to refresh target iterators by invoking the `setCurrentRowWithKey(String stringKey)` method with the *Key* attribute(s) of the selected row of the source iterator. All the UI elements bound to the target iterator will change during the subsequent render response phase in the same request processing cycle. If the new key is not found in the target iterator, you may not observe any changes on the target. For this feature to work, the key definition order and type should match between the source and target iterators.

Adding edit functionalities for a tree table

This section discusses adding edit functionalities, such as create and delete, for a data bound tree table. This is not as straightforward as we did for the table component. We will discuss this topic with an example which can be generalized for your use case.

This example uses a department-employee tree hierarchy represented using `DepartmentVO` and `EmployeeVO` view objects:

```
<af:treeTable value="#{bindings.Departments.treeModel}" var="node"
    selectionListener=
        "#{bindings.Departments.treeModel.makeCurrent}"
    rowSelection="single" id="tt1"
    binding="#{TreeBean.deptTreeTable}"
    partialTriggers="::cb1 ::cb2" editingMode="clickToEdit">
</af:treeTable>
```

Here are the generic guidelines for adding edit functionalities in a tree or tree table component.

Configuring the parent view object to retain the view link accessor row set

While you add new rows in child row sets, it is required to avoid the regeneration of a child row set every time the UI is refreshed. This is achieved by setting the **Retain View Link Accesor Rowset** flag in the parent view object. To set this flag, open the parent view object in the overview editor, select the **General** tab and expand the **Tuning** section. Check the **Retain View Link Accesor Rowset** checkbox. This ensures that the child row sets are not re-queried while you work on the tree model. Repeat this for all parent view objects in the tree hierarchy.

Creating utility methods for reading RowIterator and selected RowKey for the selected node

Define utility methods in the managed bean to read the row iterator and the row key for the selected node. Later in this exercise, we will refer to this method through EL to pass these parameters to the tree update routines defined in the application module.

Open the view controller project and create a managed bean. Add the following methods in the bean:

```
/**
 * This method returns RowIterator object for currently selected
 * row (node)
 * @return
 */
public RowIterator getSelectedNodeRowIterator() {
  RowIterator ri = null;
   //Get the treetable that we deal with in this method
  RichTreeTable depTreeTable = getDeptTreeTable();
   //Store the original Key
  Object oldKey = depTreeTable.getRowKey();
  try {
    if (depTreeTable.getSelectedRowKeys() != null) {
      for (Object opaqueFacesKey : depTreeTable.getSelectedRowKeys())
{
          depTreeTable.setRowKey(opaqueFacesKey);
           //Get the RowIterator for the lowest node
              //in the selected node path
          ri = ((JUCtrlHierNodeBinding)depTreeTable.
                     getRowData()).getRowIterator();
          break;
        }
      }
    } finally {
       //Restore the original Key
      getDeptTreeTable().setRowKey(oldKey);
    }
    return ri;
}


/**
 * This method returns Key for the selected node
 * @return
 */
public Key getSelectedNodeRowKey() {
  Key key = null;
  RichTreeTable depTreeTable = getDeptTreeTable();
   //Store the original Key
  Object oldKey = depTreeTable.getRowKey();

  try {
    if (depTreeTable.getSelectedRowKeys() != null) {

      for (Object opaqueFacesKey :
            depTreeTable.getSelectedRowKeys()) {
          //Return the Key for the lowest level
```

```
        //in the selection
    depTreeTable.setRowKey(opaqueFacesKey);
    key =
            ((JUCtrlHierNodeBinding)depTreeTable.
                getRowData()).getRowKey();
    break;
      }
    }
  } finally {
    //Restore the original Key
    depTreeTable.setRowKey(oldKey);
  }
  return key;
}


/**
 * The DeptTreeTable used in this example is bound
 * to UI treeTable component through 'binding' attribute.
 * e.g: <af:treeTable binding="#{TreeBean.deptTreeTable}"...
 * In real life application, instead of binding you can use
 * Visitor Pattern for reading the UI component. This is
 * explained in Appendix A of this book.
 */
public void setDeptTreeTable(RichTreeTable deptTreeTable) {
  this.deptTreeTable = deptTreeTable;
}

public RichTreeTable getDeptTreeTable() {
  return deptTreeTable;
}
```

If the scope of the managed bean is higher than the request, then you should not bind the UI components' elements in the JSF page with the UI component instances defined in a managed bean using the binding attribute in the component tag. If you do so, you may end up using stale references of the components when the framework recreates the component tree. Instead, you can use visitor patterns to look up the component from the component tree in your managed bean code. This method is explained in the appendix, titled *More on ADF Business Components and Fusion Page Runtime*, of this book. You can download the appendix from the Packt website link that we mentioned at the beginning of this book, in the *Preface* section.

Implementing create and delete methods in the application module

Add the following methods to create and delete children in your application module implementation class and expose them for use by the client through data control.

- The createChildren(RowIterator, Key) method adds new nodes to the child row set of currently selected nodes. The caller of this method is expected to pass the iterator holding the selected node and its Key.

- The deleteChildren(RowIterator, Key) method deletes the node identified by the Key passed by the caller. The caller of this method is expected to pass the iterator holding the selected node and its Key.

This is shown in the following code:

```
// In application module implementation class
/**
 *This method adds node to the child rowset of
 *currently selected node.
 * If no node is selected, new node is added to top
 *level parent rowset.
 * @param ri
 * @param selectedNodeKey
 */
public void createChildren(RowIterator ri, Key selectedNodeKey) {

    final String deptViewDefName = "com.packtpub.adfguide.ch8.model.
view.DepartmentVO";
    final String empViewDefName = "com.packtpub.adfguide.ch8.model.view.
EmployeeVO";
    if (ri != null && selectedNodeKey != null) {
        //Find the Row, using selected node key
      Row[] found = ri.findByKey(selectedNodeKey, 1);
      if (found != null && found.length == 1) {
        Row foundRow = found[0];
        String nodeDefname =
            foundRow.getStructureDef().getDefFullName();
        //Identify the underlying view object for the
          //selected node
        //and insert new row as child to the selected
          //node by accessing the
        //child rowset use accessor attribute
      if (nodeDefname.equals(deptViewDefName)) {
        RowSet childRows =
            (RowSet)foundRow.getAttribute("Employees");
        Row childrow = childRows.createRow();
```

```
          childRows.insertRow(childrow);
      } else if (nodeDefname.equals(empViewDefName)) {
        RowSet childRows =
                (RowSet)foundRow.getAttribute("Reportees");
        Row childrow = childRows.createRow();
        childRows.insertRow(childrow);
      }

    } else {
       //Row not found for selected node
      System.out.println("Node not Found for " +
            selectedNodeKey);
    }


  } else {
      // No node was selected when this method is called, create node
at top level parent VO
    ViewObjectImpl vo = getDepartments();
    Row foundRow = vo.first();
    Row childrow = vo.createRow();
    vo.insertRow(childrow);
  }
}

/**
 * Deletes the selected node
 * @param ri
 * @param selectedNodeKey
 */
public void deleteChildren(RowIterator ri, Key selectedNodeKey) {
  if (ri != null && selectedNodeKey != null) {
      //Finds the row using the Key passed by the caller
    Row[] rows = ri.findByKey(selectedNodeKey, 1);
    if (rows != null) {
      for (Row row : rows) {
          //Delete the row
        row.remove();
      }

    } else {
      System.out.println("Node not Found for " + selectedNodeKey);
    }
  }
}
```

Creating a new row

Drag the **createChildren** method from the **Data Controls** panel and drop it as an ADF Button on the page. Specify the parameter values using the managed bean method that we defined for the reading row iterator and selected node key. You can use the **EL Expression Builder** for picking up the right expression. Set the **ADF Button** (`af:commandButton`) as `partialTrigger` for the `af:treeTable` component.

Here is an example for `<methodAction>` binding for the `createChildren` method (in the page definition file):

```
<methodAction id="createChildren" RequiresUpdateModel="true"
    Action="invokeMethod" MethodName="createChildren"
    IsViewObjectMethod="false"
    DataControl="HRServiceAppModuleDataControl"
    InstanceName=
"data.HRServiceAppModuleDataControl.dataProvider">
  <NamedData NDName="ri"
      NDValue="#{TreeBean.selectedNodeRowIterator}"
      NDType="oracle.jbo.RowIterator"/>
  <NamedData NDName="selectedNodeKey"
      NDValue="#{TreeBean.selectedNodeRowKey}"
      NDType="oracle.jbo.Key"/>
</methodAction>
```

Deleting a row

Drag the **deleteChildren** method from the **Data Controls** panel and drop it as an **ADF Button** on the page. Specify the parameter using the managed bean method that we defined for reading the selected node row iterator and selected node key. You can use the **EL Expression Builder** for picking up the right expression. Set the **Create** command button as `partialTrigger` for the `af:treeTable` component.

Here is an example for the `<methodAction>` binding for the `deleteChildren` method:

```
<methodAction id="deleteChildren" RequiresUpdateModel="true"
    Action="invokeMethod" MethodName="deleteChildren"
    IsViewObjectMethod="false"
    DataControl="HRServiceAppModuleDataControl"
    InstanceName=
        "data.HRServiceAppModuleDataControl.dataProvider">
  <NamedData NDName="ri"
      NDValue="#{TreeBean.selectedNodeRowIterator}"
      NDType="oracle.jbo.RowIterator"/>
```

```
<NamedData NDName="selectedNodeKey"
    NDValue="#{TreeBean.selectedNodeRowKey}"
    NDType="oracle.jbo.Key"/>
</methodAction>
```

A working example illustrating the usage of APIs for performing edit functionalities on a model driven af:treeTable component can be found in the example code that we mentioned at the beginning of this book, in the *Preface* section. To access the example code, open the ADFDevGuideCh8 workspace in JDeveloper and look for the treeCRUD.jsf page in the ViewController project.

Programmatically refreshing the tree hierarchy

To forcefully refresh the tree hierarchy, executing the top level view object instance alone is not enough. This is because when you expand a parent node, if the framework identifies any existing query collection for the row filter supplied by the parent row, the existing query collection cache will be reused for displaying child nodes. To refresh specific child nodes, you will have to find the appropriate child row set and refresh it by calling the executeQuery() method. The following example executes the child Employees row set for a specific DepartmentId.

```
/**
 * Method to refresh child nodes for a specifc department
 * @param deptId
 */
public void refreshChildEmployees(Number deptId) {
    //Gets the VO used for parent node
  ViewObjectImpl vo = getDepartments();
    //Read the row using Key DeptID
  Row[] deptRow = vo.findByKey
    (new Key(new Object[] { deptId }), 1);
    //Get child rows RowSet view link accessor
    //attribute and call executeQuery on it
  RowSet childRows =
      (RowSet)deptRow[0].getAttribute("Employees");
  childRows.executeQuery();
}
```

Accessing web tier values from business components

Rich enterprise applications that we deal with today call for extensive interactions between client and server layers. Oracle ADF is designed keeping this point in mind. When you work on a business application, you may find many use cases on initializing business components (business service layer) with values from the web tier, such as the logged in user's locale and city. This raises mainly the following two questions:

- How does the client pass the web tier parameter values to the business service implementation?
- Where can the parameter values be stored for later use?

The following section will help you to find answers to both these questions.

Using ADFContext to access client specific scoped variables

ADF deploys the `oracle.adf.share.ADFContext` class to share context between the client and server. `ADFContext` exposes APIs for accessing client specific memory scopes such as request, session, page flow, and application scopes. For example, `ADFContext.getCurrent().getPageFlowScope()` returns a page flow scope map from the ADF Faces tier. Usage of ADFContext is one solution for accessing the web tier values business component. However this has serious drawbacks as discussed in the next section.

How does ADFContext provide uniform access across layers?

When a request from a client reaches the server, the framework creates an `oracle.adf.share.ADFContext` instance to hold the state (context) of the current request such as configuration settings, security context, and client state, and associate this instance with the current thread as thread local variables. When a business component class such as an application module, view object, and entity object calls `ADFContext.getCurrent()`, the framework returns an already initialized instance to the caller.

The pitfalls of using ADFContext

The following are the pitfalls of using ADFContext:

- Business services implementation that uses ADFContext to access a client specific scoped variable becomes less reusable in the long run. If your application may need to support multiple client technologies later, there is no guarantee that all these technologies will have support for all the memory scopes exposed through the ADFContext object.
- If you follow the **Test Driven Development (TDD)** methodology, the code that uses ADFContext to directly refer to the client specific memory scopes may fail as the web container is missing when you run tests in the standalone mode.
- Later when you expose application modules as business services, code that directly reads client specific scopes may fail as the request may be from a different host.

Passing web tier values as parameters to business service methods

In this approach, a business service will expose a method to read parameters from the client, which will be stored in a common storage area for later use. This approach does not suffer from any drawbacks that we discussed for the first approach. The implementation is discussed as follows.

Establishing a channel for passing web tier values to the business service layer

You can define a custom method in an application module or in a view object that takes necessary parameters. To learn how to expose a method from an application module, refer to the topic *Exposing business service methods through data control* in *Chapter 6, Introducing the Application Module*.

Using the user session data map to store values passed from the client

For the next step, we may need to decide on a storage area for parameters set by the client. Remember our discussion, in *Using user session data map*, for storing session specific data in *Chapter 6, Introducing the Application Module*. We will use the *user data map* associated with an application module for storing parameter values. Session data map from a root application module is accessible from all containing business components, either programmatically or using Groovy expressions.

When should the client invoke the method that takes web tier values?

Ideally, this should happen before the system starts processing the page which uses web tier values for processing query or business logic. ADF provides a declarative solution for this case too, as follows.

ADF Controller supports the **method call** activity in the navigation flow which can be wired to methods exposed through a view object or application module. We can use this approach to pass web tier values to the server. Apparently, the method call activity for such use cases may appear as an intermediate step for all navigation cases to the target page that contains business logic based on web tier values. At runtime, when you navigate to the target view, ADF Controller invokes the method call activity to set the parameter values to the user session data map before displaying the page.

Making the user session data map passivation safe

The previous approach works well if the business components do not need the value set by the client while serving the next request from the same client. If the business components need values stored in a user session data map across requests, you may need to make sure that the values set in the session data map survives the activation-passivation cycle of an application module. This is done by overriding the `activateState(Element)` and `passivateState(Document, Element)` methods in the corresponding application module implementation class. Refer to the topic *Programmatically passivating custom data* in *Chapter 6, Introducing the Application Module*, for code samples.

An example illustrating the usage of the user session data map for passing client side values to the middle tier is discussed later in this chapter under the section entitled *Initializing criteria item values using web tier values*.

Building data bound query search forms

The search functionality has become a very essential feature for any enterprise application which may need to deal with tons of data. The Oracle ADF framework has out of the box support for building feature rich search panels when you use the view object for querying the data source. In fact the implementation is much easier than you thought.

ADF uses the model-driven approach for building query components whose query model is derived from the view criteria that you defined in a view object. We have discussed view criteria in *Chapter 4, Introducing the View Object,* when we talked about view objects. In this section, we are revisiting the same topic to discuss some more points which we deferred then for later discussion.

Building the view criteria

To create a view criteria in a view object, perform the following steps:

1. Open a view object in the overview editor and then select the **Query** tab.

2. In the **Query** tab, expand the **View Criteria** section, and click on the green plus icon to create a new **View Criteria** icon. Doing so will display the **Edit View Criteria** dialog window as shown in the following screenshot:

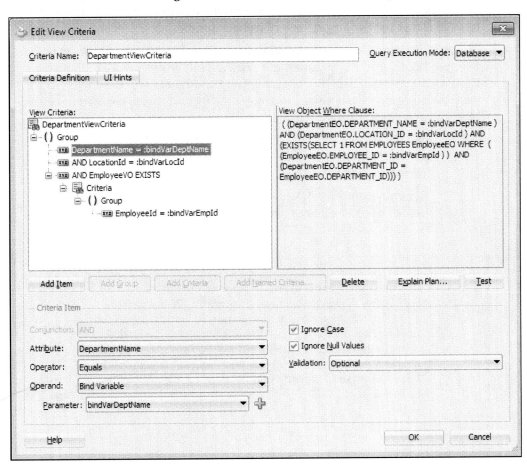

3. In **Edit View Criteria**, enter the criteria name and select the **Query Execution Mode**. The possible values for **Query Execution Modes** are as follows:

    ○ **Database**: Filtering is done on the database. This is the default mode.

    ○ **In Memory**: Filtering is performed on the in-memory row set produced by the view object.

    ○ **Both**: Filtering is performed on the database first, followed by in-memory. This mode is useful to filter out the newly added un-posted rows from the row set.

4. To add the criteria items for searching, select the **Group** node in the view criteria tree where you want the new criteria item to appear and click on the **Add Item** button. Specify values for **Attribute**, **Operator**, and **Operand**.

The view criteria item can take view accessor attributes as well. When you use the accessor attribute in a criteria item, the framework will generate the EXISTS clause for the target view object at runtime.

The criteria item value can be specified as a **literal** or **bind** variable. You may use bind variables to initialize a criteria item with some default static or dynamic values. Also, this usage has all the advantages of using a bind variable in a query such as caching query string and improved performance. Here are some tips for bind variable usage:

○ Bind variables used in a query component should be marked as Optional. Mark it as Required only if that appears in the query defined in the view object.

○ All bind variables marked as Required will be displayed in the **Search** panel as separate fields. Set the display hint to Hide to hide the bind variables from display.

If you use literal values for a criteria item, then do not assume that the framework will blindly append the WHERE clause with literal values to the query at runtime. The framework plays smarter here and creates temporary bind variables for holding literal values. This special behaviour is controlled through the useBindVarsForViewCriteriaLiterals property present in the view criteria instance. This property can be configured globally in adf-config.xml (which is true by default).

To perform a case insensitive search for each view criteria item, select the **Ignore Case** checkbox. The **Validation** option helps you to configure a "required" field validation for the criteria item. The possible options are **Required, Selectively Required**, and **Optional**. When you mark multiple criteria items as **Selectively Required**, at least one "selectively required" criteria item in this group should have a value to search.

The **Add Group** button creates new groups for holding criteria items. This is useful to group the query conditions logically based on use case requirements. The **Add Criteria** option defines new criteria which takes groups and criteria. The **Add Named Criteria** option adds existing named criteria in the current criteria.

Using UI hints to control the display for a query component

The **UI Hints** tab for the **Edit View Criteria** dialog allows you to define display hints for the view criteria which will be used by the query component at runtime to render the display. The following UI hints options are available with the view criteria definition:

- **Search Region Mode**: The search region mode allows you to specify the initial display mode such as **Advanced** or **Basic** for the query panel.

- **Show Operators**: This is the display mode in which operators for the criteria item are displayed.

- **Query Automatically**: This mode fires the query automatically when the page with search panel is loaded.

- **Show Match All Match Any**: This displays the *Match All* and *Match Any* options for criteria items in the query component. The default selected is Match All.

- **Rendered Mode**: The **Rendered Mode** controls the display of criteria items in the search screen.

- **Display Width**: The display width allows you to override the default width for a criteria item. The default width is derived from the attribute definition in the view object.

Once you are done with the model definition for the query component, next is building your UI using the named criteria definition in a view object.

Building a search UI

To build a search UI, perform the following steps:

1. Select the desired view object instance in the **Data Controls** panel and expand the **Named Criteria** node to display all the view criteria defined in the view object.

2. Drag the desired view criteria and drop it on the appropriate area in a page. From the context menu, choose **Create | Query | ADF Query Panel with Table** or **Create | Query | ADF Query Panel with Tree Table**. This is shown in the following screenshot:

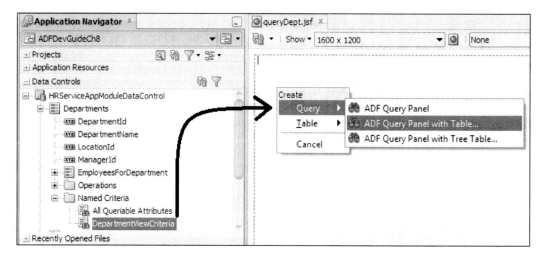

You can even build a **Query** component separately and later add the result component.

What happens when you drop a view criteria as a query component on a page?

When you build a query component by dragging and dropping view criteria on a page, the IDE generates the following:

- Code for the `<af:query>` component in the JSF page with all generic properties defaulted with values from view criteria definition though a binding EL expression

- Executable `<searchRegion>` binding for the query component

The following is an example for the executable `<searchRegion>` binding present in the page definition file:

```
<searchRegion Criteria="DepartmentViewCriteria" Customizer=
"oracle.jbo.uicli.binding.JUSearchBindingCustomizer"
Binds="DepartmentsIterator" id="DepartmentViewCriteriaQuery"/>
```

Commonly used properties of the search region binding

You are allowed to modify the default values of the `searchRegion` binding if the use cases demands so. The following are the commonly used properties of search binding:

- `TrackQueryPerformed`: This flag causes to restore queried state when you navigate back to the search page. If you want to restore the queried state between page flows, then set `TrackQueryPerformed = "PageFlow"` (which is default), otherwise set `TrackQueryPerformed = "Page"`.

  How does the framework track user search actions?

  The search binding sets the `queryPerformed` flag to `true` when you perform search. If `TrackQueryPerformed` is set as `PageFlow`, then the framework the tracks the `queryPerformed` flag at page flow level. When the user navigates back to the search page later, the framework restores the previous state by re-executing the query if `queryPerformed` is `true`.

- `InitialQueryOverridden`: Set this flag to `true` to display result of the pre-executed query result in the result table. For example, you will set this flag to `true` in order to display the result of the view object execution that happened outside the context of the current page with search binding. This flag overrides the default `AutoQuery` or `ClearRowSet` behavior of search binding. This behavior is explained in the following section.

What is AutoQuery or ClearRowSet behavior?

When a model bound query component renders, the framework will check the `Query Automatically` property set for the underlying view criteria to decide on the behavior of the query component during the page load. If this flag is true, the search binding will execute the query in the view object during page load. If this is set to false, then the search binding will clear the row set by calling the `executeEmptyRowSet()` method on the underlying view object implementation. The `executeEmptyRowSet()` method marks view objects as executed and skips further to refresh calls on the default row sets in the same page lifecycle. This is the reason why you see an empty result table when you load the search page.

To learn more about the data bound query component, refer to *Creating ADF Databound Search Forms* in *Oracle Fusion Middleware Fusion Developer's Guide for Oracle Application Development Framework*. To access the documentation online go to `http://www.oracle.com/technetwork/developer-tools/jdev/documentation/index.html` and choose **Oracle JDeveloper and ADF Documentation Library | Fusion Developer's Guide**. Use the **Search** option to find specific topics.

Initializing criteria item values using web tier values

The view criteria has declarative support for defaulting criteria item values. While defining criteria items, you can specify a bind parameter as a value which can be defaulted using a Groovy expression.

What if you need to initialize fields displayed in the **Search** panel with values from the web tier; for example, defaulting the location field with the logged in user's default location? As ADF uses view criteria to define the model for the query component, we are back to the same topic that we discussed a while ago, that is, *Accessing web tier values from business components*. This section implements the second approach that we discussed for passing web tier values. The detailed steps are as follows:

1. Generate the application module implementation class and define a method that initializes the user session data map with values passed by the client and then expose the method for use by the client. Refer to *Exposing the Business Service Method through Data Control* in *Chapter 6, Introducing the Application Module*, if you need a quick brush up on this topic. The following is an example:

```
//In application module implementation class
/**
 * Application Module method to Init User Data Map
 * @param locationId
 */
public void initSessionWithUserLoc(Integer locationId){
  getSession().getUserData().put("USER_LOC", locationId);
}
```

The data storage mechanism for holding a value passed by the client is in place now.

2. To set this user session data object as a value for the desired criteria item, open the view object in the overview editor. Select the **Query** tab and define a bind variable with a default value using a Groovy expression that accesses the session user data map, that is, adf.userSession.userData.USER_LOC. When you set a Groovy expression as a default value for bind variables make sure you selected Expression as the value type in the **Bind Variable** editor.

3. Create a view criteria whose criteria item needs to be defaulted with a value from the web tier. Select the desired criteria item and set the bind variable that we defined in a previous step as a parameter value.

4. In the next step, we may need to figure out a place to call the application module method that we defined at the beginning for passing the client side values.

5. To execute the application module method that reads client parameters before displaying the target page, double-click on the desired task flow XML file or adf-config.xml to display the navigation diagram window. Drag the desired method (initSessionWithUserLoc in our example) from the **Data Controls** panel and drop it as a method activity and set the client specific parameter as a value to the method parameter when asked, for example, #{pageFlowScope.locId}. An example navigation case is shown in the following diagram:

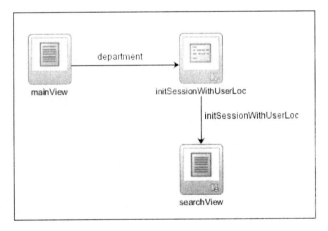

At runtime, when you navigate to the target page that displays the query component, the framework does the following behind the scenes:

1. The ADF Controller invokes the method activity before displaying the view.

2. Once the method activity is executed, the system navigates to the target view.

3. When the target page renders the query component, the framework resolves the underlying view criteria in order to build the model for the query component. During this stage, the criteria item that is mapped to the *session user data map* through the bind variable reads the value by evaluating the Groovy expression (`adf.userSession.userData.USER_LOC.`). This value is displayed in the **Search** panel as the default value for the criteria item.

Programmatically controlling the display of a query component

When a model-driven query component is rendered, the framework reads the underlying view criteria definition to render individual fields. Individual attributes used in the view criteria inherit the UI hints set at view object level.

What if you want to hide a specific criteria item based on a user profile at runtime or want to alter the display hints, such as display width or search field label, dynamically?

The **View Criteria Editor** window allows you to override basic UI hints such as display hint and display width for individual criteria. However, more granular level settings are not supported in the declarative mode as of now.

You can go for a programmatic solution for such use cases. To programmatically control the display of individual criteria items in the view criteria, you may want to do the following tasks:

1. Create a custom `oracle.jbo.AttributeHints` implementation class.

2. Override the method `getCriteriaItemAttributeHints(ViewCriteriaItem)` in the view object implementation class to return the custom implementation for `oracle.jbo.AttributeHints`.

The following is an example that returns custom `AttributeHints` implementations for a specific view criteria item. The `CustomCriteriaAttrHints` implementation used in this example is given as follows. This example returns custom format for the view criteria item. We are keeping this example simple to explain the concepts behind implementation; you can make it more dynamic by adding more realistic implementation.

```
**
*This demo implementation overrides getHint() to return
* hard coded value for Date format.
* In real life application you can take the values from a
* common user preference class:
```

```
*/
public class CustomCriteriaAttrHints extends RowAttrHintsImpl {
    ViewCriteriaItem vcItem;

    public CustomCriteriaAttrHints(ViewCriteriaItem vci) {
        super();
        vcItem = vci;
    }

    @Override
    protected AttributeHints getFormatAttributeHintsInternal
        (LocaleContext locale) {
        return vcItem.getAttributeDef().getUIHelper();
    }

    @Override
    protected AttributeHints getAttributeHintsInternal
        (String hintName, LocaleContext locale) {
        return vcItem.getAttributeDef().getUIHelper();
    }

    @Override
    public String getLocaleName
        (LocaleContext locale, String sName) {
        return vcItem.getAttributeDef().getUIHelper().
            getLocaleName(locale, sName);
    }

    @Override
    public String[][] getCompOpers(LocaleContext locale) {
        return vcItem.getAttributeDef().getUIHelper().
            getCompOpers(locale);
    }
    @Override
    public String getHint(LocaleContext locale,
        String sHintName) {
        if (AttributeHints.FMT_FORMAT.equals(sHintName)) {
            return "yyyy-MM-dd";
        } else {
            return getAttributeHintsInternal(sHintName,
                locale).getHint(locale, sHintName);
        }
    }
}
```

The next step is to override the method `getCriteriaItemAttributeHints`
`(ViewCriteriaItem)` in the view object implementation class to return the
`CustomCriteriaAttrHints` that we use in this example. This method will
be engaged every time the ADF framework renders a query component.
The following code snippet in the view object implementation class returns
the `CustomCriteriaAttrHints` implementation for the criteria item with
`oracle.jbo.domain.Date` as the attributes type. In other words, this example
provides a custom format for the `Date` data type appearing in the **Search** panel.

```
//In view object implementation class
/**
  * This method overrides the runtime display of criteria
  * items that appear inside a query component.  *
  */
@Override
public AttributeHints getCriteriaItemAttributeHints(ViewCriteriaItem
vci) {
//Apply the custom hints for VC Item type-
//oracle.jbo.domain.Date
    if ("oracle.jbo.domain.Date".equals(
      vci.getAttributeDef().getJavaType().getName())) {
    CustomCriteriaAttrHints attrHints=
        new CustomCriteriaAttrHints(vci);
    return attrHints;
    }
    return super.getCriteriaItemAttributeHints(vci);
}
```

Programmatically retrieving view criteria used for a query component

The `af:query` component allows you to intercept the query execution through the
custom `queryListener` method defined in a managed bean. The `queryListener` is
called when the user performs a search. The following `<af:query>` uses the custom
`queryPerformed(QueryEvent)` method defined in the `SearchBean` as a
query listener:

```
<af:query id="qryId1" headerText="Search" disclosed="true"
value="#{bindings.DeptViewCriteriaQuery.queryDescriptor}"
model="#{bindings.DeptViewCriteriaQuery.queryModel}"
    queryListener="#{SearchBean.queryPerfromed}"
    queryOperationListener=
"#{bindings.DeptViewCriteriaQuery.processQueryOperation}"
    resultComponentId="::resId1"/>
```

What if you want to retrieve the values set by the user in a query component, from the query listener method? The view criteria provides a model for a query component. The following example illustrates the binding APIs to retrieve the view criteria from a query component. This is useful if you need to intercept the default search invocation to customize the view criteria used for executing queries. The following code snippet appends an extra view criteria row (`DepartmentId=10`) on to the view criteria object retrieved from the query component and then processes the query.

```
//In managed bean class

/**
 * A custom queryListener
 */
public void queryPerfromed(QueryEvent queryEvent) {
    DCBindingContainer bc = (DCBindingContainer)BindingContext.
        getCurrent().getCurrentBindingsEntry();
    DCBindingContainer searchBinding = (DCBindingContainer)bc.
        findExecutableBinding("DeptViewCriteriaQuery");
    String criteriaName = JUSearchBindingCustomizer.
        getCriteriaName(searchBinding);
    ViewCriteria vc = JUSearchBindingCustomizer.
        getViewCriteria(searchBinding, criteriaName);
    ViewCriteriaRow vcr1 = vc.createViewCriteriaRow();
    vcr1.setAttribute("DepartmentId","10");
    vc.addRow(vcr1);
    invokeQueryEventMethodExpression
        ("#{bindings.DeptViewCriteriaQuery.processQuery}",
        queryEvent);

}

/**
 * Invoke Query EL
 */
private void invokeQueryEventMethodExpression(String expression,
QueryEvent queryEvent) {

    FacesContext fctx = FacesContext.getCurrentInstance();
    ELContext elctx = fctx.getELContext();
    ExpressionFactory efactory =
        fctx.getApplication().getExpressionFactory();
    MethodExpression me =
        efactory.createMethodExpression(elctx, expression,
            Object.class, new Class[] { QueryEvent.class });
    me.invoke(elctx, new Object[] { queryEvent });

}
```

Programmatically resetting a query component

In some scenarios you may need to programmatically reset the query component as part of some user action on the screen. For example, when you display a query component in a pop up, you may need to programmatically reset the previous state of the query component before displaying the pop up a second time. The following code snippet will help you to programmatically reset the query component:

```
//In managed bean class
Public void resetDeptQuery(){
//Get Query Component instance
RichQuery deptQuery = getDeptQuery();
QueryModel model = deptQuery.getModel();
QueryDescriptor qd = deptQuery.getValue();
//Reset the Query Model and refresh
model.reset(qd);
deptQuery.refresh(FacesContext.getCurrentInstance());
}
```

 Search binding will not try to refresh criteria item values on each invocation. If the criteria item in a view criteria uses some dynamic EL expression and you want search biding to re-evaluate the latest value, then call saveState() on the ViewCriteria instance.

Search on a tree table

When you use the view criteria defined in the root view object to search a tree, the framework, by default, searches only on the root view object. To filter out the child nodes based on the criteria entered by the user, you may need to override the createViewLinkAccessorRS(AssociationDefImpl assocDef, ViewObjectImpl accessorVO, Row masterRow, Object[] values) method in the parent view object implementation class and programmatically set the desired search condition for the child row set. The framework, then, invokes the previous method to create child nodes for a tree or tree table when the user expands the parent node.

The following example illustrates the tree search for a department-employee hierarchy.

This example uses the view criteria defined in DepartmnetVO to build a search form for a tree table. You can include attributes from child view objects as criteria items to make the search more meaningful. For instance, the following view criteria definition adds FirstName from EmployeeVO as a criteria item.

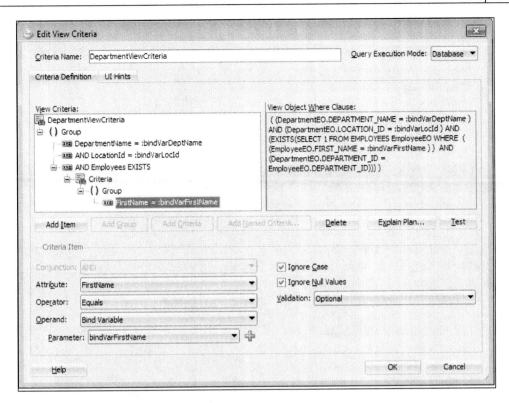

After defining the view criteria in a parent view object, define the necessary WHERE clause or view criteria in the child view object which will be used for filtering out the child rows from the method `createViewLinkAccessorRS` in the parent view object. This example uses `EmployeeViewCriteria` defined in `EmployeeVO` for filtering the employee row set. `EmployeeViewCriteria` contains `FirstName` as the view criteria item.

Open the parent view object implementation class and override `createViewLinkAcc essorRS(AssociationDefImpl, ViewObjectImpl,Row, Object[])`. The following implementation overrides `createViewLinkAccessorRS()` in `DepartmentVOImpl`. This method applies `EmployeeViewCriteria` on to the child accessor view object (`EmployeeVO`) in order to filter out employee rows. Note that this example refines the employee rows based on the value entered for `bindVarFirstName` in the search form.

```
/**
 * This method is called by framework to create view link accessor for
associated detail view objects
 */
@Override
protected ViewRowSetImpl
```

```
     createViewLinkAccessorRS(AssociationDefImpl
     associationDefImpl, ViewObjectImpl accessorVO,
     Row parentRow, Object[] object) {
    //Create View Link Accessor for detail VO that
    //is linked through view link
   ViewRowSetImpl viewRowSetImpl =
     super.createViewLinkAccessorRS(associationDefImpl,
        accessorVO, parentRow, object);

    //Get the View Criteria defined on child VO
    //and pass bind parameter values to it.
    //This will be used when framework later
    //executes child viewRowSetImplin the execution cycle
   ViewCriteriaManager vcm = accessorVO.
        getViewCriteriaManager();
   ViewCriteria vc = vcm.getViewCriteria
        ("EmployeeViewCriteria");
   VariableValueManager vvm = vc.ensureVariableManager();
   vvm.setVariableValue("bindVarEmpFirstName",
        getbindVarFirstName());
   accessorVO.applyViewCriteria(vc);

    return viewRowSetImpl;
 }
```

What happens at runtime in a tree table search?

At runtime, when you expand a parent node, the framework will invoke `createViewLinkAccessorRS` on the parent view object to identify the child row set. The logic for filtering child rows will be executed during this stage.

Building a data bound multi select list

The selection components allow the user to select single and multiple values from a list. The ADF framework offers a variety of data bound multi select UI components.

To create a data bound multi select component, drag a collection from the Data Control panel on to a JSF page. In the opened context menu, choose **Multiple Selection | ADF Select Many Choice** (or any other suitable multi select component). Select the base and display attribute in the **Edit List Binding** dialog window and click on **OK**.

When you drop a collection as multi select components, IDE generates the following:

- Component code in JSF page
- Iterator and list binding in the page definition file

Programmatically accessing selected rows

The following code snippet illustrates the binding APIs for accessing selected rows in a list binding. The list binding used in this example is built by dropping the **Departments** view object as **ADF Select Many Choice** on the JSF page. The following is the list binding entry from the page definition file:

```
<list IterBinding="DepartmentsIterator"
ListOperMode="multiSelect" ListIter="DepartmentsIterator"
id="Departments"  SelectItemValueMode="ListObject">
...
</list>
```

You can access the selected items from the managed bean code using binding APIs. The following is an example:

```
//In managed bean class
public void processSelectedItems() {
  BindingContext bctx = BindingContext.getCurrent();
  BindingContainer bc = bctx.getCurrentBindingsEntry();
  JUCtrlListBinding departsments =
      (JUCtrlListBinding)bc.get("Departments");
  int[] selectedIndices = departsments.getSelectedIndices();
  for (int indx : selectedIndices) {
    Row row = departsments.getRowAtRangeIndex(indx);
    //Work with row
      processSelectedItem(row);
  }

}
```

Overriding UI hints in a view object

The ADF framework allows you to override UI hints defined in a view object at runtime. This is done by overriding `createViewRowAttrHints(AttributeDefImpl attrDef)` in `oracle.jbo.server.ViewRowImpl` for the view object. The framework engages this method to retrieve control hints when a row is rendered on the UI.

There are two steps to supply custom row attribute hints for a view object:

1. Create a custom view row attribute hints implementation class extended from `oracle.jbo.server.ViewRowAttrHintsImpl`. This class will have the logic to return custom attribute hints.

2. Generate a view row class, and override `createViewRowAttrHints(Attrib uteDefImpl attrDef)` in the class to return customized row attribute hints implementation.

The following example illustrates the usage of attribute hints in the view object to control the runtime display of UI elements. This example hides the `ManagerId` attribute for normal business users. The term "normal user" in this example refers to the business user of the application without any special privileges.

The `CustomRowAAttrHintsImpl` class used in this example functions as follows. This implementation returns a "hide display" hint for the `ManagerId` attribute for normal users.

```
//In the view row attributes hints implementation class

class CustomRowAAttrHintsImpl extends ViewRowAttrHintsImpl {

 public CustomRowAAttrHintsImpl(AttributeDefImpl attr, ViewRowImpl
viewRow) {
  super(attr, viewRow);
 }

 @Override
public String getHint(LocaleContext locale, String sHintName) {
   //If attribute is ManagerId, execute custom hint
   if (getViewAttributeDef().getName().equals("ManagerId")) {
    if (ViewRowAttrHintsImpl.HINT_NAME_DISPLAY_HINT.
      equals(sHintName)) {
     if (isNormalUser())
        //For normal user return 'Hide'
        //else return 'Display'
      return ViewRowAttrHintsImpl.
        ATTRIBUTE_DISPLAY_HINT_HIDE;
     else
       return ViewRowAttrHintsImpl.
        ATTRIBUTE_DISPLAY_HINT_DISPLAY;
   }
  }
  return super.getHint(locale, sHintName);
 }
```

```
private boolean isNormalUser() {
    return CustomProfileChecker.getInstance().isNormalUser;
}


}
```

Generate the appropriate view row class to return the custom attribute hints implementation from the previous step (`CustomRowAAttrHintsImpl`):

```
//In the view row implementation class

public class DepartmentVORowImpl extends ViewRowImpl {
    //Other codes go here
    /**
     * Create a map to store attribute hints for this row.
     * @param attrDef The attribute definition for which
     * the hints need to be created.
     * @return an instance ofViewRowAttrHintsImpl      */
    protected ViewRowAttrHintsImpl
        createViewRowAttrHints(AttributeDefImpl attrDef) {
            //Return custom row attribute hints implementation
            return new CustomRowAAttrHintsImpl(attrDef, this);
    }
}
```

The following ADF Faces tag snippet illustrates the usage of control hints in the UI. This example hides the `ManagerId` field in the UI if `displayHint` for the `ManagerId` attribute is not equal to `Display`. At runtime, when the system evaluates the EL – `#{bindings.ManagerId.hints.displayHint}`, the framework invokes the underlying `getHint()` method on `CustomRowAAttrHintsImpl` to return the desired value.

```
<af:inputText value="#{bindings.ManagerId.inputValue}"
label="#{bindings.ManagerId.hints.label}"
        required="#{bindings.ManagerId.hints.mandatory}"
        columns="#{bindings.ManagerId.hints.displayWidth}"
        maximumLength="#{bindings.ManagerId.hints.precision}"
        rendered="#{bindings.ManagerId.hints.displayHint eq
'Display'}"
        shortDesc="#{bindings.ManagerId.hints.tooltip}" id="it7">
    <f:validator binding="#{bindings.ManagerId.validator}"/>
</af:inputText>
```

Summary

In this chapter we have explored data bound UI component features offered by the ADF framework. The major objective of this chapter was to enable you to go beyond the visual and declarative development and customize the default behaviour of the framework components without breaking the contract set by the framework. We have also covered many examples and API usages while discussing various data bound UI components.

In the next chapter, we will see how to declaratively define a navigation model in a fusion web application.

9

Controlling the Page Navigation

Most web applications display some form of visual navigations and provide navigation models to help users move around the pages. In this chapter you will learn about similar offerings from the ADF Controller layer to navigate back and forth between views in a Fusion web application. In addition to providing navigation models for the web pages, the ADF Controller is also responsible for transaction management, authorization, and managed bean lifecycle management. We will be discussing basic navigation models provided by the ADF Controller layer in this chapter. More advanced concepts will be covered in the next chapter. We will discuss the following topics in this chapter:

- The navigation model in the JSF framework
- The navigation model in ADF
- The ingredients of an ADF task flow
- Building an unbounded task flow

Introduction

As you know ADF Faces is implemented on top of the JSF framework. In other words, ADF Faces leveraged the extensibility options offered by JSF to add more features, keeping the basic architecture in aligned with that of the JSF framework. A key area where ADF Faces excels over other JSF based frameworks is the controller layer. The JSF navigation controller provides a basic navigation model for a web application and is very flexible by design. However it lacks certain functionalities such as reuse of pages, hooks for placing page initialization logic, page fragmenting, and modular development. The ADF Controller is designed to overcome these drawbacks. Let's give a glance at the features offered by the JSF controller before digging in to the details of the ADF Controller.

The navigation model in the JSF framework

The JSF framework has a very flexible navigation model which decouples navigation rules from the JSF page as well as from underlying business logic.

The JSF 2.0 navigation model supports two types of navigations:

- Rule based navigation
- Implicit navigation

Rule based navigation

The core JSF navigation model is built based on navigation rules which decide the next page in the navigation flow in response to the outcome produced by the actionable UI components. JSF uses a `faces-config.xml` file to store all the navigation rules and managed beans used in the application. The following is an example for navigation rules defined in `faces-config.xml`.

```
<navigation-rule>
  <from-view-id>/department.jsf</from-view-id>
  <navigation-case>
    <from-outcome>viewEmployees</from-outcome>
    <to-view-id>/employee.jsf</to-view-id>
  </navigation-case>
</navigation-rule>
```

In this example, the framework will navigate to the user from `department.jsf` to `employee.jsf` by clicking on any navigation UI component whose action outcome is set to `viewEmployees` in the JSF code. The following is an example for a navigation UI component:

```
<h:commandButton value="View Employees"
action="viewEmployees" />
```

If your application is huge in size, the JSF framework allows you to split `faces-config.xml` into multiple files which can be configured in the `web.xml` file as follows:

```
<context-param>
<param-name>javax.faces.CONFIG_FILES</param-name>
<param-value>
  WEB-INF/config/manage-beans.xml,
  WEB-INF/config/navigation-rule.xml,
  WEB-INF/config/config.xml
</param-value>
</context-param>
```

If you are working on a Fusion web application, you will always use ADF specific configuration files such as `adfc-config.xml` or task flow XML files for configuring navigation rules as well as for keeping managed bean definitions. By using `adfc-config.xml` or task flow XML for defining navigation rules, you can leverage the extra features offered by the ADF Faces navigation model. Note that `faces-config.xml` is still required to run an ADF Faces application. A Fusion web application may use `faces-config.xml` to store metadata definition for validation rules, converters, lifecycle phase listeners, custom component definitions, render kits, global resource bundles, and application level factory extensions.

Implicit navigation

Before winding up our discussion on the JSF navigation model, let us take a look at the new implicit navigation feature offered by JSF 2.0. The implicit navigation feature eliminates the need for navigation-rule definitions in the `faces-config.xml` file. This makes your life easier when you build demo applications or proof of concepts.

How does implicit navigation work?

When a user performs some action on the page, JSF posts a form back to the server. While processing the postback request, the framework will check all navigation cases for finding any matching outcome produced by the navigation component. If no matching navigation case is found, then the navigation handler checks to see if the action outcome corresponds to a view ID in the application. If a view matching the action outcome is found, an implicit navigation to the matching view occurs.

For example, consider the following JSF code:

```
<af:button text="View Employees" id="b1" action="empView"/>
```

When a user clicks on the **View Employees** button, the framework will check for any navigation rule definition for the action outcome `empView`. If there is no matching navigation rule found, then the framework will check for a page within the application whose extension is the same as the current page and whose filename is the same as the action string set for the component. If such a view exits, then implicit navigation will be triggered resulting in navigation to `empView.jsf`.

Implicit navigation is supported in ADF 11*g* Release 2 onwards.

The navigation model in ADF

One of the biggest challenges faced by web developers is how to deal with complex navigation requirements of huge enterprise applications. Though the control flow features offered by JSF meet the basic requirements of most of the business applications, developers may need to put extra effort in when it comes to really complex use cases. For example, consider the following navigation requirements which you might have experienced while working on rich enterprise applications:

- Implementing page hierarchies, only for top level pages, of an application should be directly accessible through a URL link

- Enforcing sequential processing for certain sets of pages to complete the transaction in a predefined order

- Reusing control flow cases and associated pages in an application

You may end up writing down custom logic to achieve these functionalities with the core JSF framework. The good news is that the Oracle ADF framework has out of the box support for all such navigation requirements. ADF uses task flows to provide the basic infrastructure for controlling the navigation cases in a Fusion web application. There are two types of task flows in ADF:

- **Unbounded Task Flow**: Unbounded task flows are designed to handle navigation between pages which do not necessarily follow any specific entry point or exit point. For example, consider the pages linked through the toolbar menu in an application. An end user can select any menu option that he or she likes, or the person can even type the URL directly in the browser for viewing the page and can exit from the page or switch to a new page at any point in time. The navigation model for such pages (unbounded view) is defined using unbounded task flow.

  Unbounded task flow defines navigation for unbounded views in a Fusion web application.

- **Bounded Task Flow**: The bounded task flow is primarily designed to implement reusable navigation cases with definite entry and exit points. A bounded task flow contains its own set of control flow rules, activities, and managed beans. The following are the unique features of a bounded task flow:

  i. They can have only one entry point for entering into the task flow. However, multiple exit points are supported.

  ii. They can take parameters from the caller before starting the execution as well as the return value to the caller after execution.

iii. They can be built either using page fragments or complete JSF pages.

iv. They support transaction aware control flow cases.

The ingredients of an ADF task flow

The ADF task flow consists of three major elements: task flow configuration files, task flow activities, and managed bean definitions. The following section discusses each item in detail.

Task flow configuration files

When you build an ADF task flow, JDeveloper IDE generates a task flow definition file that will act as a registry for keeping task flow related artefacts. These files are discussed under this section.

- `adfc-config.xml`: This file stores the metadata definition for the default unbounded task flow in a Fusion web application. JDeveloper by default creates this file in the `public_html\WEB-INF` folder of the view controller project when you generate a Fusion Web application.

  The `adfc-config.xml` file may contain unbounded task flow activities, control flow rules for pages, and managed beans interacting to allow users to finish specific business functionalities. The IDE will generate a brand new `adfc-configN.xml` file (where N is a numeric value) for new unbounded task flows created in the view controller project. At runtime, the framework will use the union of all the `adf-config.xml` files to decide the navigation case for page and also for identifying the bean definitions when referring to them in the view layer using EL expressions.

  When you ship a view controller project that contains unbounded task flow as an ADF library, the packaging tool will move the task flow definition XML file to the `META-INF` folder in the ADF Library JAR. In other words, if the project that contains unbounded task flow is shipped as an ADF library, the `META-INF` folder in the ADF Library JAR will be holding the task flow definition XML file.

- **Bounded task flow definition XML**: This file stores the metadata definition for a bounded task flow. You can specify the task flow definition XML filename and location when you generate the task flow. The task flow XML files are stored in the `WEB-INF` folder of the view controller project where you created the task flow. If the project that contains the ADF task flow is shipped as an ADF library, the `META-INF` folder in the ADF Library JAR will be holding the task flow definition XML file.

The bounded task flow XML file may contain the bounded task flow activities, control flow rules for pages or page fragments, and managed bean definitions used in the corresponding task flow.

ADF managed beans

Managed beans are Java classes used for implementing business logic or data model for your JSF page. As the name suggests, its lifecycle is managed by the underlying JSF framework. Managed beans are defined in task flow configuration files such as `adfc-config.xml` or task flow definition XML file. While defining a managed bean, you specify the bean name, the fully packaged Java class name, and scope of the bean. An example is as follows:

```
<managed-bean id="__1">
  <managed-bean-name>empBean</managed-bean-name>
  <managed-bean-class>
   com.packtpub.adfguide.ch8.view.EmployeeBean
  </managed-bean-class>
  <managed-bean-scope>request</managed-bean-scope>
</managed-bean>
```

The managed bean can be referred from a JSF page using EL expression. In the following example, the EL expression `#{empBean.firstName}` refers to the `firstName` property in the `empBean` instance.

```
<<af:inputText  id="it1" value="#{empBean.firstName}"/>
```

JSF 2.0 introduced annotations for registering a POJO class as a managed bean and also enabled **Contexts and Dependency Injection (CDI)** for managing runtime dependencies in a managed bean. As the Oracle ADF Controller layer does not have any extended implementations on these areas, we are not covering these topics in this book. Oracle ADF Controller (task flows) will continue to use the registration of beans in configuration files.

The scope specified for a managed bean decides how long it should stay in memory. The following table explains memory scopes available for managed beans in an ADF application:

Scope	Description	ADF Specific Scope (Yes/No)
backingBean	The backingBean scope exists for the duration of a request. The backingBean scope is limited to the containing task flow or UI component. If you have multiple instances of the same task flow or declarative components in a page, each instance will get its own backingBean scope memory area and they are not visible to each other. You may use the backingBean scope to store managed beans or variables for the duration of a request. The backingBean scoped memory variables are accessible only within the containing bounded task flow or within the owning component.	Yes
request	The request scope exists for the duration of a request. Unlike the backingBean scope, the request scope is shared across task flows and components in a page. You may use the request scope to store managed beans or variables for the duration of a request. If the page that uses a request scoped variable contain an embedded task flow which may accidentally use the same name for request scoped variables, then you may need to consider using the backingBean scope for such cases in order to prevent the accidental overriding of values.	No
view	The view scope is longer than the request scope, and shorter than the session scope. View-scoped memory variables or managed beans exist until the user finishes interaction with the current view. Note that JSF 2.0 introduced a View scope in the core JSF framework. ADF also provides a scope with the same name. When you use a view scope in a Fusion web application, under the covers it uses the view scope implementation provided by ADF. The difference between the two view scopes is that JSF 2.0 stores information in a map on `UIViewRoot`. This will be emptied during page refresh or a redirect to the same view. The ADF Controller view scope is refreshed only when users navigate to a new view (when the view ID changes) Thus, view scoped variables and managed beans in ADF survive refreshes and redirect to the same view.	Yes (JSF also has similar scope)

Scope	Description	ADF Specific Scope (Yes/No)
pageFlow	The pageFlow scope exists across activities for the duration of a task flow. Each task flow has its own pageFlow scoped memory area. You may use the pageFlow scope to store managed beans or variables that need to survive the transition from one page to another.	Yes
session	The session scope exists for the duration of a user session (HttpSession). It starts when the user starts accessing the application and ends when the session times out, or when the application invalidates the session object. You may use the session scope to store the user's session specific data, such as the logged-in user profile.	No
application	The application scope exists till the application ends. Application scoped memory area is shared across user session and requests. This scope is used for storing application specific configurations.	No

> Each bounded task flow in an ADF Fusion web application has its own backingBean, view, and pageFlow scoped memory areas. However, request, flash, session, and application scoped memory areas are shared across all bounded and unbounded task flows in a Fusion web application.

Along with the view scope, JSF 2.0 also introduced another scope known as the `flash` scope. The `flash` scope is longer than the request scope, and shorter than the session scope. The `flash` scope exists across a *single* view transition and survives redirects. It is automatically removed from memory before transitioning to yet another view. There is no declarative configuration support for marking a bean flash scoped. The following code snippet illustrates how you can store a managed bean in a `flash` scope. Typically, you may do this from a method action, before navigating to the destination view which requires accessing the same managed bean instance from the source view.

```
//In managed bean class
public void storeInFashScope{
    Flash   flash=FacesContext.getCurrentInstance().
        getExternalContext().getFlash();
    flash.put("myBean", this);
}
```

A flash scoped bean is accessible from EL, using the `flash` prefix as shown in the following example: #{flash.myBean.name}.

What you need to know while using managed beans in JSF code?

The following are important points you may need to keep in mind when you start using a managed bean for the first time in your Fusion web application:

- ADF inherits the request, `flash`, session, and application scopes from the underlying JSF stack. backingBean, view, and pageFlow are ADF specific scopes. If you define a managed bean in a view scope in an ADF application, under the covers it uses the view scope provided by ADF and not the one provided by the core JSF 2.0 stack.

- If a view activity defined in the task flow uses ADF specific scoped beans, then the corresponding task flow should hold the bean definitions. In other words, defining an ADF scoped managed bean in an unbounded task flow is not enough to use them from a bounded task flow. However, this restriction is not applicable for managed beans stored in memory scopes provided by JSF such as the request, session, `flash`, and application scopes.

- Prefix all ADF scoped beans with respective scope names while using them in EL expressions. For example, a managed bean stored in the pageFlow scope should be prefixed with `pageFlowScope` when referred in the EL expression. An example is as follows:

```
<af:inputText  id="it1" value="#{pageFlowScope.empBean.
firstName}"/>
```

  Similarly, backingBean scoped beans are prefixed with `backingBeanScope` as shown in the following example: #{backingBeanScope.empBean.firstName}. View scoped beans are prefixed with `viewScope` as shown here: #{viewScope.empBean.firstName}.

  Note that a managed bean with request, session or application scopes do not require any prefixing.

Task flow activities

An activity represents a unit of the task performed when the task flow runs. The task flow activity list includes view, method call, control flow router, task flow call, parent action, and task flow return. Note that the task flow return and parent action activities are specific to bounded task flows alone, and are not applicable for unbounded task flows. The following sections discuss task flow activities in detail.

View activity

The view activity represents a complete JSF page or page fragment that forms a unit of the task in the task flow. Page fragments are useful when you build a bounded task flow which requires to be embedded in a parent JSF page as a region.

To add a view activity, perform the following steps:

1. Open the desired task flow in the diagram editor.
2. Drop a view activity from the **ADF Task Flow** component palette onto the task flow diagram editor.
3. Double-click on the view to generate a physical file for the view. In the Create JSF Page dialog window, enter the filename, directory, and document type (**Facelet** or **JSP XML**) and click on **OK** to create the file.

The following is an example for a view activity in a task flow XML file:

```
<!—View Definitions -->
<view id="deptView">
  <page>/deptView.jsf</page>
</view>
<view id="empView">
   <page>/empView.jsf</page>
</view>
<!—Control flow cases using view ids -->
<control-flow-rule id="__16">
  <from-activity-id>deptView</from-activity-id>
  <control-flow-case id="__17">
    <from-outcome>employees</from-outcome>
    <to-activity-id>empView</to-activity-id>
  </control-flow-case>
</control-flow-rule>
```

You will notice that the task flow metadata definition keeps view IDs independent of the physical files. This gives more flexibility when you define control flow rules and improves reusability as well.

What document type should you choose while creating a JSF page?

ADF Faces allows you to build a view activity using either **Facelet** or **JSP XML** as a document type. You may find the same set of design time features for both these types of pages. However, they differ considerably when it comes to the rendering of views at runtime. The JSP XML uses the JSP engine at runtime to render the page which is not well tuned to accommodate the JSF lifecycle stages; whereas, Facelet is primarily built using JSF in mind and fits well with the lifecycle stages of the page. If you are building new Fusion web applications, it is strongly recommended you choose Facelet as a document type.

Bookmarking view activity

When a user navigates between views in a Fusion web application, by default, the browser URL may not reflect the actual view you are currently watching. This is because the underlying navigation handler uses a **forward** dispatching request on the JSF Controller servlet. Though this has certain performance benefits, the user may not be able to bookmark these views as the browser URL does not reflect the actual resource.

The ADF framework allows you to bookmark desired views in an unbounded task flow by setting the bookmark property to true. Note this feature is enabled only for views from *unbounded task flows*.

To create a bookmarkable view activity, perform the following steps:

1. Select the view activity in the unbounded task flow. In the property inspector, expand the **Bookmark** section and select **true**.

   This basic configuration is enough to enable bookmarking for a view. However, in real life scenarios you may want to restore the original state of the view even when it's requested, through bookmark URLs. This may call for the invocation of a managed bean method when the page loads as well as passing extra parameters through bookmarked URL. The ADF bookmarking feature has support for both these cases which is explained in the next step.

2. To add a custom initialization method for a bookmarked activity, in the property inspector, expand the **Bookmark** section and specify an EL expression referring to a managed bean method as a value for the **Method** field.

3. To add bookmark URL parameters, in the property inspector, click on the green plus icon under the **Bookmark** section. Specify the following for the newly added parameter:

    i.   **Name**: This represents the name of the parameter that may appear in the bookmark URL.

    ii. **Value**: This is value for the parameter that may appear in the bookmark URL.

    iii. **Converter**: The parameter value should always be a string value. If the parameter value is an EL expression which evaluates to an object type, you have to tell the framework how to convert the object to a string literal. This is done through a customized converter class. To implement this custom converter, define the managed bean that implements the `oracle.adf.controller.UrlParameterConverter` interface and refer it through the EL expression as a value for the converter. If no converter is specified, the system uses the default, `oracle.adf.controller.DefaultUrlParameterConverter`.

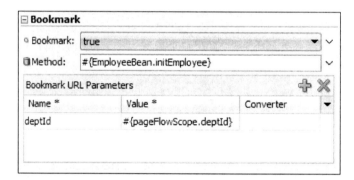

The following is an example for the custom `UrlParameterConverter` class. This example converts the parameter value from `Integer` to `String` when the bookmarkable URL is generated, and from `String` to `Integer` (before pushing the parameter values to the model) when the bookmarked URL is accessed by a user.

```
public class IntegerUrlParameterConverter implements
    oracle.adf.controller.UrlParameterConverter {

    /**
     * @param value   the value to be converted
     * into an object representation.
     * @return   the object representation of the value.
     */
```

```java
@Override
public Object getAsObject(String value) {
    // If the specified value is null or
    // zero-length, return null
    if (value == null || value.trim().length() < 1) {
        return null;
    }
    try {
        return (Integer.valueOf(value.trim()));
    } catch (Exception e) {
        throw new ConverterException(e);
    }
}


/**
 * @param value  the object to be converted into
 * a string representation.
 * @return the string representation of the value.
 */
@Override
public String getAsString(Object value) {
    // If the specified value is null, return a
    // empty String
    if (value == null) {
        return "";
    }
    try {
        return (Integer.toString(((Number)value).
            intValue()));
    } catch (Exception e) {
        throw new ConverterException(e);
    }
}
}
```

Redirect URL

As discussed in the previous section, the ADF Controller by default issues a forward request to navigate to a new view. However, you can make the ADF Controller issue a redirect request for a view activity by setting the Redirect property to true for the desired view activity. In this case, the ADF Controller issues a **redirect** dispatching request for the resource and the URL displayed in the browser will reflect the actual page that the user is working on.

To enable a redirect dispatch mode for a view activity, select the desired view in the task flow diagram and then select **True** in the **Redirect** drop-down list using the property inspector.

Note that `Bookmark` and `Redirect` are mutually exclusive properties. If you are really looking for a fully-fledged bookmarking feature, use the bookmarking itself that we discussed in the last section. `Redirect` is even enabled for abounded task flow as well.

URL view activity

The URL view activity represents URL locatable resources such as bounded task flows as a whole, view activities in an unbounded task flow and external website addresses.

To add a view activity, open the desired task flow in the diagram editor and then drop a URL view activity from the **ADF Task flow** component palette on to the task flow diagram editor. In the property inspector, specify the URL for the activity either using a static URL string or an EL expression.

The following is an example for a static URL view activity that points to an external website:

```
<url-view id="google">
   <url>http://www.google.com</url>
</url-view>
```

The following is example for programmatically specifying a URL for a view activity in the unbounded task flow:

```
<url-view id="EmpURLView">
   <url>#{DeptBean.empViewURL}</url>
</url-view>
```

The `DeptBean` code that returns `empViewURL` is as follows:

```
//In managed bean implementation class
public String getEmpViewURL() {
  String viewId = "empView";
// Generate a URL for a view activity in the
// unbounded task flow.
  ControllerContext controllerCtx = ControllerContext.getInstance();
  return controllerCtx.getGlobalViewActivityURL(viewId);
}
```

Any time an application constructs a URL pointing to a view activity, the URL must be encoded using either of the following methods from the `oracle.adf.controller.ControllerContext` class:

- `getGlobalViewActivityURL()`: This method generates a URL for a view activity in the unbounded task flow
- `getLocalViewActivityURL()`: This method generates a URL for a view activity in the bounded task flow

The usage of methods such as `getGlobalViewAtivityURL()` or `getLocalViewActivityURL()` for encoding the URL ensures that the newly constructed URL holds all state tracking parameters used by the framework. When a client requests a view, the ADF Controller will create a data control frame to serve the request and identifies the correct application module to use for a request via the state tracking parameters. If the request does not carry the right state tracking parameters, the framework will end up creating new application module instances and applications may lose their previous states. You can use the previously mentioned encoding APIs to identify the correct URL from the view ID even when you call the `redirect()` method on the `javax.faces.context.ExternalContext` instance in your code. An example is as follows:

```
//In managed bean class

public void redirectToEmpView(){

  String viewId = "empView";
  ControllerContext controllerCtx =
    ControllerContext.getInstance();
  //Gets the URL from view id
  String activityURL =
    controllerCtx.getGlobalViewActivityURL(viewId);
  try {
    extContext.redirect(activityURL);
  } catch (IOException e) {
   //Redirection failed
    e.printStackTrace();

  }
}
```

Specifying parameters for a URL view activity

If the target application referenced through the URL view activity takes input parameters, then the parameter values can be set in the following two ways:

- Specify parameters along with the URL if they are static literals
- If parameters are evaluated at runtime, then use the **url-parameter** options available with the URL view element in the task flow metadata definition

What happens when runtime invokes a URL view activity from a bounded task flow?

When runtime invokes a URL activity from a bounded task flow, before navigating to a new URL view, the framework abandons the ongoing task flow process and clears the memory scopes variables for the task flow. In other words, invoking a URL view activity is the same as exiting from a current task flow and invoking the target view.

Method call activity

Method call activity allows a task flow to call custom or built-in methods during view transitions. This is useful to execute some business logic before page renders. Method call activity represents a method defined in a managed bean, or a method exposed in data control which is referred through ADF binding.

Using a managed bean method in method call activity

To add a method defined in a managed bean as a method call activity, perform the following steps:

1. Drag **Method Call Activity** from the **ADF Task Flow** component panel and drop it in the task flow diagram. In the property inspector, specify the EL expression wiring a managed bean method for the method activity. The next steps detail the editor support for visually building the EL expression by picking up the existing bean method.

2. To enter the EL expression visually using the editor, click on the **Property Menu** option next to the **Method** field in the property inspector.

3. In the **Method Expression Builder** dialog, expand the **ADF Managed Beans** section and select the desired method displayed under the bean definitions in the tree. When you click on **OK**, IDE copies the EL expression to the **Method** field in the property inspector window.

4. You should specify the outcome for the method call activity using the following options:

    i. **Fixed Outcome**: The method activity returns a fixed single outcome on successful completion. Use this option to specify a hardcoded literal value if the method does not return any value.

    ii. **tostring()**: If specified as true, the outcome is based on calling the `toString()` method on the Java object returned by the method.

5. To specify parameters for the method, expand the **Parameters** section and enter the parameter type and value as they appear in the method signature. If the method returns any value which is required for further processing, then in the return-value field, enter an EL expression indicating where to store the method return value.

The following example represents a method call activity for the `initDept()` method defined in **DeptBean**. The **toString()** selection to `true` instructs the framework to use the returned value of the method as the outcome for this activity. The input parameter to this method is specified using the EL expression **#{pageFlowScope.departmentId}** and the retuned value from the method is stored in page flow scoped variable, **#{pageFlowScope.initDeptReturn}**.

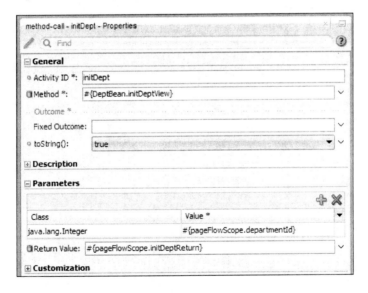

Using data control operation in method call activity

To add method call activity for a method exposed in the **Data Controls** panel, drag the desired method from the panel and drop it on to the task flow diagram. If the method takes any parameter, then IDE will allow you to specify the method parameter values through the display of the **Edit Action Binding** dialog window.

When you drop a method from the **Data Controls** panel on a page, IDE generates a page definition file for holding binding metadata and also updates the `DataBindings.cpx` file with the page mapping and page definition usage entries.

Router activity

A router activity selects one of many possible activities to execute. This takes an EL expression as selection criteria and defines possible matching navigation cases. Based on the outcome of the evaluation of the EL expression, the framework chooses the matching navigation case and continues the execution with the target activity.

To add a router activity, drag-and-drop the router activity from the **ADF Task Flow** component palette on to the task flow diagram editor. In the property inspector, specify values for the following configuration items:

- **Default Outcome**: This is the default outcome for the router activity which will be used when no control flow cases evaluate to true.

- **Navigation Cases**: The following are the navigation cases.

    i. **Expression**: This specifies an EL expression that evaluates to true or false at runtime.

    ii. **Outcome**: This specifies the outcome for the router activity if the expression evaluates to true.

The following example illustrates the usage of router activity in defining control flow cases for a task flow:

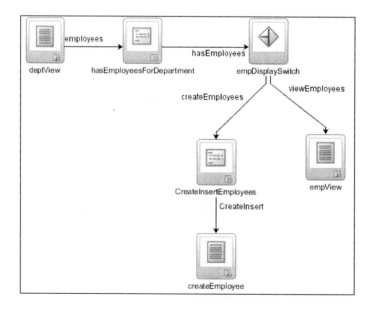

Upon selection of the **view employees** option from a department page, the application takes the user to create an employee page if there are no employees for the department. If the selected department row has employees, then the application will take the user to the employee listing page. This conditional navigation is implemented through router activity and the details of the implementation are as follows.

When the user navigates from the department view, the router activity (**empDisplaySwitch**) will check the value returned by the **hasEmployeesForDepartment** method call, and if the returned value evaluates to true, the router produces the outcome as **viewEmployees**. In other cases, the router activity will produce the outcome as **createEmployees**. The framework will take an appropriate navigation path based on the outcome produced by the router activity.

The detailed configuration for **empDisplaySwitch** router activity used in this example is displayed in the following screenshot. The router produces different outcomes based on the value of the EL expression **#{requestScope.hasEmployees}**. Note that the EL expression **#{requestScope.hasEmployees}** used in the router holds the return value from the **hasEmployeesForDepartment** method call which is executed before the router activity.

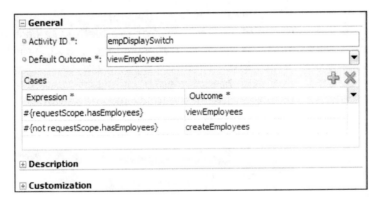

Save point restore activity

The save point feature provided by ADF Controller can be used for capturing a snapshot of the application state at a specific point in time. The **Save Point Restore** activity declaratively enables the application to restore whatever was captured when the save point was originally created. This is typically used for implementing the undo feature in task flows.

Where are ADF Controller save points created?

Save points are configured to save database tables by default. The default expiry time for a save point is 86400 seconds (24 hours). The ADF framework uses the ORADFCSAVPT table to store the save points. The framework will try to create this table if it is missing in the database when it is accessed for the first time. However the database user should have necessary privileges to create a table. Alternatively, you can define a separate database to hold this table, and configure the application to use that database for storing save points. The script for creating ORADFCSAVPT is packaged in the following folder of your JDeveloper installation:

```
<JDeveloperHome>/oracle_common/common/adfc_create_save_point_table.
sql
```

To configure the JDBC data source for storing save points, select adf-config. xml in ADF META-INF folder in the **Application Resources** panel and open it in the overview editor. In the overview editor, select the **Controller** tab and expand the **Savepoints** section. Specify the JDBC data source for the database which contains the ORADFCSAVPT table. The framework will create this table during the first access if it is missing from the database. In such cases, make sure that the username specified while configuring the data source has sufficient privileges for database table creation.

Using save points in a task flow

To declaratively define a save point in a task flow, drop a method call activity on to the task flow editor diagram and in the property inspector specify the following EL expression as a method to be invoked: #{controllerContext.savePointManager. createSavePoint}. This expression is equivalent to calling the createSavePoint() method on SavePointManager as shown in the following code snippet:

```
//In managed bean class

ControllerContext ccntxt  = ControllerContext.getInstance();
SavePointManager savePointManager =
    ccntxt.getSavePointManager();
String savePointId = savePointManager.createSavePoint();
```

When this method is called at runtime, the framework creates a save point and returns the save point ID to the caller. Store this ID to a page flow scopes variable so that it can be used later to restore the save point. For example, the following screenshot displays the property inspector for a method call activity that declaratively creates a save point at runtime and stores the save point ID to `#{pageFlowScope.spEmpBeforeEdit}`.

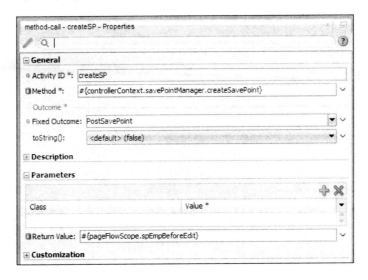

To restore the save point declaratively, drop the **Save Point Restore** activity on to task flow diagram editor. Specify the save point ID using the EL expression that points to a previously created save point ID: `#{pageFlowScope.spEmpBeforeEdit}`. The save point restore activity is typically used for implementing the undo feature when the user clicks on the **Cancel** button.

While using the declarative save point feature in a task flow, you must create the save points before entering into the task flow for which you want to restore the state, and conditionally restore the save point from the parent on exit of the task flow.

The following example illustrates the usage of save point restores activity in a task flow.

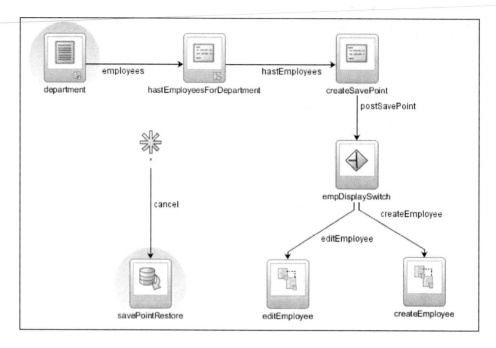

This example task flow starts with the department page that displays the department details in an ADF Form with navigation buttons. When a user clicks a command button or any other navigation component with an action outcome set as employees, the ADF runtime performs the following tasks:

1. Executes a method activity (**hasEmployeesForDepartment**) to see whether the selected department has any employees, and saves the returned value to #{requestScope.hasEmployees}.

2. Creates a save point for the current state and stores the save point ID to #{pageFlowScope.spEmpBeforeEdit}. Later in the navigation, we will use this save point to restore the state when a child task flow wants to cancel the operation.

3. The **empDisplaySwitch** router activity navigates to the **editEmployee** task flow if the EL expression, #{requestScope.hasEmployees}, evaluates to true (this implies that the department has employees). Otherwise it navigates to the **createEmployee** task flow.

4. The save point restore activity in the parent task flow will be invoked when any of the child task flow cancels the data update and returns a **cancel** outcome to the parent.

A working example illustrating the usage of save point restore activity can be found in the example code that we mentioned at the beginning of this book, in the *Preface* section. To access the example code, open the `ADFDevGuideCh9` workspace in `JDeveloper` and look for `savepoint-sample-task-flow-definition.xml` in the `ViewController` project.

What happens when you create an ADF Controller save point?

Save point captures the following state information for an application:

- **User Interface state**: This includes the selection state of selection-enabled UI components and user customizations such as table column sort state.

- **Managed beans**: This specifies the state of underlying managed beans stored in session, view, and pageflow memory scopes. Managed beans should be serializable to save their state.

- **Navigation state**: This includes task flow call stack tracks to restore the path to reach the current page.

- **ADF model state**: This specifies the state of underlying business components which includes the modified state of entity objects, conditions used for querying the data source, row currency for the row sets, and passivation-enabled transient attribute values of entity and view objects.

When the ADF Controller generates a snapshot, behind the scenes it invokes the ADF model (via the `oracle.adf.model.DataControlFrame` API) to acquire the underlying ADF model snapshot (which includes the current state of business components). The ADF model uses a similar mechanism as what is used for a model failover or for an application module recycling, to create the model state snapshot and store that state in the `PS_TXN` table. It returns the collection of the `PS_TXN` snapshot handles to the ADF Controller which then stores those handles, along with the view and controller states in the `ORAADFSAVPT` table.

Implicit save points

ADF Controller also has support for enabling *implicit save points*. This helps to automatically save the current state of the bounded task flow in two cases:

- When an Http session is invalidated
- When a browser window is closed

To enable implicit save points for the application, open `adf-config.xml` which is located in the `<application_root>\.adf\META-INF` directory in the overview editor and select the **Controller** page. Select the **Enable Implicit Savepoint** checkbox option displayed under the **Savepoints** section in order to turn on the implicit save point for the application.

When implicit save points are enabled, the framework will create in-memory save points representing the state of the application at the end of each request for task flows that are marked as critical. Later when a session is invalidated or a browser is closed, the in-memory state is pushed to the database table. The implicit save points are not restored automatically; you may need to do that programmatically.

Task flow call activity

The task flow call activity can be used to invoke a bounded task flow from a bounded or unbounded task flow. If the called (bounded) task flow takes parameters, task flow call activity will allow you to specify values for the parameters. Parameter values can be set either as a literal or an EL expression. If the called task flow returns a value to the caller on exit, you can specify memory scoped variables to store the return value using an EL expression for further processing.

Task flow return activity

The task flow return activity causes a bounded task flow to finish the execution and to return the control back to the caller. The following are the important properties of task flow return activity:

- **Outcome**: This specifies the returned outcome to the caller when the bounded task flow exits.

- **Reentry**: This property decides whether re-entry is allowed for any view activity in the task flow by clicking on the browser back button. The possible values for this property are: **reentry-allowed, reentry-not-allowed**, and **not outcome dependent**. The first two properties are self explanatory. and these properties are applicable for a task flow return activity only if the task flow level re-entry property is set as **reentry-outcome-dependent**. The Task Flow Reentry properties for a bounded task flow are explained in *Chapter 10, Taking a Closer Look at the Bounded Task Flow* under the topic Properties of a bounded task flow.

- **End Transaction**: This controls the scope of the transaction for the task flow. The possible values are commit and rollback; you can either commit an ongoing transaction or roll back the pending changes. This property is applicable if the transaction property of task flow is marked as **Always Begin New Transaction** or **Use Existing Transaction If Possible**.

> The declarative transactions settings for task flows with multiple views are by default enabled only for ADF Business Component based data model. If you are using EJB Bean or Java Bean data control, refer to the release notes to see whether this is supported out of the box. To access the release notes, go to `http://www.oracle.com/technetwork/developer-tools/jdev/documentation/index.html` and choose the **Release Notes** link displayed below the version that you are working on.

Parent action

The parent action activity is used to trigger navigation in the immediate parent or root page in the page tree from a bounded task flow running inside a region.

To add a parent action, open the bounded task flow built with page fragments in the diagram editor. Drag-and-drop the parent action activity from the **ADF Task Flow** component palette to the task flow diagram editor. Enter the following properties in the property inspector:

- **Parent Outcome**: Parent outcome triggers the matching navigation cases defined in an immediate parent task flow. This can be specified as an EL expression or a literal value which will be used by the ADF navigation handler to decide the next view for the parent page.

- **Root Outcome**: Root outcome triggers matching navigation cases defined in the root task flow. Root outcome can be specified as an EL expression or a literal value which will be used to decide the next view for the root page.

  Parent and root outcomes are mutually exclusive.

- **Outcome**: Outcome specifies the navigation case for the current view only if neither the parent view activity nor the root page navigates as a result of the parent-outcome or root-outcome sent by the parent action activity.

To learn more about control flow cases and wildcard control flow rules, refer to the topic *Getting Started with ADF Task Flows* in *Oracle Fusion Middleware Fusion Developer's Guide for Oracle Application Development Framework*. To access the documentation go to http://www.oracle.com/technetwork/developer-tools/jdev/documentation/index.html and navigate to **Oracle JDeveloper and ADF Documentation Library | Fusion Developer's Guide**. Use the **Search** option to find specific topics.

Building an unbounded task flow

When you create an application choosing the Fusion web application (ADF) template, JDeveloper generates basic view and model project structures with all the required metadata files for building a fully-fledged ADF web application. The view controller project contains an adfc-config.xml file to hold all unbounded view definitions, navigation rules, and managed bean definitions for the web project. This may be enough to meet the requirements of a simple application with a limited number of pages. What if your application grows and you have to deal with more number of pages and navigation rules? A quite obvious solution for such cases is to split the view controller project into multiple projects and use multiple task flow configuration files to hold the controller metadata definitions, and assemble all these pieces while generating the final deployable artefacts for the application. The ADF framework enables modular web development through bounded and unbounded task flows. Task flows provide a modular and transaction-aware implementation to control the page flows in an application.

In this section, you will learn to build an unbounded task flow that decides the control flow for the top level pages in an application.

To define an unbounded task flow, perform the following steps:

1. Right-click on the view controller project in the application panel, select **New | ADF Task Flow** in the context menu.

2. In the **Create Task Flow** dialog window, enter the filename and directory for the task flow. As we are building an unbounded task flow, uncheck the **Create as Bounded Task Flow** checkbox and click on **OK** to generate the task flow definition file.

3. Next is to define the activities and control flow cases for the task flow. You can drag-and-drop the task flow activities from the **ADF Task Flow** component palette and draw navigation between them.

4. To begin with, let us define a view activity which represents a page in the application. Drop the view activity from the component palette onto the task flow diagram. Use the property inspector to override the default properties for each activity. Note that when you drop the view activity on to the task flow, IDE will not generate a physical file for the same by default. To define a physical file for the view, double-click on the view activity and then create a JSF page. You can continue these steps and generate more view activities as per the business requirement.

5. Once you have generated all the view activities for the task flow, next is to define the control flow case between them. To define the control flow between two view activities, select the source view activity in the task flow diagram editor and drop **Control Flow Case** from the component palette connecting the source and destination activities. Specify **From Outcome** for the control flow in the property inspector window for enabling action-based navigation.

The following example illustrates an unbounded task flow with department and employee view activities:

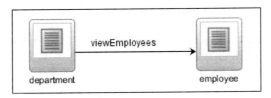

```
<control-flow-rule id="__1">
    <from-activity-id>department</from-activity-id>
    <control-flow-case id="__2">
      <from-outcome>viewEmployees</from-outcome>
      <to-activity-id>employee</to-activity-id>
    </control-flow-case>
</control-flow-rule>
```

In the previous example, the **department** view implemented the control flow rule defined to the **employee** view for the outcome **viewEmployees**. The *outcome* can be produced by any actionable components such as af:button or af:link present in **department** view. For example, if you want to trigger navigation to the employees page when the user clicks on the **Display Employee** button in the **department** page, you simply need to define a button with action = "viewEmployees as shown in the following code snippet:

```
<af:button text="Display Employees" id="b1" action="viewEmployees"/>
```

Using a managed bean to return a dynamic outcome for a navigation component

The framework also allows you to execute some business logic for deciding the outcome using action methods defined in managed beans. An action method should return either a `String` or `Object` with the `toString()` implementation. To use the outcome returned by a method defined in a bean, you must refer to the method using an EL expression for the action attribute. An example is as follows:

```
<af:button text="Display Employees" id="b1" action="#{deptBean.
handleViewAction}"/>
```

This example does not hardcode the action outcome, rather it uses the `handleViewAction()` method to return a `String` value which will be used as outcome for the action.

Conditionally executing a control flow case

If you are working on *Oracle JDeveloper 11g Release 2* or higher versions, you can specify the EL expression as a guard condition for control flow execution.

To do this, select the control flow case in the task flow diagram, expand the **Behavior** section in the property inspector and specify the EL expression that evaluates to true or false, as a value for the `If` field.

At runtime, before navigating to the target activity, the framework will read the EL expression that is set as a guard condition, and if the expression evaluates to true, navigation will continue to the target activity.

Improving the readability of control flow cases

If you have control flow cases defined from multiple source views to a single destination view, you can make it more readable using the **wildcard control flow rule** (represented by the * symbol) as shown in the following screenshot:

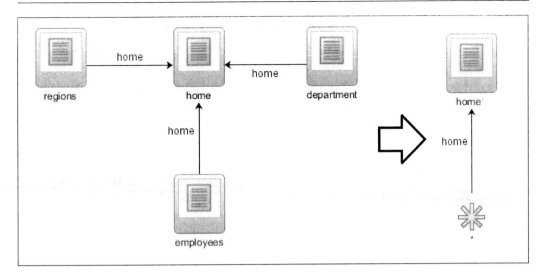

Adding an exception handler

An exception handler is the central place for handling unexpected exceptions in an application. For example, a method activity defined in a task flow may throw some business or runtime exceptions when specific conditions are not met at runtime. ADF allows you to handle such erroneous scenarios in a more user friendly way by designating one activity in a bounded or unbounded task flow as an exception handler.

To mark an activity as an exception handler, right-click on the desired activity in the task flow and select **Mark Activity | Exception Handler**.

An exception handler can be specified for a bounded or unbounded task flow. At runtime, when an error is thrown from some activity inside a bounded task flow, the framework will navigate to the exception handler activity specified for the current task flow. If there is no exception handler specified for the current task flow, the framework will check its immediate parent task flow for an exception handler activity. This repeats till the framework identifies a parent task flow with an exception handler or finishes the entire task flow call stack. If no exception handler is found, the exception will propagate to the web container.

Customizing the default exception handler

Apart from the declarative exception handler activities for task flows, ADF also allows you to add custom exception handler implementations at application level. This really helps if you want to do some application level manipulation in response to the exception. For example, for some specific exceptions you may want to display special error pages and you may want to do it globally. There are two approaches to add custom exception handlers:

- **Customizing** `oracle.adf.view.rich.context.ExceptionHandler`: This is offered by ADF and is used widely in pre JSF 2.0 time when there was no support in JSF to add a custom exception handler in a generic way. In this approach you will subclass `oracle.adf.view.rich.context.ExceptionHandler` to build a custom implementation.

  To register a custom exception handler, add a text file named `oracle.adf.view.rich.context.ExceptionHandler` in the `adf\META-DATA\services` folder. Add the fully qualified name of the custom exception handler class in the text file.

- **Customizing** `javax.faces.context.ExceptionHandler`: This is provided by the JSF 2.0 implementation. To see whether this is supported by the version of Oracle ADF that you work on, refer to the release notes. Moving forward, it is recommended to use the standard JSF exception handler mechanism for customizing the exception handling in your Fusion web application. To learn more about this class, refer to the API documentation which is available online at `http://docs.oracle.com/javaee/6/api/javax/faces/context/ExceptionHandler.html`. The steps for building a custom `javax.faces.context.ExceptionHandler` class are shown in the following section.

Building a custom javax.faces.context. ExceptionHandler

The following are the steps for building custom `ExceptionHandler` in JSF 2.0 compliant web applications.

1. Create a custom exception handler class that extends the `javax.faces.context.ExceptionHandler` class. This is an abstract class and you may end up implementing many methods if you start with this class. JSF 2.0 provides a convenience class to ease your life, `javax.faces.context.ExceptionHandlerWrapper`, which offers a simple implementation of `ExceptionHandler`. This class can be sub-classed by developers wishing to provide specialized behavior to an existing `ExceptionHandler` instance.

The following example overrides the `ExceptionHandlerWrapper::handle()` method to display a custom error page when an application throws `CustomViewException` during the request processing. This example leverages the JSF implicit navigation model to navigate to the `customErrPage` page. To make this work your application should have the `customErrPage. jsf` page in the project source.

```
public class CustomExceptionHandler extends
ExceptionHandlerWrapper {
    private ExceptionHandler wrapped;
    public CustomExceptionHandler() {
        super();
    }


    public CustomExceptionHandler(ExceptionHandler wrapped) {
        this.wrapped = wrapped;
    }
    //Override the getWrapped() method to
    //return the instance of the exception handler class
    //wrapped by this custom handler. Typically this
    //would be the original ExceptionHandler provided by
    //framework
    //See CustomExceptionHandlerFactory::getExceptionHandler()
    @Override
    public ExceptionHandler getWrapped() {
        return this.wrapped;
    }


    @Override
    public void handle() throws FacesException {
        //Iterate over all unhandled exceptions
        Iterator i = getUnhandledExceptionQueuedEvents().
            iterator();
        while (i.hasNext()) {
            ExceptionQueuedEvent event =
                (ExceptionQueuedEvent)i.next();
            ExceptionQueuedEventContext context =
                (ExceptionQueuedEventContext)event.getSource();
            Throwable t = context.getException().getCause();
            if (t instanceof CustomViewExcpetion) {

                FacesContext fc =
                    FacesContext.getCurrentInstance();
```

```
                Map<String, Object> requestMap =
                    fc.getExternalContext().getRequestMap();
                try {
                    //Use Implicit navigation model offered by
                    //JSF, Application should have
                    //'customErrPage.jsf' for this to work
                    NavigationHandler nav =
                        fc.getApplication().
                        getNavigationHandler();
                    nav.handleNavigation(
                        fc, null, "customErrPage");
                    fc.renderResponse();
                } finally {
                    //Remove the exception if it is handled
                    //by the custom handler
                    i.remove();
                }
            }
        }

        getWrapped().handle();
    }
}
```

2. Build `javax.faces.context.ExceptionHandlerFactory` to return the `CustomExceptionHandler` class that we created in step 1. The method, `getExceptionHandler()`, is called once per request. The following is an example:

```
public class CustomExceptionHandlerFactory extends
ExceptionHandlerFactory {
    private ExceptionHandlerFactory parent;

    public CustomExceptionHandlerFactory
        (ExceptionHandlerFactory parent) {
        this.parent = parent;
    }

    @Override
    public ExceptionHandler getExceptionHandler() {
        ExceptionHandler customExceptionHandler = new
            CustomExceptionHandler(parent.
            getExceptionHandler());

        return customExceptionHandler;
    }
}
```

3. Register the custom `CustomExceptionHandlerFactory` class in `faces-config.xml` as shown in the following:

```
<faces-config ...>
...
<factory>
<exception-handler-factory>
comp.packtpub.adfguide.ch9.view.CustomExceptionHandlerFactory
</exception-handler-factory>
</factory>
</faces-config>
```

Using method call activity to initialize a page

A method call activity can be used for invoking business logic while transitioning to a new view. For instance, consider a simple control flow case defined between department and employee pages in a web application. When the user navigates to employee pages by selecting a specific department row from the department page, the application should fire a query to find employees for the selected department and the result should be displayed in the employee page. The Oracle ADF framework has declarative support for invoking methods while transitioning between views.

The following control flow case diagram illustrates the usage of method activity for querying the employee data source for the selected department, while transitioning from department to employee view:

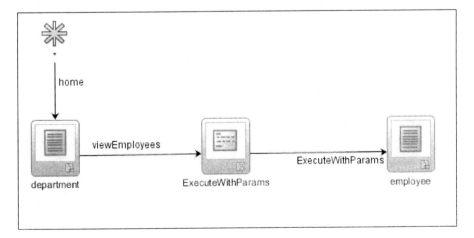

Building a task flow with method call activity

In this section we will see how to build a control flow shown in the previous screenshot:

1. Drag-and-drop the view activity for displaying department details onto the task flow diagram editor window. Double-click on the view activity to generate a physical JSF page for the view.

2. Drop the departments view object instance from the **Data Controls** panel as an ADF Form onto the department JSF page. Drop a button (`af:button`) for navigation from the component palette to department JSF page. Set the following properties for the button:

   i. Set the action attribute value as `viewEmployees`.

   ii. Add `af:setPropertyListener` to the button component for assigning the `DepartmentId` attribute value to a `requestScope` variable when a user clicks on the button to navigate to the employee page. The remaining activities in the control flow case can access the currently selected department ID using the following EL expression: `#{requestScope.deptId}`. Note that if the application needs to retain `DepartmentId` between multiple requests for pages, then you should use higher memory scopes such as `pageFlowSope` for storing the value.

   iii. The navigation button may look like the following:

```
<af:button text="View Employees" id="b5"
action="viewEmployees">
  <af:setPropertyListener from="#{bindings.DepartmentId.
inputValue}"
              to="#{requestScope.deptId}" type="action"/>
</af:button>
```

To learn more about the `af:setPropertyListener` tag, refer to the tag documentation available online at: `http://jdevadf.oracle.com/adf-richclient-demo/docs/tagdoc/af_setPropertyListener.html`.

3. The next activity in the control flow case is a method call to execute the employee view object for finding employees for the selected department id. Before adding this activity, you will have to modify the query in **EmployeeVO** to return employees for a specific department. The **EmployeeVO** is built from the **EMPLOYEES** table in the HR schema. Select the **Query** tab in **EmployeeVO** and add the following to the **WHERE** clause section in the query screen.

```
EmployeeEO.DEPARTMENT_ID = :bindVarDepartmentId
```

Create a bind variable `bindVarDepartmentId` and mark it as required. With this we have finished the ground work for reading the employees collection for a department. Refer back to the topic *Using bind variables* in *Chapter 4, Introducing the View Object*, if you need a quick brush up on bind variables.

4. Switch back to the task flow definition in the designer window. Select the **ExecuteWithParams** operation displayed under the employee view object instance in the **Data Controls** panel and drop it onto the task flow as method activity. While doing so, JDeveloper will ask you to specify a value for `bindVarDepartmentId`. Set the value as `#{requestScope.deptId}`.

5. Draw a control flow case from the department view to the **ExecuteWithParams** method activity for the outcome `viewEmployees`.

6. Drag-and-drop the view activity for displaying employee details onto a task flow. Double-click on the view activity to generate a physical JSF page for the view. Drop the same employee view object instance that you used for defining the method activity from the **Data Controls** panel as an ADF table on the page. Draw a control flow case from **ExecuteWithParams** to the employee view.

You are done with the implementation.

What happens at runtime?

At runtime, when a user transitions from the department view to employee view, the framework will execute the intermediate method activity by passing the department id. This intermediate step prepares the employees row set for display.

Building a menu model

A typical Fusion web application may contain a mix of bounded and unbounded task flows. As discussed, unbounded task flow activities can be accessed without any specific order. This makes activities in unbounded task flows, a natural choice for target for navigation components or menu items in a Fusion web application. The good news is that, JDeveloper has design time support for generating an XML menu model from unbounded task flow activities, which can be used as a data model for navigation components. The steps for declaratively building a menu model from the unbounded task flow is well explained in the online tutorial entitled *Create ADF Menus for Page Navigation*. To access this tutorial, go to the link `http://www.oracle.com/technetwork/developer-tools/jdev/documentation/index.html` and choose **JDeveloper and ADF Tutorials | Create ADF Menus for Page Navigation**.

Summary

This chapter introduced you to the navigation model used in a typical Fusion web application. Specifically, you learned about the navigation model in the JSF framework and extra offerings from the ADF Controller in the form of task flows. You also learned how to build a simple unbounded task flow towards the end.

We will take a closer look at the bounded task flow concepts and more advanced examples in the next chapter.

10
Taking a Closer Look at the Bounded Task Flow

This chapter is in continuation of the previous chapter with a special focus on features offered by the bounded task flows. This chapter will take you through the following topics:

- The properties of a bounded task flow
- Building a bounded task flow
- Working with bounded task flow activities
- Parameterizing a bounded task flow
- Consuming bounded task flows as ADF regions
- Lazy loading of an ADF region
- Refreshing an ADF region
- Displaying task flows using a pop up component
- Using contextual event for communicating to an ADF region
- Dynamically adding multiple regions to a page
- Distributing ADF task flow as ADF library
- Using a train component in a bounded task flow
- Transaction management in a bounded task flow
- The life span of a bounded task flow

Introduction

The bounded task flows improve the modularity and maintainability of a Fusion web application by splitting a single massive page flow into multiple reusable bounded page flow implementations. A bounded task flow encapsulates task flow activities, control flow cases, managed bean definitions, security checks, and declarative business transactions. When you work on a Fusion web application, you may use bounded task flows extensively to build reusable page flows. The bounded task flows can be reused within the same application in multiple places by embedding the reusable artefacts, and the same can be invoked remotely by external Fusion web applications as well.

The properties of a bounded task flow

Let us begin now with the generic properties on bounded task flows and then later focus on more advanced features offered by the task flow to handle specific use case scenarios.

The ADF framework offers many configuration parameters for a bounded task flow. You can override the default values using the property inspector in the JDeveloper IDE as shown in the following screenshot:

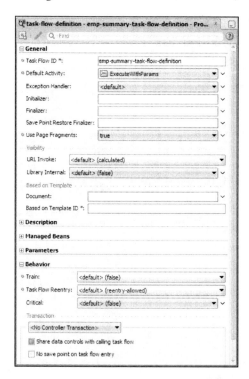

The following are the configurable properties that you may see in a bounded task flow:

- **Initializer**: This is a managed bean method that is invoked when a task flow starts execution. The value is specified using an EL expression.

- **Finalizer**: This is a managed bean method that is invoked when a task flow exits. The value is specified using an EL expression.

- **Save Point Restore Finalizer**: This is a managed bean method that is invoked when a task flow restores a save point. This is used for adding any custom method which is required to run after the execution of the framework code for a save point. If you need a quick brush up on how to define a save point in a task flow, refer back to the topic entitled *Using save points in a task flow* in *Chapter 9, Controlling the Page Navigation*.

- **URL Invoke**: This property decides whether the task flow can be invoked through URL. URL invocation should be enabled if the task flow needs to be used remotely. The following are the possible values for this flag:

  i. **url-invoke-allowed**: URL invocation is allowed.

  ii. **url-invoke-disallowed**: URL invocation is not allowed. If attempted to invoke task flow through URL, the ADF Controller will return a HTTP 403 status code in this case.

  iii. **calculated**: This is the default value for the **URL Invoke** property. This option will allow URL invocation if the bounded task flow uses the view activity as default activity and does not use any task flow initializer.

- **Library Internal**: This property controls the visibility of a task flow when packaged in an ADF library. This helps developers to expose only those task flows that are indented for reuse.

- **Parameters**: The **Parameters** section allows you to define input parameters for the task flow. Parameterization makes a task flow more generic and reusable. You can specify parameter name, type, and value. For example, when you define a task flow to display employee details for a department, you can parameterize the task flow to accept the department id from the caller so that it can be reused for any department. To learn how to specify parameters for a bounded task flow, refer the section *Parameterizing a bounded task flow*, in this chapter.

- **Return Value**: This feature allows you to define the return parameter value to the caller. You can specify return the parameter name, type, and return value. For example, suppose you are displaying the task flow in a pop up that can be used to search and select particular an employee row. The task flow should return the selected employee row to the caller in this case, which can be declaratively achieved by using this feature. This is explained in the section *Defining a task flow return value*, in this chapter.

- **Train**: This option, if set to true, generates a train model for the task flow activities. The train model can be used as a data model for various train components in the UI. For example, consider a typical shopping cart site that processes a transaction in multiple steps. You can use the `train` feature provided by ADF for such implementations. The train component summarizes the multiple steps (view activities) of a task flow as a navigational component in the UI.

- **Task Flow Reentry**: This option decides whether or not a user can re-enter the task flow by clicking on the browser's back button. The possible values are as follows:

    i.   **reentry-allowed**: Allows re-entry to the task flow.

    ii. **reentry-not-allowed**: Disallows re-entry to the task flow.

    iii. **reentry-outcome-dependent**: The re-entry permission for the task flow depends on the outcome that was received when the same bounded task flow was previously exited via the task flow return activities. Note that a task flow can take multiple return activities. If the previously used task flow return activity has a re-entry flag marked as **reentry-allowed**, then the framework allows re-entry this time as well. The framework disallows re-entry in all other cases.

    When an end user re-enters a task flow using a browser's back button, and the re-entry is allowed, the framework will re-initialize the task flow state. This includes re-initialization of input parameters used in the task flow, re-initialization of the transaction state, and re-execution of the default activity. The framework discards all the changes that are made before re-entry.

- **Critical**: If you mark a task flow as critical by setting the value to true, the framework treats the task flow with extra care.

    i.   If the application is configured to use implicit save points (configured in `adf-config.xml`), the framework will generate implicit save points on entry to all task flows that are marked as critical. Refer back to the topic *What happens when you create an ADF Controller save point?* in *Chapter 9, Controlling the Page Navigation*, if you need a quick brush up on implicit save points.

ii. The framework will keep track of uncommitted data changes for critical task flow and warn the user if the person tries to exit from the task flow without committing changes.

- **Transaction**: This property helps to declaratively manage transactions for a task flow. The possible transaction attributes are as follows:

    i. **No Controller Transaction**: The bounded task flow neither participates in existing transactions nor starts a new transaction. As the framework does not track pending changes for this setting, you will not be able to use declarative features available with **Task Flow Return** to commit changes to the database.

    ii. **Always Use Existing Transaction**: The bounded task flow will always participate in an existing transaction. If no existing transaction is found in progress, then an exception is thrown when the task flow is initialized.

    iii. **Use Existing Transaction If Possible**: The bounded task flow either participates in an existing transaction if one exists, or starts a new transaction upon entry of the bounded task flow if no transaction exists.

    iv. **Always Begin New Transaction**: The bounded task flow always starts a new transaction when entered. The new transaction completes when the bounded task flow exits.

    We will discuss these transaction attributes in detail under the section entitled *Transaction management in a bounded task flow* towards the end of this chapter.

- **Share Data Control with Calling Task Flow**: Check this property to share the data control with the calling task flow. You should not turn on this property if the transaction type is set as **Always Use Existing Transaction** or **Use Existing Transaction If Possible**.

- **No Save Point on Task Flow Entry**: On task flow entry, the framework will create model save points to store the current state of the model layer if you set the transaction as **Always Use Existing Transaction** or **Use Existing Transaction If Possible**. This save point is used later to restore the model state on the exit of the task flow if the task flow return activity is configured for restoring the save point (the **Restore Save Point** option in **Task Flow Return** activity). Apparently, save point creation on task flow entry is not really required if the task flow does not need to roll back the changes on exit. The **No Save Point on Task Flow Entry** option allows you to optionally prevent the creation of an ADF model save point on task flow entry.

Building a bounded task flow

In this section, we will build a bounded task flow to get a feel for the visual and declarative features offered by JDeveloper IDE for building reusable end-to-end navigation cases. The steps for defining activities and navigation cases for a bounded task flow are conceptually similar to that of an unbounded task flow, which we discussed in the last chapter under the topic *Building an unbounded task flow*. However there are a few additions for a bounded task flow.

To define a bounded task flow, perform the following steps:

1. Right-click on the view controller project in the application panel and then select **New | ADF Task Flow** in the context menu.

2. In the **Create Task Flow** dialog window, enter the filename and directory for the task flow. You should make sure that the **Create as Bounded Task Flow** option is selected (this is selected by default) in the **Create** dialog window. Optionally modify the **Default Task Flow ID** property that is populated by the IDE. Select the **Create with Page Fragments** option if you want to embed this task flow in a parent page using a region component. Alternatively, if you want the task flow to be built using complete JSF pages as view activities, uncheck this option. A bounded task flow built with JSF pages can be run independently.

3. Once you have generated a bounded task flow, use the property inspector window to alter the default configurations generated for the task flow. The property inspector allows you to specify all the task flow properties that we discussed in the previous section.

4. Next is to define the activities and control flow cases for the task flow. At a high level these steps remain the same as we did for unbounded task flows in the previous chapter. However, there are some additions available for bounded task flow such as default activity, parent action, and task flow return activity. These are discussed in detail in the coming section.

5. To return from a task flow, you can drop the **Task Flow Return** activity from the **ADF Task Flow** component palette and define the appropriate navigation to this activity.

The following is an example for bounded task flow with **CreateInsert** as the default activity and **Save** and **Cancel** set as the return activities.

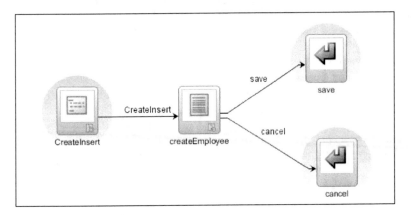

Working with bounded task flow activities

In this section we will take a closer look at the commonly used activities for a bounded task flow such as default activity, parent action, task flow call, task flow return, and exception handler.

Marking an activity as the default activity

The **default activity** is designated as an activity to run first (default entry point) in a bounded task flow. Based on the outcome of the default activity and control flow cases definitions, the framework chooses the next activity for execution.

By default, JDeveloper will mark the first activity that you added as the default activity. However you are allowed to modify the default activity at any time. To designate one of the activities as the default activity in a bounded task flow, right-click on the appropriate activity in the task flow diagram and select **Mark Activity | Default Activity** in the context menu. Note that you can mark any and only one activity in the task flow definition as the default activity.

Marking an activity as an exception handler

We have discussed the support for handling exceptions in task flows in *Chapter 9, Controlling the Page Navigation,* in the section entitled *Adding exception handler.* This section summarizes the same topic for a bounded task flow.

Bounded task flows allow you to mark any one activity in the task flow as an exception handler. Typically a view activity or a router activity is used as an exception handler. Router activity is used when you need to handle different exception types where some exceptions need special treatment.

To mark an activity as an exception handler, select the desired activity in the task flow diagram and then select **Mark Activity | Exception Handler** in the context menu.

Calling a bounded task flow using the task flow call activity

A bounded task flow can invoke another bounded task flow declaratively using the **task flow call** activity.

To use this feature, both the calling and called task flows should be built using the same page types. In other words, a bounded (or unbounded task flow) built with complete JSF pages can only call another task flow built with complete JSF pages. Similarly, a bounded task flow built with page fragments can use a task flow call activity to call another bounded task flow built with page fragments. This is because a page fragment at runtime generates a DOM fragment which cannot run independently in a browser and requires to be embedded inside an HTML DOM tree to generate the complete page. This implies also that a page fragment cannot embed a complete JSF page within it. So the runtime cannot let a page fragment part (which is embedded in a complete page) to navigate to a new complete page as it breaks the DOM hierarchy on the client side.

To call a bounded task flow using the task flow call activity from a bounded or unbounded task flow, open the calling task flow in the diagram editor. A task flow call activity can be added to it using any one of the following approaches:

- Drag-and-drop a task flow call activity from the **ADF Task Flow** component palette onto the task flow diagram. Specify the **Document** and **ID** for the target task flow using the property inspector. The **Document** represents the target task flow definition XML filename along with the path details relative to <Web Content> of the view controller project, and **ID** represents the identifier for the target task flow. The following is a sample code snippet for a task flow call:

```
<task-flow-call id="emp-detail-task-flow-definition">
  <task-flow-reference>
  <document>
    /WEB-INF/dynamic/emp-detail-task-flow-definition.xml
  </document>
  <id>emp-detail-task-flow-definition</id>
  </task-flow-reference>
</task-flow-call>
```

- Another approach to call a task flow is to drag-and-drop an existing task flow from the **Application Navigator** tab on to the task flow diagram. While doing so, if the dropped task flow takes parameters, IDE will ask you to specify values for the parameters. The following diagram illustrates the drag-and-drop features offered by the IDE.

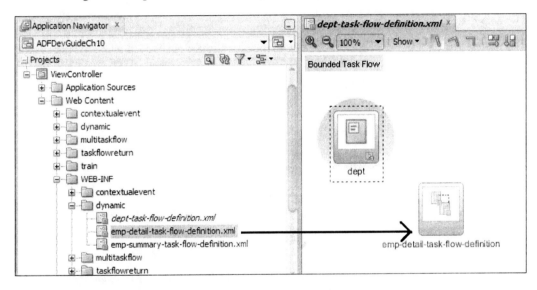

The previous approaches are good enough to invoke static task flows. What if you want to invoke a different task flow whose ID is known only at runtime?

You will use **dynamic task flows** in such scenarios as explained in the following section.

Using dynamic task flow calls

To invoke a task flow dynamically, drop a task flow call activity onto the calling (unbounded or bounded) task flow diagram editor. In the property inspector for the task flow call, select **Task Flow Reference** as **Dynamic** and provide an EL expression that returns the task flow ID at runtime. The following is an example:

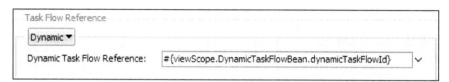

The `getdynamicTaskFlowId()` method referred in the EL `${viewScope.myBean.dynamicTaskFlowId}` is as follows:

```
//In MyBean implementation class
public class MyBean{

 //Task flow identifiers used in this e.g.
 private final String EMP_SUMMARY_TF =
       "/WEB-INF/dynamic/emp-summary-task-flow- definition.xml#emp-
summary-task-flow-definition";
 private final String EMP_DETAIL_TF =
       "/WEB-INF/dynamic/emp-detail-task-flow- definition.xml#emp-
detail-task-flow-definition";

 //Method that returns task flow id at runtime
 public TaskFlowId getDynamicTaskFlowId() {
    if("summary".equals(AdfFacesContext.getCurrentInstance().
       getPageFlowScope().get("EmpViewHint"))) {
    return TaskFlowId.parse(EMP_SUMMARY_TF);
  } else {
    return TaskFlowId.parse(EMP_DETAIL_TF);
  }
 }
}
```

The `getDynamicTaskFlowId()` method in the previous code snippet returns different task flow IDs based on the value for the page flow scope variable `EmpViewHint`. The task flow ID string used in this method is constructed by concatenating document and ID elements for the target task flow. `{document}#{id}`, where `{document}` represents target task flow definition XML filename along with the path details relative to `<Web Content>` of view controller project, and `{id}` represents identifier for the target task flow. An example is as follows: `"/WEB-INF/dynamic/emp-detail-task-flow-definition.xml#emp-detail-task-flow-definition"`.

Commonly used properties for a task flow call activity

The following are some of the commonly used properties for a task flow call activity that you must be aware of:

- **Parameters** and **Return Values**: If the called task flow takes parameters, specify parameters using the **Input Parameter** section in the **Property Inspector** window. Similarly, if the called task flow has return values, specify an EL expression pointing to an appropriate memory scoped variable for storing returned values.

- **before-listener** and **after-listeners**: ADF allows you to listen to the start and end of a task flow call activity.

  To specify the before and after listeners, expand the **Listeners** section in the **Property Inspector** window for a task flow call activity and specify the EL expression pointing to a method action binding or a managed bean method. The before listener is invoked before entering into bounded task flow and the after listener is invoked after exiting from the called task flow. These can be used to execute some custom business logic before and after the execution of a task flow. For example, if you need to log the task flow calls in your application for audit purposes, you can use these interceptors to hook the logic.

- **Run As Dialog**: Select this option to run the called task flow in a dialog window.

  To use this option, expand the **Behavior** section in the property inspector for a task flow call activity and then set **Run As Dialog** to true. Optionally select the **Display Type** as an inline-popup to run the task flow inside an inline window instead of an external popup window.

To open up the task flow in a dialog, you must set `useWindow = "true"` for the action component which triggers the navigation to the task flow call activity. The following is an example:

```
<af:button text = "Loc LOV" id = "b5" action="viewDeptTaskFlow"
useWindow = "true"/>
```

Using remote task flow calls

Oracle ADF allows you to embed bounded task flows running on a remote server in your Fusion web application.

To invoke a remote task flow select the task flow call activity in the diagram, and then in the **Property Inspector** window, specify **Remote Application URL** pointing to the task flow in a remote web application.

You have not finished yet. To invoke a bounded task flow remotely you have to enable URL access in the target task flow. To enable URL access for a bounded task, open the task flow in the diagram editor and in the **Property Inspector** window select **url-invoke-allowed**. The default is **calculated** which will allow the URL to be invoked if the task flow has a view activity as the default activity and does not have any initializer routine.

The URL syntax for calling a bounded task flow is as follows:

```
http://<server root>/<application context>/faces/adf.task-flow?adf.
tfid=<task flow definition id>&adf.tfDoc=<document name>&<named
parameter>=<named parameter value>
```

The following is an example:

```
http://127.0.0.1:7101/MyTestApp/faces/adf.task-flow?adf.
tfId=employee-task-flow-definition&adf.tfDoc=/WEB-INF/taskflowreturn/
employee-task-flow-definition.xml&departmentId=10&locationId=1700
```

The following screenshot displays the task flow call properties specified in the **Property Inspector** window for invoking the remote task flow:

What happens at runtime when a remote task flow is called?

When an application invokes the remote task flow, behind the scenes the framework constructs a remote URL for invoking the target task flow. Along with this, it also constructs a return URL using the information in the current server application, and then passes that to the remote server (using the URL parameter `_return-url`) where the task flow is executed. When the remote task flow returns, the ADF Controller serializes and URL encodes any return values, and then redirects the client to the return URL passed by the caller.

What you may need to know when you use remote task flow

When an application invokes remote task flow, the framework exits the current task flow and transfers the control to the remote task flow seamlessly. This pattern is widely used when a Fusion web application needs to display UI pages hosted in a remote Fusion web application.

When you use remote task flows, you must be aware of the following points:

- **Geometry management for the UI**: The view embedded as the remote task flow does not support geometry management set by the parent page.

- **Memory scoped variables**: Both calling and called task flow will have two separate memory areas and apparently they may not be able to share data though shared memory scopes such as request, session, and application scopes.

- **Interaction Patterns**: Task flow input parameters and return values are the only mechanisms available for enabling interaction between calling and called task flows. Contextual events are not supported when task flows are invoked from a remote server. In case you do not know what the contextual event is, here is a one line description: The contextual event helps you to define custom events in the binding layer in order to establish region to region interaction. This is explained under the section entitled *Using contextual event for communicating to an ADF region*, in this chapter.

- **Run As Dialog option**: The remote task flow call and **Run As Dialog** options are mutually exclusive. You cannot have both these options at the same time in the Oracle ADF 11.1.2.2.0 release.

- **Transaction Support and Sharing Data Control**: The remote task flow will not be able to share transaction context with the caller. In other words, the declarative transaction feature of task flows such as **Always Use Existing Transaction** and **Use Existing Transaction if Possible** will not work when accessed remotely. A remote task flow cannot share data control with calling task flow as well.

- **Security**: The calling task flow will not propagate the security context to the remotely running task flow.

Note that the task flow call activities that we discussed in this section are limited to the bounded task flow use cases. We are not repenting the general discussion on activities such as **View**, **Method Call**, **Parent Action**, **Router**, and **URL View** that we had in the last chapter. If you need a quick brush up on these items, refer to the topic *Task flow activities* in *Chapter 9, Controlling the Page Navigation*.

Parameterizing a bounded task flow

You can make a bounded task flow more generic and reusable by adding input parameters and return values.

Defining a task flow input parameter

To specify input parameters perform the following steps:

1. Open the task flow in the overview editor, select the **Parameters** tab and click on the green plus icon in the **Input Parameter Definition** section to add parameters.

2. Enter the **Name** for the parameter, Java **Class** type, **Value**, and the **Required** flag. The parameter value is specified using an EL expression. Note that an EL expression used as a parameter value is just a pointer to a memory scoped variable or managed bean property for storing the parameter's value passed by the caller. The task flow can use the EL expression set for a parameter to refer the parameter value at runtime.

Note that you can also use **Property Inspector** for a task flow to add parameters. The steps for defining parameters remain the same as we previously discussed.

Specifying input parameter values for a task flow

If a task a flow takes parameters, IDE will allow you to specify parameters when you drop it either as a region onto a page or as a task flow call activity onto a bounded or unbounded task flow diagram window.

Consider a task flow definition `emp-task-flow-definition` with **DepartmentId** as the parameter. When you drop this as a region to a page, IDE will display the **Edit Task Flow Binding** dialog with a list of input parameters.

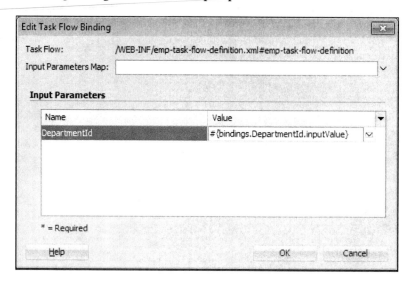

In the **Edit Task Flow Binding** editor, you will see an **Input Parameter Maps** field as well as a pre-populated **Input Parameters** list. These are two possible declarative options offered by the IDE to specify parameter values for the task flow:

- **Using Input Parameters list**: In this approach you will specify parameter values individually for each parameter. You may use this option for specifying parameter values for static task flow bindings where a region will always point to the same task flow during the page lifecycle.

  Parameter values can be specified either as static literal values or dynamic EL expressions. In this example, the value for **DepartmentId** is specified through the following EL expression: `#{bindings.DepartmentId.inputValue}`.

- **Using Input Parameters Map**: In this approach, parameter values will be specified using an EL expression that evaluates to a `java.util.Map`. In other words, this EL point to a Java property in a bean that returns a filled input parameter map of type `java.util.Map` to the caller.The parameter map will be containing parameter names and values. This is useful for passing input parameters to a dynamic region where the task flow binding changes dynamically and each task flow may have varying number of parameters.

The following example illustrates the usage of EL expressions as input parameter map values for a **dynamic** task flow.:

```
<taskFlow id="dynamicEmpRegion" taskFlowId="${viewScope.
DynamicTaskFlowBean.dynamicTaskFlowId}" activation="deferred"
xmlns="http://xmlns.oracle.com/adf/controller/binding"
parametersMap="#{viewScope.DynamicTaskFlowBean.parameterMap}"
/>
```

The `getParameterMap()` method definition in the `DynamicTaskFlowBean` class is as follows:

```java
//In DynamicTaskFlowBean implementation class

/**
 *Parameters used in the dynamically added taskflow.
 */
public Map getParameterMap() {
  //Clear the parameter map
 parameterMap.clear();
  //Get currently active task flow id
 String tfName = getDynamicTaskFlowId().
     getFullyQualifiedName();
  //Get the binding container
 BindingContainer bindings = getBindingContainer();

  //Use different input parameter values based on task flow
  //selected for display in dynamic region
 if (EMP_DETAIL_TF.equals(tfName)) {
      //This example read desired
    // attribute binding used in the UI
    // and pass the value to the task flow
    AttributeBinding deptAttrib =
        (AttributeBinding)bindings.
        getControlBinding("DepartmentId");
    AttributeBinding empAttrib = (AttributeBinding)bindings.
        getControlBinding("EmployeeId");
    parameterMap.put("DepartmentId",
        deptAttrib.getInputValue());
    parameterMap.put("EmployeeId",
        empAttrib.getInputValue());
  } else if (EMP_SUMMARY_TF.equals(tfName)) {
    AttributeBinding deptAttrib =
        (AttributeBinding)bindings.
        getControlBinding("DepartmentId");
```

```
        parameterMap.put("DepartmentId",
            deptAttrib.getInputValue());
    }
    return parameterMap;
}
//Return current binding container
public BindingContainer getBindingContainer(){
    return BindingContext.
        getCurrent().getCurrentBindingsEntry();
}
```

If you are dropping a bounded task flow onto a bounded or unbounded task flow diagram as a **Task Flow Call** activity, then you must use **Property Inspector** for the task flow call activity to configure the input parameters. However the concept remains the same as we discussed for region binding.

Defining the task flow return value

A bounded task flow has the ability to return a value to the caller. To define the return value, open the bounded task flow in the overview editor, select the **Parameters** section and click on the green plus icon in the **Return Value Definitions** section. Enter the parameter name, Java class type, and value. The parameter value can be specified as a static literal or an EL expression.

Reading a return value from a task flow

To read the returned values from a caller, you have two options as discussed in the following:

- **Reading returned values when a called task flow is run as a page**: Create the task flow call activity for calling the task flow that returns a value to the caller on exit. You can do this visually by dropping the desired target task flow on to the calling task flow diagram. Select the task flow call activity in the diagram and in the **Property Inspector** window, expand the **Parameters** section. The **Return Values** section will pre-populate all the return value names defined in the target task flow. Enter an EL expression pointing to a memory scoped variable or managed bean for storing the returned values. Use these EL expressions for referencing returned values from the calling task flow at a later point.

- **Reading returned values when called task flow is run as dialog**: The approach for reading the returned value is slightly different when the task flow is run as dialog. The following are the details:

1. Drop the target task flow as the task flow call activity onto the calling task flow diagram editor. In the **Property Inspector** window, expand the **Behavior** section and set **Run As Dialog** to true. Optionally, select the **Display Type** as `inline-popup` to run the task flow inside an inline window instead of an external pop up window.

2. To read a returned value from a custom return listener method, specify the **Dialog Return Value**. Note that this value should match with the return value defined for the called task flow.

    The following screenshot displays the task flow call activity settings to read the task flow returned parameter `selectedLoc` from the return listener method. In this example the `selectedLoc` is specified as a return value name in the **location-lov-task-flow-definition**:

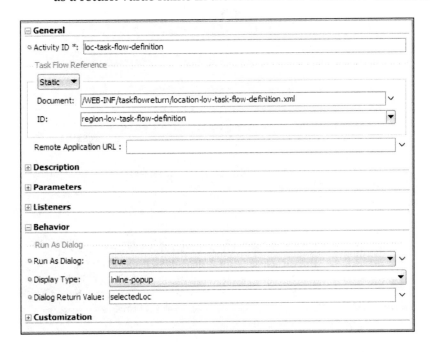

3. Now open the desired JSF page that displays the task flow as dialog. To open up the task flow in a dialog at runtime, you must set `useWindow = "true"` for the action component which triggers the navigation. To read the value returned by a task flow which is configured to run as a dialog, specify a custom return listener method as shown in the following example:

```
<af:commandButton text="Loc LOV" id="b5"
action="displayLocPopup" useWindow="true"
returnListener="#{TaskFlowBean.dialogReturnHandler}"/>
```

In this example, the command button generates the action outcome as `displayLocPopup` on button click, which causes the application to navigate to the target task flow. The `useWindow = "true"` setting for the command button tells the framework to display the target task flow in a window.

The `returnListener` will be invoked on exit from the called task flow. You can EL bind the `returnListener` to read the return value from the task flow. The `dialogReturnHandler` method used in this sample JSF code is as follows:

```
public void dialogReturnHandler(ReturnEvent returnEvent) {
//Use returnEvent.getReturnParameters() to read
//multiple return values

//Store the returned value to page flow scoped variable
  AdfFacesContext.getCurrentInstance().getPageFlowScope().
put("selectedLoc", returnEvent.getReturnValue());

//The following logic refreshes the desired part of
//the UI to display return value
//Mark the desired component for refresh
  UIComponent comp = returnEvent.getComponent().
findComponent("it4");
  RequestContext.getCurrentInstance().
addPartialTarget(comp);
}
```

A working example illustrating how to use the `returnListener` method to read the returned value from a task flow can be found in the example code that we mentioned at the beginning of this book, in the *Preface* section. To access the example code, open the `ADFDevGuideCh10` workspace in `JDeveloper` and look for `deptWithTaskflowLOV.jsf` in the `ViewController` project.

Consuming bounded task flows as ADF regions

Earlier we had discussed the usage of task flow call activity for displaying a bounded task flow built with complete JSF pages. Bounded task flows built with page fragments are displayed by using an ADF region (`af:region`) component.

The ADF region is a place holder component that allows dynamic contents to be included in the parent page. When you run a page with a region, the region component peeks into the underlying `oracle.adf.view.rich.model.RegionModel` for identifying the view to be displayed and instantiates the view. In general, ADF uses the `af:region` tag to display bounded task flows built using page fragments. ADF allows you to embed a region in a page or page fragment. Note that regions are capable of triggering the navigation of contents in its own display area (view port) without affecting the other regions or parent page. This is the reason why you are able to navigate between pages in bounded task flow added inside a region, keeping the parent view from being affected.

To build an ADF region containing task flow, perform the following steps:

1. Drag-and-drop the bounded task flow onto the page.

2. In the context menu, select **Region**. If the task flow that you dropped takes parameters, IDE will display the **Edit Task Flow Binding** dialog window for specifying parameter values.

3. Click on **OK** to save changes.

Dynamically displaying the task flow

To switch the contents displayed in a region dynamically, while dropping task flow on to the page, select **Dynamic Region** for holding the task flow. The `af:region` component generated in the JSF page remains the same for both static and dynamic regions. However, when you choose a dynamic region as a container for task flows, the `taskFlowId` referenced by the corresponding task flow binding will be pointing to an EL expression that evaluates to a task flow ID at runtime. The following is an example for task flow binding used in a dynamic region:

```
<taskFlow id="dynamicRegion1" taskFlowId="${viewScope.
myBean.dynamicTaskFlowId}" activation="deferred"
xmlns="http://xmlns.oracle.com/adf/controller/binding"/>
```

Refer to the topic *Dynamic task flow reference in a task flow call*, in this chapter, to learn the implementation of `${viewScope.myBean.dynamicTaskFlowId}`.

Lazy loading of an ADF region

When you run a page, by default, all embedded regions will be loaded at once during the initial display of the parent page. Note that if a page contains *N* regions, *N* task flows are executed during the page load. This is acceptable if all regions are exposed to the user during the initial display of the page itself. What if some regions are displayed in a pop up or inside a tabbed pane? You may definitely want to defer the execution of these regions until an end user opts to view them. ADF task flow has declarative support for such scenarios. The task flow binding provides an `activation` flag to control the activation of the underlying task flow.

To set the appropriate activation property for a task flow, open the page definition file in the overview editor. Select the desired `taskFlow` entry in the **Executables** section and then select the appropriate value for the activation property in the **Property Inspector** window. You can choose one from the following list:

- **immediate**: This option activates the region *immediately* on the initial display of parent page. This is the default value for the activation flag. Note that, with this flag, the task flow is activated if the region is hidden in the parent page.

- **deferred**: This option defers the activation of a region until it is shown to the user. In other words, the **deferred** flag enables lazy loading for task flows when used in regions. Note that this option is applicable only if the page is built by choosing the **Facelet** document type. In other words, this flag does not have any effect when the parent page is built as JSPX.

- **conditional**: This option activates the region if the EL expression specified for the `active` attribute evaluates to true. This is useful to conditionally activate the task flow bound to the region.

  In the following example, the task flow is activated only when the EL expression set for the active flag evaluates to true.

```
<taskFlow id="depttaskflowdefinition1"
    taskFlowId="/WEB-INF/hr/dept-task-flow-definition.xml#dept-
task-flow-definition"
    activation="conditional" xmlns="http://xmlns.oracle.com/adf/
controller/binding"
    active="{empty pageFlowScope.activeFlag ? false :
pageFlowScope.activeFlag}"/>
```

You can use the **Dynamic Tabs UI Shell Template (UI Shell)** page as a basic container page for Fusion web applications to have a generic look and feel and similar usability experience across applications. The UI Shell is very useful when you work on multiple enterprise applications and you want to provide a similar browsing experience for the end users. To learn more about the usage of the UI Shell template, refer to the topic *Dynamic Tabs UI Shell Template Functional UI Pattern* available on the Oracle Technology Network site: `http://www.oracle.com/technetwork/developer-tools/adf/uishell-093084.html`.

Refreshing an ADF region

While displaying a task flow using a region, the framework generates a separate view port for the region and tracks all the user actions inside the region separately from the parent page. All regions are initially refreshed during the first display of the containing page. What if you want to refresh the task flow bindings in response to some user actions outside of the region?

The ADF binding layer provides both declarative and programmatic solutions for such use cases. The following are the details:

- **Refreshing the task flow conditionally**: To refresh (restart) a task flow based on business conditions, you can specify `RefreshCondition = #{EL expression}` for the taskFlow executable binding. When you set `RefreshCondition`, the corresponding region will be refreshed (the task flow will be restarted) whenever an EL expression evaluates to true during the page lifecycle.

  Note `RefreshCondition` should only evaluate to true when you want the task flow to refresh or restart. Once the task flow is refreshed, the EL expression used for `RefreshCondition` should return false. Failing to do so will cause the task flow to restart for each post back. The easiest solution for such cases is to keep the EL expression in a request scoped memory area so that the `refresh` flag value will not survive the next request.

The following screenshot illustrates the usage of `RefreshCondition` for a dynamic task flow binding:

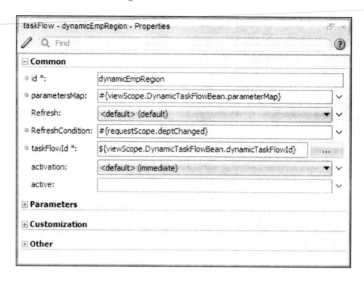

- **Refreshing the task flow when the input parameter value changes**: To refresh (restart) a task flow for input parameter value changes, set `Refresh = "ifNeeded"` for the corresponding task flow binding executable. Note that this flag is applicable only if the task flow binding defines input parameters.

  If the task flow binding uses an input parameters map instead of individual parameter definitions for passing parameter values, you must use `RefreshCondition = #{EL expression}` to refresh the binding.

  Note that you cannot use both `Refresh` and `RefreshCondition` for refreshing the task flow binding. If you specify both, the `Refresh` flag takes precedence.

Displaying task flows using a pop up component

While discussing about task flow call activity, we have seen the out of box support from ADF for running a bounded task flow built with complete JSF pages as dialog. However ADF Controller cannot run a task flow that uses page fragments as dialog. You can work around this limitation by adding a region inside a pop up as follows.

To display a bounded task flow with page fragments in a pop up, drop the **Popup** component onto the JSF page and then add a panel window to the pop up. The panel window component displays contents inside a window and does not display any predefined action buttons in the window. You can drop the desired bounded task flow with page fragments as a region into the panel window.

The following JSF code illustrates the use of the `af:popup` component for displaying a task flow.

```
<!-- Popup with a region that contains a bounded task flow -->
<af:popup childCreation="deferred" autoCancel="disabled" id="p1">
  <af:panelWindow id="pw1" title="Demo">
  <af:region
      value="#{bindings.mytaskflowdefinition.regionModel}"
      id="r1"/>
  </af:panelWindow>
</af:popup>
<!-- Button for displaying popup -->
<af:commandButton text="Display Task Flow" id="cb1"
    action="tf3" partialSubmit="true" immediate="true">
  <af:showPopupBehavior popupId="p1" triggerType="action"/>
</af:commandButton>
```

Lazy activation for a task flow when displayed in a pop up

When the parent JSF page is of a Facelet type and the activation flag for the task flow executable is set as deferred, then the framework will postpone the activation of the task flow until the region component is added to the pop up. The addition of child components is controlled by setting `childCreation = "deferred"` for the `af:popup`. With the `deferred` flag, the child components will be added only when a pop up is shown to the user.

If the parent page is a JSPX page (not Facelet), then you should use activation and active flag for lazy initialization of task flow. We have discussed these properties under the topic *Lazy loading of an ADF region*, in this chapter. When you use an EL expression that evaluates to a boolean flag as a value for an active flag, the memory scope used for holding the condition in the EL expression should be either `pageFlowScope` or `session` scope. You cannot use a `request` scope variable to build the condition in the EL, because the `request` scope is live only for the current requests and for each request, a new `request` scope will be created. If you use a `request` scope variable to build the condition, then during the postback from the activated task flow, the EL will be evaluated to false. Note that the view scope will not work when you use a pop up as the dialog window cannot access the `view` scope variable set by the parent page.

In the following example, the task flow becomes active when the `activeFlag` stored in the `pageFlowScope` memory scope is set to true.

```
<taskFlow id="employeetaskflowdefinition1"
   taskFlowId = "/WEB-INF/employee-task-flow-definition.xml#employee-
task-flow-definition"
   xmlns = http://xmlns.oracle.com/adf/controller/binding
   activation="conditional"
   active = "#{empty pageFlowScope.activeFlag ? false : pageFlowScope.
activeFlag}"/>
```

Using a contextual event for communicating to an ADF region

A Fusion web page can have multiple task flows added as region components. The task flows added in regions works independent to each other and with limited interactions with the parent page. What if you want a region to respond to some user actions in the parent page? How do you establish a channel for passing messages or data from the containing page to the task flow activity displayed in the view port of a region component?

Oracle ADF provides a **Contextual Events** framework for handling such scenarios. The contextual event enables communication between the following items:

- Parent page to region (and vice versa)
- Region to region

Contextual event model

Contextual event model is based on a publisher subscriber pattern. The event framework allows you to define custom event types and wire them with standard UI events through the binding container. Whenever a UI event is raised, the framework will trigger the associated contextual event as well. The contextual event dispatcher takes care of the queuing and propagating of events to the registered subscribers. The following diagram illustrates the contextual event model and its key players when used for region to region communication.

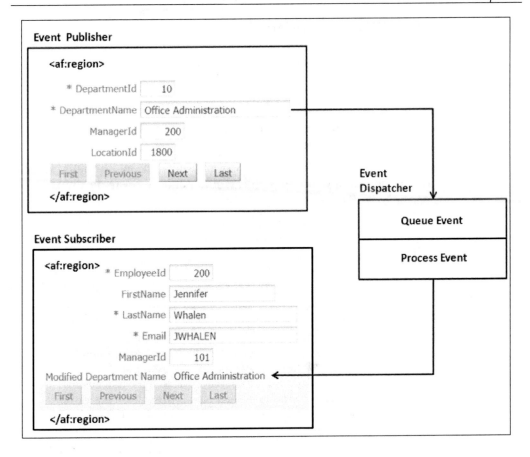

Using a contextual event

Unlike JSF events, contextual events are very dynamic and flexible in nature. The contextual event model allows you to choose the event types, payload, and event publishers. An event can be subscribed to by multiple interested parties.

To use a contextual event, you will have to define an event publisher and subscribers as explained in the next sections.

Defining an event publisher

JDeveloper IDE allows you to declaratively define contextual event and wire the event to a producer component. To define a contextual event for a UI component, perform the following steps:

1. Select the desired component in the JSF page design editor and then navigate to the **Contextual Events** section in the **Property Inspector** window. This is located inside the **Behavior** section.

2. Click on the green plus icon to add a new event entry. In the **Publish Contextual Event** dialog window, you can either choose to create a new event or use an existing event.

3. To define a new event, enter the event name and type (if the event type is not pre-populated). The following are the default contextual event types supported for various components:

Event Type	Description
Currency Change Event	This event can be published by any tree, table, or list navigator binding in the binding container.
	You may use this event type with any data bound table, tree table, or list control (for example, `selectOneChoice`) in the UI. The contextual event associated with this event type is fired when the current selection in the underlying data model changes at runtime.
Value Change Event	This event can be published by any attribute binding in the binding container.
	You may use this event type with any data bound editable component in the UI. The contextual event associated with this event type is fired when the attribute value changes at runtime.
Action Event	This event can be published by any action binding.
	You may use this event type with any actionable component such as the command button in the UI. The contextual event associated with this event type is fired when the user actions the component at runtime.

4. Select the **Payload** tab to specify the custom data that you want to pass as event payload for use by the event subscribers.

5. Select the **Pass Custom Value** checkbox and then select the payload data type. Based on the payload type selection, IDE will display various options to select the payload data. The payload can take the following types: page binding data, return value from managed bean and data control method, string literal, or any other EL expression. Optionally, you can specify raise conditions for the event using a Groovy expression in the **Raise Condition** tab. You can document the event in the **Documentation** tab.

6. Click on **OK** to save changes.

While defining the contextual event for a value change event or for a currency change event, mostly you do not need to specify any event payload. Why is that so?

If you do not specify any payload while defining the contextual event publisher for a value change event on an attribute, then the framework will pass `oracle.adf.model.binding.DCBindingContainerValueChangeEvent` as a default event payload at runtime. Similarly, the default payload type for a row currency change event is `oracle.adf.model.binding.DCBindingContainerCurrencyChangeEvent`.

The following screenshot illustrates the contextual event definition for a value change event. This event is defined for the department name field in the JSF page.

In this example, the `DepartmentName` attribute binding value is set as an event payload. Note that this is done just to illustrate how to supply the custom event payload. If you do not set the event payload explicitly, the framework supplies `DCBindingContainerValueChangeEvent` as the payload which has APIs to read the new value as well as the current row.

 There is no direct support for specifying multiple payloads for an event. To pass multiple payloads for an event, you should wrap them in a custom Java object or in a `java.util.Map` object and return it either using a method in a managed bean or using a method exposed in a data control.

Defining an event subscriber

Subscribing to a contextual event involves two subtasks.

- Defining an event handler method
- Subscribing to desired events

Defining an event handler method

You can designate an operation exposed through a data control or a method defined in a managed bean as handler methods for contextual events. A handler method can take any number of arguments. The method signature depends on the event payload and use case specific requirements. The following is an example for a contextual event handler method that takes the `String` type as payload:

```
public class ContextualEventEHandlerBean {
    //Event handler method
    public void deptNameChanged(String deptName){
        //Business logic goes here
        this.departmentName= deptName;
        refreshDeptComponent();
    }
...
}
```

Once you defined an appropriate handler method with the right signature in a plain Java class, you will have to create a data control for it in order to refer to it from an ADF binding layer. To create a data control, select the appropriate Java class, right-click and choose **Create Data Control**. You can also make use of methods exposed through the application module as event handlers.

The next step is to generate a method action binding in the consuming view's page definition file. To generate a method action binding for a data control method, perform the following steps:

1. Open up the desired page definition file in the overview editor.

2. In the **Bindings** panel, click on the green plus icon to create a new binding entry.

3. In the **Insert Item** dialog window, select **Generic Bindings | methodAction**.

4. In the **Create Action Binding** dialog window, select the appropriate method and click on **OK** to save changes.

If you want to use the method in a managed bean as an event handler, then the method action binding generation is bit tricky as there isn't a direct editor support for the same. You may need to add it manually as shown in the following code.

The `methodAction` binding syntax referring managed method syntax is as follows:

```
<methodAction DataControl="<DataControlName>" id="<methodAction
identifier>"
    InstanceName="${<bean instance name>}" MethodName="<event handler
method name in the bean>">
    <NamedData NDName="<param name>" NDType="<Java type>"/>
</methodAction>
```

The `DataControl` name in the previous binding definition is **not** related to the managed bean instance that we supplied as the value for `InstanceName`. It could be any data control instance used in the page definition and is required to handle any exception that might occur during invocation. The bean `InstanceName` should use the immediate evaluation syntax, that is, `${bean instance name}` instead of `#{bean instance name}`.

The following is an example:

```
<methodAction DataControl="HRServiceAppModuleDataControl"
id="DeptNameChangedHandler"
    InstanceName="${viewScope.ContextualEventEHandlerBean}"
MethodName="deptNameChanged">
    <NamedData NDName="deptName" NDType="java.lang.String"/>
</methodAction>
```

Subscribing to desired events

To consume a contextual event from a region or from a parent page, perform the following steps:

1. Open up the desired page definition file in the overview editor.

2. Select **Contextual Event | Subscribers**. Click on the green plus icon on the **Event Subscribers** panel to register a new subscriber.

3. In the **Subscribe to Contextual** event dialog window, enter the event name that you want to subscribe to. If you are subscribing from a parent page, you can use the **Search** button to locate the event instead of manually entering the name. Optionally, specify the publisher (producer region) for the event. Note that this field is enabled only when IDE can locate the producer. By default a subscriber is set to listen to any producer which is denoted by region = "*" (displayed as <Any> in the editor) in the eventMap definition present in the page definition file. To specify an event handler, click on the search icon close to the **Handler** field and in the **Select Handler** dialog window. Select an appropriate method action that you defined for handling events. Enter the parameters' **Name** and **Value** for the method handler. To use the event payload as a value for parameter, specify the EL expression as #{data.payLoad}. Note that you can also use the **Variables** dialog window to declaratively specify the payload EL expression. Optionally specify **Handle Condition**.

4. Click on **OK** to save changes.

The following screenshot illustrates the subscriber definition for the **DeptNameChanged** event. The **Consumer Parameters** section contains the handler method parameter name and value.

Remember that if you do not specify any payload while defining a contextual event publisher for the value change event, the framework will implicitly pass an `oracle.adf.model.binding.DCBindingContainerValueChangeEvent` object as an event payload. Similarly, for a currency change event, the default payload type is `oracle.adf.model.binding.DCBindingContainerCurrencyChangeEvent`. You can have an event subscriber with appropriate argument types to read these implicit payload objects. The following code snippet illustrates a sample event handler method that takes an implicit `DCBindingContainerValueChangeEvent` object as payload:

```
//In event handler Java bean class

public void implicitPayLoadHandlerMethod(Object payLoadObj) {
  DCBindingContainerValueChangeEvent payload = (
    DCBindingContainerValueChangeEvent)payLoadObj;
  //Read the new value
  Object newValue = payload.getNewValue();
  //Following line reads the row used in event producer
  //Row row= payload.getRow()
  //Business logic goes here...
}
```

Contextual event propagation at runtime

When a region triggers a contextual event, it's first propagated to the producer region itself. Then the event is bubbled up to the parent container, up to the root level. While bubbling to the parent container, the framework will see whether any region is referenced in the parent container and if so, the event is bubbled down to the referenced child regions as well. Once the event propagation reaches the topmost container, the framework starts dispatching the event to binding containers that have wildcard regions as event producers.

The framework allows you to turn off the event dispatch to regions that have subscribed to all publishers with the producer region set to any (*). The following are the details:

To turn off the event dispatch at page level, set **DynamicEventSubscriptions** = "false" in the page definition file. The following is an example:

```
<pageDefinition xmlns="http://xmlns.oracle.com/adfm/uimodel"
  version="11.1.2.61.83"  id="empcePageDef"  ...
DynamicEventSubscriptions="true">
```

Dynamically adding multiple regions to a page

ADF allows you to add or remove regions to a page at runtime. This feature is useful if you do not know the number of regions that render in the page at design time. For example, consider a page with panel tabbed display, each tab holding a region. An end user can add or remove tabs at runtime. This section discusses a solution for such use cases.

You can use a page definition file's `multiTaskFlow` element to reference a list of bounded task flows that are added at runtime. Each region in the UI may hold a reference to a task flow in the list. The following are the implementation details:

1. **Implementing the logic to return a task flow binding attributes list**.

   The first step is to build a managed bean to return a dynamic task flow list containing `oracle.adf.controller.binding.TaskFlowBindingAttributes` instances. Each `TaskFlowBindingAttributes` entry describes a task flow added at runtime. The following is an example for `TaskFlowBindingAttributes`:

   ```
   TaskFlowBindingAttributes tfBindingAttrib2 = new
   TaskFlowBindingAttributes();
   tfBindingAttrib2.setId("region2");
   ```

```
tfBindingAttrib2.setTaskFlowId(
new TaskFlowId(
    "/WEB-INF/multitaskflow/emp-task-flow-definition.xml",
   "emp-task-flow-definition"));
//Task flow parameters set through EL expression
tfBindingAttrib2.setParametersMap(
   "#{pageFlowScope.MultiTaskflowBean.parameterMap}");
```

You can specify parameters for a dynamically added task flow by calling setParametersMap() on the TaskFlowBindingAttributes instance as shown in the following:

```
//Parameter is set as EL expression
pointing to java.util.Map tfBindingAttrib.
setParametersMap("#{pageFlowScope.
MultiTaskflowBean.parameterMap}");
```

An example for a managed bean returning a list for TaskFlowBindingAttributes is given in the following code snippet. In the code snippet the buildTaskflowBindings() method adds TaskFlowBindingAttributes to the taskFlowBindings list at runtime in response to the action event for a button in the UI. The order of this list defines the order of the region objects in the multitask flow binding.

```
//In managed bean class

public class MultiTaskflowBean {

    private Map<String, Object> parameterMap =
        new HashMap<String, Object>();
    private List<TaskFlowBindingAttributes> taskFlowBindings =
        new ArrayList<TaskFlowBindingAttributes>();

/**
* Build task flow bindings at runtime in response to
* button click. You can do this from any action event.
*/
public void displayTaskflows(ActionEvent actionEvent) {
   buildTaskflowBindings();
}

/**
 * This constructs TaskFlowBindingAttributes list dynamically
 */
```

```
public void buidTaskflowBindings() {

    //Define TaskFlowBindingAttributes that holds
    // dept-task-flow-definition
    TaskFlowBindingAttributes tfBindingAttrib1 = new
        TaskFlowBindingAttributes();
    //Set identifier for the binding
    tfBindingAttrib1.setId("region1");
    //Set task flow id
    tfBindingAttrib1.setTaskFlowId(
        new TaskFlowId(
        "/WEB-INF/dept-task-flow-definition.xml",
        "dept-task-flow-definition"));
    taskFlowBindings.add(tfBindingAttrib1);

    //Define TaskFlowBindingAttributes that holds
    //emp-task-flow-definitionn
    TaskFlowBindingAttributes tfBindingAttrib2 = new
        TaskFlowBindingAttributes();
    tfBindingAttrib2.setId("region2");
    tfBindingAttrib2.setTaskFlowId(
        new TaskFlowId("/WEB-INF/emp-task-flow-definition.xml",
"emp-task-flow-definition"));

    //Init input param map for the task flow
    initPramaMap();
    //Pass parameters to task flow
    tfBindingAttrib2.setParametersMap(
        "#{pageFlowScope.MultiTaskflowBean.parameterMap}");
    taskFlowBindings.add(tfBindingAttrib2);
}

/**
 * Parameters used in dynamically added taskflow.
 * EL #{pageFlowScope.MainBean.parameterMap} refers this map.
 * DepartmentId is hard coded in this sample. In real life
 * application you will recreate this Map dynamically each
 * time when you rebuild TaskFlowBindingAttributes list.
 */
public Map getParameterMap() {

    return parameterMap;
}
```

```
//Initialize the input parameter map for a task flow
private void initPramaMap() {
   parameterMap.put("DepartmentId", new Integer (80));
}
/**
 * @return TaskFlowBindingAttributes list
 */
public List<TaskFlowBindingAttributes> getTaskFlowBindings() {
   return taskFlowBindings;
 }


//Class ends
}
```

2. **Generating the executable entry for the multitask flow**.

   The next step is to supply the dynamic task flow list from step 1 to the binding container. To add an executable binding for a multitask flow, perform the following steps:

   1. Open the page definition in the overview editor and select the **Bindings and Executable** tab.

   2. Click on the green plus icon on the **Executables** panel. In the **Insert Item** dialog window, select **ADF Task Flow Bindings** in the binding category and then select the **multiTaskFlow** binding in the corresponding item list.

   3. In the **Insert mulitTaskFlow** dialog window, enter the unique ID for the multitask flow binding and then specify an EL expression that returns the list of TaskFlowBindingAttributes as values for **taskFlowList**. The EL expression used in this example is #{pageFlowScope.MultiTaskflowBean.taskFlowBindings}.

   4. Click on **OK** to create the necessary binding entries.

   5. Select **activation** as **deferred** in the **Property Inspector** window.

   Now the binding entry for **multiTaskFlow** may look like the following:

```
<multiTaskFlow id="multiRegion1"
    taskFlowList=
    "#{pageFlowScope.MultiTaskflowBean.taskFlowBindings}"
    xmlns="http://xmlns.oracle.com/adf/controller/binding"
activation="deferred"/>
```

3. **Adding regions that refers to multi task flow binding entries in the JSF page**.

This is the last step in this exercise. Open the JSF page and add the necessary code for displaying dynamic regions using the `multiTaskFlow` bindings. You can use the following EL syntax to refer the multitask flow binding in the UI:

`#{bindings.<multiTaskFlow  Id>.taskFlowBindingList}`

The following example uses the `af:forEach` tag to insert region components for each element in `taskFlowBindingList`:

```
<af:forEach var="tf" items="#{bindings.multiRegion1.
taskFlowBindingList}">
  <af:region value="#{tf.regionModel}" id="reg#{tf.name}"/>
</af:forEach>
```

While adding a region dynamically, you may need to ensure that each region is assigned a unique identifier at runtime. This example uses the following EL expression to generate unique identifiers for each region: `id= "reg#{tf.name}"`

To alter the task flow list at runtime, call the appropriate method in the managed bean that modifies the task flow list in response to some user action. For instance, this example uses the `MultiTaskflowBean::display Taskflows(ActionEvent)` method (See step 1 for the managed bean source) to alter the task flow list in response to the action event on a button.

A working example illustrating the use of a `multiTaskFlow` binding for dynamically adding task flows can be found in the example code that we mentioned at the beginning of this book, in the *Preface* section. To access the example code, open the `MultiRegionSample` workspace in JDeveloper and look for `main.jsf` in the `ViewController` project.

Distributing ADF task flow as the ADF library

The **ADF Library JAR** is a very commonly used mechanism to distribute reusable ADF artefacts such as task flows, page templates, declarative components, and business services within the same application or across different applications. The ADF library follows the **Java Archive (JAR)** file format with some extra metadata files for use by JDeveloper to manage dependencies.

Packaging the task flow into the ADF library

To distribute a task flow as an ADF library, perform the following steps:

1. Right-click on the view controller project and select **New | Deploy | Deployment Profile**. In the **Create Deployment Profile** dialog window, select **ADF Library Jar File as Profile Type** and enter **Deployment Profile Name**. Click on **OK** to continue.

2. To specify dependencies, select **Library Dependencies** in the **Edit ADF Library Jar Deployment Profile Properties** dialog and edit the desired dependency by clicking on the **Edit Dependencies** icon. In the **Edit Dependencies** dialog window, select each dependent project and specify whether to include the **Build Output** directly or specify the deployment profile to the class path. The build output option will add all the dependencies and class files to the final artefact which is fine for this example. Select **Build Output** and click on **OK** to continue.

3. In the **Edit ADF Library Jar Deployment Profile Properties** dialog window, select the **Connections** property in the list and specify how you want to include the connection details in the ADF library. You can either include the connection with all the connection details (excluding the password) or just add the connection name. In both cases, the database connection needs to be edited in the project which imports the ADF library. Optionally, you can edit the **Jar Options** and **ADF Validations** properties.

4. Click on **OK** to save changes.

To deploy the ADF library, right-click on the view controller project that contains the bounded task flow and then select **Deploy | <Deployment Profile>**.

Consuming task flows added into an ADF library

JDeveloper provides a **Resource Palette** window to manage ADF libraries used in applications. Before starting to use an ADF library, you may need to add it to the **Resource Palette window**. You can open the **Resource Palette** window from the **Windows** menu in the main menu bar or by pressing *Ctrl + Shift + O*. To add a new ADF library into the resource palette, perform the following steps:

1. Click on the new folder icon in the resource palette and select **New Connection | File System** in the context menu.

2. In the **Create File System Connection** dialog window, enter the connection name and specify the directory path pointing to the folder containing the ADF Library JAR file. This directory path could be a network path which can be accessed by all developers working in a team. Click on **OK** to continue.

Once you added the ADF library to the resource palette, it will be listed in the **IDE Connection** window under the **File System** node.

To use the ADF library from a project, select the desired project in the **Application Navigator** and then go to the **IDE Connection** window and select the ADF library. Right-click on the desired JAR file and choose **Add to Project** in the context menu. Behind the scenes this action creates an ADF library entry to the project libraries and also sets up the component palette. If the library that you added to the project contains the model project with a database connection, you may also notice the following:

- A new database connection name used by the newly added library will appear in the **Application Resources** panel. Note that you may need to edit this connection either by specifying the connection string or password depending upon the *include setting* for the connection in the ADF library deployment profile.
- Data control from the library will be appearing in **Data Controls** window.

To locate the task flow exposed by the ADF library, select the ADF Library JAR in the **Component Palette** drop-down list. IDE will then display the task flows and regions in the component palette. You can drop the desired task flow or region item from the component palette onto the desired location. The rest of the steps are the same as you consume a task flow local to the application.

To learn more about reusing application components as an ADF library, refer to the topic *Packaging a Reusable ADF Component into an ADF Library* in *Oracle Fusion Middleware Fusion Developer's Guide for Oracle Application Development Framework*. To access the documentation go to http://www.oracle.com/technetwork/developer-tools/jdev/documentation/index.html and choose **Oracle JDeveloper and ADF Documentation Library | Fusion Developer's Guide**. Use the **Search** option to find specific topics.

Using a train component in a bounded task flow

A typical web application may have some business transactions that span across multiple pages and take a sequential path to complete. Most of the rich enterprise applications provide visual indicators pointing to the current step when the user navigates around different activities in a multi-step process.

ADF Faces provides an `af:train` component to display a series of stops in a multi-step process. Each train stop displayed in the train component represents an activity in a multi-step process flow. The following is an example for an `af:train` component display at runtime:

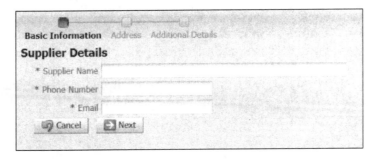

 To learn more about the `af:train` component, refer to the tag documentation available online at `http://jdevadf.oracle.com/adf-richclient-demo/docs/tagdoc/af_train.html`.

Creating a train in a bounded task flow

You can enable train stops for activities in a bounded task flow in the following two ways:

- Enabling train support while creating a bounded task flow: When you create bounded task flow, you can check the **Create Train** checkbox in the **Create Task Flow** dialog window. This action will enable train stop support for all activities in the corresponding task flow.

- Enabling train support for an existing bounded task flow: This can be done in the following two ways:

  i. Right-click on the task flow and select **Train | Create Train** in the context menu.

  ii. Open the task flow in the overview editor, select the **Behavior** tab and check the **Train** checkbox. Alternatively, you can set the **Train** property in the **Property Inspector** to **true**.

Once you enable the train for a task flow, all task flow activities will bear a visual indicator representing train stop support for the task flow. Note that this action will just enable train support across activities in a task flow. However, to display the train component on view activities, you have to explicitly add the appropriate train component on to the page as explained in the following section.

To display the train component in a JSF page, double-click on the desired view activities in the task flow diagram editor. JDeveloper will display the **Create ADF Page** dialog window if the view activity is not yet associated with a page. Drop **Train** or the **Train Button Bar** component from the **Component Palette** panel onto the page. In the **Property Inspector** window for the train component, enter **Value** as: `#{controllerContext.currentRootViewPort.taskFlowContext.trainModel}`.

Setting display names for train stops

To set display names for train stops generated for the view activities in a bounded task flow, select the desired view activity in the task flow diagram editor. In the **Property Inspector** window, expand the **Description** section and enter **Display Name** for the train stop. If you want to localize the display name of the train stop, use the following EL expression format to refer to a specific key in the resource bundle: `#{adfBundle['ResourceBundleName'] ['SomeKey']}`. The following is an example: `#{adfBundle['com.packtpub.adfguide.ch9.view.ResourcesGenBundle']['CreateEmp']}`

Customizing the display for train stops

ADF allows you to customize the train display using the `af:navigationPane` component. The hint attribute in `af:navigationPane` decides the display component. The following are the possible hints for `navigationPane` components: bar, buttons, choice, list, and tabs. The following is an example illustrating the usage of `af:navigationPane` for displaying customized train stops:

```
<af:navigationPane hint="tabs"
    value="#{controllerContext.currentViewPort.
            taskFlowContext.trainModel}"
    var="trainNode" id="np1">
  <f:facet name="nodeStamp">
  <af:commandNavigationItem
            text="#{trainNode.textAndAccessKey}" id="cni1"
        visited="#{trainNode.visited}"
            disabled="#{trainNode.disabled}"
        action="#{trainNode.action}"
            selected="#{TrainBean.currentTab}"  />
    </f:facet>
</af:navigationPane>
```

You can directly map the properties of `af:commandNavigationItem` to the appropriate properties exposed by a train node in the train model. If required, you can also provide custom implementation for any of these properties. For example, the `selected` property of `af:navigationPane` in this example is an EL expression wired to the `isCurrentTab()` method in `TrainBean`. This method returns true for the selected navigation tab. The code for the `currentTab` property defined in `TrainBean` is as follows:

```java
//In managed bean class
public boolean isCurrentTab() {
    //Get current stop
  TaskFlowTrainModel model =
    ControllerContext.getInstance().
        getCurrentViewPort().getTaskFlowContext().
        getTaskFlowTrainModel();
  TaskFlowTrainStopModel currentStop =
        model.getCurrentStop();

  //Following code helps you to get current
  //view activity in the task flow
  FacesContext fctx = FacesContext.getCurrentInstance();
  ELContext elctx = fctx.getELContext();
  Application app = fctx.getApplication();
  ExpressionFactory expressionFactory =
        app.getExpressionFactory();
  //trainNode is the name of the variable
  //attribute defined in af:navigationPane
  ValueExpression ve = expressionFactory.
        createValueExpression(elctx, "#{trainNode}",
        Object.class);
  TaskFlowTrainStopModel renderedTrainNode =
        (TaskFlowTrainStopModel)ve.getValue(elctx);
  String renderedActivityId =
        renderedTrainNode.getLocalActivityId();
  //Check whether renderedActivityId is same as current stop
  if (renderedActivityId.
        equalsIgnoreCase(currentStop.getLocalActivityId())) {
    return true;
  }
  return false;
}
```

Programmatically navigating between train stops

Apart from using declarative navigation features provided by the train component, you can also use train model APIs to programmatically navigate between train stops. The following example illustrates train model APIs used for navigating to the next stop in the train model:

```
//In TrainBean bean class
public String nextTrainStop() {
    //Get current stop
  TaskFlowTrainModel model =
              ControllerContext.getInstance().getCurrentViewPort().
              getTaskFlowContext().getTaskFlowTrainModel();
  TaskFlowTrainStopModel currentStop = model.getCurrentStop();
    //Next train stop
  TaskFlowTrainStopModel nextStop = model.getNextStop(currentStop);
  if (nextStop != null)
    return nextStop.getOutcome();
  else
    return currentStop.getOutcome();
}
```

The following commandButton code EL binds the action attribute with the previously mentioned method in TrainBean. When the user clicks on the button at runtime, the system navigates to the next available train stop.

```
<af:commandButton text="Go to Next Stop" id="b5"
action="#{pageFlowScope.TrainBean.nextTrainStop}"/>
```

Executing methods while navigating between train stops

In the last chapter you learned about using method call activities to initialize a view. Navigation to the method activity is decided based on the outcome from the preceding activity. What if you want to execute a method activity before a specific train stop? You will not be able to directly put a method call activity before a train stop because ADF does not allow you to mark a method call activity as a train stop.

To execute a method call activity before a specific train stop, perform the following:

Select the desired train stop in the task flow diagram editor. In the **Property Inspector** window, expand the **Train Stop** section and specify an **Outcome** value for the train stop. You will use this outcome to define the control flow case to the method activity (or to any valid task flow activity) that you want to execute before the train stop. Draw a wildcard control flow rule to the method activity and specify the **From Outcome** for the control flow case. The **From Outcome** value should be the same as the outcome, set for the train stop.

At runtime, whenever the control navigates to a train stop, the framework will check for any navigation case that matches the outcome set for the train stop. And if any matching navigation case is found, then the control flow takes that path. You can use this approach for overriding default navigation provided by the framework.

For example, in the following task flow, the user is allowed to navigate to **empView** from **deptView** using the train component only if the currently selected department row has more than five employee rows (display threshold). This check is done using the method call activity, **hasMinimumEmployees** and if the number of employees is less than the display threshold, the system will not allow the navigation. To enable automatic execution of the method call before displaying **empView**, the outcome set for the **empView** train stop is used in defining the control flow case to the **hasMinimumEmployees** method call activity. This is shown in the following screenshot:

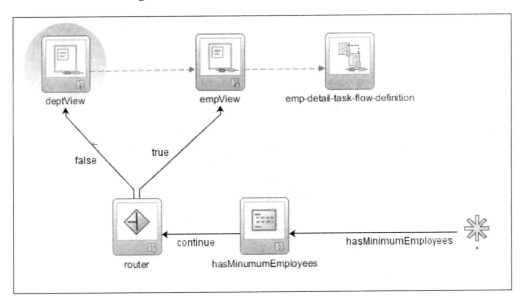

At runtime, the system displays **deptView** to the user as the default view. When the user clicks on the train stop for accessing **empView**, the framework executes the method activity **hasMinimumEmployees** and if this method returns as true, the system navigates to **empView**, otherwise the system takes the user back to **deptView**.

Transaction management in a bounded task flow

One of the great advantages of a bounded task flow is its out of the box support for declarative transaction management. Without this support you may end up writing a lot of plumbing code for managing transactions. In this section, we will take a closer look at the declarative transaction settings available for a task flow and how the framework manages the transaction behind the scenes.

The bounded task flow supports the following declarative transaction settings:

- **No Controller Transaction**: The called bounded task flow does not participate in any declarative transaction management. However you can programmatically manage the transaction, if required. This is explained in the next section entitled *Programmatically managing transactions for a task flow*.

- **Always Begin New Transaction**: The called task flow starts a new transaction.

- **Always Use Existing Transaction**: The called task flows participate in the existing transaction.

- **Use Existing Transaction If Possible**: The called task flow will join the existing transaction from the caller, if it exists, otherwise it starts a new transaction on entry to the task flow.

A bounded task flow also has a declarative option to share data control with the calling task flow. When you mark a data control as shared, the called task flow reuses the same database connection instance and data control instances from the calling task flow. The following screenshot displays the default transaction settings as well as the data control sharing option for a bounded task flow:

What happens at runtime?

Now that you have seen the transaction value setting for a task flow, this section will explain to you how the framework manages the transaction behind the scenes at runtime.

When you run a page with a nested region, the framework does the following behind the scenes.

During the **Before Restore View** phase of the JSF lifecycle, the framework creates a new root view port for the top level page. During the view port initialization, the framework will build a data control frame to hold data controls and bind containers used in the root view port (parent page). You can consider a data control frame as a bucket for holding data controls used in the binding container. Note that each data control frame will use a local transaction handler to manage all transaction related activities such as commit and rollback of transactions, save point creation, and restore. The transaction handler will delegate the calls to the respective data controls as and when required.

During the **Render Response** phase of the JSF lifecycle, if the page contains a region while encoding the region tag, the framework creates a new child view port as well as a separate controller state for the child region and then starts processing the task flow as explained in the following:

- If the child task flow is configured to share data control with the calling task flow, then the framework will use the data control frame from the parent page (caller) to serve the child region as well. Alternatively, if the data control scope for the child task flow is set to **isolated**, the framework will create a new data control frame for the task flow and add it as a child to the parent data control frame.

- If the transaction for the task flow is set to **Always Begin New Transaction**, then the framework will open a new transaction on the data control frame. If the data control frame has already started a transaction, then the framework throws an error and stops further processing.

- If the transaction for the task flow is set to **Always Use Existing Transaction**, then the framework will ensure that the transaction is already started on the data control frame and then continue the processing. If the parent data control framework has not started the transaction, then the framework throws an error and stops further processing.

- If the transaction for the task flow is set to **Use Existing Transaction If Possible**, then the framework starts a new transaction if there is no transaction open on the data control frame, or uses an existing transaction if one exists.

Later in the lifecycle, when the UI component starts rendering a value, the framework will instantiate associated data controls for reading a data collection, and adding them to the appropriate data control frame, which is associated with the current view port.

When a task flow commits a transaction, the framework will call commit on the data control frame which in turn will call commit on all data controls present in the data control frame. The same logical sequence repeats for transaction rollback as well, with rollback calls on the data controls.

> Refer to the section entitled *Transaction management in Fusion web applications* in the appendix of this book, *More on ADF Business Components and Fusion Page Runtime*, for a detailed discussion on transaction management in a Fusion web application. You can download the appendix from the Packt website link that we mentioned at the beginning of this book, in the *Preface* section.

Programmatically managing transactions for a task flow

Sometimes you may need to move out of the boundaries of declarative settings to realize specific use cases. For example, consider a scenario where a task flow's transaction setting depends on complex business conditions and the declarative transaction setting fails to meet the requirement. In such cases, you can use the model APIs for programmatically starting a transaction.

The following task flow illustrates the usage of APIs for programmatically starting a transaction on a data control frame:

```
//In managed bean class
/**
 * The following method programmatically starts
 * transaction on the data control frame
 */
public void beginTransaction() {
  BindingContext context = BindingContext.getCurrent();
   //Get the name of Data Control Frame
  String dcFrameName = context.getCurrentDataControlFrame();
   //GetData control Frame
  DataControlFrame dcFrame = context.
      findDataControlFrame(dcFrameName);
  dcFrame.beginTransaction(new TransactionProperties());
}
```

The following is a task flow that makes use of method activity to start a transaction. Note that as the transaction is managed programmatically, the declarative transaction property for this task flow is set to **No Controller Transaction**.

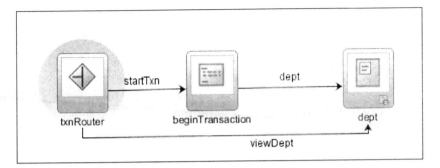

The following code snippet illustrates the usage of APIs for programmatically committing a transaction open on a data control frame.

```
//In managed bean class

/**
 * The following method commits transaction on a
 * data control frame
 */
public void commitTransaction() {
  BindingContext context = BindingContext.getCurrent();

  //Get the name of Data Control Frame
  String dcFrameName = context.getCurrentDataControlFrame();
  //GetData control Frame
  DataControlFrame dcFrame = context.
      findDataControlFrame(dcFrameName);
  dcFrame.commit();
}
```

The life span of a bounded task flow

A bounded task flow becomes eligible for garbage collection in the following scenarios:

- When a task flow return activity is executed
- When the region holding a task flow reference switches to a new task flow (by changing the task flow ID)
- When the user navigates away from the parent page that contains the task flow
- When a pop up displaying a task flow is dismissed by the user

Summary

Bounded task flows play a very crucial role in a Fusion web application. It allows you to split a single massive control flow structure into multiple reusable modules. A well designed application will reduce the development cost considerably. In this chapter, you have learned how to build bounded task flows, their various configuration properties, and real life usage patterns. With this chapter, we are done with the ADF Controller layer.

In the next chapter we will discuss the ADF validation cycle for a page and the basic infrastructure services offered by ADF for handling validation exceptions.

11
More on Validations and Error Handling

This chapter summarizes the discussion on validation that we have had so far. In this chapter we will explore the ADF validation cycle for a page and the infrastructure for handling validation exceptions. The following topics are discussed in this chapter:

- Adding validation rules in a Fusion web application
- Displaying validation exceptions on a page
- Where in the page lifecycle does validation occur?
- Error handling in ADF
- Programmatically throwing validation exceptions in business components
- Customizing default business component error messages
- Skipping validation

Introduction

Validation is the process of ensuring the completeness and sanity of business data before posting to the underlying data source. Validating user input is very important for any business application that you build. We will start by discussing the features offered by ADF for adding validation rules to a page. Next, we will see how the framework handles the validation exceptions and reports it to the end user.

Adding validation rules in a fusion web application

A typical enterprise application may want to perform certain validations at client-side and certain things at server-side. The idea is to detect and report the errors as soon as possible to the end user. Oracle ADF allows you to perform validations on both client- and server-side. For a fusion web application, client-side validation is performed in the browser itself without performing a server round trip. Client-side validation is typically used to validate the basic syntax and semantics of the user input. More business critical validations, which involve pulling data from database or interaction with third party services, are performed on the server. This is done when the user submits a page.

For an ADF web application, you can enable validations at three different layers as follows:

- ADF view (ADF Faces)
- ADF model
- ADF Business Components

The validations added in different layers are triggered at different stages in a page life cycle. When a page is posted back to the server, the validations defined in the view layer are executed first, followed by validations in the binding layer (model), and then in business components. The following diagram represents validation support for various layers in a fusion web application:

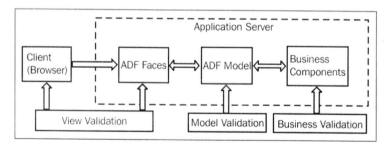

As you can see in the diagram, view layer validations can be split between the client (browser) and the server. The client part of the view layer validation is done using JavaScript and the server part is done in Java code. The next section discusses this topic in detail.

Defining validations in the ADF view layer

You will use ADF Faces validation to perform validation on the view layer. The view layer validations in ADF Faces are performed on both the client (web browser) and server. You can add validation rules to an ADF Faces component used in a web page using one of the following approaches, as appropriate:

- Enable simple validations for a component using built-in validation attributes such as required flag, minimum and maximum value checks, and maximum length check. An example is here:

```
<af:inputText value="#{dpetBean.jobId}" label="Job Id:"
 columns="5"    required="true"     maximumLength="5"
   id="it6"/>
```

- Add more business specific validation for components by EL binding the **validator** attribute to a method in a managed bean. An example is here:

```
<af:inputText  id="it2" value="#{deptBean.DepartmentName}"
   label="DepartmentName:" autoSubmit="true"
   validator="#{deptBean.validateDepartmentName}" />
```

In this example, the `validator` attribute for the `af:inputText` is wired to the `validateDepartmentName()` method in the `DeptBean` class through an EL expression. This is implemented as follows:

```
//In managed bean class
public void validateDepartmentName(FacesContext facesContext,
   UIComponent uIComponent, Object value) {
   //This checks DepartmentName value using custom
   //business rule by calling
   //validateDeptUsingCompanyRules() method
   if ( !validateDeptUsingCompanyRules(value)) {
     FacesMessage message = new
       FacesMessage(FacesMessage.SEVERITY_ERROR,null,
       "Department Name is invalid);
   throw new ValidatorException(message);
   }
}
```

Note that the method signature for the validator method defined in the managed bean should be as follows:

```
public void methodName(FacesContext, UIComponent, Object){...}
```

- If the validation rules repeat across multiple components, then build reusable validator component classes that implement the `javax.faces.validator.Validator` interface. This can be reused across the application as explained in the following section.

Defining a custom ADF Faces validator

The ADF Faces framework ships with a wide variety of built-in validation types. If the built-in validations are not meeting your application's needs, you can create custom reusable JSF validators by implementing the `javax.faces.validator.Validator` interface. The JSF validators by design run on the server. However, ADF Faces overcomes this shortcoming by allowing you to combine both client-side and server-side validation rules in the validator. In fact, this feature is inherited from **Apache Trinidad**. Validators that wish to run on both client-side and server-side should implement `javax.faces.validator.Validator` and `org.apache.myfaces.trinidad.validator.ClientValidator` interfaces.

The following is an example for the ADF Faces validator class that implements both client-side and server-side validation rules for validating an e-mail field on the UI. Here are the details of the implementation.

Step1: Defining client-side validation in JavaScript

The first step is to write a client-side validation using JavaScript. The client-side validation implementation used in this example makes use of `TrValidator`, which is from the Trinidad Java Script library. This is conceptually similar to `javax.faces.validator.Validator` in JSF. In client-side JavaScript, you do not have access to the component or any of its properties. So, all the required parameters need to be passed while initializing script objects. This example stores the JavaScript implementation in the `emailValidator.js` file, which is shown as follows:

```
// In emailValidator.js

function EmailClientValidator() {
  // This is added for debugging
  this._class = "EmailClientValidator";
}


// TrValidator is from Trinidad Java Script library. This is
// conceptually similar to javax.faces.validator.Validator
// in JSF

EmailClientValidator.prototype = new TrValidator();
/**
 * Validates the email field on client side.
 * If any violations are found, a TrValidatorException will
 * be thrown which contains TrFacesMessage describing the
 * reason for failure.
 * @param value - value to be validated
 * @param label- label to identify the input field to the user
 * @param converter - converter to format error string
```

```
 * properly
 */
EmailClientValidator.prototype.validate = function (value, label,
  converter) {
  var emailPattern = /^[a-zA-Z0-9._-]+@[a-zA-Z0-9.-]+\.
    [a-zA-Z]{2,4}$/;
  //If email is invalid, then throw error
  if (!emailPattern.test(value)) {
    var fm = new TrFacesMessage("Email validation failed",
      "Invalid Email", TrFacesMessage.SEVERITY_ERROR);
      throw new TrValidatorException(fm);
  }
}
```

Step 2: Defining the validator Java class

Once you have defined JavaScript for performing client-side validation, the next step is to plug in the JavaScript code to the validation framework and also implement the logic for performing extra validation at the server. To do this, you can create a custom validator class implementing the following interfaces:

- `org.apache.myfaces.trinidad.validator.ClientValidator`: This is the interface which requires to be implemented by objects that wish to perform client-side validation in addition to server-side validation. This is from the Apache Trinidad library.

  The method `getClientLibrarySource()` in the `ClientValidator` returns the URI to the JavaScript file that contains the client-side validation logic. The method `getClientValidation()` returns the appropriate client validation code to be used from JavaScript.

- `javax.faces.validator.Validator`: This is the interface that requires to be implemented by objects for performing validation at server-side. This is from the core JSF stack.

The following example illustrates the implementation of the e-mail validator that performs validation at both client-side and server-side. Here is the implementation:

```
public class EmailValidator implements Validator,
  ClientValidator {
  //Pattern for email validation
  Pattern emailPattern = Pattern.compile
    ("^[a-zA-Z0-9._-]+@[a-zA-Z0-9.-]+\\.[a-zA-Z]{2,4}$");

  public EmailValidator() {
    super();
  }
```

```
/**
*This is used to import the built-in scripts
*provided by Apache Trinidad.
*If this function returns null, built in
*"Validator()" will be used.
*/
@Override
public Collection<String> getClientImportNames() {
  return null;
}


/**
* Implementation for
* ClientValidator::getClientLibrarySource()
* Gets the URI specifying the location of the js
* lib resource.
*/
@Override
public String getClientLibrarySource(FacesContext context)
{

  return context.getExternalContext().
    getRequestContextPath() + "/resources/js/email.js";
}


/**
 * Implementation for ClientValidator::getClientScript()
 * Opportunity for the ClientValidator to return
 * script content.
 */
@Override
public String getClientScript(FacesContext context,
  UIComponent component) {
  return null;
}


/**
 * Implementation for
 * ClientValidator::getClientValidation()
 * Called to retrieve the appropriate client
 * validation code(JavaScript method) for the
 * current field
 */
@Override
```

```java
public String getClientValidation(FacesContext context,
  UIComponent component) {
    return ("new EmailClientValidator()");
}


/**
 * Implementation for Validator::validate()
 * This validates the value on server.
 */
@Override
public void validate(FacesContext facesContext,
  UIComponent uIComponent, Object object) throws
  ValidatorException {
  //This method does the following:
  // 1. Validates email format using regular expression
  // 2. Validates the existence of email using
  //third party service
  Matcher matcher = emailPattern.
    matcher(object.toString());
  if (!matcher.matches()) {
    if (!validateEmailBySendingMail(object)) {

      FacesMessage msg = new FacesMessage
        ("Email validation failed", "Invalid Email");
      msg.setSeverity(FacesMessage.SEVERITY_ERROR);
      throw new ValidatorException(msg);
    }


  }
}


/**
*This method validates the existence of email
*/
public boolean validateEmailBySendingMail
  ( Object email) {
  //Email Service tests the validity of an email
  //It's implementation is not shown here
  return EMailService.validate(email);
}
}
```

Step 3: Configuring and using the validator

The last step is to configure the custom JSF validator class in `faces-config.xml` for use in the UI. The following code snippet in `faces-config.xml` illustrates how to configure `EmailValidator` in `faces-config.xml`:

```
<validator>
  <validator-id>EmailValidator</validator-id>
  <validator-class>
    com.packtpub.adfguide.ch11.view.validator.EmailValidator
  </validator-class>
</validator>
```

To add the newly added validator to a UI component, use the `f:validator` tag as shown in the following example:

```
<af:inputText label="Email" id="it5"
  value="#{ValidateBean.email}">
<f:validator validatorId="EmailValidator"/>
<!-- EmailValidator is the validator-id configured in
  faces-config.xml -->
</af:inputText>
```

At runtime, when you finish editing the e-mail field in the page (on tabbing out), the client-side validation gets executed. Server-side validation is fired when the form is submitted to the server.

> To learn more about **client-side converters and validators** used in ADF Faces (inherited from **Apache Trinidad**), refer to the online documentation available at http://myfaces.apache.org/trinidad/devguide/clientValidation.html

Defining validations in the ADF model layer

ADF allows you to add validations in the model (binding layer) layer as well. The model level validations are added on the binding definitions present in a page definition file. This feature is useful if the underlying business service implementation, which is wired to the UI through the ADF model, does not provide the necessary validation support.

To add a model layer validation rule, do the following:

1. Open the desired page definition file.

2. In the structure window, right-click the desired binding item and then select **Edit Validation Rule** in the context menu.

3. You can add validations on attribute, list, table, or tree binding entries in the binding section. In the **Validation Rule Editor** dialog window, select the attributes for which validation needs to be set. Click **New** in the **Validation Rule Editor** dialog to add new validation rules.

4. In the **Add Validation Rule** dialog window, select the appropriate rule types from the drop down. Use the dialog settings to configure the new rule. You can specify the error message and error severity in the **Failure Handling** tab.

5. Click **OK** to save the settings and dispose of the dialog.

The UI is bound to the model validation rules though the binding EL expression specified using `<f:validator>` tag. An example is here:

```
<af:inputText value="#{bindings.PhoneNumber.inputValue}"
   ... lid="it1">
<f:validator binding="#{bindings.PhoneNumber.validator}"/>
</af:inputText>
```

The model validation rules will be fired when the user submits a page, before pushing the changes to the underlying business components.

Defining validations in the ADF Business Components layer

ADF business component framework provides great support for validating data passed by the client. The advantage of adding validations at the business service layer is that validations stay independent of the client, and it also provides great flexibility in building validation rules. The business component framework offers many built-in declarative validation rules which can be added to entity attributes, entity rows, or transient attributes in the view object. If the declarative validation rules offered by the framework are not enough for building specific use cases, then developers can add custom validation logic as well.

> We have discussed the support for adding validation rules to attributes and entity objects a while ago under the topic *Adding validation* in *Chapter 3, Entity Objects*. Refer back to this topic if you need a quick brush up on declarative validation support offered by business components.

Remember from our discussion in *Chapter 3, Entity Objects* on Validations that validations can be defined in an entity object at three levels: attribute level, entity level, and transaction level. They primarily differ in the execution sequence as explained below:

- **Attribute level**: The validations added on the attributes will be fired before pushing the value to the underlying model.

- **Entity level**: The validations added at entity level will be fired during entity row selection changes in the binding layer, during post back action on the UI, or when the transaction is committed.

- **Transaction level**: The behaviour of transaction level validation is a bit confusing for developers. As the name suggests, it is fired when a transaction is committed for sure. However, when you work on fusion web applications, you may notice that transaction level validation rules are also getting fired even during the post back of the page to the server. This is because for a web application the application module instances (which act as a container for business components) are not really bound to a specific client throughout the user session. As the load increases, runtime will recycle the least recently used application module instances to serve new clients. Due to this reason, the framework will validate underlying data controls while posting data from client to server, every time. This validate call in turn triggers both entity level and transaction level validations.

If you really want to defer the transaction level validation to the commit phase of a transaction, then set `SkipValidation="skipDataControls"` in the page definition file of the appropriate JSF page that displays the edit form. This setting causes the framework to skip all transaction-level validations during the post back of a page. The `SkipValidation` property of a page definition file is discussed in detail under the section *Skipping validations in the business components*. Following code snippet from a page definition file illustrates this setting:

```
<pageDefinition id="deptPageDef" ...
   SkipValidation="skipDataControls"> ...
</pageDefinition>
```

Validations using custom domain objects

ADF Business Components allows you to define custom data types known as domain object types. This is typically used for representing custom complex data types in an application. The custom domain object can hold the basic data validation check and data conversion logic. An example for a custom domain is an e-mail domain object.

To define a custom domain object, do the following:

1. Right-click the model project in the application panel and select **New**.

2. In the **New Gallery**, select **Business Tier | Business Component | Domain**.

3. In the **Create Domain** dialog window, enter the domain name and package. Click **Next** to continue. In the **Settings** page, select the database column type and click **Finish**.

To add custom validation logic to the newly built domain class, open the generated domain class in the source editor. You can do this by clicking the **Domain Class** link in the **Java** tab of the domain object. The custom domain class implements the oracle.jbo.domain.DomainInterface interface. To add validation logic, locate the validate() method in the domain class and add the validation as appropriate. The following is an example for an e-mail domain object:

```
// A custom domain object

public class EmailDomain implements DomainInterface,
  Serializable {

private String mData;

public EmailDomain(String val) {
  mData = new String(val);
  validate();
}

protected EmailDomain() {
  mData = "";
}

/**
  * Implements domain validation logic for email and throws
  * a JboException on error.
  */
protected void validate() {
  // Compiles the given regular expression
  //into a pattern object.
  Pattern emailPattern =
    Pattern.compile(
      "^[a-zA-Z0-9._-]+@[a-zA-Z0-9.-]+\\.[a-zA-Z]{2,4}$");
  //Creates a matcher that will match the given input
  // against this pattern
```

```
  Matcher matcher =
    emailPattern.matcher(getData().toString());
  if (!matcher.matches()) {
    // CustomErrorMessageBundle is extended
    //from ListResourceBundle, shown below
    throw new DataCreationException
      (CustomErrorMessageBundle.class,
      CustomErrorMessageBundle.INVALID_EMAIL,null, null);
  }
}
public Object getData() {
  return mData;
}

/**
 * Applications should not use this method.</em>
 */
public void setContext(DomainOwnerInterface owner,
  Transaction trans, Object obj) {
}

//Other methods such as equals() and toString() go here...

}
```

The `CustomErrorMessageBundle` class used in this example is created by using the **Create Message Bundle Class** option available in the model project properties dialog.

Here is the implementation of a `CustomErrorMessageBundle` class:

```
public class CustomErrorMessageBundle extends ListResourceBundle {
  public static final String INVALID_EMAIL =
    "INVALID_EMAIL";
  private static final Object[][] messageKeyValues =
    new String[][] {
      {INVALID_EMAIL, "Invalid Email" }
    };

  /**Return String Identifiers and corresponding Messages
   * in a  two-dimensional array.
   */
  protected Object[][] getContents() {
    return messageKeyValues;
  }
}
```

The detailed steps for creating custom message bundles are as follows.

Creating and registering custom message bundles

To register a custom message bundle with the model project, do the following:

1. Right-click the desired model project in the application navigator and select **Project Properties** in the context menu.

2. In the **Project Properties** dialog window, expand the **ADF Business Components** node in the tree and select the **Options** node.

3. Go to the section entitled **Custom Message Bundles to use in this Project**, displayed at the bottom of the dialog. Click on the **New** button to define a new list bundle class. This is shown in the following screenshot:

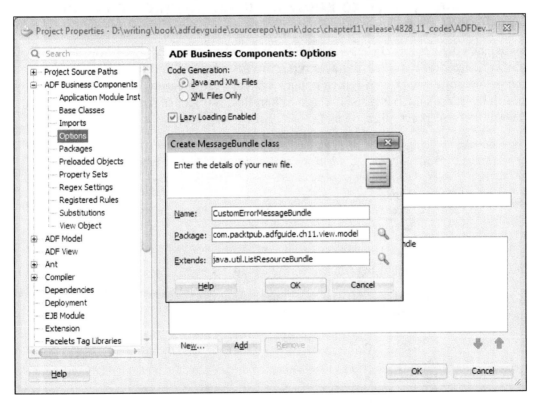

4. In the **Create MessageBundle class** dialog window, enter the **Name** and **Package** for the custom message bundle class. Click on **OK** to generate the custom message bundle class. While doing so, IDE will update the `<Modedl Project>.jpx` with the message bundle class name.

5. Open the generated message bundle class and provide message strings as appropriate. See `CustomErrorMessageBundle` that we used in the previous example to get a feel for the implementation.

Note that a message bundle is backed up by a subclass of the `java.util.ListResourceBundle` class. To add support for an additional class, you can create another message bundle class with the appropriate locale identifier appended to the source file and compile it into a class file. For example, you may create `CustomErrorMessageBundle_ja_JP.class` in order to store messages in Japanese. In a nutshell, you create a separate message bundle class file (with the appropriate locale identifier appended to the source file) for every locale that your application is required to support.

What you may need to know while using custom domain types on the UI

To display custom domain types on the UI, you have to specify an appropriate faces converter for handling the data type conversions back and forth. The ADF framework comes packaged with a generic converter implementation, **oracle.genericDomain**, which is good enough to handle a number of jbo domain types. This converter is preconfigured in `faces-config.xml` as follows:

```
<converter>
  <display-name>Generic Domain Converter</display-name>
  <converter-id>oracle.genericDomain</converter-id>
  <converter-class>
    oracle.adfinternal.view.faces.convert.GenericDomainConverter
  </converter-class>
</converter>
```

The following component tag illustrates the usage of `oracle.genericDomain`:

```
<af:inputText value="#{bindings.Email.inputValue}"
  label="#{bindings.Email.hints.label}"
  required="#{bindings.Email.hints.mandatory}"
  converter="oracle.genericDomain"  id="it4">
</af:inputText>
```

If the `oracle.genericDomain` is not enough to display custom domain objects in the UI, then you have to create a custom JSF converter. To learn how to do this, refer to the topic *Creating Custom JSF Converters in Oracle Fusion Middleware Web User Interface Developer's Guide for Oracle Application Development Framework*. To access the documentation go to `http://www.oracle.com/technetwork/developer-tools/jdev/documentation/index.html` and choose **Oracle JDeveloper and ADF Documentation Library | Web User Interface Developer's Guide**. Use the search option to find specific topics.

When does the framework validate the custom domain object?

The validate routine for the custom domain types takes a slightly different path than the normal validation cycle. The framework calls `validate()` on the domain instance during the object instantiation itself. Custom domain objects mapped to a field in a web page are instantiated in the following two scenarios:

- When the framework populates the row containing custom domain object typed field for displaying on the UI
- When the framework pushes submitted values to a custom domain object typed field in the model

The error handler used by the binding layer (`DCErrorHandlerImpl`) is not involved in the formatting of error messages thrown by the custom domain types. The framework handles the validation errors thrown by domain types by converting it in to `javax.faces.convert.ConverterException`.

Where to put validation in a Fusion web application

As ADF offers options to validate data at different layers, you might be wondering where to put the validation in an application. There are no right or wrong answers for this question. It all depends on use cases and business needs. A typical fusion web application may use validations at both the view layer and business service layer. All critical business functionalities should be validated at the business component level irrespective of whether you validate it at view or other layers. The model layer validation is a very rarely used feature for a fusion web application. This is because the validation rules in the business component layer are a superset of the model layer. Also, validations added on the business components can be reused when their values are accessed by any page.

Displaying validation exceptions on a page

When a validation fails during the post back of a page, the framework adds the validation error messages in `javax.faces.context.FacesContext` object displaying it during the **RenderResponse phase** in the page life cycle. ADF input components, in general, supports automatically displaying their own messages. However, if you want to override the default display of messages (including validation exception), the following ADF Faces components are available for you:

- **af:message**: To override the default error display for a component, you can use the `af:message` component. The following example overrides the default error display for the `deptName` field using a separate `af:message` component:

```
<af:inputText id="deptName" value="#{deptBean.departmentName}"
validator="#{deptBean.validateDepartmentName}"
  label="Departmnet Name:" autoSubmit="false"/>
<af:message for="deptName" id="msg1"/>
```

This code will produce the following validation error display at runtime:

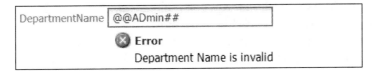

- **af:messages**: Use this component to display messages that may or may not be directly related to specific components. You can use this to override the default error pop up provided by the framework. Note that the default error pop up that you see on the validation error is enabled for all pages with the `af:document` tag, that use the `oracle.adf.rich` render kit.

Where in the page lifecycle does validation occur?

It is always good to know the sequence of actions that happens at the client and server when a page with validation-enabled components is submitted. In this section, we will explore the validation cycle for a typical fusion web page.

Client-side validation

The client-side validation is triggered when the user finishes editing the data on the UI. During the client-side validation cycle, the client-side peer component for the UI control performs basic data sanity checks which include basic data type checks as well as executing client-side validation rules such as mandatory field, maximum length, and max-min value check. If any error is found during this cycle, it will be immediately reported back to the user.

Server-side validation

The server-side validation is triggered when a page is posted back to server, after the successful completion of client-side validation. When the request reaches the server, the framework intercepts the request and starts the fusion page life cycle for the page. We have already discussed the fusion page life cycle in detail in *Chapter 7* under the topic *What happens when you access a fusion web page*. In this section, we are revisiting the fusion page life cycle to answer the following question—when does validation occur during the page life cycle?

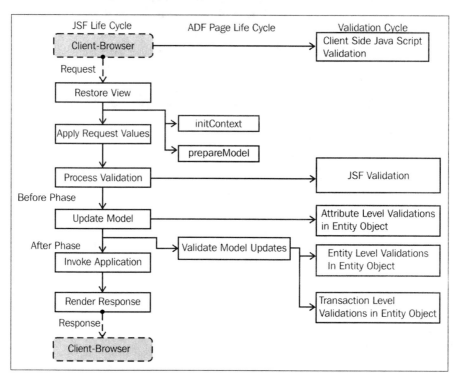

We will now have a look at the different phases:

- **Restore View**: In the Restore View phase of the life cycle, the component tree (view) for the submitted page is restored. This is followed by the initialization of binding context and prepares model phases.

- **Apply Request Values**: During the Apply Request Values phase in the cycle, the framework extracts the submitted values and applies them to the corresponding component in the tree.

- **Process Validation**: During the Process Validation phase, ADF Faces converts the submitted value to the corresponding model objects, and then runs validation rules over them. The validation rules include standard and custom validations added to the component. If any validation fails, the error messages are queued as `javax.faces.application.FacesMessage` in the `FacesContext` instance and life cycle execution skips to the **Render Response** phase.

- **Update Model**: On successful execution of the Process Validation phase, the life cycle proceeds to the Update Model phase during which the submitted values are pushed into the model. During the Update Model phase, attribute level validations added on the entity objects are fired. These validations are triggered before pushing changes to entity.

  ○ **Validate Model Update:** This is extended from JSF life cycle phase for meeting special validation requirements of the ADF framework. After the Update Model phase, the framework proceeds to Validate Model Updates. Entity level validations are fired during this phase. If you have any validations (such as method validator or key exists validator) marked to "defer execution to transaction level", then they are also executed during this phase, by default. If any validation fails during the Update Model or during the Validate Model Updates phase, the error messages are queued in the `FacesContext` instance and the life cycle is skipped to the Render Response phase.

- **Render Reponses**: The component tree is rendered during this phase. If any validation exception is thrown during the processing of the request, then the framework renders the validation error messages on the UI as appropriate.

Error handling in ADF

So far in this chapter, we have explored the validation support in ADF and also discussed the validation cycle for a page. Now you must be curious to know how the framework handles the validation or system exceptions during the page life cycle and reports it to the user. The rest of the chapter discusses this topic.

Exception handling in a web application is a challenging task for many developers and the solutions may vary according to scenarios. Support for graceful handling of all business and system exceptions, and reporting the relevant error messages to the end user, is essential for any application framework. The good news is that the Oracle ADF framework offers extensible, out of the box solutions for handling both checked and unchecked exceptions.

In general, a fusion web application may need to handle two categories of exceptions; exceptions thrown by the business components when accessed in binding context, and exceptions thrown during task flow execution. The ADF model deploys an exception handler in the binding container for handling exceptions thrown by business components when accessing them in the binding context. Exceptions during navigation are handled by the exception handler deployed by the controller layer. The following diagram illustrates this concept:

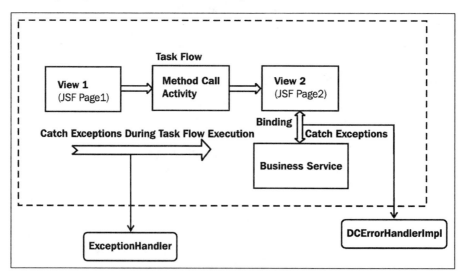

In the diagram, you may notice the presence of two exception handlers: one in the binding layer and another in the controller layer. Let us take a quick look at these items:

- Exception handling in the binding layer: ADF binding layer uses a default `oracle.adf.model.binding.DCErrorHandlerImpl` class for handling all the exceptions thrown by the business components when invoked through the binding layer. This involves all validation exceptions as well as system exceptions.

- Exception handling in the controller layer: The exceptions handler deployed by the controller layer handles all the exceptions that are raised during the execution of the task flow. This includes exceptions thrown from an intermediate method call activity while navigating from one view to the next. The ADF 11*g* release (in pre-JSF 2.0 time) uses the implementation of `oracle.adf.view.rich.context.ExceptionHandler` for handling all controller layer exceptions. This solution was proprietary to ADF. The JSF 2.0 release has standardized the exception handling by introducing `javax.faces.context.ExceptionHandler`. To see whether this is supported by the version of Oracle ADF that you work on, refer to the release notes.

You will have to customize the default exception handler only if the default mechanism provided by the controller is not meeting your application's needs. To gracefully handle exceptions during navigation, all you need to do is designate an activity in a task flow as an exception handler. Each task flow can have its own exception handler. It does not mean that all task flows should have an exception handler. At runtime when an exception is thrown during navigation in a task flow and if there is no exception handler activity specified for it, then the framework will walk up the hierarchy of the task flow to find an exception handler.

> We discussed the basic steps for configuring a custom exception handler for the controller layer (task flow) in *Chapter 9* under the topic *Adding an exception handler*. Revise this topic if you need a quick brush up.

- Exception handling in the view layer: If the controller layer and binding layer are not involved in the context where the exception is thrown, then the exception is caught by the view layer. The exception handling by the view layer is specific to the implementation and not extensible as in the other two cases.

Taking a closer look at DCErrorHandlerImpl

The oracle.adf.model.binding.DCErrorHandlerImpl is the default error handler used by the binding container to handle exceptions thrown by business service implementation when accessed in the context of a binding container. For a fusion web application, DCErrorHandlerImpl handles exceptions in two steps:

1. In the first step, exceptions are intercepted and cached in the binding container. This typically happens during the validate phase, update model phase, or during the invoke application phase in a page life cycle.

2. In the second step, cached exceptions are formatted and displayed to the user. The framework executes this step during the rendering of the page.

The following diagram will help you to understand how the framework engages `DCErrorHandlerImpl` during the page life cycle for handling exceptions thrown by business components when accessing them in the binding context:

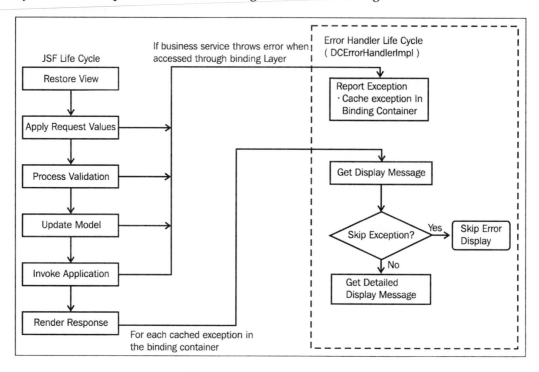

If an exception is thrown while accessing business components through the binding layer, the binding container intercepts the exception and takes over further processing. To decide how to proceed with the exception, the binding container then invokes `reportException(DCBindingContainer formBnd, Exception ex)` on the `DCErrorHandlerImpl` class. The `reportException()` routine does the following:

- Wraps non JboException using the `JboException` instance
- Caches the exception in the binding container allowing the framework to complete the life cycle for the page

During the Prepare Render phase of the fusion page life cycle, the framework will iterate over all the cached exceptions in the binding container and prepare them for display. The framework executes the following steps for preparing validation exception for display:

- To get a human-readable error message text for each cached exception, the framework calls `getDisplayMessage(BindingContext, Exception)` on the error handler class passing the exception.

- The `getDisplayMessage(BindingContext, Exception)` method in turn invokes `skipException(Exception)` on the error handler implementation for skipping duplicate and irrelevant wrapper exceptions. This step is required because while processing exceptions, `DCErrorHandlerImpl` wraps non-JboException using a `JboException` instance. Apparently this wrapper needs to be removed before reporting to the user. The framework will skip processing an exception if `getDisplayMessge(BindingContext, Exception)` returns null.

- If `getDisplayMessge(BindingContext, Exception)` returns a not null message for the exception, then, as the next step, the framework invokes `getDetailedDisplayMessage(BindingContext, RegionBinding, Exception)` on the error handler for reading detailed messages for exception.

  The returned value from `getDisplayMessge(BindingContext, Exception)` and `getDetailedDisplayMessage(BindingContext, RegionBinding, Exception)` are used for building the `javax.faces.application.FacesMessage` object with summary and detail fields. The `FacesMessage` represents a single validation (or any other failure message) message, which is typically associated with a particular component in the view.

- The framework adds `FacesMessages` to the `FacesContext` instance which is later used in the Render Response phase and displayed to the user.

Programmatically throwing validation exceptions in business components

Sometimes you may want to programmatically throw validation exceptions from custom business service methods if certain business conditions are not met in the middle of a process flow. In this section, you will learn to use appropriate exception classes for programmatically throwing validation exceptions with localized messages from business component classes.

In this section, we will start with the localization of validation messages, then we will move forward to discuss the validation class hierarchy, and finally we will see APIs from throwing various validation exceptions.

Localizing validation error messages

ADF allows you to localize messages that are displayed when a validation is triggered or an error is thrown. ADF business components such as entity objects and view objects have declarative support for associating property resource bundles with their definitions. Runtime will pick up the appropriate property resource bundle based on the user locale. The following sections explain how you associate resource bundles to business components.

Resource bundle usage in entity objects and view objects

When you define validation error messages or UI hints such as label, tool tip, and display format for attributes in an entity object or in a view object, JDeveloper IDE will allow you to choose a resource bundle using the **Select Text Resource** dialog window. You can open up the **Select Text Resource** dialog window by clicking on the search icon displayed close to the localizable UI hints fields in the respective business component overview editor. When you select a resource bundle for use in an entity object or in a view object definition, JDeveloper will generate mapping for the resource bundle in the respective component descriptor XML file. The following is an example for the ResourceBundle mapping entry in an entity object XML file:

```
<Entity
  . . .
  <ResourceBundle>
  <PropertiesBundle
    PropertiesFile="com.packtpub.adfguide.ch11.
      model.HRDataModelBundle"/>
  </ResourceBundle>
</Entity>
```

Resource bundle usage in the application module

The application module lacks visual support for configuring resource bundles as you see for entity object or view objects. The resource bundle reference is needed in an application module when you want to customize the validation messages thrown from an application module. There are two possible ways you can associate a resource bundle with an application module definition:

1. Manually specify the resource bundle entry in the desired application module XML file as follows:

```
<AppModule
  ...
  <ResourceBundle>
    <PropertiesBundle
      PropertiesFile=
        "com.packtpub.adfguide.ch11.model.HRDataModelBundle"/>
  </ResourceBundle>
</AppModule>
```

2. Programmatically specify the resource bundle for an application module.

To programmatically specify the resource bundle for an application module, generate application module definition class for the desired application module and then override the `finishedLoading()` method to set the resource bundle definition as follows:

```
//In application module definition class

public class HRServiceAppModuleDefImpl extends
  ApplicationModuleDefImpl {

  //Other methods go here...

  @Override
  protected void finishedLoading() {
    super.finishedLoading();
    PropertiesBundleDef propBundleDef = new
      PropertiesBundleDef(this);
    //Specify property resource bundle
    propBundleDef.setPropertiesFile
      ("com.packtpub.adfguide.ch11.model.HRDataModelBundle");
    //Attach the resource bundle definition to the component
    setResourceBundleDef(propBundleDef);
  }
}
```

The `finishedLoading()` method is invoked once the definition object is loaded during the creation of an instance. Note that the above approach is not limited for the application module alone; rather it can be used for dynamically specifying the resource bundle for entity objects or view objects (using their respective definition classes). The resource bundles mapped to business components such as the entity object, view object, and application module can be read using the `getResourceBundleDef()` method in their respective implementation classes.

Reading the resource bundle definition from the business component

Sometimes you may want to access the resource bundle attached to the business component definition from the code. For example, when you programmatically throw a validation exception from an entity object implementation class, you may want to localize the error messages by supplying the error description from the resource bundle attached to the corresponding entity object definition. The following code snippet illustrates the use of APIs for reading the resource bundle attached to a business component's implementation class:

```
//You can use this in the implementation classes of
//application module, view object or entity object as
//appropriate
/**
 * This method returns the localized message string the value
 * for a key from the resource bundle associated with the
 * containing business component. This method can be used in
 * the implementation class of an application module, an
 * entity object or a view object.
 *
 */
public String getLocalizedValue(String key) {

  ResourceBundleDef resourceDef = this.
    getResourceBundleDef();
  Locale locale = this.getDBTransaction().getSession().
    getLocale();
  String retVal = StringManager.
    getLocalizedStringFromResourceDef
      (resourceDef, key, null, locale, null, false);
  return retVal;
}
```

Programmatically throwing validation exceptions

The following code snippet illustrates the APIs for throwing `oracle.jbo.ValidationException` from a custom business method defined in an application module implementation class. The `processEmployeesForaDepdt()` method shown in this example checks whether the supplied department has any employees and if not found, it throws `ValidationException` to the caller. You can use the same APIs for throwing `ValidationException` from methods defined in an entity object as well as in a view object.

```
//In application module implementation class
/**
 * This is a custom business method defined in an application
 * module implementation class
 */
public void processEmployeesForaDepdt(Row deptRow) {
  //Throw exception if no employees found
  //for department
  if (!hasEmployeesExists(deptRow)) {
    throw new ValidationException
      (deptRow.getAttribute("DepartmentName") +
        " does not have   any employees configured!");
  }
  //The following method is invoked only if
  //the supplied department has employee rows
  reviseSalaryForEmployees((RowSet)deptRow.getAttribute
    ("Employees"));
}

//Method to check whether supplied department row has any
//existing employees
private boolean hasEmployeesExists(Row dpetRow) {
  //Access empployee row set through view link accessor
  RowSet empRowSet = (RowSet)dpetRow.
    getAttribute("Employees");
  empRowSet.reset();
  Row r = empRowSet.first();
  //Check whether first rows is null
  if (r != null)
    return true;
  else
    return false;
}
```

Building a validation exception using message strings from the resource bundle

The previous example uses a hardcoded message string. To localize the error message, you can change the code to read the message from the resource bundle using the `getResourceBundleDef()` method in the business components, as follows:

```
//In application module implementation class.

/**
 * This is a custom business method defined in an application
 * module implementation class
```

```
  */
public void validateDeptRow(Row deptRow) {

    //Throw exception if no employees found
    //for department

    if (!hasEmployeesExists(deptRow)) {
      //getResourceBundleDef returns property resource bundle
      //mapped to the application module
      ResourceBundleDef resourceBundle = getResourceBundleDef();
      throw new ValidationException(resourceBundle,
        "ERROR_MESSAGE_NULL_EMPLOYEES",
          new Object[] { deptRow.getAttribute
            ("DepartmentName") });

    }

    //The following method is invoked only if
    //the supplied department has employee rows
    reviseSalaryForEmployees(
      (RowSet)deptRow.getAttribute("Employees"));
}
```

The property resource bundle file (`HRDataModelBundle.properties` file) used in this example contains the following message key (error code) entry:

```
ERROR_MESSAGE_NULL_EMPLOYEES = The department {0} does not have any
employees configured!
```

Validation class hierarchy

Before proceeding with more complex use cases on validation, let us understand the validation class hierarchy. The following class diagram represents the class hierarchy for validation exceptions used in the ADF business component framework. All the validation exceptions are subclassed from the `oracle.jbo.JboException` class which provides a single point for the localization and formatting of exception messages.

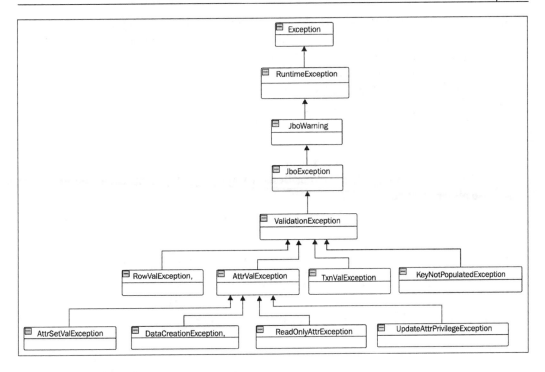

Wrapping exceptions

Java language does not allow you to directly throw multiple exceptions at a time. However, you can work around this by wrapping multiple exceptions using a parent exception. The same idea is used by the validator classes in ADF business components to report multiple exceptions associated with an attribute or a row. When multiple validation exceptions need to be thrown to the client, they are bundled together by appropriate top-level exceptions as shown in the following diagram (an example) and thrown to the caller:

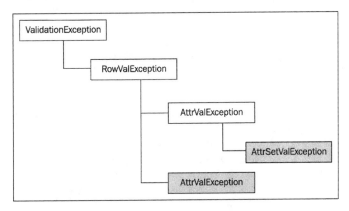

The business component framework does not insist on a definite exception hierarchy when you need to bundle multiple exceptions under a parent JboException. You can decide top-level exceptions as appropriate to the context. As discussed earlier, the default error handler used by the binding layer will skip all the top-level exceptions during the display of messages.

The following thumb rules may help you to build and bundle multiple exceptions programmatically:

- Use **AttrSetValException** to report failed attempts to set an attribute value. If there are multiple exceptions for an attribute, wrap them using **AttrValException**.

- If there are multiple AttrValException for a row, then wrap them using a **RowValException**.

- If there are multiple RowValException, then wrap them using a **ValidationException** or a **TxnValException**.

Programmatically throwing multiple RowValException

The following is a custom validate method in the application module that illustrates the APIs for validating multiple rows in one go and finally throwing a single ValidationException, bundling all the oracle.jbo.RowValException exceptions. The method validateEmployeeAndDepartment() shown in this example takes the department row and employee row as input parameters. This method validates the e-mail field from the employee row and the department name field from the department row. On validation error, one or more RowValExceptions are bundled in an array list and thrown to the caller by wrapping it inside a ValidationException.

```
//In application module implementation class

/**
 * A method illustrating the APIs for bundling
 * multiple RowValException exceptions wrapped through
 * ValidationException class
 * @param employeeRow
 */
public void validateEmployeeAndDepartment(ViewRowImpl deptRow,
  ViewRowImpl employeeRow) {

  //Read the employee entity object that back up employee Row
  Entity employeeEO = employeeRow.getEntity(0);
  //Create a list for storing RowValExceptions
```

```
ArrayList<RowValException> exceptions = new
  ArrayList<RowValException>();

//Validate Email
//Method body for isValidEmail(String) is not shown
//in this sample

if (!isValidEmail((String)employeeRow.
  getAttribute("Email"))){

  //Invalid email, create a new  RowValException
  //and add it to the exceptions list

  //Param 'ERROR_MESSAGE_INVALID_EMAIL' is the key to
  //identify message from resource bundle
  exceptions.add(newRowValException
    ("ERROR_MESSAGE_INVALID_EMAIL", employeeEO,null));
}

//Read the department entity object that back up dept Row
Entity deptEO = deptRow.getEntity(0);
//Validate DepartmentName
//Method body for isValidDept(String) is not shown
//in this sample
if (!isValidDept((String)deptRow.getAttribute
  ("DepartmentName"))){

  //Invalid DepartmentName, create a new RowValException
  //and add it to the exceptions list

  //Param 'ERROR_MESSAGE_DEPTNAME_INVALID' is the key to
  //identify message from resource bundle

  exceptions.add(newRowValException
    ("ERROR_MESSAGE_DEPTNAME_INVALID", deptEO, new
      Object[]{deptRow.getAttribute("DepartmentName")}));
}

//Bundle all exceptions by wrapping it using a
//ValidationException and throw it to the caller
if (exceptions.size() > 0) {
  // CSMessageBundle.class Defines the error codes and
  // default error messages for operations
  //on business objects
  ValidationException val = new ValidationException
    (CSMessageBundle.class,
      CSMessageBundle.EXC_VAL_VR_VALIDATE_FAILED, null);
```

```
      val.setExceptions((Exception[])exceptions.toArray(new
        Exception[exceptions.size()]));
      throw val;
    }
  }


  /**
   * Helper method to create RowValException
   * @param messageBundleKey
   * @param e
   * @param errorMessageParams
   * @return
   */
  private RowValException newRowValException(
    String messageBundleKey, Entity e, Object[]
      errorMessageParams) {
    //Create a new RowValException for the supplied
    //entity object
    RowValException rowVal= new
      RowValException(getResourceBundleDef(),
        messageBundleKey, e.getStructureDef().getFullName(),
          e.getKey(), null, null);
    rowVal.setErrorParameters(errorMessageParams);
    return rowVal;
  }
```

The property resource bundle file used in this example contains the following
message key (error code) entries:

```
ERROR_MESSAGE_DEPTNAME_INVALID = Department Name - {0} - is not valid

ERROR_MESSAGE_INVALID_EMAIL = Invalid Email
```

The property file used by the application module in this example is manually added
to the application module XML descriptor file as shown in the following block of code.
This helps us to access the property bundle by calling getResourceBundleDef() on
the application module component:

```
  <AppModule . . .>
  ...
  <ResourceBundle>
    <PropertiesBundle
    PropertiesFile=
    "com.packtpub.adfguide.ch11.model.HRDataModelBundle"/>
  </ResourceBundle>
  </AppModule>
```

Programmatically throwing AttrValException

The following example illustrates how you can bundle multiple
AttrSetValException using an AttrValException and throwing it to the caller.
The AttrSetValException used in this example is created for the DepartmentName
attribute in the department entity object.

```
//In application module implementation class
/**
 * Custom validate method illustrating the APIs for throwing
 * multiple AttrValException
 */
public void validateDepartmentName(Row deptRow) {

  //Get the entity object that back supplied row
  Entity e = ((ViewRowImpl) deptRow).getEntity(0);
  //Creates list for storing AttrSetValException
  ArrayList<AttrSetValException> exceptions = new
    ArrayList<AttrSetValException>();

  //Check if department name already exists in data store.
  //Method body for isDeptNameAlreadyExisting()
  //is not shown in this sample
  if (isDeptNameAlreadyExisting(deptRow)) {

    // Department name is in use, so
    // create AttrSetValException for DepartmentName field

    //Param 'ERROR_MESSAGE_DEPTNAME_DUPLICATE' is the
    //key to identify message from resource bundle

    AttrSetValException asve = new AttrSetValException
      (AttrValException.TYP_DEF_ENTITY_OBJECT,
        this.getResourceBundleDef(),
          "ERROR_MESSAGE_DEPTNAME_DUPLICATE",
            e.getStructureDef().getFullName(), "DepartmentName",
              deptRow.getAttribute("DepartmentName"), null);

    //Supply parameter values for the error message
    //from properties file
    asve.setErrorParameters(new Object[]
      {deptRow.getAttribute("DepartmentName")});
    //Add the exception to the list
    exceptions.add(asve);
  }
```

```
//Check if department name is well formed
if (!isValidName(deptRow)) {

    //Invalid department name, so
    //create AttrSetValException for DepartmentName field

    //Param 'ERROR_MESSAGE_DEPTNAME_INVALID' is the
    //key to identify message from resource bundle

    AttrSetValException asve = new AttrSetValException
      (AttrValException.TYP_DEF_ENTITY_OBJECT,
        this.getResourceBundleDef(),
          "ERROR_MESSAGE_DEPTNAME_INVALID",
            e.getStructureDef().getFullName(), "DepartmentName",
              deptRow.getAttribute("DepartmentName"), null);

    //Supply parameter values for error message
    //from properties file
    asve.setErrorParameters(new Object[]
      {deptRow.getAttribute("DepartmentName")});
    //Add the exception to the list
    exceptions.add(asve);
}

//If any exception occurred?
if (exceptions.size() > 0) {

  //Bundle the list of AttrSetValException in
  //AttrValException and throw to the caller

  //CSMessageBundle.class parameter defines the
  //error codes and default error messages for operations
  //on business objects
  AttrValException ave = new AttrValException
  (CSMessageBundle.class,
    CSMessageBundle.EXC_VAL_VR_VALIDATE_FAILED,
      e.getStructureDef().getFullName(), "DepartmentName",
        deptRow.getAttribute("DepartmentName"),
          exceptions, false);
  throw ave;
}
}
```

The property resource bundle file used in this example contains the following message key (error code) entry:

```
ERROR_MESSAGE_DEPTNAME_INVALID=DepartmentName - {0} - is not well
formed

ERROR_MESSAGE_DEPTNAME_DUPLICATE=DepartmentName - {0} - is in use
```

Customizing default business component error messages

ADF business components allow you to customize default business component error messages, such as unique constraint violation or foreign key constraint violation, by providing an alternative message string for the error code in a custom message bundle.

The following example will help you to understand the steps for customizing the message bundle used by business components. In this example, we will override the default error message displayed for the violation of the unique constraint 'EMP_EMAIL_UK' defined on the Email field in the Employee table. By default, when you commit a transaction with a duplicate Email field, the error message thrown by the application is as follows:

"ORA-00001: unique constraint (HR.EMP_EMAIL_UK) violated"

This does not make any sense to an end user and he or she cannot judge anything from this error. Let us see how to convert this error in to more user friendly message:

"Email is in use"

Step1: Creating and registering a custom message bundle

The first step is to generate a custom message bundle to override the default error message thrown during unique key violation for the database constraint 'EMP_EMAIL_UK'.

To generate a custom message bundle, you can use the create option available in the project properties window of your model project. If you need detailed steps for building a custom message bundle, refer to the section *Creating and registering custom message bundles*.

Once the custom message bundle class is created, open the generated class and override the message string array by providing a meaningful error message for the error code 'EMP_EMAIL_UK', as shown in the following example:

```
/**
 * This is ListResourceBundle implementation that
 * overrides default error message for
 * EMP_EMAIL_UK  unique constrains violation
 */
public class CustomMessageBundle extends ListResourceBundle {
  //EMP_EMAIL_UK is the Unique Key constraint defined
  //on EMPLOYEE table
  private static final Object[][] messageKeyValues =
    new String[][] { { "EMP_EMAIL_UK",
      " Email is in use"} };

  /**Return String Identifiers and corresponding
   * Messages in a two-dimensional array.
   */
  protected Object[][] getContents() {
    return messageKeyValues;
  }
}
```

Step 2: Customizing the DCErrorHandlerImpl

The previous step localizes the error message for an error code present in an exception. Now we may need to customize the default error handler to include the constraint violation exception (which carries the localized message) in the final error display list. This is discussed here.

Remember that the binding layer catches and caches the exceptions thrown by the business components during the page life cycle. While rendering the page, the framework invokes skipException() on DCErrorHandlerImpl before displaying each cached exception. If the method skipException() returns true, then the exception is skipped and is not displayed to the user. The default DCErrorHandlerImpl will skip the exception in the following scenarios:

- If the current exception wraps (caused by) a oracle.jbo.JboException
- If the current exception is JboException and it bundles detailed exceptions

As DMLConstraintException contains child exceptions, the default DCErrorHandlerImpl will skip this exception during the error display. In this example, we will override this behaviour to display customized messages for DMLConstraintException.

To define a custom error handler for use by the binding layer, create a Java class extending `oracle.adf.model.binding.DCErrorHandlerImpl`. In the custom error handler, override `skipException(Exception ex)` method to display nested `DMLConstraintException` as shown in the following code snippet:

```
//Custom error handler class

public class CustomErrorHandler extends DCErrorHandlerImpl {

  public CustomErrorHandler() {
    super(false);
  }

  public CustomErrorHandler(boolean b) {
    super(b);
  }

  /**
   * This method does the following:
   * 1. Tells framework to display DMLConstraintException
   * by returning false.
   * 2. Tells framework to skip
   * SQLIntegrityConstraintViolationException by returning
   * true.
   * 3. Method follows the default display rule for
   * other exceptions which is as follows-
   * If an exception is a RowValException or a
   * TxnValException
   * and they have nested exceptions, then this method
   * return true for not to display the exception in the UI.
   * It returns false for all other exceptions.
   */
  @Override
  protected boolean skipException(Exception ex) {

    if (ex instanceof DMLConstraintException) {
      return false;
    } else if (ex instanceof
      SQLIntegrityConstraintViolationException) {
        return true;
      }
    return super.skipException(ex);
  }
}
```

Step 3: Registering the CustomErrorHandler

The last step in this exercise is to make the binding container to use the custom error handler for handling exceptions from business components. To register the custom error handler for use by the binding layer, follow the steps listed:

1. Select the `DataBindings.cpx` file in the application navigator editor. You can find this file under the `<view Controller>/adfmsrc/<project package>` folder.

2. Select the **root node** of the **CPX** file in the structure window. In the property inspector for the root node of the CPX file, enter the fully qualified name of the custom class that you created as the value for the **ErrorHandlerClass** field.

How does the CustomErrorHandler implementation work?

At runtime, when the user updates an employee row in the UI with an e-mail address used by another record and commits the changes, the database throws a unique key violation error to the caller. The ADF framework catches the error thrown by the database and creates `DMLConstraintException` which contains details about the error as well as the constraint name that caused the exception (`EMP_EMAIL_UK`). During the render response phase of the page, the ADF framework engages the error handler implementation (`DCErrorHandlerImpl` or its customized version) to format the errors for presenting on the UI. At this stage, `DMLConstraintException` resolves the error message for the constraint name `'EMP_EMAIL_UK'` from the associated message bundle classes. The `CustomMessageBundle` class used in this example is queried during this phase. The error handler implementation passes this message to the view layer for display.

Skipping validation

Support for skipping validation by a framework is as important as support for triggering validation. You might want to skip validation under certain circumstances. For example, skip validation when the user clicks the **Cancel** button on the page to undo the changes. The following are the offerings from Oracle ADF for skipping validations.

Skipping validations in the ADF Faces layer

ADF Faces allows you to alter the normal processing sequence for command components and input components using the immediate attribute. This property is in fact inherited from the underlying JSF stack. You can use this property to skip validation cycles as explained here:

- When you set immediate property to true for a command component, the framework will execute the associated actionListener or action method during the Apply Request Values phase, which otherwise would have happened during the Invoke Application phase. After the "immediate" execution of an action event, if there are no input components with the immediate attribute set as true in the submitted page, then the life cycle proceeds to the Render Response phase.

- When you set the immediate property to true for an input component, the framework will execute the ValueChangeEvent method during the Apply Request Values phase, which otherwise would have happened at the end of the Process Validations phase. If there are no input components with immediate set as true in the submitted page, then the life cycle proceeds to the Render Response phase.

As the events for the components with the immediate property set as true are processed before the Process Validations and Update Model phases, no validation errors are encountered for the component. You can use this property to avoid unwanted validation execution during the page life cycle.

The following example uses the immediate="true" setting for a Cancel button:

```
<af:commandButton actionListener=
  "#{bindings.Rollback.execute}" text="Cancel"
    immediate="true" id="cb13">
  <af:resetActionListener/>
</af:commandButton>
```

Skipping validations in the business components

You can use the `SkipValidation` property associated with the page definition file for bypassing validations initiated through the binding layer. The `SkipValidation` property is applicable only for those validations defined at entity level or transaction level. In other words, none of the attribute level validations are affected by this property.

To set the `SkipValidation` property for a page:

1. Open the page definition file in the editor.
2. Select the root node of the page definition file in the structure window.
3. Select the appropriate value from the **SkipValidation** drop down in the property inspector window.

The following are the possible values for the `SkipValidation` property:

Skip Validation property value	Description
false	This is the default value for `SkipValidation`. This setting just ensures the normal flow for validation during form submission.
custom	Use this property if you don't want the framework to execute the default validation logic. If you set `SkipValidation="custom"`, then you should specify a `CustomValidator` implementation in the page definition file. The value for the `CustomValidator` property should be an EL expression that evaluates to a bean which implements the `oracle.binding.BindingContainerValidator` interface.
skipDataControls	This setting skips validations defined at transaction level in an entity object. However, the framework will execute validation rules defined at attributes level or at entity objects level for rows which are modified in the current transaction.
true	This setting makes the framework skip all validations defined at entity or transaction level during post back of the form. With this setting, all entity level and transaction level validation happens when you commit a transaction.

Summary

You now should have an understanding of the validation exceptions and error handling in ADF. Specifically, you learned about the validation support in the different layers of a fusion web application and the validation life cycle in an ADF application. You also learned how to customize the default validation error handler for an application. Towards the end of the chapter, you saw how to declaratively skip validations defined in business components.

The next chapter summarizes the best practices and coding tips that developers will find useful when building ADF applications. This chapter is very important for you as a developer and it is worth spending time on each item that we discuss.

12

Oracle ADF Best Practices

This chapter summarizes the best practices and coding tips that developers will find useful when building ADF applications. Learning the best practices will help you to avoid common pitfalls that others might have faced. The content for this chapter is based on input from various teams who have successfully used ADF. The following topics are discussed in this chapter:

- Setting up the project structure for your Fusion web application
- The lifespan of ADF Business Components
- The best practices and performance tuning for ADF
- Internationalization of Fusion web applications
- Ensuring high availability for Fusion web applications

Introduction

In this chapter you will learn standards, conventions, and tips and tricks that you can apply to your Fusion web applications today. Let us begin with the best strategies for application source setup. Moving forward, we will discuss better practices and tips for ADF development.

Setting up the project structure for your Fusion web application

The very first step before starting to build an application is to decide on the architecture and setting up the source structure. You must consider the following factors while deciding on the application architecture and application source layout; size of the application, deployment requirements, release cycles for each module, degree of interaction between various modules, and interaction with external applications. The project structuring should be a well-thought decision and it should be driven by the business use cases and technology requirements of the target application. Let us take a quick look at the commonly used application source layouts for ADF applications. In the discussion that follows, we assume that JDeveloper is the IDE used for building applications and OJDeploy is the tool used (which comes with JDeveloper by default) for packaging and deploying the source.

Single application workspace comprising of multiple projects – monolithic approach

This is the simplest architecture for a Fusion web application. In this model the entire application uses a single JDeveloper workspace, which may contain one or more model and view controller projects based on the complexity of the application. In a real-life scenario, you may see the following variations in the single monolithic workspace approach:

- **Single view controller** and **model project**: This is the simplest application model. This could be the right choice for simple demo applications or proof of concepts.

  The view controller project can contain JSF pages, page fragments, task flows, and managed beans. The model project may contain entity objects, view objects, one or more application modules, and Java classes.

  The advantage of this model is its simplicity. This is suitable for small applications where a single developer will be working in most of the cases and no code sharing is involved with other applications. The major disadvantage is the poor reusability of modules.

- **Single view controller** and **multiple model projects**: This project structure contains a single view controller project and multiple model projects. When you split a project into multiple projects, special care must be given to decide what depends on what. You must avoid the possibility for a cyclic dependency between projects in an application. This is discussed under the topic *How to avoid cyclic dependency between modules in this chapter*.

This source layout approach will fit for small to medium sized business applications where the numbers of UI pages are minimal (below 50 pages) and the degree on interaction (through binary reusability) with applications is less.

- **Multiple view controller** and **model projects**: This is a slight variant of the previous structure. This application structure may contain multiple view controller projects and model projects in a single application workspace. One of the view controller projects will be logically designated as the *master view controller* which will act as a master module for the entire application. The master view controller project stores application-specific configuration files, build script, and dependency details. The main view controller project will be referring to other view controller projects in the application workspace for the purpose of accessing bounded or unbounded task flows. Numbers of projects in an application are driven by the business functionality and modularity that you may require for an application. The view and model projects are split into multiple projects based on business functionality and reusability requirements.

This structure will fit for small to medium sized applications with a relatively large number of UI pages (above 50 pages).

Multiple application workspaces controlled by a single master application– microkernel approach

The single application workspace approach may work for most of the real-life applications. However this is not a universal solution. This approach may fail if your organization has multiple applications talking to each other and one application wants to use services as libraries from the other applications. Interestingly some organizations may have different strategies on bundling binaries as well. For example, based on market demand, an enterprise may want to bundle services exposed by multiple applications into a new product and release it in line with their existing product portfolio. A solution for such a scenario is to keep business modules loosely coupled. You can split the business functionalities across multiple subsystems and create separate application workspaces for each subsystem. Also, you must have a single master application workspace which controls the final application artefact. Most of the large scale applications follow this structure. The advantages of this model are as follows:

- Improves modularity of the system
- Maintenance becomes easier

- Rapid development time, new modules can be tested independently
- Improves reusability of the modules

Though there are definite advantages with this approach, it comes with certain challenges. The management of development processes requires more effort with this approach. Some of the points you should keep in mind with this approach are as follows:

- As the components used in the final application artefact are scattered across multiple application workspaces, default dependency management mechanisms provided by the JDeveloper IDE may not work. You may need to follow a certain discipline during development.

- Extra effort is associated with the management of multiple application workspaces. Each workspace needs to be managed independently and version controlled.

Guidelines for setting up the application source using the microkernel approach

If you have multiple ADF based applications talking to each other and sharing some common artefacts, you may eventually go for the microkernel approach for setting up the applications source. The following are a few tips for setting up the project source that is scattered across multiple applications:

- Make sure you create one workspace for each deployable **Enterprise Archive (EAR)** file. This is very important because JDeveloper (and ADF in particular) stores application level configuration metadata files such as `jps-config.xml`, `connections.xml`, and `adf-config.xml` at the application workspace level.

    If you have multiple workspaces, make sure that the workspace contents are logically independent and they do not overlap each other.

- An application can have multiple model and view controller projects. Business functionality should be the major driving factor in deciding the projects, second comes the technology specific constrains. For example, you might have a view controller project and a model project for HR Services. Note that a project represents a unit of deliverables. You can split large projects into sub projects to achieve the desired modularity and reusability.

- Projects are also organized by how they want to share that code with others. For example, in a real-life scenario you might actually have two model projects for the HR Services application – one that is public which can be shared with other projects or applications, and one that is private which is private to the application. If needed, you can pull out the UI specific functionalities from the public model project and keep them in a separate UI model project. The following diagram illustrates this concept:

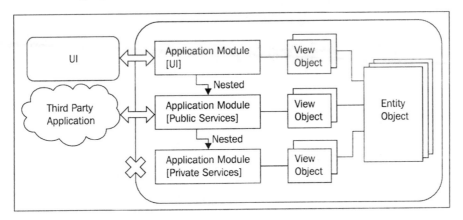

- Each project creates a single **Java Archive (JAR)** file. If you use JDeveloper as IDE for building an application, typically this JAR would be packaged as an ADF library (a JAR file with ADF specific metadata that eases the application assembly).

- If you have multiple applications sharing common resources then follow some guidelines which may make your life easier.

  Make sure all "public projects" generate JARs to a public location `<CommonNetworkPath>/apps/public/jlib`. Less public ones get created in a more specific location (public folder located under an application folder), for example, `<CommonNetworkPath>/apps/hr/public/jlib`. JARs that are completely private to the workspace go under the application folder, for example, `<CommonNetworkPath>/apps/hr/components/master/jlib`.

The following diagram summarizes the points that we discussed in this section. This diagram shows how you can set up the project source for your application that uses artefacts provided by other ADF applications. Note that all the artefacts are shared as an ADF library. If you use Maven or any other build tool you can use JAR artefacts.

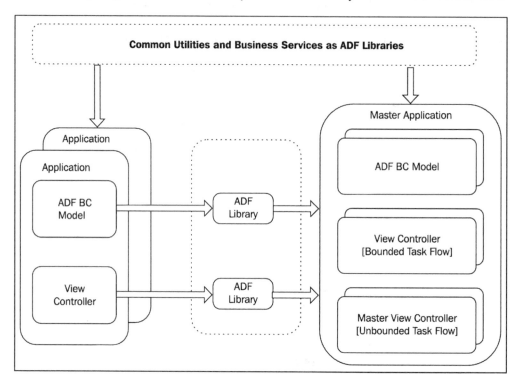

In the previous diagram the master application workspace consumes the ADF libraries from other applications. The ADF libraries may contain business services (model project) or UI components such as page template, custom components, or task flows.

How to avoid cyclic dependency between modules

When you split a single module to multiple sub modules, the biggest challenge is how to decide what goes to what module and avoid cyclic dependencies between them. You can use the following thumb rule for splitting a single monolithic model into multiple projects, which may make your life much easier:

4. Identify the common services and utilities for the application and move them to a common project.

5. Identify logically independent business modules for the application and build the model project for them. They can consume services (that they are dependent on) from the common project, but not from any other business modules.

6. Identify a more granular level of business modules and build model projects for them. Make sure these modules are dependent only on those modules identified in the previous steps. In other words, the dependency should always be linear. Continue this process until you finish the logical splitting of model projects for all business use cases. Note that there is no hard-and-fast rule on the number of modules; sometimes you may even need to refactor existing modules during the development phase to avoid cyclic dependencies.

While adding more model or view controller projects, you must make sure that each one bears unique package names. This is very important as ADF expects certain configuration files in specific folders relative to the package names. Keeping unique package names ensures that they don't override each other at runtime.

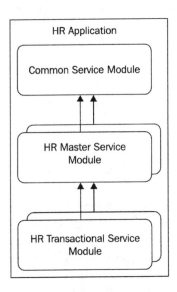

The previous diagram illustrates how the business logic layer of an HR application is split into three modules. You can see that common utilities (helper classes) are placed in a common module which is consumed by all other modules in the system. The next level contains all the master data setup related modules. The business components for your lookup tables or code tables come under this module. All the transactional modules come next on the ladder which can consume services exposed by both common and master setup modules.

We are not discussing coding standards for Fusion web applications in this chapter. To learn about naming conventions and coding standards for ADF applications, refer to the topic *Naming Conventions* in the chapter *Reusing Application Components* in *Oracle Fusion Middleware User's Guide for Oracle Application Development Framework*. To access the documentation go to `http://www.oracle.com/technetwork/developer-tools/jdev/documentation/index.html` and choose **Oracle JDeveloper and ADF Documentation Library | Fusion Developer's Guide**. Use the **Search** option to find specific topics. You can also refer to the ADF coding standard documentation created by the Oracle ADF Enterprise Methodology Group, available online at `https://sites.google.com/site/oracleemg/adf/files`.

The life span of ADF Business Components

This section discusses the lifespan of business components used in a Fusion web application. This will help you in fine-tuning the performance of your ADF application.

We will start our discussions on lifespan with an application module first and then move towards view object, row set, and entity objects. As we move forward, you will also see different declarative options to fine-tune the business components participating in the page lifecycle.

Life span of an application module

When you access a data bound ADF Faces page from your browser, the application server receives the request and routes it to the appropriate application. This request is intercepted by the binding filter which initializes the binding context for the requested page. During this stage, the framework grabs the data controls used in the page binding for accessing the underlying application module. Data control acts as a thin wrapper (proxy client) over the application module. The ADF Faces rich client framework takes over the processing thereafter and starts the page lifecycle. During the early stages of request processing, the framework creates a component tree which is a runtime representation of the JSF page.

The framework acquires an instance of the application module from the application module pool when it is referenced within the request for the first time. This happens during the render response phase when the data bound UI elements require to read data. When components ask for data, the framework will evaluate the associated binding EL expression. The EL evaluator used by ADF delegates the call to the binding layer classes which will check out the appropriate application module instance from the pool for use.

By default, the framework eagerly loads all the components added to an application module, such as view object instances and nested application modules, when it is instantiated. You can specify the `jbo.load.components.lazily` parameter to JVM to control this behaviour as `java -D jbo.load.components.lazily = true` or `false`. Alternatively, you can override this property for individual application module definition by setting `LoadComponentsLazily = "default"`, `"true"` or `"false"` in the application module XML file. If you set `LoadComponentsLazily = "default"` in the XML file, then the runtime will observe the default value set for the JVM. If there is no value set for the JVM, then the default runtime behavior is the eager loading of components. If this flag is set as "true", then child components such as view objects or nested application modules are instantiated and added to the application module only when the client refers to them by calling through `Applicat ionModule::findViewObject(String voName)` or `ApplicationModule::findApp licationModule(String amName)`.

 To learn the life cycle stages for an application module, refer back to the topic *Lifecycle of an application module* in *Chapter 6, Introducing the Application Module*.

How the framework allocates an application module for serving a client request

By now you must have a basic understanding of how binding layers grab application module instances from the pool when it is referenced in a page lifecycle. In this section you will see how the framework manages instances in an application module pool and performs garbage collection whenever required. The initial application module pool size is determined by the initial pool size parameter (`jbo.ampool.initpoolsize`) specified in the application module configuration file (`bc4j.xcfg`). Alternatively, you can configure this property at the application level using the `adf-config.xml` file located under the `META-INF` folder. This is treated as 0 by default. The framework will use this parameter to create the specified number of application module instances when the pool is initialized for the very first access.

To reduce the delay in instantiating application modules, it is recommended to keep this value at 10 percent (buffer size) more than the expected number of concurrent application module instances required to service the concurrent users. When a client request tries to grab an application module instance and if there are no un-referenced instances available in the pool, then the following algorithm is used by the framework to allocate an application module instance for serving the request:

1. The framework will check to see whether the application module used for serving the last request from the current requestor is available in the pool and if found, then allocate it for serving the current request. Continue to the next step if no application module is allocated for the requestor in this step.

2. If the previously used application module is not available in the pool, then the framework creates a new instance using the following algorithm:

    i. The framework creates a new application module instance if the number of application module instances in the pool which were released in the managed state (session affinity) is less than the recycle threshold value (`jbo.recyclethreshold`).

    ii. The framework creates a new application module instance if all the instances in the pool are in use, and the current pool size is less than the maximum pool size (`jbo.ampool.maxpoolsize`).

    Continue to the next step if no application module is allocated in this step.

3. If the number of application module instances in the pool, which were released in a managed state, has reached the recycle threshold value then the framework will look for the least recently used (LRU) instance in the pool and will allocate it for the current requestor. While doing so, the runtime will start the passivation and activation cycle for the chosen application module. Continue to the next step if no application module is allocated in this step. This typically happens if all application modules in the pool are in use.

> **Passivation** is the process of disassociating an application module instance from its client session so that the instance can be reused to conserve memory. **Activation** is the process of associating an application module instance with a client session so that it can service a request.

4. If all instances in the pool are currently in use and the number of instances in the pool has reached the maximum pool size, then the framework will notify of the development by throwing an exception to the caller.

If you want to refresh on application module activation cycle, refer to the topic *Lifecycle of an application module* in *Chapter 6, Introducing the Application Module*.

More configuration options for an application module

This section lists some more configuration options that you may want to know while tuning an application module. Refer to the section entitled *Overriding default properties of an application module* in *Chapter 6, Introducing the Application Module*, to learn about the editor support for configuring the properties of an application module.

- **jbo.recyclethreshold**: The recycle threshold value (`jbo.recyclethreshold`) decides the maximum number of application module instances in the pool that are released in the managed state mode by the previous clients. The framework maintains them in the pool till the limit crosses the recycle threshold value anticipating that the previous client may ask for it again in the future. In other words, the framework starts the passivation-activation cycle for the application modules in a pool when the number of concurrent users exceeds the recycle threshold value. The default value for the recycle threshold parameter is set as 10.

- **jbo.doconnectionpooling**: This setting forces the application module to release the JDBC connection back to the connection pool each time it is checked-in back to the pool at end of the request. You can configure this property by selecting the **Disconnect Application Module upon Release** checkbox in the application module configuration editor.

- **jbo.txn.disconnect_level**: By default when an application module is disconnected from a client, all the associated view object instances and its row sets are closed and removed from the memory. They will be recreated upon activation. This behavior can be controlled by configuring `jbo.txn.disconnect_level` for the application module. The default value for this property is `0`. You can set `jbo.txn.disconnect_level = 1` to bypass the database centric passivation cycle of business components. When setting `jbo.txn.disconnect_level = 1`, the application module, view objects, and row sets all remain in memory but their corresponding references to JDBC objects, such as open cursors, are closed and cleaned up. Typically in-memory passivation of view object and row set is used in conjunction with connection pooling.

- **jbo.maxpassivationstacksize**: This property controls the number of snapshots that the business component framework manages for performing the undo (rollback) operation. These snapshots can be used either programmatically or declaratively to restore the state of the application later on. The default value for the maximum passivation stack size is 10 which is good for most of the generic use cases. The passivation stack size is used by the framework to limit the entries in the following scenarios:

  i.   When you explicitly call `passivateStateForUndo(String id, byte[] clientData, int flags)` on application module for the purpose of creating a snapshot of its state.

  ii. When the task flow acquires save points on entry.

When an application module is removed from the pool

Cleaning up an unused application module is very important for the health of the system. The framework deploys an application module pool monitor on each **Java Virtual Machine (JVM)** to clean up the unused instances. The application module pool monitor scans through the instances in the pool at the time interval of every 600000 milliseconds (10 minutes) by default. This default pool polling interval can be overridden by using the `jbo.ampool.monitorsleepinterval` parameter. When the pool monitor performs the cleanup, it will try to bring down the number of instances in the pool to the maximum available size configured using the `jbo.ampool. maxavailablesize` parameter. The default maximum available size is 25. You must override this default value based on the number of concurrent users for the application module. Again these values depend upon usage patterns of the services exposed by the application module.

If you do not want the pool monitor to clean up the entire pool when all the instances are eligible for removal, you can specify the minimum available size for the pool using `jbo.ampool.minavailablesize`. The default minimum available size is 5.

The pool monitor uses the following algorithm to remove unused application module instances. It uses two independent strategies to identify the candidates for removal:

1.   The application module pool monitor will remove all the unused application module instances which have been living in the pool for more than 3600000 milliseconds (one hour) without bothering about the minimum available size for the pool. You can override the maximum time to live for an application module by setting the `jbo.ampool.timetolive` configuration parameter. The default value is one hour. In real life applications, you may not use this property. To ignore this property at runtime, you can set the value to -1.

2. The application module pool monitor will remove all the application module instances that are idle for 600000 milliseconds (10 minutes). This clean up will be stopped when the number of instances in the pool reaches the minimum available size. The idle timeout for an application module can be configured using the `jbo.ampool.maxinactiveage` parameter. The default idle timeout is 10 minutes.

If you do not want your application module to be removed from the pool, you can set `jbo.ampool.timetolive` and `jbo.ampool.maxinactiveage` to -1.

Configuring the application module pool parameters – a case study

Consider a human resource management application built using Oracle ADF. The runtime statistics of this application shows an increased use of application module instances in the morning between 10 A.M. and 11 A.M. (when office hours start). During this period, average use of the application module instances vary from 100 to 120. The rest of the time the average use is around 100 application modules. For this application, you can set the parameter `jbo.ampool.minavailablesize` to 100 and `jbo.ampool.maxavailablesize` to 120. If you set the `jbo.ampool.minavailablesize` to 100, then the pool of available instances will shrink to 100 after the period of heavy use ends. How quickly this happens is determined by the `jbo.ampool.maxinactiveage` parameter and by how frequently the pool monitor reclaims unused instances, which is determined through `jbo.ampool.monitorsleepinterval` parameter.

Though the previously mentioned configuration parameter values will work for the use case that we discussed in the previous example, in real life, coming up with accurate values for these parameters may not be an easy job. In such cases you can follow the following thumb rule:

- Keep `jbo.ampool.maxavailablesize` 20 percent higher than normal use.
- Keep `jbo.ampool.minavailablesize` the same as `jbo.ampool.maxavailablesize`. This ensures that application module pool is always prepared to meet a high load.

Life span of a view object, row set, and query collection in a regular application module

The lifecycle of a view object starts when a client calls `executeQuery()` on a view object instance in order to retrieve the data collection from the underlying data source. For a data bound web page, the execution of a view object happens when it is referenced for the first time in page lifecycle.

During view object execution, the framework will engage the appropriate callback methods in the view object implementation class as it finds appropriate. Refer back to *Chapter 5, Advanced Concepts on Entity Objects and View Objects*, if you need a quick brush up on lifecycle callback methods for a view object.

Once the query is executed, the framework will populate the default row set of the view object with the rows in the result set returned by the JDBC call. While doing so, if the view object is backed up by entity objects, the framework will partition attributes based on the entity usages and will generate appropriate entity instances to back up the view rows. The newly instantiated entity objects will be added to the appropriate entity cache based on the entity definition type. View row instances are backed up by the query collection object. If the view object is based on an entity object, then each row in the query collection will point to the entity row as shown in the following diagram:

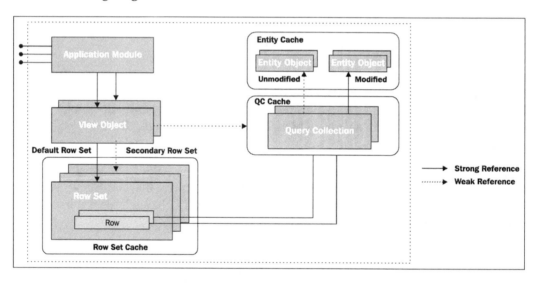

The entity object acts as the actual data storage for a view row in this case. At runtime, each attribute in the view row will actually be referring to the underlying entity object instance while reading or writing attribute values. If you need a quick brush up on this subject, refer back to *Chapter 4, Introducing View Objects*.

A view object can have multiple row sets for managing a collection of rows from a query. As shown in the previous diagram, every row set in a view object is backed up by a query collection object that stores the result set returned by the JDBC APIs. All query collections belonging to a view object in a regular application module are cached as weak references. A query collection is referenced by one or more row sets in a view object instance if they share the same row filter values (search parameter values). All the secondary row sets in view objects are also weakly referenced by the parent view object. This is done to hide the complexities of memory management from an application developer.

 A **weak reference**, simply put, is a reference that is not strong enough to force an object to remain in memory. The garbage collector will remove all the weakly referenced objects during the next garbage collection cycle if they are not strongly referenced in the programme and reachable by traversing only a weak reference.

During a query execution, if the framework finds that the query collection backing the row set is no longer available, it creates a new query collection and refreshes it to bring in the result set from the database. On the contrary, if the weak reference was not cleaned up and if the query collection is still around, the framework will re-use the cached query collection, and if the cached query collection is already in an executed state, it will not be executed again.

Note that the parent view object gives special treatment to the default row set. The default row set resulted from the query execution is strongly referenced by the parent view object. Obviously, the default row set will survive the garbage collection cycle and stay in memory along with the parent view object instance till the owning application module is recycled.

The query collection cache and view accessor row set

When a client accesses a view accessor attribute in a parent view row, the framework will return the row set from the cache if it is found for the current row filter. If you do not want the framework to read from the cache, override the `createViewLinkAccessorRS()` method in the parent view object and call `clearCache()` on the access view object as shown in the following code snippet. This tip is useful if you want `af:tree` or `af:treeTable` to query the database each time you expand the parent node.

```
//In view object implementation class
@Override
```

```
//This method is invoked each time client access view accessor
//attribute. E.g. When you expand parent tree node,
// createViewLinkAccessorRS() in parent view object is
//invoked to read child rows
    protected ViewRowSetImpl createViewLinkAccessorRS
       (AssociationDefImpl
        assocDef, ViewObjectImpl accessorVO,
    Row masterRow, Object[] values){
    if ("<viewlink accessor attribute name>".equals
        (assocDef.getName())) {
      accessorVO.clearCache();
    }
    return super.createViewLinkAccessorRS
        (assocDef, accessorVO, masterRow, values);
}
```

The life span of entity objects

Entity object cache implementation stores unmodified rows in a weakly referenced hash map (`java.util.WeakHashMap`). When you insert, modify, or delete rows, they will be transferred to a strongly held list which will survive the garbage collection cycle. All weakly referred entity rows in the cache will be cleaned up in memory pressure, leaving dirty (new, modified, and deleted) rows intact.

What if you want to clear an entity cache at specific points in time?

If you want to clear an entity cache at definite points in the application lifecycle, the following are a few tips:

- **Configuring an application module to clear the cache during transaction rollback or commit**: You can configure the application module to clear its query collection (query collections cache all row sets used in a view object instance) and entity cache during transaction commit or rollback by using `ClearCacheOnCommit` (default is false) and `ClearCacheOnRollback` (default is true) properties in the application module XML file. An example is as follows:

```
<AppModule
  xmlns="http://xmlns.oracle.com/bc4j"
  Name="HRServiceAppModule"
  Version="11.1.2.61.83"
  ClearCacheOnRollback="true" ClearCacheOnCommit="true"
  ComponentClass="com.packtpub.model.HRServiceAppModuleImpl"
  LoadComponentsLazily="default">
```

You can set this property at runtime by calling
`setClearCacheOnCommit(true)` on the `oracle.jbo.Transaction` instance
read from an application module.

* **Programmatically clearing cache**: Apart from the declarative approach for
clearing cached entity rows, you can also use APIs for clearing the cache. Call
`clearEntityCache(String entityName)` on `oracle.jbo.Transaction`
for programmatically clearing *unmodified* entity rows in the cache. This call
will also clear all view row caches based on this entity object. This method
will throw `oracle.jbo.InvalidOperException` if you are trying to clear
an entity object cache with pending changes. The following code snippet
illustrates how you can programmatically clear the entity cache:

```
//This is defined in application module implementation
//class.
//This method clears specified entity cache.
public void clearEntityCache(String fullEOName){
    /**
    * Clears the cache of the specified Entity Object.
     * You should use fully qualified EO name
     * A value of null clears the caches of all Entities.
     * If a View Object uses the Entity Object,
    * the View Object's cache will also be cleared.
    * */
    this.getDBTransaction().clearEntityCache(fullEOName);
}
```

The life span of row sets in a shared application module

All the query collections in shared application modules are strongly referenced.
The framework deploys a shared query collection pool monitor to clean up the
inactive query collection objects in a shared application module. The shared query
collection pool monitor polls the shared query collection pool at an interval of
1800000 milliseconds (30 minutes). The default polling interval can be overridden
by configuring appropriate values for the `jbo.qcpool.monitorsleepinterval`
parameter using the application module's **Edit Configuration** screen. During polling,
if any inactive shared query collection is detected, then the framework will remove
it from the memory. The default idle timeout is 900000 milliseconds (15 minutes).
This can be overridden by setting the value for `jbo.qcpool.maxinactiveage`. Once
all the inactive query collections are removed from the cache, the pool monitor
will check to see if the total weight of the pool (total number of rows in all query
collections for a view object) exceeds the maximum weight allowed for all the query
collections in a view object.

If the total weight exceeds the maximum weight allowed, the pool monitor will start removing the least recently used (LRU) query collections until the weight falls below the limit. This is configured using `jbo.qcpool.maxweight` for an application module. By default there is no limit set for query collections in a view object.

The life span of binding objects

When we talk about the lifespan of business components, the story is incomplete without referring to the ADF binding layer that wires the UI with business components. When a data bound page is accessed from a browser, `ADFBindingFilter` intercepts the request and creates the `BindingContext` object that represents the content of the `DataBindings.cpx` file at runtime. The binding context is cached in the HTTP session object for use in subsequent requests from the same user. During the page lifecycle, before starting the restore view phase of the JSF page, the ADF framework creates the binding container that represents the contents of the page definition file for the requested page and caches it inside the binding context. This contains the data control frame, control bindings definitions, and executables. The UI components will be wired to the model data through the binding definitions objects. Note that when the client components refer to the model data through binding EL expressions, it is the binding layer that fetches the data collection by executing the appropriate view object instance. At the end of the request, ADF runtime will reset the values associated with all the control binding objects. However, the binding context and binding containers are retained for serving postback requests from the same client or user.

The framework will remove all the cached binding containers when the user navigates away to a new data bound page with a page definition file behind it. The binding context is removed from the session cache on session timeout, session invalidation, or on session failover.

The best practices and performance tuning for Oracle ADF

This section examines the best practices and tuning options around the Oracle ADF framework. We will start with ADF Business Components. As we move forward we will cover the best practices for the ADF model (binding), controller, and view layers. Tips under each section are further categorized for ease of reading and quick reference.

 Note that we are not repeating topics that we discussed in the previous section of this chapter. To get the complete picture, make sure that you read the previous section as well, that is *Life span of ADF Business Components*.

Tuning tips for an application module

The following are a few tips for building scalable business services using an application module. These tips are categorized for ease of reading and quick reference.

Tips for optimizing an application module initialization

This section discusses tips for optimizing the initialization phase of application modules.

- Enable lazy loading for application module contents, such as view object instances and nested application module instances. When you turn on the **Lazy Loading** option, ADF runtime will defer the creation of view object instances and nested application modules until they are requested. Possible lazy loading options are **Lazy Loading**, **Non-Lazy Loading**, and **Runtime Instantiation** (default). When you leave the option as default, the framework will observe the default value set for `jbo.load.components.lazily` at the Java Virtual Machine level (which is specified through `-Djbo.load.components.lazily = true` or `false`), and if any value is found, the framework uses it for the application module. We have covered the usage of this parameter in the *Life span of an application module* section previously in this chapter.

- Sometimes you may need to explicitly create application module instances by calling `oracle.jbo.client.Configuration.createRootApplicationModule (String qualifiedAMDefName, String configName)`. This kind of use case arises only when you need to access the application module outside the binding context, for instance, accessing the application module from the `javax.servlet.http.HttpServlet` class or from a batch job. If you create an application module via the `Configuration.createRootApplicationModule(String qualifiedAMDefName, String configName)` API, you should call `Configuration.releaseRootApplicationModule(ApplicationModule appModule, boolean remove)` to release it. Failing to do so will keep the application module instance in memory and will potentially result in a memory leak. When you use the `releaseRootApplicationModule(ApplicationModule appModule, boolean remove)` API make sure you are passing `false` to the `remove` flag to keep it in the pool for future use. This will give you the benefit of potentially reusing that application module (after it was reset) over creating a new application module instance which is slightly expensive. If the `remove` flag is set as true in the `releaseRootApplicationModule(ApplicationModule appModule, boolean remove)` call, the framework will remove the application module from the pool. An example is as follows:

```
//In client Java code
public void invokeAMMethod(){
 ApplicationModule applicationModule = null;
 try{
   String amDefName = "com.packtpub.model.HRServiceAppModule";
   String configName = "HRServiceAppModuleLocal";
    //Create AM instance
   applicationModule =
       Configuration.
       createRootApplicationModule(amDefName, configName);
   //Business logic goes here.......
 }catch(Exception ex){
   //Handle Error
 }finally{
   //Release AM instance back to the pool
   if(applicationModule != null)
     Configuration.releaseRootApplicationModule
         (applicationModule, false);
 }
}
```

Tips for optimizing resource usages in an application module

This section discusses tips for optimizing resource usage in an application module at runtime.

- If the web page or business logic implementation demands data from multiple application modules, then you can build composite services by nesting the desired application modules under a root application module. The nested application modules will share the same transaction context and database connection with the root application module. When the application modules are nested, the configuration for the top-most parent application module overrides all the child application modules' configurations.

- You should avoid adding multiple application modules to your page. If you need to logically segregate business functionalities into multiple application modules, nest them under a root application module whenever possible. While dropping view object instances onto a page, make sure that you are using view object instances from the nested application module, which is displayed underneath the root application module in the **Data Controls** panel.

All nested application modules share the same database connection and transaction context. Note that a nested application module cannot have different database connections and you should avoid the nesting of application modules if they need to talk to different databases.

When you call `commit()` or `rollback()` on a transaction object associated with a root application module, the framework invokes commits or rollbacks on all the nested application modules as well. The following example shows how to call commit on a transaction associated with the root application module:

```
//This is defined in application module implementation class
public void commitAllAMs(){
  this.getRootApplicationModule().
      getTransaction().commit();
}
```

- The shared application module allows the sharing of a single application module instance with multiple requests. They are typically used for caching the shared static data. For example, when you need to build an LOV to display seeded data which does not change very frequently at runtime, you can use shared application module for holding such view objects. When you use the shared application modules for accessing read only data, you do not really need to have a separate transaction context for each usage. This can be achieved by setting a string value for the `jbo.shared.txn` property for the desired application module. ADF enforces application modules with the same `jbo.shared.txn` (named transaction) parameter configuration value (a string value) to share the same transaction object at application level. The transaction object holds the database connection and entity cache. By configuring the same value for `jbo.shared.txn` you can avoid multiple instances of the shared application module from creating a new transaction context. Note that connection pooling is disabled for shared application modules by design.

  For better performance, enable connection pooling and in-memory passivation by setting `jbo.doconnectionpooling = true` and `jbo.txn.disconnect_level = 1` respectively. The `jbo.txn.disconnect_level=1` instructs the framework to manage the partially fetched JDBC `ResultSets` in memory rather than passivating their state. To learn more, refer back to the topic *More configuration options for an application module* in this chapter.

Tips for fine-tuning the JDBC API use

This section discusses tips for fine-tuning the JDBC API use in your web application.

- If you want to limit the caching of JDBC cursors used in a session, override `jbo.max.cursors` to a lower value in the application module configuration. The default value is 50.

- Use JDBC data source over JDBC Connection URL in an application module so that your application can leverage the features offered by the container.

- If you have multiple application modules connecting to the same database, make sure the same JDBC data source name is used in all application modules so that you just need to configure a single JDBC data source and maintenance will be easier.

Coding guidelines for application modules

This section discusses coding guidelines for application modules.

- Do not call `postChanges()` on `DBTransaction` in an application module if you are not going to commit the transaction within the same request. Also avoid using the global temporary table or PLSQL global variable to hold the result across requests. This is because as the database connections are getting pooled for a Fusion web application, there is no guarantee that all the client requests in a user session will be using the same database connection. When the framework releases a connection object to the pool, all pending changes on that connection will be rolled back.

- Avoid defining member variables in an application module and view object classes. Note that custom member variables added to the business components will not survive the activation-passivation cycle. If you have member variables defined in an application module class whose state needs to be maintained across requests, or if you have variables stored in a `UserData` hash table associated with the application module session, then you must make sure that they are activation safe. In other words, ADF framework does not take care of serialization and deserialization of user defined objects during passivation and activation of application module. To learn more, refer back to the topic *Programmatically passivating custom data* in *Chapter 6, Introducing the Application Module*.

- At the end of a request, the framework releases the application module instance used for serving the request. By default, the application module is released in the managed (stateful) mode which means that the framework would try to preserve the application module's state across requests within a user session. You can override this behavior by explicitly invoking `resetState()` on `DCDataControl` at the end of the request. This call will release the application module in the unmanaged (stateless) mode. This is useful for scenarios such as user logout where the system does not need to maintain the state after logout. Note that this call only affects the current application module instance in the current request. The framework will again use the managed release level for the next request onwards. The following example illustrates the use of this API:

```
//In managed bean class.
//This method is triggered when user clicks logout
public void handleLogout(ActionEvent act){
    //Get the binding context and look up data control
    BindingContext bcContext = BindingContext.getCurrent();
```

```
DCDataControl dcDCDataControl = bcContext.findDataControl
    ("AppModuleDataControl");
  //Release the application module in unmanaged state
dcDCDataControl.resetState();
  doLogoutTasks();
}
```

- Query the data source to use a view object whenever possible. If you want to use JDBC APIs such as `java.sql.Statement`, `java.sql.PreparedStatement`, or `java.sql.CallableStatement` directly in your code, use the appropriate create functionality exposed by the `oracle.jbo.server.DBTransaction` class for obtaining the desired statement instance. The following example, call `createPreparedStatement(String str, int noRowsPrefetch)` on `DBTransaction` to create the `PreparedStatement` object.

```
//In application module implementation class

public String getDepartmentName(int deptId) {
  PreparedStatement preparedStatement = null;
  ResultSet rs = null;
  try {
    String sql =
      "SELECT Departments.DEPARTMENT_NAME FROM DEPARTMENTS"
        +"Departments WHERE Departments.DEPARTMENT_ID=?";
      int noRowsPrefetch=1;
      //Creates PreparedStatement object
    preparedStatement = getDBTransaction().
        createPreparedStatement(sql, noRowsPrefetch);
    preparedStatement.setInt(1, deptId);
    rs = preparedStatement.executeQuery();
    if (rs.next()) {
      return rs.getString(1);
    }
  } catch (SQLException e) {
    throw new JboException(e);
  } finally {
    if (preparedStatement != null) {
      try {
        //Close the statement
        preparedStatement.close();
      } catch (SQLException e) {
        e.printStackTrace();
      }
    }
  }
  return null;
}
```

- Use the native Java types instead of jbo data types whenever possible. This is especially useful when you need to expose the business service for public use. The client code will be clean and neat in this case without any dependency to custom jbo data types. Refer to the section *Attribute types in an entity object* in *Chapter 3, Introducing Entity Object*, to learn more on data types use.

Tuning tips for view objects

The following are tips for building a scalable data access layer using a view object. These tips are categorized for ease of reading and quick reference.

Tips for optimizing query execution in a view object

This section discusses query optimization tips for a view object.

- If the query executed by a view object is expected to have a WHERE clause all the time, add the WHERE clause directly to the query at design time. This will ensure that in all cases the view object executes the query with the appropriate WHERE clause.

- Use the named bind parameters over indexed bind parameters wherever possible. This makes your code more readable. Also, if the named bind parameter repeats multiple times in a query, you just need to bind only once.

- Avoid using SELECT * FROM <TABLE_NAME> in a query for a view object. This may easily break your code if the table definition changes in the future.

- Use declarative query mode whenever possible. Declarative view objects have the capability to dynamically adjust the SELECT clause to include only those columns used in the binding definition. Also this mode helps you to build the query declaratively. However, you may not be able to use the declarative query mode if the query contains the complex WHERE clause which cannot be built using declarative query mode.

- Build view objects are backed up by entity objects whenever possible. Note that both updatable view objects and read only view objects can be backed up by entity objects. While building a read only view object, backed up by entity objects, make sure you are choosing non-updatable entity objects. The following are the advantages of using entity based view objects:
    i.   Out of the box support for managing newly created rows across view objects through the view link consistency feature.
    ii. View row instances backed up by (updatable) entity objects are updatable and they participate in the transaction post cycle.

    iii. Multiple view objects backed up by the same entity objects will be referring to the same data storage. This reduces the memory foot print and also helps to reflect the changes performed on an entity object across all view objects.

Tips for optimizing database read operations

This section discusses tips for optimizing database read operations for a view object.

- If you want to use a view object for creating rows alone, select the option **No Rows** under the **Tuning** section in the **General** tab of the view object editor. This will avoid unwanted data retrieval when you use this view object in a JSF page. If the same view object is used in both create and query mode in the same application module, then you should call setMaxFetchSize(0) on the view object instance programmatically when it is being used in insert mode. You should unset or set an appropriate maximum fetch size when the same instance is used in the query mode.

- You must set an appropriate fetch size for view objects. To configure the fetch size, open the view object in the editor and set the appropriate value for the **in Batches of** field in the **General | Tuning** section. If the view objects are used in the UI, the fetch size must be the range size of the iterator in the page definition file +1. This is because the binding layer always fetches an extra row to see if it has hit the end of the collection or not. In range paging cases (UI with pagination), it should be the range size of iterator +3.

- You should not set a very high value for the fetch size. When you use JDBC API for executing a SELECT statement, JDBC implementation pre-allocates memory to hold the returned result set based on the fetch size. For view objects used in the UI, the fetch size should be ideally less than 30. Note that the ADF BC framework would use the fetch size only if the SQL flavor is Oracle.

- You can override the fetch size at the view object instance level when exposed through an application module, and at view accessor level when used in another view object.

- When you need to display a large number of rows in the read-only mode, specify the **Access Mode** for the underlying view object as **Range Paging** or **Range Paging Incremental**. This mode keeps only the current range of rows in memory. However this may not be the right choice if you need to edit the rows.

- Specify **Range Size** for the view object so that only required rows are fetched to the middle tier.

  Note that if the access mode is one of the range paging type (**Range Paging, Range Paging Auto Post**, or **Range Paging Incremental**), then the runtime will use the range size to build paginated queries restricting the resulting rows to be less than or equal to range size. For Range Paging Incremental, the page size in the query is equal to the range size multiplied by the cache factor. The framework will not generate a paginated query if the view object uses other access modes such as **Scrollable** or **Forward Only**.

Tips for setting a global row fetch limit for view objects

This section discusses how to globally limit the rows returned by a view object for an application, and related use cases.

- You can globally specify the row fetch limit for all view objects used in an application by configuring the row fetch limit in adf-config.xml. This property prevents a poorly formulated query from fetching a huge number of rows to the middle tier .When a client tries to access rows beyond the row fetch limit, the framework will log an oracle.jbo. RowLimitExceededWarning message.

  If you want to bypass a row fetch limit for a certain view object, choose one of the following approaches as appropriate:

  i. Specify the maximum fetch size on a view object to a large value (that is large enough to accommodate all possible rows returned by the query). You can specify this programmatically via the setMaxFetchSize() call on the view object instance, or declaratively via the **Only up to row number** setting which is displayed under the **Tuning** section of the **General** tab of the overview editor for the view object. The maximum fetch size can be set at the view object definition level, the view object usage (in the application module) level, or at the view accessor level. Specify the value where you really want to override it. In most cases, you really do not need to specify the maximum fetch size at the view object definition level, rather set it at the view object usage level, or the view accessor level where it will make the view object more reusable.

ii. Override `getRowLimit()` in `ViewObjectImpl` to return `-1`. An example is as follows:

```
//In view object implementation class
/**
* A limit may be applied on the number of rows in a
* query collection. When
* a new row is requested from the database and the limit is
* exceeded a warning is raised. By default the limit is
* configured as an application wide setting in adf-config.
xml.
*
* @return a limit on the number of rows in a query
collection. If no row limit is enforced
*/
@Override
protected long getRowLimit(){
  //-1 means no limit on rows returned
    return -1;
}
```

iii. Set the access mode of the view object as Forward Only (`FORWARD_ONLY`). Forward Only view objects are not subjected to a row limit as they do not cache any row set.

Tuning view criteria in view objects

In this section you may find some useful tips for optimizing view criteria defined in a view object.

- Define the appropriate view criteria in a view object if you need to conditionally append the WHERE clause to the query. View criteria definitions are also useful for declaratively building a search panel in the UI. You can also expose it in the service interface as appropriate. As a bonus, the view objects with view criteria definitions become more reusable and user friendly.

- While using a search panel backed up by view criteria, if an empty search results in thousands of rows, then you should mark at least one view criteria item as **Required** or **Selectively Required** in order to make sure the query contains at least a search condition in all cases that limits the number of rows read from the database. To improve the query performance in a database, you can index the columns that form a view criteria item, especially for those view criteria items which are marked as **Required** or **Selectively Required**. Avoid both the **Contains** and **Ends With** operator for **Required** or **Selectively Required** view criteria items. These operators result in inefficient queries as they fail to use the database indices while scanning through the table.

- The view criteria items defined in the view criteria can take string literals as values for the attributes. To force the runtime to generate temporary bind variables instead of directly using literal values while generating the WHERE clause for the view criteria, set useBindVarsForViewCriteriaLiterals as true in adf-config.xml. The following is an example:

```
<adf-config ...>
  <adf-adfm-config xmlns="http://xmlns.oracle.com/adfm/config">
    <defaults changeEventPolicy="ppr"
     useBindVarsForViewCriteriaLiterals="true"/>
  </adf-adfm-config>
  ...
</adf-config>
```

This feature will help you to improve the performance of query execution by caching SQLs and it will also reduce the chance for SQL injection.

Tips for optimizing LOV definitions

This section discusses tuning tips for the LOV defined in a view object (model driven LOV definitions).

- Use smart LOV definitions whenever possible. You can define a smart LOV by choosing the **Filter Combo Box** option in the LOV editor. This may help you to restrict the number of rows returned by the combo box LOV.

- Avoid choosing the **Query List Automatically** feature for the LOVs with search pop ups such as **Input Text with List of Values** and **Combo Box with List of Values**. This setting will cause the framework to execute the LOV view object query when the LOV pop up is displayed.

- The number of rows returned by an LOV data source view object is decided by the ListRangeSize value set in the list binding definition in the view object XML file. The list range size for the range fetch enabled LOV components such as **Input Text with List of Values** and **Combo Box with List of Values** should be equal to the number of rows to be displayed on the LOV +1. Only **Choice List**, **Combo Box**, **List Box**, and **Radio Group** list types require ListRangeSize as -1. The value ListRangeSize = "-1" for a list binding implies all rows are read in one go. The following is an example for the <ListBinding> definition present in a view object:

```
<ListBinding
    Name="LOV_DepartmentId"
    ListVOName="DepartmentVA"
    ListRangeSize="25"
    NullValueFlag="none"
    MRUCount="0">
    <AttrArray Name="AttrNames">
```

```
        <Item Value="DepartmentId"/>
    </AttrArray>
    <AttrArray Name="ListAttrNames">
        <Item Value="DepartmentId"/>
    </AttrArray>
    <AttrArray Name="ListDisplayAttrNames">
        <Item Value="DepartmentName"/>
    </AttrArray>
    <DisplayCriteria/>
</ListBinding>
```

- By default, IDE sets `RowLevelBinds` as `true` in the view accessor definition. This settings means that the values for the LOV may change for each row and the framework will fire separate database queries for each row if there is no query collection found for the query filter in the cache. Set this flag to false if LOV's row set does not depend on any bind variables driven by attribute values in the current row, in other words, set this flag to false if the set of LOV values is the same for every row. An example is as follows:

```
<ViewAccessor
    Name="DepartmentVA"
    ViewObjectName="com.packtpub.model.view.DepartmentVO"
    RowLevelBinds="false"/>
```

- Do not specify unwanted dependency attributes on an LOV enabled attribute. This will result in unwanted refresh (query execution) of the underlying LOV row set whenever the dependency attribute value changes.

- Choose the LOV types judiciously. Use **Input Text with List of Values** or **Combo Box with List of Values** if the LOV displays more than 25 elements. These LOV types are loaded with data only when the user opts to view the list.

General tips for tuning view objects

This section discusses some general tips for tuning your view objects.

- When a view object is used only in validation or in business logic to query the data source and not to be displayed in the UI, define it as a read-only view object with the access mode set as **Forward Only** to avoid the caching of rows in the middle tier.

- When you add view link instances between master and child view objects, the framework will actively execute a child view object while you navigate between master rows. Avoid using view link instances if you do not need them.

- While dealing with master detail view objects linked through a view link instance, the framework by default does not cache any child row set. To enable the caching of child row sets, select the **Retain View Link Accessor** option for the child view object.

- If a view object contains transient attributes whose value can be derived from other persisted attributes, you must turn off passivation for those attributes; this gives better performance. To disable passivation for a subset of a view object's transient values, deselect the **Include All Transient Values** checkbox in the **General** tab of a view object editor, and check the **Passivate** checkbox only for those transient attributes which cannot be derived from the existing attributes.

- If you need to display data in the read-only mode, use either of the following:

    i.   Define read only view object.

    ii. Define view object based on non-updatable entity object.

Coding guidelines for view objects

This section discusses coding guidelines for the view object implementation class.

- When you need to define a view object at runtime, consider using (if feasible) APIs for creating `oracle.jbo.server.ViewDef` over the method `createV iewObjectFromQueryStmt(String voName, String sqlStatement)` in `oracle.jbo.server.ApplicationModuleImpl`. In the later case, there will be an additional round trip to the database to read the table metadata for constructing the view object definition. Refer to the appendix titled *More on ADF Business Components and Fusion Page Runtime*, to learn about the APIs for creating dynamic view objects. You can download the appendix from the Packt website link that we mentioned at the beginning of this book, in the *Preface* section.

- While accessing attribute values of a view object row or entity row, use the `getAttribute(int index)` API which takes the attribute index as a parameter over the `getAttribute(String name)` call which takes the attribute name as the parameter. The latter performs an extensive scan to look up the index before reading the value.

- Create a secondary `RowSetIterator` if you need to iterate over rows of view objects in your business logic. Note that the default `RowSetIterator` is typically bound to the UI components and use of it in business logic will give you weird results at runtime. Call `closeRowSetIterator()` on the `RowSetIterator` instance once you are done with the iteration. An example is as follows:

```
//In application module implementation class

public void reviseEmployeeSalary() {
  RowSetIterator empRowSetIter = null;
  try {
```

```
        //Create secondary row set iterator
      empRowSetIter = this.getEmployees().
        createRowSetIterator("MyEmpRI");
      while (empRowSetIter.hasNext()) {
        Row empRow = empRowSetIter.next();
        processEmployeeRow(empRow);
      }
    } finally {
      //Close the secondary row set iterator
      if (empRowSetIter != null)
        empRowSetIter.closeRowSetIterator();
    }


  }
```

- When you want to execute a query with different bind variable values without affecting the default row set used in the UI, you must create a secondary row set and execute the same. It is best practice to close the row set once you are done with it. If you use the **Retain Association Accessor RowSet** option, then you should not call `closeRowSet()`.

```
//In application module implementation class
public boolean validateEmployeeSalary(Integer empId) {
    //Create secondary rowset
  RowSet empRowSet =
      this.getEmployees().createRowSet("MyEmployeeRS");
   empRowSet.setNamedWhereClauseParam("bindVarEmpId",
      empId );
  empRowSet.executeQuery();
  while(empRowSet.hasNext()){
    EmployeeEO empRow = (EmployeeEO)empRowSet.next();
    if(empRow.getSalary() < 1) {
        //close rowset
      empRow.closeRowSet();
      return false ;
    }
  }
   //Close rowset
  empRowSet.closeRowSet();
  return true ;
}
```

- Do not add attributes to a view object after executing it. You cannot add dynamic attributes to a view object once it is executed.

- If you need to populate transient attribute values based on complex business logic or using data from a third party data source and you want to avoid re-execution of this initialization logic for each access to the attribute, then you can override `createRowFromResultSet(Object qc, ResultSet resultSet)` in the `oracle.jbo.server.ViewObjectImpl` class. The following is an example:

```
//In view object implementation class

public class EmployeesVO extends ViewObjectImpl {


    /**
     * executeQueryForCollection - overridden for
     * custom java data source support.
     */
    protected void executeQueryForCollection(Object qc,
        Object[] params, int noUserParams) {

        getThirdPartyDataSource().filterOutValues(params);
        super.executeQueryForCollection(qc, params,
            noUserParams);
    }


    /**
     * createRowFromResultSet - overridden for custom
     * java data source support.
     */
    protected ViewRowImpl createRowFromResultSet(Object qc,
        ResultSet resultSet) {
        EmployeesViewRowImpl rowImpl =
            (EmployeesViewRowImpl)super.
            createRowFromResultSet(qc, resultSet);
        rowImpl.populateAttribute(
            EmployeesViewRowImpl.LOCATIONDETAILS,
            getThirdPartyDataSource().getValueForAttribute(
            EmployeesViewRowImpl.AttributesEnum.
                LocationDetails.toString(),
            rowImpl.getKey().getAttributeValues()));
        return rowImpl;
    }

    //This part of the sample deals with custom data source
    //Added for demo purpose.
    ThirdPartyDataSource thirdPartyDataSource = null;
```

```
        public ThirdPartyDataSource getThirdPartyDataSource() {
            if (thirdPartyDataSource == null) {
                thirdPartyDataSource = CustomServiceFactory.
                                        getDataSource(this);
            }
            return thirdPartyDataSource;
        }

    }
```

- Prevent the caching of row sets in the access mode of the view object to **Forward Only**. Setting forward only will prevent the caching of previous sets of rows as the dataset is traversed. For example, you may use this access mode when you just need to iterate over the row set in order to process rows one by one, or check for some conditions by taking one row at a time. If you want to conditionally set the access mode at runtime, call setForwardOnly(true) on the view object. You can restore the original access mode later based on the use case. The advantage of doing this programmatically is that you can use the forward-only mode only when needed, while other users of the view object will not be affected. The following is an example:

```
//In application module implementation class
public void processEmployees() {
   //Get view object instance
   ViewObject empVO = getEmployees();
   byte origMode = empVO.getAccessMode();
   //Set access mode to FORWARD_ONLY
   empVO.setAccessMode(ViewObject.FORWARD_ONLY);
   while (empVO.hasNext()) {
     Row row = empVO.next();
     processRow(row);
   }
   //Restore the access mode
   empVO.setAccessMode(origMode);
}
```

- When you modify the WHERE clause fragment of the view object by calling setWhereClause() on a view object, make sure that you use bind variable for supplying the parameter values. For example, if you use the following approach for building the WHERE clause, each time when the employee ID changes, the database engine will has to parse the query and compile it before execution.

```
//In application module implementation class
public Row findEmployee(Integer empId) {
   //Get the employee VO
```

```
ViewObject empVO = getEmployees();
//Define WHERE clause
String whereClause = "EmployeeEO.EMPLOYEE_ID = '"
    + empId + "'";
empVO.setWhereClause(whereClause);
empVO.executeQuery();
return empVO.first();
}
```

The previous code can be rewritten using a bind variable as follows:

```
// In application module implementation class
public Row findEmployee(Integer empId) {
  //Get the employee VO
  ViewObject empVO = getEmployees();
  //Define WHERE clause with bind variable
  String whereClause = "EmployeeEO.EMPLOYEE_ID = :empId";
  empVO.setWhereClause(whereClause);
  empVO.setNamedWhereClauseParam("empId", empId);
  empVO.executeQuery();
  return empVO.first();
}
```

- There are multiple ways to supply bind variable values for a view object. You must know what means what when you build business components. The following are the details:

    i. Using `setNamedWhereClauseParam(String name, Object value)` on `ViewObject`: This method sets the value on a default row set of the view object instance. In other words, this does not affect the secondary row sets that you or the system generates.

    ii. Using `setVariableValue()` on `VariableValueManager`: The variable value manager manages named variables and their values for a view object instance. The bind variable value set by calling `setVariableValue(String name, Object value)` on `oracle.jbo.VariableValueManager` may reflect across all row sets if the bind variable values have not been set on them by explicitly calling `setNamedWhereClauseParam(String name, Object value)`. This is because the call to `setNamedWhereClauseParam()` on a row set takes precedence over the variable value manager's copy of the bind variable value. The following example uses the `VariableValueManager` API to initialize the bind variable value:

```
//In application module implementation class

public void executeEmployeeVOForEmpId(Integer emptId) {
    //EmployeesVO has WHERE clause set as
    //WHERE EmployeeEO.EMPLOYEE_ID = :bindVarEmpId
    ViewObject employeeVO = findViewObject("EmployeesVO");
    VariableValueManager vm = employeeVO.
        ensureVariableManager();
    vm.setVariableValue("bindVarEmpId", emptId);
    employeeVO.executeQuery();


}
```

iii. Using `setWhereClauseParam(int index, Object value)` on the view object: You will use this method for view objects with the binding style of **Oracle Positional** or **JDBC Positional**. An example is as follows:

```
//In application module implementation class

public void executeEmployeeVOForEmpId(Integer empId) {
    ViewObject employeeVO = findViewObject("EmployeesVO");
    //Define WHERE clause with JDBC style bind var :NNN
    String whereClause = "EmployeeEO.EMPLOYEE_ID = :1";
    employeeVO.setWhereClause(whereClause);
    employeeVO.setWhereClauseParam(1,empId);
    employeeVO.executeQuery();
}
```

- You must avoid the unwanted execution of the count query by the framework whenever possible. Count queries make sense when the client really needs the total number of recodes. For example, it is used by the ADF Faces framework to size the scroll bar for a table or tree table. However you must try avoiding the execution of expensive count queries in your business logic. The following are the various APIs exposed in a view object that you may use in your business logic to find the number of rows returned by a query.

    i. When you call `getEstimatedRowCount()`, `getCappedQueryHitCount()`, or `getCappedRowCount(cap)` on a view object, the framework fires a count query on the underlying database tables

    ii. When you call `getRowCount()` on a view object, the framework will fetch all the rows from the underlying table that matches the search criteria and iterates the rows to find the total number

Use the previous APIs only when you really need to identify the total number of rows. Don't use them just to find out whether a query retuned any rows. For example, the following code snippet illustrates how you can check whether a view object query returned any rows without firing a count query:

```
//In application module implementation class

public void processEmployeeRows() {
  ViewObject employeeVO = getEmployees();
  employeeVO.executeQuery();
  Row r = employeeVO.first();
  //Check whether first rows is null
  if (r != null) {
    //Query returned some rows
    //Your business logic goes here
    processEmpRows(employeeVO.getRowSet());
  }
}
```

Similarly, don't use a count query in your code just for setting the "upper limit" for iterating over all rows returned by view object. Instead, you can call hasNext() on the row set and iterate over rows if it returns true.

* To assign bind variable values at runtime or to modify the WHERE clause used in the query or to apply view criteria at runtime, just before the query execution, override the method prepareRowSetForQuery(ViewRowSetImpl vrs) in oracle.jbo.server.ViewObjectImpl and add your logic. If you want this modification to happen across all row sets for a view object, you can override the prepareVOForQuery() method instead. The following example overrides prepareRowSetForQuery(ViewRowSetImpl) to supply the value for the bind variable bindVarDeptId just before executing the query. An example is as follows:

```
//In view object implementation
public void prepareRowSetForQuery(ViewRowSetImpl vrs) {
  //Set the value for bind variable ':bindVarDeptId' only
  //for default row set
  if(vrs.isDefaultRowSet()){
    vrs.setNamedWhereClauseParam( "bindVarDeptId",
getUserDeptId());
  }
  super.prepareRowSetForQuery(vrs);
}
```

On a related note, you should not override `executeQueryForCollection(O bject qc, Object[] params, int noUserParams)` to make changes to the WHERE clauses and bind parameters used in the query because this method is getting engaged late in the view object data fetch cycle. By the time the control reaches this method, the bind parameter values are already extracted to build the WHERE clause. Also this method will not get engaged with the `ViewObjectImpl::getEstimatedRowCount()` call which is typically fired during the rendering of the UI components, such as table and tree table, for identifying the total row count.

- Avoid using SQL conversion functions such as `to_date()`, `to_number()`, and `to_char()` in the query. You must do this in the middle tier Java class instead. This will keep your business logic independent of the underlying data source.

- You can use Groovy expressions to initialize bind variables used in a view criteria as well as in the SQL WHERE clause with runtime values. For example, use the Groovy expression `now()` for the current date and time, and `today()` for the current date.

Tuning tips for entity objects

The following are tips to build scalable data persistence logic using ADF entity objects. These tips are categorized for ease of reading and quick reference.

Design guidelines for entity objects

When you define an entity object, make sure that it has unrestricted access to the underlying database table. This is required for the proper functioning of certain framework functionalities, such as unique key validation, which requires access to all records in a table. In other words, if you build an entity object based on a database view or synonyms, make sure that the framework is able to read all the required records to perform out of the box functionalities enabled on it.

Tips for validating entity objects

The following tips may help you to use validation features offered by ADF entity objects more effectively in your ADF application.

- You must use the validation feature provided by business components to validate business data whenever possible. Use the appropriate attribute level validation to validate individual attribute values. To perform validation across attributes in a row, such as `fromDate` should be less than `toDate`, use entity level validation. Avoid adding validation to attribute setter methods or to any other entity object lifecycle method.

- To create custom validation that needs to be triggered once for the entire entity collection before committing the transaction, define a method validation in the entity object and in the **Validation Execution** tab select **Defer the execution to Transaction Level**. To avoid the firing of transaction level validation, during the postback of a page that uses this entity object, keep SkipValidation = "skipDataControls" in the page definition file. Avoid the list validator if the list size is large. List validator implementation reads the list elements in sequential order which may not be an ideal choice if the size is huge.

General tips for tuning entity objects

In this section you will learn general tuning tips for entity objects.

- Always define primary keys for an entity object. The IDE will add the RowId attribute to an entity object if the underlying table is missing a primary key definition. You should not use RowId as a primary key for an entity object in a real-life application because it is not guaranteed to be unique when the database runs in a clustered environment.

- You need not set the foreign key values for a child entity object in a composite association; this is taken care of by the framework.

- Retain the association accessor row set in an entity object as appropriate. You can traverse the association accessor attribute in an entity object to read rows returned by destination entity objects. The following code snippet is copied from the DepartmentEO entity object. This example illustrates how you can iterate over EmployeeEO entity instances returned through the association accessor:

```
//In entity object implementation class

public void processEmployess(){
  //
  RowSet empRowSet = this.getEmployees();
  while(empRowSet.hasNext()){
    EmployeeEO r = (EmployeeEO)rs.next();
    //Do something  with each entity row
    _processEmployeeEORow(r);
  }
}
/**
 * @return the associated entity oracle.jbo.RowIterator.
 */
public RowIterator getEmployees() {
  return (RowIterator)getAttributeInternal(EMPLOYEES);
}
```

Each time you access a target entity object using the association accessor, the framework creates a new row set object with a default iterator object which will enable you to iterate over the associated entity row collection. If your code needs to read rows using the association accessor multiple times within the same transaction, then ideally you should avoid the creation of a row set for each access. The ADF Business Components framework gives you an option to retain a previously used association accessor for future use. This option is available in the **General | Tuning** section of the entity object editor. Note that this option comes with side effects of increased memory usage. Use this option if it gives clear benefits. When you choose to retain the association accessor, you must call reset() on the row set before iterating over it. The reset() call resets the default row set iterator to a slot before the first row.

- If your table has a column to hold the version for the row, mark it as **Change Indicator**. This will save some CPU cycles whenever the framework needs to check whether any other user has modified the row in the database that is updated by the current user. If you have changed the indicator columns set for an entity object, then only those columns will be used for the *stale data* check.

- You can override the default query generated for an association through **Where** and **Reverse Where** clauses properties in the association XML. When you override **Where** or **Reverse Where** clauses, the framework, by default, will turn off association consistency for the target. This means that the target row set will not see un-posted rows. If you want the row set to see the un-posted rows, you need to call setAssociationConsistent(true) on the entity row set by overriding createAssociationAccessorRS(A ssociationDefImpl assocDef, ViewObjectImpl accessorVO, Row masterRow, Object[] values) on the source entity object. You should call setRowMatch(RowMatch rowMatch) on the association accessor view object in the overridden method to add the in-memory filter in order to prevent all un-posted rows appearing in the row set. Refer to the topic *In-memory filtering with RowMatch* in *Chapter 4, Introducing the View Object*, if you need a quick brush up on using RowMatch.

- Do not select transient attributes when you define associations between entity objects. You must use SQL derived attributes in such cases. Note that transient attributes from an entity are not guaranteed in internal view objects created by the framework for performing various utility services.

Coding guidelines for entity objects

This section discusses coding guidelines for entity object classes.

- If you use a surrogate primary key for an entity object, initialize it by either using a Java unique ID generator or using the database sequence. Using these techniques makes sure that the surrogate primary key attribute is initialized during the instance creation itself. You can do this by setting a default value expression built using Groovy or by overriding the `initDefault()` method in the entity object implementation class.

- You must override the `initDefaultExpressionAttributes(AttributeLi st nameValuePair)` method in the `oracle.jbo.server.EntityImpl` class to add the logic for the defaulting attribute values which need to be called during row creation as well as when the entity row is refreshed back to the initialized status.

- While accessing the attribute values of a entity object row or entity row, it is better to use `getAttribute(int index)` over the `getAttribute(String name)` API. The latter performs expensive scans to look up the index before reading the value. If you need to read or update attribute values of an entity object multiple times in a transaction, you can generate an entity object class with attribute accessors (getter and setter methods) included. Accessing attribute values using `get<AttributeName>()` or `set<AttributeName>(value)` internally uses an index to identify the attributes which gives better performance and improves the readability of your code.

- If you have many entity rows participating in a transaction, use the **Update Batching** option. Note that in the following scenarios, the framework will not support batch update:

    i. If the entity object contains one or more CLOB or BLOB attribute types.

    ii. If one or more attributes are marked as either **Refresh on Insert** or **Refresh on Update**.

    iii. If you have overridden the `doDML()` method of the entity object to use custom logic or PLSQL procedure for posting changes to the data source.

- Override the `create()` method in the entity object implementation to change the status of the entity object when attributes are defaulted. When you create a new row in the UI using the `CreateInsert` action binding, the binding framework marks the state of the entity object as `STATUS_INITIALIZED`. Even if you have default values configured for some attributes, the status does not change and such entity objects will not participate in the transaction commit cycle. If you want to override this behavior, then override the `create()` method in the entity object implementation class and invoke `setAttribute(value)` for defaulting attribute values.

- Never import any client side classes or binding classes in your business service implementation code. This will help you to keep your business service layer independent of the client technology and make the implementation more scalable.

- To read the current database time in the middle tier, call the `oracle.jbo.server.DBTransactionImpl.getCurrentDbTime()` method. If you need the current time as `java.sql.Date`, then you may want to use the following API: `new java.sql.Date(((DBTransactionImpl)(this.getDBTransaction()))).getCurrentDbTime().getTime());`.

  To read the current database date using Groovy expressions, use the following: `DBTransaction.currentDbTime`.

Tuning tips for ADF model

When you run a data bound Fusion web page, it is the ADF binding that is doing the job of executing the underlying data source and returning the collection for use in the view layer. This section discusses the best practices and tuning tips for an ADF binding layer. These tips are categorized for ease of reading and quick reference.

Tips for tuning executable bindings

You will learn coding tips for executable bindings present in a page definition file in this section.

- Do not use `Refresh = "always"` for the executable iterator binding. This may result in refreshing the corresponding iterator multiple times during a page lifecycle. The default refresh setting (`Refresh = "deferred"`) will meet most of the use case requirements.

- You should not use the `<invokeAction>` executable to execute initialization logic during the page load. This is because the `<invokeAction>` executable will be invoked multiple times during the page lifecycle. To avoid multiple invocations you will end up setting `RefreshCondition` for `<invokeAction>` which will have serious side effects when the ADF Faces page works in a streaming mode. For example, a UI table component with lazy content delivery paints the table in multiple requests from the browser. If you want to execute some initialization logic before the page runs, it is recommended to use method call activity in the task flow.

  Although `<invokeAction>` is not recommended, if you are working on legacy implementations you may still want to use `<invokeAction>`. For example, you may want to invoke a fusion web page from a non-ADF application, which is not necessarily part of any task flow. In case you use `<invokeAction>` make sure that the appropriate value for `RefreshCondition` is set to avoid multiple invocations during the page lifecycle. The refresh conditions `"always"` or `"default"` are not valid for `<invokeAction>`.

- If your page uses the `<methodIterator>` executable to populate the UI table component, make sure that the corresponding `<methodAction>` binding definition has `CacheReturnDefinition = "true"`. This property ensures that the data collection returned by the method is retained across requests from the client. This is required to enable sort, search, and edit on a UI table bound to the `<methodIterator>`.

- You should not leave any unused executables or binding entry in a page definition file. Note that, by default, executables such as `<invokeAction>` and `<taskFlow>` will get executed even if they are not referenced in a UI. When you remove any data bound component from the JSF page during development, make sure you remove the corresponding binding entries from the page definition file.

- The EL expression when used in a page definition should always start with `${}` or `#{}`. The framework will not bother to evaluate the EL expression which comes in the middle of literal values. For instance, in the following parameter definition, the EL expression set for the parameter value will not be evaluated as the EL comes in the middle of the literal. An example of this is shown as follows:

```
<taskFlow id="deptTaskFlow" ...>
<parameters>
 <parameter id="path"  value="/oracle/demo/page/#{param.
virtualPath}/" />
</parameters>
</taskFlow>
```

The valid parameter value in this example is: value="#{param.virtualPath}.

Tips for optimizing data traffic between a binding layer and business components

The ADF data binding layer declaratively binds the UI controls to a data collection returned by a business service implementation. This section discusses tips to optimize the data traffic between a binding layer and a business component layer.

- The RangeSize property specified for an iterator binding decides the number of rows (page size) to be fetched to the client. To improve the data read performance, the RangeSize property must be set appropriately so that only the required rows are fetched to the middle tier.

- You can see similar RangeSize settings in the view object as well (**General | Tuning** section of view object editor). The RangeSize setting for the iterator binding will override the view object's range size at runtime if the value is greater than 0. If you want the runtime to use a range size set for a view object, keep RangeSize = "0" for the iterator binding in the page definition file.

- You should set RangeSize = "-1" for executable iterators bound to non-paginated list components (UI components without any scrollable behavior or pagination) such as af:selectOneChoice. This setting ensures that all rows are read by the iterator binding during the rendering of the page.

- If there are multiple UI components bound to the same iterator binding definition, the range size should be set as the maximum of all rows to be read for the components.

- The FetchSize property set for a view object instance in an application module should be the maximum range size configured for all iterators bound to the view object instance.

- The FetchSize property set for a view accessor used as data source for model-driven UI components such as LOV should not be lower than the number of rows displayed in the UI + 1. Keeping this value as 16 looks like works for most of the applications in general.

Tips for optimizing count query executions

This section discusses optimization techniques for count queries fired by certain UI components such as `af:table` and `af:treeTable`. These components execute count queries during the rendering of the page in order to find out the total rows returned by the underlying view object.

- When you use the `<af:table>` component to display data at runtime, the framework will fire a count query to size the table scroll bar accurately. This is essentially a SQL `SELECT Count (1)` query wrapping the `SELECT` query specified for the underlying view object. The count query is harmless if the number of records in the database table is less. However this becomes a very expensive affair if there are millions of records. You can configure the `<iterator>` binding to skip the count query execution altogether, or to put an upper cap on the total rows scanned using the `RowCountThreshold` property as shown in the following:

  i. If `RowCountThreshold = 0` (which is the default value), the iterator binding will execute the count query and return the row count.

  ii. If `RowCountThreshold < 0`, then the iterator binding will not execute the count query.

  iii. If `RowCountThreshold > 0`, then the iterator binding will execute the count query with `RowCountThreshold` as an upper limit. If the estimated row count is less than the value of `RowCountThreshold`, then the framework returns the number of rows in the estimated row count. If the estimated row count is greater than the value of `RowCountThreshold`, then it returns `-1`.

Coding guidelines for ADF binding APIs

This section takes you through the coding guidelines for ADF binding APIs. You may use these APIs in a managed bean to access the underlying model data.

- To programmatically execute a method binding, you can either call `execute()` or `invoke()` on the `JUCtrlActionBinding` instance. Though both usages are perfectly valid, if you want your custom error handler to be involved during this invocation use `invoke()` over `execute()`. The following is an example:

```
//In managed bean class
public void invokeUpdateDeptService(Integer deptId, String
deptName){
   // Get binding container
```

```
BindingContainer bc = BindingContext.getCurrent().
    getCurrentBindingsEntry();
  //Get action binding
JUCtrlActionBinding methodBinding = (JUCtrlActionBinding)
    (bc.getControlBinding("updateDept"));
Map params = methodBinding.getParamsMap();
params.put("departmentId", deptId);
params.put("departmentName", deptName);
methodBinding.invoke();


}
```

- If you want to invoke business methods exposed in an application module from a managed bean, use the binding API whenever possible. To do this, define the <methodAction> binding for the desired method in the page definition file and then use the binding API to invoke it. The following is an example:

```
public String updateEmployees() {
   // Get binding container
  BindingContainer bindings = BindingContext.
      getCurrent().getCurrentBindingsEntry();
  //Get operation binding for updateEmployees
  OperationBinding ob = bindings.
      getOperationBinding("updateEmployees");
  Object result = ob.execute();
  //Any error during execution
  if (!ob.getErrors().isEmpty()) {
    return "error";
  }
  return "success";
}
```

You should not bypass the binding layer while accessing business methods exposed by the data control. The use of binding APIs decouples the view layer from the business service implementation. As you are accessing methods through the binding layer, the error handler used by the current binding container would be available to report any error during invocation and this apparently provides a consistent error reporting experience.

- If you want to make use of an error handler provided by the binding container for reporting exceptions in a non-binding context, call `reportException()` on DCBindingContainer. The following example finds a view object from the iterator binding and invokes methods on it. The direct invocation of methods on business components occurs outside the binding context:

```
public void refreshDeptCollection() {

  try {
    //your business logic goes here
    DCBindingContainer bc = (DCBindingContainer)
        BindingContext.getCurrent().
        getCurrentBindingsEntry();
      //Finds iterator
    DCIteratorBinding iter = (DCIteratorBinding)bc.
        findIteratorBinding("DepartmentsIterator");
      //Get the view object
    ViewObject vo = iter.getViewObject();

      //Here you are working directly on VO instance
      //bypassing binding layer.
      //On error use DCBindingContainer to report error
    vo.executeQuery();
  } catch (JboException je) {
    //All the exceptions are reported
      //through DCBindingContainer
    DCBindingContainer bc = (DCBindingContainer)
        BindingContext.getCurrent().
        getCurrentBindingsEntry();
    bc.reportException(je);
  }
}
```

Tuning tips for ADF Controller and task flows

The following are tips for building high performing task flows. These tips are categorized for ease of reading and quick reference.

Tips for optimizing resource usage in a task flow

This section discusses tips for optimizing the resource usages in a task flow.

- Avoid eager initialization of task flows whenever possible; go for lazy loading as appropriate. You can use any one of the following for lazy initialization of task flow embedded in a region:

    i.   For a Facelet page, set the `activation = "deferred"` on the `<taskFlow>` element in the page definition file.

    ii. If the default activation setting is not feasible for you and your task flow still requires lazy initialization, then conditionally activate the task flow based on the EL expression set for `active` flag. To do this set the `activation` property on the task flow executable binding to `conditional` and EL bind the `active` property. When you specify activation as conditional, the framework will evaluate the EL expression set for the `active` property during the page lifecycle and if it returns true, the task flow will be executed.

- When you define a task flow, choose the **share data control with calling task flow** option whenever appropriate. This will cause the called task flow to share the data control with the caller. In simple words, with this setting both the calling and called task flow work on the same instances of data collections.

- Avoid unwanted save point creations whenever possible. If the transaction setting of a task flow is **Always Use Existing Transaction** or **Reuse Existing Transaction if Possible**, the framework automatically creates an ADF model save point (model save points store only the business component state, not the UI state) when you enter the task flow. This is useful only if the task flow leverages the declarative rollback feature. To avoid unwanted save point creation, deselect the **No save point on task flow entry** checkbox in the overview editor.

General guidelines for building successful task flows

This section discusses general guidelines for building best performing task flows.

- Avoid unwanted regions in the page. It is recommended to have a maximum of 10 regions in a page. There is a cost associated with a region. Each region added to a page will produce a different binding container and query execution which will eventually result in more memory and CPU usage.

- Use the `<multiTaskFlow>` binding to add regions at runtime. This is useful if you don't know the number of task flows to be rendered while designing the page. We discussed this topic in detail under the section *Dynamically adding multiple regions to a page* in *Chapter 10, Taking a Closer Look at the Bounded Task Flow*.

- It is recommended to go for an application-specific pattern for the purpose of handling authorization failure errors for task flows or views. You can disable or hide the navigation components based on user privileges for viewing a target view or task flow. This will give you consistent behavior across applications. By default, if a user does not have access to a task flow rendered in a region, then the framework handles it in the following ways based on the context of invocation:

  i. If the task flow is directly added to a page in an unbounded task flow, then an empty region is displayed to the user

  ii. If the task flow is added inside another bounded task flow view as a nested region, then the user will see an authorization check failure error message at runtime when he or she accesses the region

- If you need to redirect to a JSF page programmatically from the code, you must encode the URL using the `ControllerContext.getInstance().getGlobalViewActivityURL(viewId)` API. This call will do all the required encoding of the URL. Failing to do so will skip necessary tokens in the URL which are used to track the state of the view.

- You should be careful when you display a task flow in a pop up. By default, a task flow added as a region in a page gets executed when the parent page loads. You can use one of the following approaches to defer the execution of the task flow till the system displays it:

To process the pop up only when the client requested for it, set the `childCreation` property on the `af:popup` to `deferred` and `contentDelivery` to `lazyUncached`. When you keep `childCreation = "deferred"`, children will not be added to the component tree until the content delivery is made. Along with the UI settings, you must keep the `activation` property as `deferred` in the task flow executable binding. Note that when you use `childCreation = "deferred"`, you won't be able to use the following tags in the `af:popup` component: `f:attribute`, `af:setPropertyListener`, `af:clientListener`, and `af:serverListener`. Use `popupFetchListener` to initialize the popup contents as an alternative.

Coding guidelines for managed beans

This section discusses coding guidelines for a managed bean used in a Fusion web application.

- Define managed beans only in the task flow definition XML files. Do not mix the bean definitions across `faces-config.xml` and the task flow definition XML files.

- While using dynamic regions, make sure the scope of the managed bean returning the task flow ID is higher than the request. Otherwise, the framework will recreate a bean for each postback which may result in returning the default task flow ID in all cases.

- Never cache the binding context or binding container objects in a managed bean. Look up these objects as and when required.

- Never cache any memory scoped map object in a managed bean. If you do so, you will end up using stale data. You must read the scoped map whenever required. The following code snippet will help you to identify the right API usage to read various memory scoped maps:

```
ADFContext.getCurrent().getApplicationScope();
ADFContext.getCurrent().getSessionScope();
ADFContext.getCurrent().getPageFlowScope();
ADFContext.getCurrent().getRequestScope();
ADFContext.getCurrent().getViewScope();
```

- Do not evaluate the EL expressions in a program code if the corresponding API exists for reading the object. API usage is always faster than EL expressions. For example, API usage to get `DCBindingContainer` is more performant than using the EL expression `#{bindings}`.

```
//In managed bean class
BindingContext bc = BindingContext.getCurrent();
DCBindingContainer bindingContainer = (DCBindingContainer)
bc.getCurrentBindingsEntry();
```

Tuning tips for ADF Faces

The following are the tips for building high performing ADF Faces pages.

General tips for ADF Faces pages

This section discusses the best practices used for improving the performance of the ADF Faces components at runtime. We also discuss common coding mistakes that you may want to avoid.

- Use **Partial Page Refresh (PPR)** whenever possible. Make sure that you set the `partialSubmit` attribute to true for all actionable components, whenever possible, to optimize the page lifecycle. When `partialSubmit` is set to true, then only the components that have values for their `partialTriggers` attribute will be processed through the lifecycle.

- Do not generate a client component for the UI component if you do not need to access them from the client-side JavaScript. You can disable the client component creation by keeping `clientComponent = "false"` for the desired component.

- Always avoid long identifiers (ID) for User Interface components. Long identifiers for components increase the size of the generated HTML content.

- Do not use `jsp:include` to include pages with page definitions. Runtime will load only the page definition file of the parent page.

- The ADF Faces application displays session timeout messages if the user performs some action on the page after being idle for an extended period that exceeds the session timeout period specified in `web.xml`. If you want to suppress the session expiry message for a specific page (for example, login page) and want this message to be displayed for other pages, then you must set `stateSaving = "client"` for an `af:document` component tag for the page in which you don't want to display a session timeout. An example is as follows:

  ```
  <af:document title="login" id="d1" stateSaving="client">
  ```

- Do not EL bind the same data element to multiple editable UI components.

- Do not use more than 10 task flows in a page as `af:region`. It will adversely affect the performance of the parent page.

- Use an appropriate content delivery mode for the table and tree table. The following `contentDelivery` modes are supported by these components: `immediate`, `lazy`, and `whenAvailable` (default). In the `lazy` mode, the browser initiates separate requests for reading data after painting the table frame. `whenAvailable` acts as `lazy` if the model does not return the value immediately. You can override the default setting and keep `contentDelivery = "immediate"`, if you want the table content to be delivered in-line with the page content. Note that immediate delivery avoids multiple requests from the browser during page rendering. If the data read is reasonably faster, then `contentDelivery = "immediate"` gives better results as it avoids multiple round trips between the browser and the server.

- Use the `click-To-Edit` mode over the `edit-All` mode for tables. The `click-To-Edit` mode table lets the end user edit the selected rows in a lockstep fashion, one row at a time. This has the following advantages:

    i.   In `click-To-Edit`, non-editable rows are rendered as output components which tend to generate less HTML than input components.

    ii. Client components are not created for the read-only rows.

    iii. Validation phase is also optimized to handle one row at a time.

    iv. Lesser request and response data size.

Best practices for ADF Faces UI components

This section discusses about the best practices for ADF Faces components when used in the UI design.

- Do not mix HTML tags with ADF Faces components tags.

- Minimize the use of components with stretchable behavior. These components are low on performance than fixed size containers. If you are using geometry management enabled containers, try minimizing the number of child components. The following components are capable of stretching child components (geometry management): `af:panelAccordion`, `af:panelStretchLayout`, `af:panelTabbed`, `af:navigationPane`, `af:pannelSplitter`, `af:toolbar`, `af:toolbox`, and `af:train`.

- Minimize the use of column stretching in `af:table`. A table with column stretching takes more time to render on the client side.

- Minimize the use of `af:carousel`, `af:table`, `af:tree`, and `af:treeTable` in a page.

- Do not use multiple root components in a page fragment file. Regions with multiple root components will not perform well in the browser. You must wrap them using a top level container.

- Go for the deferred child component creation for `af:panelTabbed` by setting `childCreation = "lazy"`. With this setting, components are added to the DOM tree when the user opts to view it. This will help you to reduce the page component size. For `af:popup` components use `childCreation = "deferred"`.

Internationalization of Fusion web applications

Internationalization enabled applications offers its content in languages and formats tailored to target audiences. It can be adapted to various languages and regions without an engineering change. This section discusses internationalization guidelines for a Fusion web application in general:

- All the labels displayed in the UI must be stored in resource bundles: If the UI displays data rows from a view object backed up by entity objects, then you can define labels and tool tips for each attribute in the underlying entity object. If required, these labels can be overridden in the view object or in the JSF page as appropriate. To reduce the resource usage at runtime, you must define UI hints only for those attributes displayed in the UI. Avoid reusing labels for multiple attributes within the same entity object (or view object) or between entity objects (or view objects). This may make your life easier if you need to change specific labels alone based on the context of usage.

- Avoid hard coding locale in JSF pages: Avoid the hard coding format mask or pattern strings for locale sensitive data types such as date, date time, currency, and number in a JSF page. You can use resource bundles for storing locale specific format patterns. If your application allows the user to define locale specific patterns at runtime, a better option is to use a session scoped preference bean for the purpose of managing locale specific data.

```
<af:inputDate value="#{bindings.Date.inputValue}"
label="#{bindings.Date.label}">
    <af:convertDateTime pattern="#{userPrefBean.
dateFormatPattern}"/>
</af:inputDate>
```

- Use skinning as appropriate: Avoid hard coding fonts such as font name, family, and size. You must use standard locale aware skins instead.

Configuring the time zone for a Fusion web application

You can specify the time zone for a Fusion web application by configuring `<time-zone>` in `trinidad-config.xml` located in the `WEB-INF` folder of the application. To read the time zone object configured in `trinidad-config.xm`, use the following API:

```
TimeZone tz=AdfFacesContext.getCurrentInstance().getTimeZone();
```

You can access the time zone code by following the EL expression in the view layer `#{adfFacesContext.timeZone.ID}` which is equivalent to calling the API: `AdfFacesContext.getCurrentInstance().getTimeZone().getID();`

Note that the previous API or the EL expression does not return the time zone used by the client browser; rather it returns the `<time-zone>` value configured in `trinidad-config.xml`. If the time zone is not configured, then the framework returns the time zone read through the API `java.util.TimeZone.getDefault()`, which is usually the web container or application server's time zone.

To display the time zone for a user, use a user preference screen and allow the user to specify the time zone over there, which can be EL wired to the `<time-zone>` element in `trinidad-config.xml`, as shown in the following:

```
<trinidad-config xmlns="http://myfaces.apache.org/trinidad/config">
  <time-zone>#{UserPrefBean.timeZoneID}</time-zone>
</trinidad-config>
```

To learn more about configuring `trinidad-config.xml`, visit the following link `http://myfaces.apache.org/trinidad/devguide/configuration.html#trinidad-config.xml`.

The previous configuration is valid only for the view controller layer. ADF Business Components use the time zone configured using the element `<user-time-zone-config>` in the `adf-config.xml`. This value can be retrieved by calling `getUserTimeZone()` on the `oracle.jbo.common.DefLocaleContext` instance. The following is an example:

```
DefLocaleContext context = DefLocaleContext.getInstance();
TimeZone tz = context.getUserTimeZone();
```

If the time zone is not configured, the value is read from the underlying Java Virtual Machine, which is usually the application server's time zone.

The following example illustrates how you can configure `adf-config.xml` to use the time zone used in the view layer:

```
<?xml version="1.0" encoding="windows-1252" ?>
<adf-config xmlns="http://xmlns.oracle.com/adf/config"
  ...
<user-time-zone-config xmlns="http://xmlns.oracle.com/adf/
usertimezone/config">
<user-timezone expression="#{adfFacesContext.timeZone.ID}"/>
</user-time-zone-config>
```

Ensuring high availability for Fusion web applications

High availability for an application refers to the ability to keep a system continuously operational for a desirably long period of time. Ensuring high availability is a top priority for many enterprise applications nowadays. The following are the points you must consider when you need to build highly available Fusion web applications:

- If you want to enable high availability for your application and want to deploy it in a clustered environment, you have to select the **High Availability for ADF Scopes** option in the adf-config.xml editor under the **Controller** tab. If you select this option, at runtime, the ADF Controller will track changes to the ADF memory scopes and replicate the page flow scope and view scope objects within the server cluster:

```
<adf-config ...
  <adf-controller-config xmlns="http://xmlns.oracle.com/adf/
controller/config">
    <adf-scope-ha-support>true</adf-scope-ha-support>
  </adf-controller-config>
</adf-config>
```

- To configure a client session failover, edit the weblogic.xml file to add the replicated_if_clustered option as shown in the following example:

```
<weblogic-web-app ... >
    <session-descriptor>
    <persistent-store-type>
    replicated_if_clustered
    </persistent-store-type>
    </session-descriptor>
</weblogic-web-app>
```

- To enable high availability for business services built using ADF business components, set jbo.dofailover = "true" for the application modules used in the application as appropriate. You can configure this property visually by using the configuration editor for the application module. In the editor, select the **Pooling and Scalability** tab and then choose **Failover Transaction State upon Managed Release**. This will ensure that the application module state is saved at the end of each request. ADF runtime will restore the saved state of the application module from the data store in case of node failure.

- All the managed beans whose scopes are higher than the request should implement the `java.io.Serializable` interface. A serialization enabled managed bean should not contain any non serializable member variables, such as UI component or business component objects. In case your code contains references to UI components, use `org.apache.myfaces.trinidad.util.ComponentReference` to hold the component reference. The following code snippet from a managed bean will help you to understand how you can use `ComponentReference` to hold a non serializable UI component if required:

```
//In managed bean class
public class MyBean implements java.io.Serializable{

 //ComponentReference holds the reference to the component
 private ComponentReference someUICompReference;

 //Getter for the component
 public UIComponent getSomeUIComponent(){
   return someUICompReference == null ?
           null : someUICompReference.getComponent();
 }
 //Setter for the component
 public void setSomeUIComponent(UIComponent component) {
    // Create a new reference the first time,
    // all other references for this page would be identical
    if (someUICompReference == null)
    someUICompReference =
        ComponentReference.newUIComponentReference(component);
 }
}
```

- Another solution for a higher scoped managed bean, holding reference to a non serializable UI component, is to refactor the bean (splitting) to hold UI components in a request or lesser scopes and refer to it from the managed bean. To do this, split the bean into two. The first bean is a request scoped bean and is used for holding a UI component reference alone. The second bean stores the business logic and if it needs to refer to any UI component, it will make use of the request scoped bean for obtaining the reference.

- You should not use transient member variables in a managed bean with a scope higher than the request, to hold UI component reference. This hard reference will prevent the UI component tree from being cleaned up.

- Make sure that all the task flow parameters are serializable when you run it in high availability mode.

- Mark the ADF scopes as dirty to enable state replication: When the high availability mode is on, the application server will call serialize on any object that is put into the session scope in order to create a serialized backup. This serialization process happens at the end of the request and the resulting serialized data is copied to other nodes participating in the server cluster. Note that, by default, the runtime will serialize the session scoped objects only when you store them in the session for the first time. To force serialization during the next request, the runtime removes the state object from the session scope at the end of the request and then immediately adds it back. You must know that the ADF Controller uses session scoped objects to hold the view scope and page flow scope. This is to ensure that all the scopes are part of the same object graph and will be serialized and replicated within a cluster together. ADF optimizes the serialization of the ADF scoped beans by avoiding blind serialization of the object state. So you may need to ask for state replication by marking them as dirty if any property changes in a request. You can use the API `ControllerContext::markScopeDirty(Map<String, Object> scopeMap)` to ensure the state replication for `ViewScope` or `PageFlowScoped` bean if they are modified for any request. In other words, `ControllerContext:: markScopeDirty(...)` is used for the purpose of handling the case of a bean mutation that does not directly change the memory scope map. The following example illustrates the use of API `markScopeDirty()`:

```
//In managed bean class
public void updateEmpBean(){
    Map<String, Object> viewScope =
        AdfFacesContext.getCurrentInstance().getViewScope();
    EmpBean empBean = (EmpBean)viewScope.get("emp");
    empBean.setFirstName("Chinmay");
    empBean.setLastName("Jobinesh");
    ControllerContext.getInstance().markScopeDirty(viewScope);
}
```

Note that when you assign values to variables stored in `pageFlowScope` or `viewScope` memory scope maps through listener tags such as `af:setActionListener` and `af:setPropertyListener` or using APIs, the framework will take care of marking the scope as dirty. The following example illustrates how you can use the `af:setPropertyListener` tag to copy the value to the `pageFlowScope` variable:

```
<af:commandButton text="View City Details" id="cb1"
action="cityView">
  <af:setPropertyListener from="#{bindings.City.inputValue}"
    to="#{pageFlowScope.cityName}" type="action"/>
</af:commandButton>
```

However, the previous rule is not applicable when you assign values to properties of a managed bean using these assignment tags as shown in the following code snippet. In such a case, you have to manually mark the scope as dirty in the setter method of the `CityBean` class:

```
<af:commandButton text="View City Details" id="cb1"
action="cityView">
  <af:setPropertyListener from="#{bindings.City.inputValue}"
    to="#{pageFlowScope.CityBean.cityName}" type="action"/>
</af:commandButton>
```

If you want to use `javax.servlet.http.HttpSession` directly in your code to modify the session object, call `HttpSession::setAttribute(String name, Object value)` which will update that object across the cluster. Similarly, to remove a session object, call `HttpSession::removeAttribute(String name)`.

How does a bean data control participate in session replication in high availability mode?

When you use EJB bean data controls in high availability mode, state saving and restoring is done by the data control handler configured in the `DataControls.dcx` file. The default for the data control handler for EJB is the `oracle.adf.model.adapter.bean.jpa.JPQLDataFilterHandler` class, and this class is capable of doing the serialization and de-serialization of the state on application server failover. You need not provide any implementation in your EJB bean to handle the application server failover.

However, for Java Bean data control you should enable it explicitly. To make your Java Bean data control work in high availability mode, make sure that the corresponding bean data control class implements `oracle.adf.model.ManagedDataControl`. The framework invokes `createSnapshot()` for saving the state immediately following each request, and on node failure, the framework invokes `restoreSnapshot()` to restore the state on another node. An example is as follows:

```java
public class DeptBean implements Serializable,
    oracle.adf.model.ManagedDataControl {
  private BigDecimal departmentId;
  private String departmentName;
    /**
     * Creates a snapshot of the state of the DataControl.
     * Returns a serializable handle to the snapshot.
     *
     * @return a snapshot handle
     */
    @Override
    public Serializable createSnapshot() {
        return this;
    }

    /**
     * Removes the snapshot associated with the snapshot
     *   handle.
     */
    @Override
    public void removeSnapshot(Serializable handle) {
      //No special handling required in this sample
    }

    /**
     * Restore the state of the DataControl with the snapshot
     *    state that is referenced by the handle.
     */
    @Override
    public void restoreSnapshot(Serializable handle) {
      if (handle instanceof DeptBean) {
          DeptBean restoredBean = ((DeptBean)handle).
            getDeptBeanCollection();
        //restore the member variable
      this.departmentId = restoredBean.departmentId;
          this.departmentName = restoredBean.departmentName;
      }
    }

}
```

Summary

That was a lengthy chapter providing a number of important explanations and useful tips on ADF. Feel free to refer back to this chapter while working with ADF.

We started this chapter by discussing different approaches for setting up the project source structure for a Fusion web application. Then we moved out from the infrastructure setup and dived into the ADF runtime optimizations techniques. We discussed the life span of business components and the role of the garbage collector. We also discussed the best practices and performance optimization tips for Fusion web applications. Towards the end, we discussed tips to ensure high availability for a Fusion web application.

By now you must have learned how to build successful enterprise applications using Oracle ADF.

Index

attribute binding
accessing 283
associated view object, accessing 283, 284
iterator binding, accessing 283, 284
attribute level
about 448
validation rule 92
Attribute Mapping page 113
attributes
annotating, UI hints used 118, 119
attribute settings page 112
Attributes navigation tab 76
attributes page 112
AttrSetValException
using 468
AttrValException
about 468
throwing, programmatically 471, 473
AutoQuery behavior 339, 340

B

backingBean scope 359
batch update
enabling, in entity object 98
bc4j.xcfg file 33, 49, 220
behavior tab, composition association
Cascade Update Key Attributes option 91
Implement Cascade Delete option 90
Lock Level option 91
Optimize for Database Cascade Delete
option 90
properties 90
Update Top-level History Columns option
91
Use Database Key Constraints property 90
Binary Large Object. *See* **BLOB data type**
binding container
accessing 279
binding editor
using 278
binding objects
life span 498
Bindings and Executables tab 278
bindings, page definition file
action binding 277
attribute value binding 277

boolean value binding 277
data visualization components binding 277
list binding 277
method action binding 277
table binding 278
tree binding 278
bind parameter 56
bind variable
about 56, 107, 129
accessing, programmatically 141
oracle.jbo.domain.Array using as, view
criteria item used 190-193
value, specifying for 129, 130
Bind Variable page 113
BLOB, database column type 73
BLOB data type 204
boolean binding 277
boolean remove flag 245
bounded task flow
about 356, 390
activities, working with 395
activity, marking as default activity 395
activity, marking as exception handler 396
building, steps for 394
calculated option 391
calling, task flow call activity used 396, 397
consuming, as ADF regions 409
critical option 392
definition XML file 357
dynamic task flow calls using 398, 399
finalizer property 391
initializer property 391
input parameter values, specifying 403-406
library internal property 391
life span 437
parameterizing 403
parameters section 391
properties 390, 391
remote task flow calls, using 400, 401
remote task flow, pointers for using 402
return value feature 392
save point restore finalizer property 391
task flow call activity, properties 399
task flow input parameter, defining 403
task flow reentry option 392
train component, creating 429, 430
train component, using 428, 429

F

Facelet document type 363
faces-config.xml file 24, 354
FacesContext object 287
facet 301
FetchSize property set 524
FileStorageEO entity object 204
FileStorageVO view object 204
finalizer property 391
final parameter option 306
findApplicationModule() method 240
findApplicationModule(String amName)
     method 240
findByKey()
  about 144, 168
  using, on view object 144
findByPKExtended() method 82
findByPrimaryKey() 80, 102
findByPrimaryKey method 80, 168
findByViewCriteria() 141
findDepartmentsForDepartmnetNames(..)
     method 189
finishedLoading() method 463
Fusion page lifecycle customization
  URL 296
Fusion web application
  application, deploying 37
  application module, building 31, 32
  application, running 37
  application running, integrated webLogic
    server used 37
  application, running on standalone
    application server 38
  application template, selecting 21
  business services, generating 26
  comparing, to Java EE web application 12
  creating, steps for 22, 23
  database, connecting to 25
  data model, generating 26
  entity objects, building 26-28
  high availability mode, ensuring 535-538
  internationalization 533
  JDeveloper IDE, starting 20, 21
  metadata files, analyzing 23, 24
  model project source 33, 34
  project structure, setting up 482

time zone, configuring 533
user interfaces, building from model 34-36
validation 454
validation rules, adding 440
view controller project source 36
view objects, building to shape business
    data 29, 30
Fusion Web Application template 266
fusion web application workspace
  building, steps for 266
Fusion web page
  accessing, consequences for 284-290

G

General navigation tab 87
getAttribute(attrIndex,EntityImpl.ORIGI-
    NAL_VERSION) 162
getCriteriaItemClause()
  overriding in view, tips for 186
getCriteriaItemClause(ViewCriteriaItem
    vci)
  overriding, in view object implementation
    class 184, 185
getDynamicTaskFlowId() method 399
getEntityState() method 161
getGlobalViewAtivityURL() method 367
getHistoryContextForAttribute() method
    177
getLocalViewActivityURL() method 367
getParameterMap() method 405
getPostedAttribute(int attribIndex) 162
getPostState() method 161
getResourceBundleDef() method 463, 465
getViewCriteriaClause()
  overriding in view, tips for 186
getViewCriteriaClause(boolean forQuery)
  overriding, in view object implementation
    class 183
global row fetch limit
  setting, for view objects 507, 508
Graphical User Interface (GUI) 50

H

hasEmployeesForDepartment method 371
hasNext() 154

hierarchical view object instances
adding 224
hierarchical view objects
buidling 317, 318
high availability mode
bean data control, participating in session replication 538
ensuring, for fusion web application 535-538
history types
creating, steps for 175, 176
custom history types, building 175
HRServiceAppModule.xml file 33
HttpServlet
ADF binding APIs, using 293, 294
Configuration::createRootApplicationModule(), using 291

I

IDE 15, 306
immediate option 410
immediate property 477
Implement Cascade Delete option 90
implicit navigation
about 355
working 355
implicit save points
enabling 375, 376
inheritance hierarchies
creating, for entity objects 80, 81
in entity objects 80
subtype entity objects, defining 82
initDefaultExpressionAttributes(AttributeList nameValuePair) method 166
initDefaultExpressionAttributes() method 165
initDefault() method 166, 521
Initialize Business Components dialog box 67
initializer property 391
InitialQueryOverridden property 339
initSharedQCPoolProperties() 234
in-memory filtering
by overriding rowQualifies() in ViewObjectImpl 136

by overriding, rowQualifies() in ViewObjectImpl 135
of row set 132
with RowMatch 132-135
in-memory mode, view criteria 137
Input Parameters list 404
Input Parameters Map 404
input parameter values
specifying, for task flow 403
Insert mulitTaskFlow dialog window 425
Integrated Development Environment. *See* IDE
integrated webLogic server
used, for running application 37
internationalization, fusion web application 533
invoke application 290
iterator binding
accessing 283, 284
ChangeEventPolicy 309
RangeSize 309
RowCountThreshold property 310
iterator bindings
attributes, commonly used 309, 310

J

Java Archive (JAR) file 426, 485
JavaBean Data Control 264
Java classes
creating, for entity components 69
entity collection class 70
entity definition class 70
entity object class 70
generating, for application module 223
generating, for view object 116, 117
generating optionally, for ADF view object 116, 117
Java Database Connectivity (JDBC) 59
Java EE 7
Java EE components
ADF Business Components, using with 260
Java EE web application
and Fusion web application, comparing 12
Java Extended For Oracle 67
Java Management Extensions (JMX) 264

New Connection option 25
New Deployment Profile option 38
New Entity Constraint option 87
No Controller Transaction 393, 434
non-polymorphic entity usage
  inheritance hierarchies, on view objects 123
Non-translatable property 87
No save point on task flow entry property
    393
NOT operator 135
NUMBER, database column type 72

O

Object Relational Mapping (ORM) 42
One to Many entity instance 88
One to One entity instance 88
Optimize for Database Cascade Delete
    option 90
optional parameter option 306
Oracle ADF
  about 7
  advantages 9
  architecture 10
  need for 8
Oracle ADF, architecture
  business service layer 12
  controller layer 11
  model layer 11
  view layer 11
oracle.adf.model.binding.DCErrorHandler-
    Impl class 458
Oracle ADF Model Tester 50-52
Oracle ADF runtime components
  database list, URL 64
oracle.adf.view.rich.context.ExceptionHan-
    dler
  customizing 382
Oracle Application Development Frame-
    work. *See* Oracle ADF
Oracle Database SQL Language Reference
    documentation
  URL 69
Oracle Enterprise Manager (OEM) 49
Oracle Fusion Middleware Administrator's
    Guide documentation
  URL 38

oracle.jbo.domain.Array
  used, for passing parameters to SQL IN
    clause, 188
  using, as bind variable for view criteria item
    190-193
  using, as NamedWhereClauseParam value
    189, 190
oracle.jbo.domain.Array parameter type 190
oracle.jbo.JboException class 466
oracle.jbo.RowValException exceptions 468
oracle.jbo.server.ViewObjectImpl class 268
Oracle Platform Security Services (OPSS)
    26
Oracle Platform Security Services (OPSS)
    policy provider 285
Oracle Team Productivity Center
  about 17
  components 18
Oracle Team Productivity Center,
    components
  Team Productivity Center client software
    18
  Team Productivity Center connectors 18
  Team Productivity Center server software
    18
org.apache.myfaces.t rinidad.validator.
    ClientValidator interface 443
originally retrieved value
  reading 162
OR operator 135
outcome property 376, 377

P

page
  validation exceptions, displaying 454, 455
page binding elements
  accessing, programmatically 279
  binding container, accessing 279
page contents
  organizing 300-302
page definition file
  <executables> section 275
  < parameters> section 275
  about 275
  binding editor, using 278
  bindings section 277, 278

pageFlow scope 360
page initialization
  method call activity, using 385
page layout
  art 298
page layout components
  URL 299
page laying out
  art 299
page lifecycle
  client-side validation 455
  server-side validation 456, 457
  validation triggered 455
Page Templates
  URL 267
panelGridLayout component 302
parameter binding
  accessing, programmatically 280
  method action binding, executing
    programmatically 280
parameters
  passing, to SQL IN clause,
    oracle.jbo.domain.Array used 188
parameters section 391
parent action activity
  about 377
  adding 377
  outcome property 377
  parent outcome property 377
  root outcome property 377
parent outcome property 377
parent view object
  configuring, to retain view link accessor
    row set 325
Partial Page Refresh (PPR) 310, 531
participate in row delete property 111
passivation 490
PDef 215
placeholder data control 265
Plain Old Java Object (POJO) class 264
polymorphic entity usage
  inheritance hierarchies, on view objects
    123, 124
pool parameters 493
pop up component
  used, for displaying task flow 413
postChanges() method 169

prepareForDML() method 103, 169
prepare render 290
prepareRowSetForQuery() method
    59, 153, 187
prepareVOForQuery() method 517
primary key
  defining 79, 80
processEmployeesForaDepdt() method 464
process validations 289
programmatically managed entity object
  building 170, 172
programmatically managed view objects
  building 180, 181
property inspector window 20
property set
  about 74
  associating, with entity object attributes 75
  creating, steps for 74

Q

queriable checkbox option 84
query
  counting, in view object 180
  customization logic 181
  customizing, at runtime 186
  customizing, for row set 187
  customizing, for view object 187
  custom view criteria adapter, using 182,
    183
query collection
  about 45, 56, 58, 108
  life span 493-495
query collection cache 495
query execution
  optimizing in view object, tips 505, 506
query mode
  scan database tables mode 126
  scan entity cache mode 126
  scan view rows mode 126
  specifying, for view object 126
query page 112, 113

R

RangeSize property 309, 524
readXML() method 199
  using, on view object 200

V

validateDepartmentName() method 441
validation
    adding 92
    attribute level validation rule 92
    client-side validation 455
    Custom ADF faces validator, defining
        442-446
    custom domain objects used 448-451
    custom validation rule, defining 95
    defining, in ADF business components
        layer 447, 448
    defining, in ADF model layer 446, 447
    defining, in ADF view layer 441
    entity level validation rule 92
    putting, in fusion web application 454
    rule, adding to attribute 92-94
    rule, adding to entity object 94
    rules, adding in fusion web application 440
    server-side validation 456, 457
    transaction level validation 95
validation class hierarchy 466
validation error messages
    localizing 462
validation exception
    building, message strings from resource
        bundle used 465, 466
    displaying, on page 454, 455
    multiple exception, building 468
    multiple exception, bundling 468
    resource bundle usage, in application
        module 462, 463
    resource bundle usage, in entity object 462
    resource bundle usage, in view object 462
    throwing programmatically 464
    throwing programmatically, in business
        components 461
    validation error messages, localizing 462
    wrapping 467
ValidationException 468
Validation Execution tab 95
validation listener list 102
validator attribute 441
validator Java class
    defining 443
Value Change Event, event type 416

ValueChangeEvent method 477
value change events 303
VARCHAR2, database column type 72
view accessor 107
view accessor row set 495
view activity
    adding, steps for 362
    bookmarking 363, 364
    example 362
    redirect URL 365
    router activity 371
    task flow return activity 377
view criteria
    about 107, 136
    applying, to view object instance 230
    architecture 136-138
    database mode 137
    in-memory mode 137
    removing 139
    tuning, in view object 508, 509
View Criteria Editor window 342
view criteria item
    oracle.jbo.domain.Array, using as bind
        variable 190-193
ViewCriteria object 139
view definition
    building with entity usage, at runtime
        212-215
view definition class 107
View definition XML file 106
View Employee button 355
view employees option 371
view layer 11, 13
view link 108
view link consistency
    about 147
    configuring 147, 148
    working 148, 149
View link instances 46
View Link Properties page 122
view object. *See also* ADF view object
view object
    about 44, 56
    building, to shape business data 29, 30
    building 208-210
    coding, guidelines 511-518

W

weak reference 495
weblogic-application.xml file 24
web page
    building 267
Web Service Data Control 264
Web Services Description Language
        (WSDL) 264
web tier values
    accessing, from business components 332
    passing as parameters to business service
        layer, channel establishing for 333
    passing, as parameters to business service
        methods 333
    user session data map passivation, making
        safe 334

user session data map, using to store client
        side passed values 333
web.xml file 24
WHERE Clause
    appending, at design time 128
    appending, at runtime 128
While New attribute 83
wildcard control flow rule 380
    URL 378
writeXML() method 199
    using, on row object 199
    using, on view object 200

X

XA data source 261

Thank you for buying
Oracle ADF Real World Developer's Guide

About Packt Publishing

Packt, pronounced 'packed', published its first book "Mastering phpMyAdmin for Effective MySQL Management" in April 2004 and subsequently continued to specialize in publishing highly focused books on specific technologies and solutions.

Our books and publications share the experiences of your fellow IT professionals in adapting and customizing today's systems, applications, and frameworks. Our solution based books give you the knowledge and power to customize the software and technologies you're using to get the job done. Packt books are more specific and less general than the IT books you have seen in the past. Our unique business model allows us to bring you more focused information, giving you more of what you need to know, and less of what you don't.

Packt is a modern, yet unique publishing company, which focuses on producing quality, cutting-edge books for communities of developers, administrators, and newbies alike. For more information, please visit our website: www.packtpub.com.

About Packt Enterprise

In 2010, Packt launched two new brands, Packt Enterprise and Packt Open Source, in order to continue its focus on specialization. This book is part of the Packt Enterprise brand, home to books published on enterprise software – software created by major vendors, including (but not limited to) IBM, Microsoft and Oracle, often for use in other corporations. Its titles will offer information relevant to a range of users of this software, including administrators, developers, architects, and end users.

Writing for Packt

We welcome all inquiries from people who are interested in authoring. Book proposals should be sent to author@packtpub.com. If your book idea is still at an early stage and you would like to discuss it first before writing a formal book proposal, contact us; one of our commissioning editors will get in touch with you.

We're not just looking for published authors; if you have strong technical skills but no writing experience, our experienced editors can help you develop a writing career, or simply get some additional reward for your expertise.

Oracle JDeveloper 11gR2
Cookbook

Over 85 simple but incredibly effective recipes for using Oracle
JDeveloper 11gR2 to build ADF applications

Foreword by Frank Nimphius
Senior Principal Product Manager, Oracle Application Development Tools

Nick Haralabidis [PACKT] enterprise

Oracle JDeveloper 11gR2
Cookbook

ISBN: 978-1-84968-476-7   Paperback: 406 pages

Over 85 simple but incredibly effective recipes
for using Oracle JDeveloper 11gR2 to build ADF
applications

1. Encounter a myriad of ADF tasks to help you
   enhance the practical application of JDeveloper
   11gR2

2. Get to grips with deploying, debugging, testing,
   profiling and optimizing Fusion Web ADF
   Applications with JDeveloper 11gR2

3. A high level development cookbook with
   immediately applicable recipes for extending
   your practical knowledge of building ADF
   applications

Oracle BPM Suite 11g
Developer's Cookbook

Over 80 advanced recipes to develop rich, interactive
business processes using the Oracle Business Process
Management Suite

Vivek Acharya [PACKT] enterprise

Oracle BPM Suite 11g Developer's
cookbook

ISBN: 978-1-84968-422-4   Paperback: 512 pages

Over 80 advanced recipes to develop rich, interactive
business process using the Oracle Business Process
Management Suite

1. Full of illustrations, diagrams, and tips with
   clear step-by-step instructions and real time
   examples to develop Industry Sample BPM
   Process and BPM interaction with SOA
   Components

2. Dive into lessons on Fault ,Performance and
   Rum Time Management

3. Explore User Interaction ,Deployment and
   Monitoring

Please check **www.PacktPub.com** for information on our titles

CPSIA information can be obtained
at www.ICGtesting.com
Printed in the USA
FFOW01n1340200615
14455FF

9 781849 684828